Globalization and Language Vitality

Globalization and Language Vitality

Perspectives from Africa

Edited by

Cécile B. Vigouroux
Salikoko S. Mufwene

continuum

Continuum International Publishing Group

The Tower Building   80 Maiden Lane, Suite 704
11 York Road   New York
London SE1 7NX   NY 10038

British Library Cataloguing-in-Publication Data
A catalogue record for this book is available from the British Library.

ISBN: 978-0-8264-9514-3 (Hardback)
         978-0-8264-9515-0 (Paperback)

Library of Congress Cataloguing-in-Publication Data
The Publisher has applied for CIP data.

Typeset by Newgen Imaging Systems Pvt Ltd, Chennai, India
Printed and bound in Great Britain by MPG Books, Cornwall

Contents

Contributors

Neville Alexander is currently the director of the Project for the Study of Alternative Education in South Africa (PRAESA) at the University of Cape Town. He was appointed to chair the South African Language Plan Task Group (LANGTAG) and was a special advisor on language policy and planning to the minister of arts, culture, science and technology until December 2005 and is a member of the Western Cape Language Committee. His recent publications include: (i) *English Unassailable But Unattainable. The Dilemmas of South African Language Policy in Education* (PRAESA 2000); (ii) *An Ordinary Country. Issues in the Transition from Apartheid to Democracy* (University of Natal Press 2002); and (iii) *The African Renaissance and the Use of African Languages in Tertiary Education* (PRAESA 2003).

Herman M. Batibo is professor of African linguistics at the University of Botswana. He has worked on language endangerment and loss in both eastern and southern Africa, particularly Tanzania and Botswana. His recent major publications include *Language Decline and Death in Africa: Causes, Consequences and Challenges* (Multilingual Matters 2005), *Botswana: The Future of Minority Languages* (edited with B. Smieja 2000) and *The State of Khoesan Languages in Botswana* (edited with J. Tsonope 2000).

Jan Blommaert is professor of linguistic anthropology at Tilburg University, The Netherlands, and part-time professor of African linguistics and sociolinguistics at Ghent University, Belgium. He has conducted ethnographic research in East, Central and South Africa, focusing on language policies and ideologies in the present globalization era. His publications include *Discourse: A Critical Introduction* (Cambridge University Press 2005), *Language Ideological Debates* (Mouton de Gruyter 1999), *State Ideology and Language in Tanzania* (Koeppe 1999) and *Debating Diversity* (Routledge 1998).

Eyamba G. Bokamba is currently a professor of linguistics and African languages, and director of the language program at the University of Illinois at Urbana–Champaign. His sociolinguistics interests lie primarily in multilingualism, language planning, language policy, African Englishes and language in literacy. His relevant publications include the following: 'Language and national development in Sub-Saharan Africa: A progress report' (*Studies in the Linguistic Sciences* 11.1–26, 1981); 'The politics of language planning in Africa: Critical choices for the 21st century' (in *Discrimination through Language in Africa?* Mouton de Gruyter 1995); and '[The spread of] Lingala' (in *Encyclopedia of Twentieth-Century African History*, Routledge 2003).

Ahmed Boukous is 'Professeur de l'enseignement supérieur' at IRCAM, Morocco. He has served on some of the advisory councils of the Organisation Intergouvernementale de la Francophonie, especially regarding the partnership between French and minority languages. His recent publications in sociolinguistics include: *Société, langues et cultures au Maroc* (Rabat: Université Mohammed V 1995); *Dominance et différence: essais sur les enjeux symboliques* (Casablanca: Le Fennec 1999); and *L'amazighe dans la politique linguistique et culturelle au Maroc* (Rabat: Centre Tarik Ibn Zyad 2004).

Robert Chaudenson is professor emeritus of linguistics and Francophone studies at the Université d'Aix-Marseille 1. He is widely published on the development of creoles and their place in school, on globalization and the future of French in Africa and on language endangerment in the same part of the world. His publications include: *The Creolization of Language and Culture* (Routledge 2001); *La créolisation: théorie, applications, implications* (L'Harmattan 2003); *Les situations linguistiques de la francophonie: état des lieux* (with D. Rakotomala, Montréal: AUF 2004); and *Vers une autre idée et pour une autre politique de la langue française* (L'Harmattan 2006).

Alamin Mazrui is a professor in the Department of African–American and African Studies at Ohio State University. His research is on language and urbanization, language and globalization, and language and law. A member of the board of directors of the Kenya Human Rights Commission, he has a special interest in human rights and civil liberties and has written policy reports on these subjects. He is author and/or editor of several books including: *The Power of Babel: Language and Governance in the African Experience* (with Ali Mazrui, Univerity of Chicago Press 1998) and *English in Africa: After the Cold War* (Multilingual Matters 2004).

Fiona Mc Laughlin is an associate professor of African linguistics at the University of Florida. She has worked on the sociolinguistics of Senegalese languages, especially in the urban context and served as director of the West African Research Center in Dakar, Senegal. Her relevant recent publications include: 'Haalpulaar identity as a response to Wolofization' (*African Languages and Cultures* 8:153–168); 'Dakar Wolof and the configuration of an urban identity' (*Journal of African Cultural Studies* 14:153–172); and 'Senegal: The emergence of a national lingua franca' (*Language and National Identity in Africa*, ed. by Andrew Simpson, 79–97, Oxford University Press, 2008).

Rajend Mesthrie is professor of linguistics at the University of Cape Town. He was formerly deputy director of the Centre for Language Studies and Services in Africa at the same university. His sociolinguistics research focuses mainly on language contact in southern Africa. His relevant publications include: *Language in Indenture* (Routledge 1992); *English in Language Shift* (Cambridge University Press 1991); and *Language in South Africa* (Cambridge University Press, 2002).

Salikoko S. Mufwene is the Frank J. McLoraine Distinguished Service Professor of Linguistics and the College at the University of Chicago. His current research is on language evolution, including also questions of language vitality and endangerment. He is the author of *The Ecology of Language Evolution* (Cambridge University Press 2001); *Créoles, écologie sociale, évolution linguistique* (L'Harmattan 2005); and *Language Evolution: Contact, Competition, and Change* (Continuum 2008).

Christopher Stroud is professor of linguistics at the University of the Western Cape and a professor of bilingual research at Stockholm University. He has worked on the sociolinguistic ethnographies of practice and representation of Portuguese and African languages, including multilingualism, in Mozambique. His relevant publications include: 'Portuguese as ideology and politics in Mozambique' (in *Language Ideological Debates*, ed. by J. Blommaert, Mouton, 1999) and 'Framing Bourdieu socioculturally: Alternative forms of linguistic legitimacy in postcolonial Mozambique' (*Multilingua* 21.247–273, 2002).

Cécile B. Vigouroux is an assistant professor in the Department of French at Simon Fraser University (Canada). She has conducted ethnographic research on Francophone African migrants to South Africa since 1994. Her relevant publications include: 'Rencontre d'un autre type: dynamique identitaire et stratégies discursives en situation d'entretien' (*Revue de Linguistique et de Didactique des Langages* 29, 2004); '"There Are no Whites in Africa": Territoriality, Language, and Identity among Francophone Africans in Cape Town' (*Language and Communication*, 2005); and 'The "smuggling of la *Francophonie*": Francophone Africans in Anglophone Cape Town (South Africa)' (*Language in Society*, 37: 415–37, 2008).

Acknowledgements

The editors wish to express their heartfelt thanks to Emily Pelka and Nicholas Kontovas for drafting the translations of, respectively, the chapters by Robert Chaudenson and Ahmed Boukous. This helped in saving a great deal of time towards the production of this volume. They are also very grateful to Kay Yang and Matt Marsik for producing, respectively, Map 1.1 representing the different parts of Africa discussed in this book and Map 7.1 situating the Senegalese languages discussed in Chapter 7.

Chapter 1

Colonization, Globalization and Language Vitality in Africa: An Introduction

Salikoko S. Mufwene and Cécile B. Vigouroux

1.1 Historical Background

The word *colonization* in the title of this chapter is intended to conjure up the fact that much of the current debate on the impact of globalization on language vitality[1] does not make sense without also invoking the relocation of populations to new places and often the domination of the indigenous ones by the newcomers. We argue here that one cannot make sense of *globalization* without connecting it to *colonization* and articulating the different ways in which the latter proceeds. Languages are affected because colonization and sometimes globalization entail the following: population movements; the spread of the migrants' languages and the ensuing contacts of the latter with those of the indigenous, dominated populations; the emergence of new language repertoires and new divisions of labor among the coexistent languages, as well as new dynamics of competition and selection among them; and differential evolution regarding their vitality.

To start with a strong and provocative observation, we'd like to submit that both colonization and globalization are as old as the dispersal of Homo sapiens out of East Africa forty to sixty thousand years ago, although both phenomena have evolved significantly and diversified in ecology-specific ways since then. The first primitive adaptations must have taken place with the colonization of hunter–gatherers by agriculturalists and pastoralists at the dawn of modern human civilizations (Mufwene 2008). They must have complexified again with the invention of writing and the emergence of the first trade empires, such as the Babylonian and Phoenician (see Ostler 2003). Forerunners of recent and present-day styles of colonization and globalization may be identified in the Hellenic and Roman empires, though one cannot overlook the role of Chinese and Arab trade routes by sea and land during the Middle Ages as antecedents of the European expansion since the fifteenth century. Then the differential history of human migrations and the ensuing diasporas

(Cavalli-Sforza and Cavalli-Sforza 1995) and of language spread and language loss becomes altogether more intriguing and in need of more ecology-specific accounts.

As observed by Fiona Mc Laughlin in the introduction to Chapter 7, this book is an overdue complement to the ever-growing literature on the now popular subject matter of language endangerment. It provides information about Africa that reminds us that language evolution has not proceeded uniformly at all, not any more than colonization and globalization have, at least in the way we discuss them in the following paragraphs. While language dynamics in Africa undoubtedly vary as much as elsewhere in the world, overall the recent history of language vitality on this continent questions some of the claims of the rapidly vanishing linguistic diversity that are based on the experience of especially North America and Australia. It is debatable whether the colonial European languages that now function as official languages in Africa are (general) threats to the continent's indigenous vernaculars. It generally appears one must first distinguish between rural and urban Africa since they have not experienced European colonization, let alone globalization as this is commonly discussed in the current literature, in the same way. One must also articulate the particular ethnographic domains, and even the socioeconomic classes, in which competition obtains between the relevant European and indigenous languages, among the indigenous languages and now also between European languages, notably English and the traditional official language, which is in general the ex-colonial European language. Complementing the chapters in this book, we try to explain here why the story from Africa is so different from that of North America and Australia.

Although colonization and globalization[2] certainly account for why the linguistic landscapes of the world have changed, sometimes dramatically, over the past few centuries, it is also noteworthy that the colonial history of Africa has not been the same as that of North America and Australia. The trade colonization phase, marked especially by the establishment of (mostly coastal and riverine) trade posts and egalitarian exchange relations between the Europeans and the Natives, lasted much longer in Africa than in the Americas and Australia. Overall, they preceded any other form of the colonization of the non-European world by Europeans, although they were periods of overlap. This is more evident in the case of the Americas, where settle-colonization started early on along the Atlantic coast. Europeans secured concessions quite soon after discovering the New World, treated them as new homes, sort of Europe outside Europe (Crosby 1986), and traded with Native Americans from these strategic bases. Westward expansion would gradually replace former trade colonies with settlements, which would eventually lead to the establishment of European-style socioeconomic structures and the emergence of European demographic majorities. Even this evolution suggests a geographical complementary distribution of trade and settlement colonies, until the former was completely replaced by the latter and the Natives were forcibly relocated in reservations by the nineteenth century.

With the exception of South Africa, occupied permanently by the Dutch in the mid-seventeenth century, Europeans practised only trade colonization in mainland Africa until the mid-nineteenth century, staying typically on the coast. However, as reported by Fiona Mc Laughlin in Chapter 7, they opened up some riverine trade posts in the interior, an expansion that would lead to the exploitation colonization of the continent. Only the off-shore islands would be colonized on the settlement model, but the Europeans would remain minorities there, due largely to the development of agricultural industries that thrived on huge slave labor, which, like in the Caribbean, grew much larger and faster than the European populations. Moreover, the lucrative attraction of the Brazilian colony would lead the Portuguese to abandon their plantations, creating conditions for the emergence of creoles, at the expense of the African languages the slaves had brought with them, especially on the Islands of Cape Verde, São Tomé and Principe (Mufwene 2008). The French settled in the Mascarene Islands, where creoles have also developed, but would eventually colonize the larger island of Madagascar partly on the exploitation model, like continental Africa. The continent would thus serve as the source of raw materials to be exported to the European metropoles, where the colonizers (rather than colonists) would retire on the completion of their service for their countries or companies.

The trend of the exploitation colonization of Africa, in lieu of trade colonization, started in the second half of the nineteenth century, when Western European colonial powers found it profitable to take control of the whole continent and carved it geographically among them in the Berlin Treaty (1885), the outcome of a conference that had started in 1884. South Africa is doubly unique in having been colonized on the settlement model since the mid-seventeenth century, and experiencing a overlay of exploitation colonization by Britain since the late eighteenth century, an evolution that would lead the Boers (Dutch settlers) to proclaim themselves as Afrikan(d)ers and their new, colonially evolved language variety as Afrikaans (see also Mesthrie, this volume). We can claim that, unlike the settlement colonization of the Americas and Australia, the exploitation colonization of Africa has hardly contributed directly to the endangerment or extinction of indigenous African languages. That of the Khoesan languages has been caused by the settlement colonization of Southern Africa by both the Bantu population, during their geographical expansion southward, and the Afrikaners.

All these observations are relevant because different colonization styles can be associated with different socioeconomic structures, therefore different interactional and linguistic regimes, which have engendered different dynamics of language competition between the languages in contact (Mufwene 2008). During the trade colonization phase, Europeans were just happy to be able to communicate with the indigenous populations, initially through interpreters, which facilitated trade. As this intensified, new lingua franca emerged, which have been identified as pidgins. An important difference between the Americas and Africa is that in the former these new languages (such as Delaware Pidgin, Mobilian Jargon and Lingua Geral Amazônica, now known as Nheengatu) were based on Native American languages, whereas in the latter they were based on European languages.[3] It now appears that a Portuguese contact variety had served as the trade language used by all Europeans traders before pidgin English varieties emerged in the late eighteenth or early nineteenth centuries (Huber 1999). Expanded pidgins such as Nigerian and Cameroon Pidgin Englishes owe their existence, maintenance and expansion (structural and demographic), as well as their continuing divergence from their 'lexifier', to the intensification of the trade, the growing insufficiency of interpreters, the fact that more and more Natives would interact directly with the Europeans or their auxiliaries in approximations of the new lingua franca and the subsequent emergence of large trade and/or administrative centers during the exploitation colonization period (Mufwene 2005). That the pidgins have survived in Africa, unlike in the Americas, is in itself evidence of different language policies and practices that must distinguish settlement colonies from their exploitation counterparts, a topic to which we return shortly.

Overall, trade colonization did not create any threat to indigenous languages, because the new communicative needs and functions it introduced were met by Native languages in the case of the Americas and by European languages elsewhere, originally through interpreters in both cases. The dynamics of language coexistence would change only after the trade colonization would be replaced by settlement colonization; that is, although trade colonization did indeed introduce some form of *globalization* from the perspective of population movements and transportation of goods over long distances, it did not need to proceed in the language of the economically more powerful, least of all to impose the language of the latter as a vernacular over the trading 'partners'. As a matter of fact, even today, globalization in the sense of worldwide network of economic interconnectedness and interdependencies is not imposing English or French as a vernacular on any non-European populations outside the European settlement colonies.

During the exploitation colonization of Africa, the European colonizers were no more interested in sharing their languages with the indigenous populations than they were in India, where the Macaulay Doctrine was passed in the early nineteenth century (see also Brutt-Griffler 2002). Unlike in the settlement colonies of the New World and Australia, the colonizers did not develop the kind of socioeconomic structure that would entice the Natives to acquire the colonial languages as their vernacular either. In fact either education was made accessible in the indigenous languages with the teaching of European languages dispensed past the third–fifth grades to the elite who passed all sorts of difficult requirements and challenges, and/or schooling was accessible only to a small fraction of the population. The French and Portuguese assimilation system was designed less for universal education (as is obvious from Chapter 8, by Robert Chaudenson) than to create an elite class of colonial auxiliaries who became a buffer between the colonized and the colonizers and ultimately worked for the metropole.

The very artificial technique of transmitting a language through the school system rather than through daily interactions with native or fluent speakers contributed to spreading the European colonial languages as elite lingua francas rather than as vernaculars. The attachment of the elite class of colonial auxiliaries to their traditions and their continued interactions with their less fortunate relatives in the extended family structures hardly gave the European languages a chance to evolve ethnographically into vernaculars as they would appear to be snobbish and uprooted (Mufwene 2005, 2008).

One might expect the colonial languages now adopted as (co-)official languages of the independent African countries to have spread and vernacularized like Vulgar Latin in parts of the former Western Roman Empire in continental Europe, where the Romance languages are now spoken. This happened especially because Latin became the urban vernaculars of the towns and cities that developed during the Roman colonization and because of the spread of the Roman style economic system even after the Romans had left. However, exploitation colonization in most of Africa produced new indigenous urban vernaculars, which have remained very African despite extensive lexical borrowings from the European languages. The colonizers had set up a two-tier economic system in which the vast majority of the indigenous labor was in the blue collar sector, which has functioned in the urban vernaculars, which also function as regional lingua francas. Since Independence, the economies of most of the countries have at best stagnated; in most cases it has collapsed. This evolution has hardly provided any incentive for the masses of the populations, more than half of which are still rural, to learn the European languages. These remain the privilege of an elite that have perpetuated the colonial exploitation system and are distrusted, together with the political leadership. If there is any *globalization* that is supposed to make the world more and more uniform economically and culturally, it has certainly left most of the African populations on the margins, though variably.

1.2 The African Experience of Language Coexistence and Competition since the Seventeenth Century

As noted earlier, South Africa is an interesting case of two layers of European colonization. The Bantu populations were already settling the Khoesan territory when the Dutch first settled in the Cape area. Then the latter moved east and

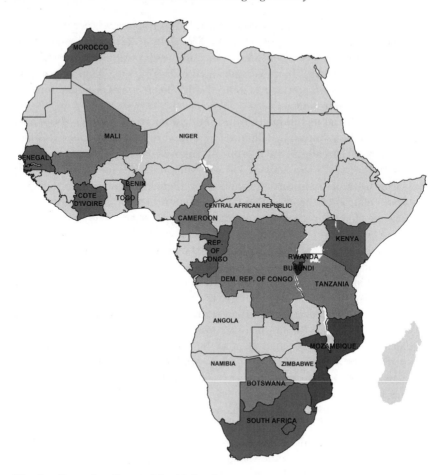

MAP 1 Countries discussed in this book.

into the interior after the Britons colonized the land, in the exploitation style, in the late eighteenth century. This latter colonization never put an end to the Dutch settlement colonization, although it created a situation where the Afrikaners have had to learn English too as either an additional vernacular or just as a lingua franca. The various dynamics of land appropriation and distribution have created an interesting population structure in which the Khoesans have been largely absorbed by the expanding Bantu populations and the Dutch settlers. Overall, from the perspective of language coexistence and competition, very few Khoesan groups have been left alone, while important proportions of the Bantu populations in South Africa are still rural, despite recent migrations into the townships and large squatter camps surrounding these.

As Rajend Mesthrie shows in Chapter 2, the dynamics of language competition have been quite complex. Although most Khoesans have lost their languages to the Bantu and Dutch colonists, there are no reported cases of Bantu populations shifting massively from their heritage languages to either Afrikaans or English, unlike the experience of Native Americans or Australian Aborigenes. This is noteworthy, in spite of the recent emergence of an urban segment of the Bantu and Colored populations that speaks English as their vernacular, along with the South African Indians, who, as a group, had shifted earlier to English, producing their own ethnolect (Mesthrie 1992). Quite interesting in this particular polity is the extent to which the vitality of Afrikaans has been affected by the presence of English and its growing status as a global language of business and diplomacy, creating a situation where Afrikaans is being redefined as an ethnic language, being abandoned by especially the urban Colored elite (Broeder et al. 2002; Giliomee 2003). This is an interesting case of a language spoken by millions whose feature may be at risk, especially if some Afrikaner children too start investing themselves more in English than in their heritage language (Mufwene 2008). Noteworthy here is also the fact that the less affluent and rural Bantu populations have remained in their respective regions, which pre-empts competition among them, as in the rest of Black Africa.

Being also the only polity in Black Africa whose economy continues to develop, South Africa has attracted migrants, earlier from neighboring countries for work in the mines and recently from almost all of Black Africa (see Chapter 11 by Cécile B. Vigouroux). It has also become an interesting contact setting that can inform us about the particular conditions under which migrants maintain or give up their heritage languages. As explained in Mufwene (2008), this is an interesting colonial history that is in some ways reminiscent of that of the United States (up to their segregation policies) and yet also quite different from the perspective of language vitality. To understand all this, one must remember that *settlement colonies* differ from *exploitation colonies* in that the colonists intended to settle new homes in the former, or, as Crosby (1986) expresses it, to develop new and better Europes than what they had left behind. Under this particular ideology, they developed in the colony a socioeconomic structure that was essentially European and different only in respects that they wanted to improve it. Generally they ignored, marginalized and/or eradicated any indigenous structures from which the Natives had to shift gradually once the colonists had reached a critical mass and were powerful enough to rule them. The shift to the European world order, including their languages, has proceeded more rapidly since the time the colonists became the majority populations and started to claim more and more of the land that the Natives had managed to keep for themselves.

South Africa is thus a case of partial settlement, or perhaps an incomplete one arrested or disturbed by the British exploitation colonization. To be sure, the Bantu populations have become the majority compared to the more indigenous Khoesans, most of whom they have assimilated. On the other hand, they have also remained the majority compared to the Afrikaners and other (white) populations combined, although they have been marginalized from the socioeconomic system that the latter developed. It is in this disenfranchising that the explanation for the maintenance of the Bantu languages lies, an experience that they share only with those Native American languages whose speakers remain on the reservations, marginalized from the American socio-economic structure.

The competition between Afrikaans and English is itself reminiscent of that which occurred between various European national languages and English in North America, as they 'collided' (Joseph et al. 2003) within the same socio-economic structure and lost to English. As we are reminded by Robert Chaudenson (Chapter 8), this is a competition that French is still facing in Quebec, lost in Nova Scotia and various other places in North America and is still losing in Louisiana. It is against this general backdrop of patterns of colonization that the reader should read, especially, the chapters by Rajend Mesthrie and Herman Batibo, where settlement and exploitation colonizations of Southern Africa by various non-Khoesan populations account for the extinction of many Khoesan languages, the current endangerment of some and the division of labor between the Bantu and European languages.

Regarding the recent Black African migrants, while the fate of the languages they brought with them remains subject to speculations, we also know from publications such as Mesthrie's (2006) that the children of the migrants from Mozambique, Zimbabwe, and so on have been no more loyal to their heritage languages than those of the Indian contract laborers. Such shifts have been facilitated by the integration of the Bantu migrant workers within the local Bantu populations. The difference in outcomes from that of language shift among South African Indians lies in the fact that the latter were segregated from the local Bantu populations and were given more access to schooling and to the socioeconomic system run by the British colonizers (Chapter 2, by Mesthrie). After all, it was the Britons who brought them to South Africa, concurrently with those other Indian contract laborers they imported to the British Caribbean and Fiji and who have all become Anglophone (a category in which we are deliberately subsuming the varieties typically disfranchised as creole).

The socioeconomic system in South Africa is otherwise as in the rest of Black Africa, where the modern industry is to be found in cities, mines and wineries, as well as on large farms held by the Afrikaners, while the rural villages where most of the Bantu and Khoesan populations live still practice traditional hunter gathering, subsistence farming or cultivate some cash crops. Overall, the populations the most isolated from the socioeconomic structure inherited from the colonial regimes are those that have held on to their languages and other cultural practices. Social and geographical segregation is what has protected South African Bantu and Khoesan languages the most. Thus, it appears that the answers to the question of what is the future of especially Bantu languages in South Africa depends largely on the answers to the following questions on its socioeconomic system: (i) Will the South African new socioeconomic structure expand to the rural areas? (ii) Will the economy develop to where residents of the ever-growing squatter camps will no longer be disenfranchised and benefit from the growth? and (iii) Will any of the indigenous South African languages be used in the modern, Western-style economic sector, or will English and, to some extent, Afrikaans continue to prevail in this ethnographic domain? The reader will hopefully benefit from these considerations in processing the details that Rajend Mesthrie provides in Chapter 2.

Some of these considerations will also help the reader put Chapter 3 by Herman Batibo in the right historical perspective, as he contributes yet another dimension to language competition, the fact that some Bantu languages have driven some others out to extinction. It is absolutely important to pay attention to the particular ecological factors that have permitted it, especially the relative demographic sizes and political strengths of the populations in contact. Another important dimension is the colonial history that has promoted some indigenous vernaculars to the status of regional lingua francas and 'national languages', thus associating them with modernity and making them more attractive to speakers of other ethnic vernaculars. In this chapter too it is evident that the indigenous languages all compete more among themselves than with the European colonial languages that have been adopted as official languages and are used in communicative domains introduced by the Europeans. It is interesting to know that some indigenous languages are indeed expanding demographically and in domains of usage, contrary to the standard literature, traditionally based on the Americas and Australia. That literature has given the wrong impression that major European languages have been expanding uniformly at the expense of the indigenous languages in the colonies.

The significance of the factor of *modernity* is also highlighted by Christopher Stroud in Chapter 4, where it is problematized as not being uniform and as possibly meaning different things in different socioeconomic structures and polities. The author argues that *multilingualism* is conceptualized differently in center-economy states such as the United States than in economically peripheral states (within the context of globalization) such as Mozambique. It appears that in the latter, languages are associated with different ethnographic functions or communicative domains (such as public or private life, technological or vernacular communication, national or transnational transactions, etc.), whereas in the former they compete in the same domains, which has led to the endangerment and loss of the less advantageous ones. Also noteworthy is the fact that Portuguese is spoken mostly in the city, as a mother tongue by no more than 3 per cent of the population and as an L2 by 25 per cent of the population. There is also more multilingualism in the city than in the rural areas, both in terms of number of languages one can speak and in terms of individuals who are multilingual. African languages remain the dominant vernaculars of about 75 per cent of the population, although Portuguese is rated above them.

The Portuguese colonizers do not seem to have intended to Europeanize the indigenous Mozambicans, at least not during the first half-century of colonial period, as they barred most Natives from the city and limited their access to schools. It is only in 1930 that they thought of converting the exploitation colony into a settlement, introducing the policy of *assimilados*, which required mastery of Portuguese. However, the demographics presented earlier suggest that the segregated population structure of the colony must have not facilitated the spread of the colonial language, not at all as a vernacular. Besides, the protestant missionaries, who were in charge of education, were more invested in proselytizing in major indigenous languages than in spreading Portuguese. Thus, the requisite socioeconomic structure for its spread nationwide has never been set up. In fact, the current limited spread of Portuguese as an urban L2 is also a recent phenomenon, whose catalyst was the revolutionary war for Independence, as it functioned as the uniting language of the militants, in the absence of a common major indigenous lingua franca that could unify all. Interestingly, although, since Independence, Portuguese has been promoted as the statewide language of education – a conjunction of various factors, including the civil war and the promotion of cultural diversity. This evolution has contributed more to defining the ethnographic functions of Portuguese than in discouraging usage of the indigenous languages. The history of post-Independence Mozambique appears to be one of shifting markets driven by different ideological forces that have promoted both Portuguese and (major) indigenous languages in the interest of diversity without giving a privileged advantage to the (ex-)colonial language.

In Chapter 5, Eyamba Bokamba invites the reader to revisit *multilingualism* and *linguistic markets* again in the context of the Democratic Republic of Congo (DRC), as he shows that the different languages are not uniformly weighted. The ethnographic significance of ethnic vernaculars varies depending on whether one is in Kinshasa, the capital city, which is more associated with modernity and where the language varieties associated with it (Lingala and French) are highly valued, or in a provincial capital, such as Mbandaka, where the residents maintain close ties with their ancestral origins in the ethnic vernaculars. Just as there is no constant socioeconomic structure that is emerging worldwide today (as a by-product of globalization) and is uniformly endangering the vitality of 'indigenous' languages all over the world, there are no uniform linguistic markets in DRC that are (dis)advantaging them in the same ways from one contact setting to another. Linguistic markets depend on the local socioeconomic structures of the populations that produce them through their daily interactions. Settings such as secondary urban centers where populations maintain regular ties with their relatives in the rural areas continue to provide ecologies in which even minor ethnic languages are not endangered, whereas major urban centers provide an ecology that is less advantageous to them. It is in the latter that the presence of the European language and the external pressures of globalization as an international phenomenon are felt.

Yet, as Bokamba's study also shows, the domains of use of the colonial, now official language only overlap with those of the indigenous urban vernacular, Lingala in this particular case; the ensuing competition is not always resolved in favor of the European language. Bokamba shows how the behavior of the ruling class can also diminish interest in the language that is emblematic of their social status. Within the low class, the association of French with socio-economic exploitation, a form of internal colonization, has often aroused attitudes of distrust and/or contempt, causing even those who learned to speak it somewhat in high school (if they did not drop out) not to want to use it. At the same time, the prestige of French has been challenged by English, a major language associated with better-paying jobs, independent of its alleged global status or of the greater economic and military might of the countries that export it.

In the final analysis, the case of language coexistence and competition in DRC is far from supporting the 'gravitational' model proposed by Swaan (2001) and Calvet (2006), which is intended to foster alliances among languages to resist the expansion of the 'supercentral' languages such as English. As explained in Mufwene (2008), decisions to use one language or another are very local, and the cumulative resolution of the competition in favor of one language or another is unconsciously influenced typically by factors that do not include dynamics of language practice outside the small socioeconomic structures in which they evolve. Locally, people learn a language because of the benefits, usually socioeconomic but often also symbolic (à la Bourdieu 1991), that they hope to derive from them rather than because of whether or not they feel connected to the outside world. Bokamba reminds the reader of the utilitarian dimension of languages, as assets that one accumulates only if they have local market values that are significant to them.

These dynamics lead us to consider the case of societal multilingualism in Morocco and the ecological pressures that govern the coexistence of Amazigh (Berber), Arabic, French and English. In Chapter 6, Ahmed Boukous reminds us that North Africa has experienced several documented layers of colonization since the Phoenician trade ventures, the current situation being the ultimate outcome of that long history of language contacts. For the Amazighs, the recent exploitation colonization of Morocco by the French is just another layer over the earlier settlement colonization by the Arabs whose language and culture have been threats to theirs and must have driven various other minor languages to extinction (Mufwene 2001). These historical layers of entrenchment also appear to correspond to the current ethnographic stratification of the coexistent, if not really competing, language varieties, namely, Amazigh, Colloquial Arabic, Standard Arabic, French and English. Thanks to global, post-colonial economic pressures, English, the latest newcomer, emerges at top of the scale, while Amazigh, the most indigenous of the languages, lies at the bottom. The latter also happens to be predominantly rural, functioning in ethnographic domains where it faces no competition from French, least of all English, but is threatened by Colloquial Arabic, its urban counterpart.

Morocco is, according to Boukous, an interesting arena where the dynamics of language practice suggest that the foreign languages represent important social capitals, contrary to the Arabization promoted by the policy makers. Here too one must factor in the local population structure, in which native speakers of Arabic find no need to learn Amazigh and can even afford to be monolingual if they are not educated in French or English, whereas the Amazighs cannot, although their language is emerging from centuries of marginalization. Since the colonial period, French has been associated with modernity, especially in economics and technology, domains in which English is introducing competition, whereas Standard Arabic is associated with 'Arabo-Muslim tradition', especially regarding Islamic studies, and with cultural Independence. One might want to conclude that there is a neat division of labor that keeps French and English out of domains devoted to Standard and Colloquial Arabic. However, Arabization policies in education and technology are creating competition for French.

Overall, the foreign languages derive their social capital locally from the fact that Morocco has developed a Western-style economic system and they connect the national economy to the international markets. They are also favored by fear among some Moroccans that Arabization policies are nothing more than attempts to eliminate cultural diversity by assimilating ethnic minorities and to provide to working-class children second-rate education that is not competitive with that provided to children of the more affluent in French or English. This is quite consistent with Robert Chaudenson's observation (Chapter 8) that it is often the parents themselves who are opposed to their children being schooled in indigenous languages.

In the current socioeconomic structure of Morocco, French and English are greater assets on the local job market than Arabic, at least for jobs that are more highly valued. There is indeed competition taking place among the languages but in a very ecology-specific way, with English competing with French and French also being threatened by Arabization policies. Because of the division of labor between Standard Arabic and Colloquial Arabic, only the latter is a threat to Amazigh, in vernacular domains of oral communication, and more in the urban than in the rural environment. The latter is protected only to the extent that a movement is developing that promotes indigenous cultures and diversity, and Amazigh is entering political discourse. The traditional population structure has thus managed to slow down the extinction of this most indigenous language. Perhaps the current reforms will help it thrive again, but can it if the reforms are only linguistic and cultural but do not affect the socioeconomic structure that has kept it at the very bottom of the ladder of symbolic capitals?

In Chapter 7, Fiona Mc Laughlin gives us a glimpse into another facet of the varying linguistic effects of exploitation colonization in Black Africa, namely, the promotion, deliberate or accidental, of some indigenous languages to the status of major urban vernacular, regional lingua franca and national language – a phenomenon discussed only in passing by Eyamba Bokamba in Chapter 5. Focusing on Wolof, Mc Laughlin tells the story of its ascent from an ethnic language to the dominant and national language now spoken as a vernacular or as a lingua franca by at least 90 per cent of the Senegalese population, many more than the 10–15 per cent who speak French, the official language, with variable levels of competence. Like Kikongo-Kimanyanga in present-day DRC, which evolved into Kikongo-Kituba and became a regional lingua franca cum national language (Mufwene 1994, 1997), Wolof already functioned as a trade language before colonization. Its speakers controlled much of the center of Senegal by the time the first Europeans arrived and developed trade colonies. They had already traded with the Portuguese and the Dutch by the time the French arrived in 1638. They became the majority residents of the first towns to emerge (St. Louis, Dakar, Gorée and Rufisque, among others), and many of them functioned as interpreters. Their language would soon develop into an urban vernacular, by the founder principle (Mufwene 2001), and it would also spread with the Dakar–Niger railroad project in the late nineteenth century.

Mc Laughlin thus shows how urbanization and economic development can play a central role in the spread of a language. The spread of Wolof, thanks to its function as an urban vernacular, is in fact reminiscent of that of Latin in today's Romance countries, where it expanded geographically from the urban centers where it was associated with a Roman-style socioeconomic system, which would be emulated by the rural areas. It is also in the (major) urban centers that Wolof came to compete with other ethnic languages as a vernacular, with more and more children ignoring their (grand)parents' languages – in a way similar to Eyamba Bokamba's account of language shift in Kinshasa, DRC. The towns also fostered an asymmetrical multilingualism that favored Wolof among the adults who have migrated to the city, as more non-Wolof speakers learn to speak Wolof than the other way around.

In addition, urbanization has had the effect of obliterating traditional ethnic distinctions, leading the residents to identify themselves, for instance, as 'Dakarois' (in association with the city) rather than by any traditional ethnic name. Thus, more than French, Wolof has been a major threat to other indigenous Senegalese languages typically in the urban centers. Although there is pressure to speak it as an indigenous lingua franca even in rural areas, people stick here to their ethnic languages as their vernaculars. In a number of cases, the languages are also spoken outside Senegal in places where they are major languages, which encourages their speakers to hold on to them in Senegal.[4] Militantism for the maintenance of languages such Pulaar has also warded off any threat that Wolof can constitute to other (minority) languages. Overall, a clear division of labor exists among many speakers in rural areas between usage of Wolof as a lingua franca and speaking their ethnic language as a vernacular and ethnicity marker. It also appears that in an ecology with a long tradition of egalitarian societal multilingualism, acquisition of a language of wider communication just to speak with people of different ethnic groups entails no pressure to give up one's heritage language. This is a general ecological factor that has protected most African languages in especially the rural areas, where almost half the indigenous population continues to live (unlike in the West), against the spread of European languages and indigenous urban vernaculars and lingua francas (Mufwene 2008).

It is also noteworthy that despite all the prestige it has, French functions in Senegal, as in several other Francophone African countries, primarily as a lingua franca, marginally as vernacular, which is why it is not endangering the indigenous languages. Generally, vernaculars compete with other vernaculars within the socioeconomic ecologies of their speakers, and lingua francas with other lingua francas. Moreover, rising sentiments of national pride that now promote usage of national languages even in domains formerly reserved to European colonial languages, such as political speeches and radio and TV broadcasts, are slowing down the expansion of the latter if not reversing it altogether.

Studies invoking globalization as the constant cause of the endangerment of indigenous languages around the world oversimplify a situation that is heterogeneous and complex. The introduction of English to Senegal has no more endangered the indigenous languages than French has over centuries of contact, although it has relativized the importance of French as a means to connect with the outside world. On the other hand, the fact that non-local globalization has enabled many Senegalese to emigrate has also promoted Wolof to function as a unifying national language among the expatriates, without being the reason why some of these may give up their ethnic languages. When expatriate minorities give up their ethnic languages, it is usually because they hardly come across anybody who speaks them, the same kind of experience that slaves had endured in the New World and in the Indian Ocean (Mufwene 2008), aside from the pressure that the host society exerts on immigrant children to speak the local (dominant) language as a vernacular.

In Chapter 8, Robert Chaudenson puts in historical perspective a prediction made by several linguists since soon after the access of African states to Independence, namely, that the (ex-)colonial languages that now function as official languages endanger the indigenous languages and would drive them to extinction, an experience suffered more specifically by the patois in France. Focusing on former French colonies he explains why such 'futurology' has been proven wrong: the futurologists did not take into account differences in the socioeconomic structures of Europe and Black Africa. They were as naïve as the new, indigenous rulers of the African nations, who generally thought that the ex-colonial languages, associated with better education, would spread widely within their populations through the school system, which they hoped to make accessible to all. On the other hand, they were not developing the requisite socioeconomic infrastructures that would make the ex-colonial and now official languages useful or necessary to all citizens of their nations. The economies of the new states have all collapsed, taking down with them the educational systems left by the colonizers. Even the command of the European languages themselves has statistically gone down.

Highlighting the distinction that must be made between, on the one hand, *glocalization* as locally adapted state of interdependencies between components of a complex socioeconomic structure and, on the other, *globalization* as inter-connectedness between various branches of especially multinational companies, Chaudenson shows, like Blommaert (2003) and Pennycook (2007), how the latter is far from making the world more and more uniform or equal. He under-scores the fact that the gap between the economic North and South is getting wider and wider, making it almost utopian to expect Black Africa to evolve in the same way as Europe or North America, although, as he shows, there have been some surprising developments on the Internet with regard to language vitality. A little over a decade ago, it was generally feared that English (above any other Western European language) would prevail as *the* language of the Inter-net and this situation would precipitate the extinction of minority or marginalized languages. On the contrary, this electronic medium has availed another sphere where the putatively endangered languages can be used, as long as some graphic system has been developed for them and their users can access the new technology. As Chaudenson puts it, the Internet provides a 'quasi-ideal mode(. . .) of managing linguistic diversity and language partner-ship'.[5] He argues that the audiovisual media can likewise be used wisely to serve the needs of all the languages that coexist in a polity, as they bypass the problem that arises with developing a graphic system (see also Chapter 9 by Alamin Mazrui) and of printing materials for the practice of the relevant languages. They can be used to satisfy the needs of both those who want more exposure to the European languages and those who are interested in seeing the indigenous language (re)valorized. Readers will have to assess the economic feasibility of this proposal and fit it with demands for more and more democracy, especially if some languages are given more air time and receive more financial invest-ment than others. They will have to think over whether using a language in the media really guarantees or strengthens its vitality.

Much of the discussion in this chapter makes it obvious that the vitality of languages depends largely on an adequate socioeconomic infrastructure (in the author's words, 'economic, social, political, psychological, technical, etc') that can support them. Agreeing with Mufwene (2005), Chaudenson explains, with more arguments, why efforts to revitalize Gaelic/Irish were doomed to fail in Ireland, while the recreation of Hebrew in Israel and the revitalization of French in Quebec benefited from a number of circumstantial factors, other than the support of the economic system, which favored their success. However, he doubts whether the revitalization of French in Quebec will last. While the state has set up the right economic ecology for the maintenance of French as a useful language, one cannot overlook the fact that the bilingual policy of the federal government provides its citizens the alternative of favoring the language that is likely to offer more advantages to their children in the larger region where English is the dominant language. Moreover, citizens of non-French origin can invoke their human rights to reject the imposition of French on them. As argued in Mufwene (2008), the 'language rights' advocated by linguists often clash with the human rights of speakers, and it appears that the latter will usually prevail.

In the case of Quebec, militancy for a separate state may have worked against the efforts to revitalize the French culture and language, as it has aroused resentment among those who see the language and culture imposed on them against their human rights. It has thus created a situation comparable to that of Afrikaans in South Africa first in the 1970s, when the Bantu populations rioted to resist its imposition on them (Chapter 2 by Rajend Mesthrie), and then now when more and more non-Bantu non-Afrikaners are raising their children with English as mother tongue or placing them in English-medium schools (Mufwene 2008, citing Broeder et al. 2002; Giliomee 2003). In the case of both Quebec and South Africa, the situation is complicated by migrations of those who are ethnically associated with French and Afrikaans, respectively, to areas or spheres where another major language, English, is dominant and their children may not invest themselves in the ethnic language.

The reader can revisit the topic of the usage of less prestigious languages on the Internet in Chapter 9 by Alamin Mazrui. By his own admission, Africans represent only 2.2 per cent of the world's Internet users, and Swahili speakers constitute 6.6 per cent of that population. Yet, several Kenyans are excited by the fact that Microsoft has decided to produce some software in Swahili, arguing that Swahili can now compete more with English and can even spread. They are encouraged to think so by the fact that generally 'the forces of economic globalization are seen to have developed great interest in penetrating world markets through local languages'. The question is: Can the Internet really help a language spread any more than it can help maintain its vitality? Mazrui concludes that 'far from supporting the nationalist agenda of empowering Kiswahili in its perceived competition against English through the localization program, the Internet in Kenya has generally favored the use of "global English"'. English continues to carry a very high symbolic value in Kenya and has prevailed as the preferred lingua franca of the elite; it even functions as a vernacular for some, though it is not evident what proportion of the population the latter represents. Does this really mean that English is endangering

Kiswahili or any other indigenous languages? What should we think of the fact that most Kenyan users of the Internet prefer it to Kiswahili? Does this entail that English is being more widely used in Kenya than this major indigenous lingua, which is also associated with urbanity and modernity, at least to the masses of the population? The study also reveals that there is much more usage of Kiswahili than is generally acknowledged in the survey, albeit as a code-mixed variety. As is evident from the contributions to this volume by Eyamba Bokamba and Fiona Mc Laughlin, code-mixing between an indigenous language and the official one is widespread phenomenon in Black Africa and may perhaps be considered part of normal linguistic practice. It may be observed in urban Lingala in DRC and urban Wolof in Senegal, and the behavior is confirmed by the rich literature on code-switching. Mazrui also reveals that an important reason why Swahili is not as much used on the Internet is the discontinuity between the variety prescribed by purist Kiswahili advocates and what they normally speak. Another is that, although both Kiswahili and English are promoted in the school system, the former was taught as a medium and the latter as an instrument; their literacy has been shaped more in English than in Kiswahili. This appears to be a common experience of the African elite. However, although their language of literacy and scholarship is a European language, they have not necessarily given up usage of their ethnic languages, urban vernaculars or regional lingua francas. It is also important to know what Kenyan and other users of electronic mail use this medium for. Who do they communicate with and about what? Could these factors have contributed to privileging English without concurrently reducing the opportunity for the same Internet users to practice their indigenous languages? The subject matter of language practice and the conditions under which it can cumulatively drive indigenous languages out to extinction is made more complex by the fact that most indigenous African languages have survived the experience of European colonization and the post-Independence retention of the colonial languages as official languages, which are the most emblematic of elite status. English may very well be spreading even into the rural areas of Kenya, but it is quite a different matter whether the spread entails endangerment of the indigenous languages.

The reader will thus be quite interested in the ethnographic significance of the literary creation that Jan Blommaert discusses in Chapter 10. Arguing against the metaphor of 'killer language', he states that dominant languages are not always oppressive and exclusive; they often 'also offer new communicative possibilities and opportunities for creating new sociolinguistic identities'. He finds 'more promising' such metaphors as 'center' and 'periphery' that are found in globalization studies and applies them to a critique of the political novel *Miradi Bubu* (1992) by Tanzania's writer Gabriel Ruhumbika, who he claims both used 'a form of cultural vernacularization' that highlights the locality of its characters, situated in Tanzania, and took advantage of his life abroad to 'globalize' Swahili, a language of the periphery in the *worldwide interconnectedness* conception of globalization.

Blommaert assumes that globalization enables cultures not only to coexist within the same geographical and social spaces but also to spread over discontinuous geographical ones, placing 'emphasis on situatedness, (. . .) flows, trajectories, movements, and thus (. . .) *relative* spatiality'. He explains how Ruhumbika uses place indexicalities to juxtapose several intersecting centers and peripheries at the world and national levels and within the city of Dar es Salaam. Characters' geographical and social trajectories connect these indexicalities both in time and space, highlighting socioeconomic disparities even within a part of Africa considered uniformly peripheral relative to the West. This is all to indicate that things do not evolve uniformly within African nation-states or within urban centers, which sheds light on how differentially African languages must have evolved in their contact with major Western languages. It is possible for different languages to be allocated their respective geographical, social and functional spaces in which they are maintained, despite the spread of major and global languages.

Diasporas are an in important dimension of worldwide globalization insofar as they are among the outcomes of population movements. Although written in Swahili, *Miradi Bubu* is a global novel because it is intended for literate Tanzanians and other literate Swahili speakers all over the world who can grasp the 'translocalizations' and make sense of the local Tanzanian experience that it presents from a world-system perspective. The novel is thus an example of how the global/world-system dimensions of modern life can be interlocked symbiotically with the local. The paper is an invitation to reflect over the idealization of culture, society and particular language practices in a world where people are constantly on the move and must reshape their identities and adapt to new communicative needs. Just as deterritorialization entails reterritorialization (Vigouroux 2005), every new situation at home or away from home may entail new communicative practices, including a reallocation of new ethnographic roles to the languages of one's repertoire. Relocation, translocation and related notions need not be interpreted only geographically; they can be interpreted even socially and also in both ways. This is indeed what Ruhumbika's novel shows successfully. These considerations must be part of our reflections on language vitality and endangerment, from which the rights of speakers as adaptive individuals tend to be subordinated to the rights of languages.

Migrations, the formation of (ethnic and linguistic) diasporas, the integration of the migrants in the host country and the role that language (practice) plays in the process is the focus of Cécile B. Vigouroux in Chapter 11. As longitudinal as her study is, the period of 10 years or so covered by her field research does not enable her to determine what particular languages other than the particular lingua francas of the migrants' countries of origin, including French, enjoy some vitality in the host country and which ones are falling into attrition.

For countries such as DRC and Cameroon, where more than one indigenous lingua francas are spoken, it would also be interesting to find out which particular languages are gaining more speakers and, conversely, which ones are losing speakers, among the migrants. Equally informative would be knowledge of the particular diasporic ecological conditions that favor these evolutions. For instance, are DRC migrants socializing among themselves in ways that reflect regional divisions in the home country and therefore competitive maintenance of the "national languages" or in novel ways that favor one over the others? Do the migrants often meet other migrants that speak the same ethnic languages with whom they continue to speak the same traditional vernaculars in private or are the occasional phone calls at home the only opportunities they have to practice these? On the other hand, does technology constrain the particular languages that one can use, such as French on the Internet, not only because this is the dominant language of literacy among Francophone Africans but also because the correspondents that can have access to it at home are more likely to be affluent and among the privileged few that have access to this technology? The language would thus be emblematic of this economically privileged position. By the same token, does the telephone as an urban phenomenon disfavor usage of ethnic languages and therefore condemn them to attrition among the migrants who do not come across speakers of the same languages? Are there any shifts of vernaculars as languages of day-to-day communication among the migrants and according to what particular interactional patterns?

These are all interesting questions about language maintenance and loss among (im)migrants that a more extensive investigation, extending over a longer period of time than Vigouroux's ethnographic field research, could have focused on. However, the author capitalizes on dynamics of socio-economic integration within the host "social space" and the impact that they make both on language acquisition among the migrants and on language practice with and among the host population, which is multilingual. In this respect Vigouroux articulates the distinction between Pierre Bourdieu's notions of "market value" and "symbolic value." The distinction helps explain why the recent Francophone migrants are more interested in learning IsiZulu, spoken in the eastern part of South Africa, than IsiXhosa and Afrikaans, the local indigenous languages. To the migrants, the symbolic value that IsiZulu derives from its association with the historic leader Shaka Zulu is more significant than the important local market value of IsiXhosa, which they find less useful than English. This imbalance is largely due to the availability of business opportunities locally and to the possibility of moving outside Cape Town and South Africa to places where English is more likely to be used.

However, what kind of English do the migrants learn and how do they manage their language repertoires? Chapter 11 sheds light not only on the above dynamics but also on the way IsiXhosa's ethnographic space has been extended because of the presence of the migrants in Cape Town's city-center. The migrants have made Blacks' presence more conspicuous in the city-center especially through the marketing of art crafts from all over Black Africa and the employment of local women as helpers and occasional interpreters in both English and IsiXhosa. By the same token, they have contributed to spreading IsiXhosa from the townships and squatter camps to the city-center. The latter phenomenon has hardly received much attention in linguistic studies of migrations under conditions other than those of colonization. To what extent do the migrants directly or indirectly affect language practice within the host population?

Another, more applied perspective on the complex question of the co-existence of the ex-colonial and (more) indigenous African languages is contributed by Neville Alexander in Chapter 12, where he focuses on policies for the promotion, maintenance and/or revitalization of the indigenous languages. Arguing that language planning is not a futile enterprise, he addresses the following specific question: 'under what conditions can language policy and planning influence decisively the direction and depth of social change?' He admits that scholars should avoid social engineering, arguing that language planning projects should be undertaken in consultation with their speakers. The same is certainly true of attempts to revitalize some languages, an activity that we consider different from the related scholarly interest in documenting moribund languages for the purposes of future research on language universals and typology, which need not be claimed as useful to the would-be speakers of the languages in question.

Alexander acknowledges that the ex-colonial European languages have become part of the normal linguistic landscape of Africa and 'our objective is to develop the use of [the more indigenous] African languages in high-status functions *next to*, rather than *in place of*, the current languages of European origin'. His goal is to reduce their 'hegemony'. One of the questions is whether the current ethnographic ranking of languages inherited from the colonial period, which has associated the non-European languages with less prestige, can be changed. On the other hand, one can also ask whether the (Black) African experience is unique. Continental European scholars have increasingly been holding conferences and publishing their research findings in English, a practice against which Phillipson (2003) and Hagège (2006) write.[6] And why should anyone worry this much if, as is obvious from most of the other contributions to this volume, indigenous African languages are indeed not at all endangered by the ex-colonial languages in the first place? Why should anyone worry since the latter have actually been indigenized and are no less African than the Romance languages are non-Roman? As a matter of fact, are they not meeting communication needs that are as important as the now indigenized languages themselves? Isn't Africa actually contributing a new form of linguistic diversity with an African touch? Do the more indigenous African languages actually have less value because they are not usually used in the domains allocated to the Euro-African language varieties?

Alexander's chapter is not as much about language endangerment as it is about the current marginalization of large segments of the indigenous populations from modern knowledge, just like during the colonial days. His argument is for a wider diffusion of knowledge in languages that should empower more citizens and to have their governments function in languages that should make their transactions more transparent. As a matter of fact, provided the economies of African nations stop stagnating or degrading, citizens better educated in their own languages could, like their Western counterparts, participate more in the global qua worldwide networks of economic interdependencies instead of being marginalized from them or just being exploited to the benefit of the West. Note that the Japanese and Taiwanese, for instance, participate in the worldwide global economy not because every Japanese or Taiwanese can speak English – as a matter of fact, most of them do not – but because they are empowered to function in successful economies that operate in the indigenous languages. Only a small elite in the white collar sector interface and communicate with the foreign nodes of the worldwide networks of the global economic system in the dominant lingua franca, English. Alexander's essay can thus be interpreted as a plea for decreasing, if the current political systems are incapable of stopping it, the marginalization of the vast majority of African populations from the education systems and the politics of their respective nations, thus for a 'radical democratization of African societies'. The reader is invited to think over this alternative approach to the coexistence of ex-colonial and more indigenous languages in Africa.

1.3 Some Relevant Interpretations of *Globalization*

In this introduction, we have so far not anchored our discussions in globalization and have referred to it without really discussing what it is. There are two important reasons for this. First, there is an obvious correlation between the variable speeds at which language endangerment and loss have proceeded over the past half-millennium and the particular style in which European nations have colonized particular parts of the world. Indigenous languages have vanished the most in settlement colonies than elsewhere. Trade colonies and exploitation colonies have actually introduced new language varieties (Mufwene 2001ff), although the latter have concurrently created new ecologies of language coexistence (especially through urbanization) that have triggered new dynamics of competition among the indigenous languages themselves. This particular correlation between style of colonization and the fate of the indigenous languages has in fact prompted Mufwene (2001ff) to take a retroactive perspective on human history of population movements and contacts, hoping to better understand whether the consequences of recent history of language contacts is that different from the linguistic consequences of, for instance, the colonization of England by the Germanics, of especially continental southwestern Europe by the Romans, and of Europe and South Asia by the Indo-Europeans. From this perspective, we can also determine whether world-wide globalization, rather than local globalization dynamics, is the main reason why indigenous languages have been vanishing so fast in some parts of the world. Can worldwide globalization be dissociated from colonization, be it political or economic, in modern terms?

The second reason for our approach in this introduction is that language practice in Africa today is largely a legacy of colonial traditions, one of which is the imposition of the European colonial languages as emblems of socio-economic status and political power (Mazrui and Mazrui 1998). It is a tradition that has also perpetuated them as tools of socioeconomic exclusion, of oppression and exploitation. We think that understanding these 'local' ecologies of language coexistence and competition, without dwelling too much and preco-ciously on worldwide globalization, can shed interesting light on why the current experience of language endangerment and loss does not sound as grim in Africa as in the rest of world. We do not of course ignore the heavy toll that the Bantu expansion over the past five thousand years or so has inflicted on the Pygmy and Khoesan languages, nor that suffered by the Khoesan languages from the settlement of South Africa by the Dutch in the seventeenth and eighteenth centuries especially. On the contrary, we think that there is some-thing to learn from all this differential evolution of languages in assuming that the Indo-European dispersal continues to date, although its linguistic conse-quences are not uniform around the world (Mufwene 2008). We may even want to consider the alternative that what has been acknowledged recently as worldwide economic globalization is yet another facet and consequence of a new form of colonization in which trade and exploitation have become difficult to extricate from each other and Western metropolitan states have disengaged from political accountability to the exploited populations, although they can intervene militarily to protect the interests of multinational companies in which their citizens are heavily invested.

It is thus deliberately that we have left globalization on the back burner in this introduction, although much of the current literature on language endan-germent and loss has just done the opposite, often invoking colonization only implicitly. Unfortunately, the same literature has not bothered much to explain *globalization* itself nor question whether worldwide rather than local globalization was really responsible for the current experience of language endangerment and loss. We would be remiss not to invite the reader to put its different interpretations, or perhaps just facets of the same phenomenon, in perspective, so that they can appreciate the contributions to this volume against the prevailing literature in a more informed way. We focus on the relevant meanings of the term, on which of them bear(s) on language vitality, and on whether it is accurate to consider it a recent phenomenon.

We start with two interpretations of *globalization* that stand out. The first is what Francophone linguists have typically identified as *mondialisation,* in reference to the interconnectedness of different parts of the world thanks to better networks of communication and transportation, which have facilitated both world exchanges of goods manufactured in different parts of the world and more movements of people who now can remain connected to their places of origins while residing (permanently) in the host country. Thanks to improved communication and transportation technologies, we can now also witness almost instantaneously what is going on in distant parts of the world, consume fresh produce originating in distant climates, communicate almost in the same limited number of European languages, chiefly English, with colleagues and business partners at various points of the planet, and, among other things, sustain the emergent ethnic diasporas as if we all lived in adjacent neighborhoods. These developments have led some optimists to claim that geographical distances and time zone differences have been reduced if not eliminated, that the world has become smaller and more uniform and that cultural and linguistic diversities are vanishing. Little attention has been given to observations that globalization has either widened inequities between the economically more and less developed parts of the world (Stiglitz 2002) or introduced new forms of diversity (Tomlinson 1999). As many contributions to this book show, Africa is still far from experiencing either linguistic Westernization or any kind of cultural and linguistic homogenization. The linguistic Westernization of Africa has remained very much contained by its current socioeconomic structure, limited to a small elite socioeconomic class. If we can speak of some parallel evolutions that set most of Africa in a separate category of its own from the perspective of language vitality, the European languages are not the ones prevailing at the expense of the indigenous ones, and language endangerment is being experienced more in the city than in rural areas, subject to various other ecological factors.

This variable evolution is driven primarily by the second interpretation of globalization as interdependencies that obtain locally among various components of a complex socioeconomic system. Although local economic systems are very much influenced by worldwide global economic trends, populations of different localities adapt primarily, though not exclusively, to local socioeconomic ecological pressures, which affect them directly. Although multinational companies have been at the center of the literature on globalization, especially in linguistics, global economic systems need not cross national or regional boundaries. They are fundamentally local, based on some sort of complementary distribution among the different components, such as (i) dependable transportation and communication infrastructures (for the traffic of ideas, manufactured goods, farming produce and people) and (ii) reliable utility services (in water, electricity and healthcare, which support the industry and labor) within the same town or cluster thereof, as well as (iii) interdependencies between different domains of expertise (such as between masons, carpenters, electricians and other utility service men in the housing industry). Even the plantation slave system operated on this local globalization model, which led everybody operating within the same system to shift quickly to the dominant language of the system, while independent farms evolved at their own separate pace towards the emergence of a common national vernacular in the statewide colony.[7] Communication between the different sectors of such complex systems requires a common language, a phenomenon that becomes evident in urban centers, which have tended to evolve toward monolingualism, unless different parts of the city are highly ethnicized or racialized and each one is almost autonomous, while they are united by a central administration that is bi- or multilingual, as in Brussels.

It is not surprising that language endangerment and loss are the most advanced in polities where urbanization, industrialization and local globalization are the most advanced. These are also territories where a dominant majority of the population is urban and the economic gap in industrial development and buying power per capita between the rural and urban environments is less and less significant, as in North America and Western Europe. Language shift has been driven more by ecological pressures from the socioeconomic system than by any national language policy, which makes the case of Israel quite exceptional, with the peculiar history of its foundation and its relations with its neighbors, as explained in Chapter 8 by Robert Chaudenson. The experience of language endangerment and loss in Africa is so different because its local globalization is nowhere close to what can be observed in the West. The continent is little industrialized and the few industries to be found there are typically urban phenomena and more than half of its indigenous people are still rural (averaging recently to 57 per cent, according to a United Nations 2004 report.), experiencing little pressure for shifting from their traditional languages or cultures. Note also that even the massive migrations of the latter to the city have proceeded in quite peculiar ways. Cities have become bigger faster than anywhere else in the world over the past few decades, often due to economic desperation in the countryside; and they have grown not by some design but rather by the mushrooming of shanty towns around the pre-Independence urban centers, with populations that are only partly urbanized and straddle between the urban and rural ways. The less integrated populations continue to function in their ethnic vernaculars at home and/or neighborhoods. Although their children typically acquire the urban vernacular as their mother tongue, continued migrations from the rural areas has continued to supply speakers of the ethnic vernaculars and other regional lingua francas. This is more remarkable in second-order cities and smaller towns, as explained by Eyamba Bokamba in Chapter 5.[8]

The notion of *glocalization*, more commonly invoked in multicultural studies and invoked in this volume by Robert Chaudenson (see also Mufwene 2008), is ultimately relative to the degree of advancement of local globalization and the integration of the latter in the *mondialisation* phenomenon. The connection between glocalization and *mondialisation* articulates the gap between the haves and have-nots, making some parts of the world more alike than others, despite the undeniable local cachets that can be observed across, for instance, MacDonald eateries and Hilton hotels around the world (Marling 2006). A factor bearing on it is also socioeconomic class, which creates the kinds of local, intranational divides well illustrated by the novel that Jan Blommaert discusses in Chapter 11, with some segments of the national population, especially in the urban centers, being more connected to the world outside their polities than others. As Blommaert articulates this, it depends largely on whether one lives in the town center and thus has access to some socioeconomic privileges or in its periphery and is excluded from the privileges. It also depends on whether one evolves in a geographical area that has benefited the most from industrialization and some Westernization of has been excluded from such evolution . Thus globalization qua *mondialisation* does not bear uniformly on the interactions of citizens of the same country, as Eyamba Bokamba and Fiona Mc Laughlin show so well in relation to the coexistence of French and the indigenous languages in DRC and Senegal, respectively. Almost the same experience is true of Morocco, as is explained by Ahmed Boukous in Chapter 6, which portrays Amazigh as primarily rural and represents lack of both Arabization and Gallicization. It is all so reminiscent of the fact that in North America, the indigenous languages and cultures have survived the most in places least exposed to European influence, typically on the reservations, as long the Native Americans themselves were not mixed among themselves and/ or European Americans did not move in to claim some of their lands too (Banner 2005). As explained in Mufwene (2008), the ensuing hardship and the concurrent lure of the world outside the reservation exerted pressure to shift to the language and culture of the new population majority, predominantly of European descent and speaking English. The Brazilian Amazon is another interesting example of how marginalization from the ongoing economic changes can protect indigenous languages. Until its deforestation started, the Native Americans who inhabit(ed) this rain forest hardly came in contact with the Western-style culture and language(s) that had spread in the rest of Brazil. These contacts have exerted new ecological pressures on the populations to either shift from their traditions and/or relocate to join the dominant population and its more glocalized socioeconomic system. They have thus endangered the Natives' ancestral languages and cultures.

It is myopic to assume that either fundamental interpretation of *globalization* is a recent development or to assume that globalization qua *mondialisation* is disconnected from colonization. As is obvious from Smith (2005), the colonization of Africa by Europe was in itself already an instance of Africa's connection to the world economy, albeit as a source of raw materials, with the modes of exploitation and the rate of production determined by institutions outside the continent. As is evident from Ostler (2003) and well explained by economic historians such as Cowen (2001), globalization is an old phenomenon in human history, though it has become more and more complex in modern times. It has always been characterized by convergence in the modes of production and consumption styles facilitated by wider diffusion of goods through long-distance trade routes.

Long before the European 'Great Explorations' of the fifteenth and sixteenth centuries, the Phoenicians had established trade colonies around the Mediterranean, the Greeks and Macedonians had built a Hellenic Empire that consisted primarily of trade colonies and the Romans had already set up a vast empire straddling in style between the exploitation and settlement models all in the interest of Rome, bequeathing us, among other things, the saying 'all roads lead to Rome'. The forerunners of all such ventures appear to lie in the colonization of hunter–gatherers everywhere, at the dawn of civilization, by farmers and pastoralists. As pointed out by Cowen (2001), they have repeatedly been enhanced by the invention of better and faster means of transportation, with inequities in the control of wealth following from unequal inventions of technology and developments of armies, as well as from advantages that writing and literacy provided to those who controlled technology and power. Colonization of any style and some form of globalization and its inequities in how the benefits are shared have thus proceeded hand in hand. In Africa, the geographical expansion of the Bantu population, which has resulted in the domination and assimilation, sometimes in further marginalization, of the Pygmy and Khoesan populations is reminiscent of the Indo-European expansion, which continues to date in the world. As explained by Herman Batibo in Chapter 3 (see also Mufwene 2001) it caused the gradual loss of the Khoesan languages and cultures (not without their partial impacts on those of their colonizers) in basically the same way that Indo-European languages expanded geographically and speciated in Europe, while the pre-Indo-European languages were vanishing. This was of course the effect of settlement colonization, which has triggered similar effects recently in the Americas and Australia.

Just like the Hellenic Empire was replaced by the Roman Empire, the colonization of the Pygmies and Khoesans by the Bantu has been replaced by that of Africa by the Europeans. On the other hand, just like the Hellenic Empire, the European colonization of Africa has little affected the linguistic landscape of Africa, except in introducing the European languages as lingua francas for communicative functions considered ethnographically high, occasioning the emergence of indigenous urban vernaculars such as urban Wolof and urban Lingala, concurrent with the wider spread of some indigenous languages (e.g., Swahili, Hausa), and the emergence of Afrikaans. Thus, European languages have generally been associated with functions in which they hardly compete with the indigenous languages, in more or less the same ways that Aramaic and Ancient Greek once did. The position of European languages in Africa is even more similar to that of Latin in today's Romance countries of Europe after the collapse of the Western Roman Empire, as an emblem of the socioeconomic elite and largely an urban phenomenon. Their future appear likewise to be tied to how African economies have been evolving, though, as in the case of the Romance countries, one must also factor in the role that nationalisms play in the vitality and restructuring of languages. This is one of the ramifications of Neville Alexander's contribution to this volume.

As noted earlier, from the point of view of the spread of European languages and their impact on indigenous languages, language evolution has proceeded differently in Africa than in the Americas (especially North America) and Australia. This differential evolution appears to be strongly correlated with differences in colonization styles and in the nature of the ensuing glocalization. A dimension of this has involved human traffic and, more recently, migrants perceived as a problem. As a matter of fact, migrations caused either by economic hardship in the country of origin or by armed political conflicts, which have forced many people to seek refuge in other countries, have become part of the demographic dynamics in Africa today. They raise a host of questions regarding language vitality that have seldom been investigated.

In the case of massive refugee exoduses, one of the questions regards the extent to which the vacuum left in the home country affects the vitality of languages. Will the few members of the same ethnolinguistic group left behind shift to another language in order to protect their identity and get their children to speak nothing else but the other language? Will those who left ever return to rebuild the critical mass that their language needs in order to thrive? What happens in the host countries? Are the refugees kept together and in isolation from the host populations, in places where they can continue to evolve in their own cultures and languages? Or are they given refuge in places where they can interact regularly with the host populations and their children acquire the latter's languages as their vernaculars? Is there any hope for them to return home or are they settled almost for good? For instance, during the Angolan struggle for Independence, many Angolans lived in the DRC, integrated within the host population. By the time of Independence, many were connected to Angola more by ideology and nationality than by any knowledge of its languages and other cultural realities. We have met a few of them in the West who are better speakers of Lingala and French than of Kizombo and Portuguese, or any other Angolan language. In this case, as in many others, of refugee exodus caused by armed conflicts, more important proportions of speakers of the language were left home than fled to other countries. The question is whether cases exist where most speakers of a particular language left, leaving behind a small number who need to join other groups that welcome them to survive?

There are also many (im)migrants whom the late American president Gerald Ford once identified as economic refugees. They have generally relocated not as groups but as individuals, have settled where they could find a roof and earn a living, have often not found people speaking the same ethnic vernacular and have communicated with people from the same country either in one of the national languages or in their ex-colonial European official language. Many of them have experienced attrition of their knowledge of their ethnic languages and have not transmitted them to their children. The dynamics of language competition in exile is precisely one way to consider the practice of Wolof as a Senegalese language among Senegalese expatriates, as discussed by Fiona Mc Laughlin in Chapter 7. Similar observations have been made by Vigouroux (2008; also Chapter 11, this volume) about usage of Lingala and Swahili among DRC Congolese in Cape Town (South Africa) and by Meeuwis (1997) and Meeuwis and Blommaert (1998) about Lingala among the same Congolese immigrants to Belgium, where a particular neighborhood in Brussels is nick-named *Matonge* (after a neighborhood in Kinshasa) because of the exceptionally high concentration of them. There are undoubtedly many Congolese who have learned Lingala there rather than in DRC.

All in all, such cases of competition of languages indigenous to Africa abroad shed light on the fact that even at home indigenous African languages compete more among themselves than with the European languages of their respective countries. While globalization has dispersed speakers to various places around the world and subjected the competence of some of them to attrition, it has not changed the nature of the competition among first-generation immigrants, even when the host country's language has imposed itself as the new vernacular of many.

Notes

[1] As becomes obvious later, we use *vitality* as an umbrella term for the maintenance, endangerment and loss of languages.

[2] In the interest of avoiding digressions, we will specify the relevant meanings of these terms only at critical points of this chapter, when it is evident that the reader would be confused if we did not make obvious which particular interpretation applies. The wealth of interpretations that the reader should be aware of will thus emerge gradually.

[3] This peculiarity of the American trade colonies still calls for an explanation. Elsewhere, even in Canton, where the Chinese kept the English at bay and stipulated the conditions of trade with them, the lingua franca was generally a European language, regardless of whether or not it evolved into a pidgin. The adoption of indigenous languages in the colonization of continental Africa, which would lead to the emergence of new varieties such as Kikongo-Kituba, Lingala and Sango and the further expansion of others such as Hausa, Swahili and Songhai, was concurrent with the exploitation colonization of the land (Mufwene 2008).

[4] This raises interesting questions. For instance, what is the impact of the national boundaries inherited from the European colonial regime on how different indi-viduals identify the boundaries of their ethnic affiliations. When ethnicity straddles across national boundaries, do the latter affect their sense of ethnolinguistic

identity? How do populations' attitudes toward ethnicity affect the vitality of the languages of their repertoires?

5 Chaudenson's comment here partly echoes a curious ideology within the Organisation Intergouvernementale de la Francophonie according to which partnerships can be formed between French and the indigenous languages of member states to ward off the dangerous expansion of English. This official position is akin to Swaan's (2001) and Calvet's (2006) 'gravitational' model of language constellations, according to which, as explained in passing earlier, 'peripheral languages' can be rallied around 'central' languages to support each other against external influences such as the expansion of English, a 'supercentral language' in the context of globalization as a worldwide network of interdependencies. Ironically, Robert Chaudenson (p.c. 2005) does not believe that the gravitational model is an adequate representation of the coexistence of languages within national boundaries or of the ethnographic division of labor between them.

6 Ironically, Claude Hagège himself, a Frenchman, has also published in English!

7 It is informative that in the North American a Frenchman, colonies the first immigrants who shifted languages were the economically most destitute, namely, the African slaves and the European indentured servants, who had immediately been integrated in the socioeconomic architecture of the relevant colonies. It took the populations that were economically more autonomous and settled by nationalities a longer time, sometimes up to the twentieth century, to shift to the prevailing language, English (Mufwene 2008). As is quite evident from the histories of Quebec and Louisiana in particular, the socioeconomic pressures are felt the most when the relevant populations have access to the relevant job markets or are absorbed in the relevant socioeconomic structures.

8 While Mufwene (2008) is correct in analogizing the loss of African languages on the plantations of slave colonies with the emergence of monolingualism among the indigenous populations in African cities, we must note that his emphasis was on the role of children as the central factor in language shift at the population level. Otherwise, the shift is not complete yet.

References

Banner, Stuart. 2005. *How the Indians Lost Their Land: Law and Power on the Frontier.* Cambridge, MA: Belknab Press.

Blommaert, Jan. 2003. A Sociolinguistics of Globalization. Commentary. *Journal of Sociolinguistics* 7.607–623.

Bourdieu, Pierre. 1991. *Language and Symbolic Power.* Cambridge, MA: Harvard University Press.

Broeder, Peter, Guus Extra and Jeanne Maartens. 2002. *Multilingualism in South Africa, with a Focus on KwaZulu-Natal and Metropolitan Durban.* Cape Town: PRAESA, University of Cape Town.

Brutt-Griffler, Janina. 2002. *World English: A Study of its Development.* Clevedon: Multilingual Matters Ltd.

Calvet, Louis-Jean. 2006. *Towards an Ecology of World Languages.* Cambridge: Polity.

Cavalli-Sforza, Luigi Luca and Francesco Cavalli-Sforza. 1995. *Great Human Diasporas.* Cambridge, MA: Perseus Books.

Cowen, Noel. 2001. *Global History: A Short Overview.* Cambridge: Polity Press.

Crosby, Alfred W. 1986. *Ecological Imperialism: The Biological Expansion of Europe, 900–1900.* Cambridge: Cambridge University Press.

Giliomee, Harmann. 2003. *The Rise and Possible Demise of Afrikaans as a Public Language.* Cape Town: PRAESA, University of Cape Town.

Hagège, Claude. 2006. *Combat pour le français: au nom de la diversité des langues et des cultures.* Paris: Odile Jacob.

Huber, Magnus. 1999. Atlantic Ceoles and the Lower Guinea Coast: A Case Against Afrogenesis. In *Spreading the Word: The Issue of Diffusion among the Atlantic Creoles,* ed. by Magnus Huber and Mikael Parkvall, 81–110. London: University of Westminster Press.

Joseph, Brian, Johanna DeStefano, Neil Jacobs, and Ilse Lehiste. 2003. *When Languages Collide: Perspectives on Language Conflict, Language Competition, and Language Coexistence.* Columbus: Ohio State University Press.

Marling, William H. 2006. *How 'American' is Globalization?* Baltimore: Johns Hopkins Press.

Mazrui, Ali A. and Alamin M. Mazrui. 1998. *The Power of Babel: Language and Governance in the African Experience.* Oxford: James Currey; Nairobi: E.A.E.P.; Kampala: Fountain Publishers; Cape Town: David Philip Publishers; Chicago: University of Chicago Press.

Meeuwis, Michael. 1997. *Constructing Sociolinguistic Consensus: A Linguistic Ethnography of the Zairian Community in Antwerp, Belgium.* Doctoral thesis, University of Antwerp.

Meeuwis, Michael and Jan Blommaert. 1998. A Monolectal View of Code-Switching: Layered Code-Switching Among Zairians in Belgium. In *Code-Switching in Conversation,* ed. by Peter Auer, 76–100. London: Routledge.

Mesthrie, Rajend. 1992. *English in Language Shift: The History, Structure and Sociolinguistics of South African Indian English.* Cambridge: Cambridge University Press.

—2006. Subordinate Immigrant Languages and Language Endangerment: Two Community Studies from Kwa-Zulu Natal. *Language Matters* 37.3–15.

Mufwene, Salikoko S. 1994. Restructuring, Feature Selection, and Markedness: From Kimanyanga to Kituba. In *Historical Issues in African Linguistics,* ed. by Kevin E. Moore et al., 67–90. Berkeley Linguistics Society.

—1997. Kituba. In *Contact Languages: A Wider Perspective,* ed. by Sarah G. Thomason, 173–208. Amsterdam: John Benjamins.

—2001. *The Ecology of Language Evolution.* Cambridge: Cambridge University Press.

—2005. *Créoles, écologie sociale, évolution linguistique.* Paris: L'Harmattan.

—2008. *Language Evolution: Contact, Competition, and Change.* London: Continuum Press.

Ostler, Nicholas. 2003. *Empires of the World: A Language History of the World.* New York: Harper Collins.

Pennycook, Alastair. 2007. *Global Englishes and Transcultural Flows.* London: Routledge.

Phillipson, Robert. 2003. *English-Only Europe? Challenging Language Policy.* London: Routledge.

Ruhumbika, Gabriel. 1992. *Miradi Bubu ya Wazalendo.* Dar es Salaam: Nkuki na Nyota.

Smith, Stephen. 2005. L'Afrique paradoxale. In *Les faces de la mondialisation,* ed. by Thierry de Montbrial and Philippe Moreau Defarges, 111–24. Paris: Dunod, for L'Institut Français des Relations Internationales.

Stiglitz, Joseph E. 2002. *Globalization and its Discontents.* New York: W.W. Norton & Co.

Swaan, Abram de. 2001. *Words of the World: The Global Language System.* Cambridge: Polity Press.

Tomlinson, John. 1999. *Globalization and Culture.* Chicago: University of Chicago Press.

Vigouroux, Cécile B. 2005. 'There Are No Whites in Africa': Territoriality, Language and Identity Among Francophone Africans in Cape Town. *Language and Communication* 25.237–255.

—2008. The 'Smuggling of la Francophonie': Francophone Africans in Anglophone Cape Town (South Africa). *Language in Society* 37.415–434.

Chapter 2

Trajectories of Language Endangerment in South Africa

Rajend Mesthrie

2.1 Introduction

South Africa is an important site for evaluating the impact of the colonial and (now) global onslaughts upon indigenous peoples, their ecologies, cultures and languages. In Mufwene's terms (2001:9) South Africa is historically a 'settlement colony' in which speakers of European languages, with the aid of colonial networks, partially altered the local landscapes, economies and socio-cultural patterns towards European models of development. Which of the European languages themselves prospered and which gave way is an interesting question in its own right, though necessarily of lesser significance than their own impact upon the local languages. In this chapter I examine clear-cut cases of language shift and death in recent South African history. I argue that these cases are not necessarily typical of, or precursors to, further language loss in the post-colonial globalizing era. To uncover patterns of language maintenance and loss it is necessary to differentiate between different levels of indigenity, and to identify different types of colonial networks.

2.2 On the Term *Indigenous*

The OED defines *indigenous* as follows: 'Born or produced naturally in a land or region or belonging naturally *to* (the soil, region etc). (Used primarily of aboriginal inhabitants or natural products)'. On the other hand, the term *aboriginal* is defined as 'First or earliest so far as history or science gives record'. Such terms are problematic insofar as there is no way of deciding how far back one is to go to find the original local inhabitants. Current usage, both learned and popular, assigns indigenous status to the majority of Black people in South Africa speaking a Bantu language, as well as to the descendants of the Khoesan, who are often classified in South African terms as 'Colored'. (Like all racial designations these terms are controversial and contested: but the nomenclature has survived the collapse of apartheid for complex reasons.) History tells us that Khoesan people were the first peoples of South Africa, and in fact constitute the oldest 'genetic material' not just in South Africa, but in Africa and, ergo, the world, given geneticists' consensus regarding Africa as the cradle of human-kind. On the other hand, the presence of Bantu-speaking groups in the territory now called South Africa dates to about 300 AD, themselves probably displaced and absorbed by later migrants of similar linguistic affiliation around 1000 AD (Herbert and Bailey 2002:50–51). No one doubts that these dates are old enough for their latter-day descendants to be considered 'indigenous' in South Africa. The Microsoft Encarta dictionary (1999) in fact offers the definition of *indigenous* as people belonging to a territory at the time of colonial contact. There is, however, a case to be made for differentiating between 'older indige-nous' (aka *first nations* or *authocthones*) and indigenous. Khoesan exemplifies both, Bantu only the latter for South Africa. The term *aboriginal*, which was defined earlier as part of the meaning of *indigenous*, is not used in South Africa; a synonym *native* in apartheid-speak came to refer to 'Bantu-speaking Africans' rather than 'Coloreds' (many of whom are of Khoesan or part-Khoesan descent). Relations between the Khoesan and incoming Bantu varied. Some scholars stress inimical relations between them in the earlier periods of contact (Bryant 1929:5; Ownby 1981). Herbert (2002) and others find evidence of peaceful coexistence too, leading to language transfer, most spectacularly of clicks from Khoesan languages to Xhosa, Zulu, and, to a lesser extent, a few other Southern Bantu languages. The main reason for differentiating these 'degrees of indi-genity' is that there are linguistic ramifications regarding degrees of contact and bilingualism, as well as who shifted to whose language. These aspects are explored further in Section 2.3.

   The apartheid regime tried to promote the idea that the first European set-tlers from the Netherlands were as indigenous as the Bantu in the Cape in the sixteenth century. Their claim that it was a contemporaneous settlement and expansion that saw Afrikaners moving northwards from the Cape and Bantu speakers heading south has been disproved by historians and archaeologists. Nevertheless the claim that Afrikaans is an indigenous language of Africa per-sists (as suggested by its name, which means 'of Africa'). Central to the claim is the fact that the form of the language took shape in South Africa and has no exact equivalent in Europe. The fact that the language has a large proportion of speakers who are not White (i.e., mostly 'Colored' and some 'Black') and whose linguistic norms are even further removed from Europe is also used to substantiate the claim. It is not the aim of this chapter to concentrate on language politics, but it is already clear how politicized the discussion of lan-guage status can become. One intriguing point is seldom noted in the language policy literature: that Afrikaans (in its Dutch and Cape Dutch incarnations) is of older lineage in South Africa than the 'smaller' official Bantu languages, Tsonga (chiTsonga), Venda (luVenda) and Swazi (siSwati), which emanated mostly in the nineteenth century from adjacent southern African territories. (This raises another intriguing debate about the status of adjacent territories and countries in defining indigenous).

2.3 Khoesan Endangerment

As far as South Africa is concerned, the history of Khoesan languages follows the dismal record of colonial destruction that one finds in North America and Australia.[1] The history is slightly different insofar as Bantu languages also impacted upon the fate of Khoesan. Once thriving languages of different families spoken all over the territory, Khoesan languages have become eroded to the point where most of them are now extinct and the rest endangered. In the century of first colonization of the territory later called South Africa (the seventeenth), there were languages of the Central (Khoekhoe) and Southern (Bushman) groupings. Traill (2002:29) estimates that at this time there were approximately eleven closely related Cape Khoekhoe varieties spanning a wide area from what is now Cape Town to as far east as the Fish River. Their total number of speakers is estimated to have been somewhere between one hundred thousand and two hundred thousand. The Southern Bushman languages were at that time even more widespread, covering the rest of South Africa as shared territory with the Bantu languages. Wright (1971) estimates the number of San in South Africa to have been about ten thousand–twenty thousand at that time. Their languages were thus much less densely distributed than the Khoekhoe varieties.

The Khoekhoe languages of the south western Cape, which included Hesse (Hai-se), Chainou, Cocho, Guri, Gorinhai (!uri-//'ae) and Gorachou (!ora-// xau), were the ones to be eroded first, within a hundred years of the arrival of Dutch colonization (Elphick 1985:211; Traill 2002:31). Traill's summary of the causes of language death in the Western Khoe languages is as follows:

> It has been argued that the processes that destroyed the social, political and economic structures of the western Cape Khoekhoe were far advanced only sixty-one years after van Riebeeck landed in Table Bay (Elphick 1985); the smallpox epidemic of 1713, which virtually wiped out the Khoekhoe in the western Cape, merely consummated this breakdown. The result for the Khoe language spoken there was that within a hundred years of van Riebeeck's arrival in 1652 it too had largely succumbed, and was largely replaced by Afrikaans. (31)

Apart from the breakdown of traditional Khoekhoe social structure, Traill mentions prejudice against their language, with even the missionaries generally failing to come to terms with them; as well as the social pressures caused by the arrival of large numbers of slaves from the East Indies, Madagascar and Mozambique. All of these factors favored the emergent lingua franca, a modified form of Dutch that was eventually to be labelled *Afrikaans.*

The Khoekhoe languages that were taken into the interior by their communities survived longer. The closely related Kora (or !ora) and Gri (Xiri) varieties of Khoekhoe, whose speakers migrated into the Orange and Vaal River areas, survived until the early twentieth century. Gri had undergone advanced shift by 1801, but Kora survived well into the 1830s as a significantly monolingual speech community at Bethany in the southern Orange Free State (Traill 2002:35). In the northern part of the Cape frontier the Griqua became dominant over the Korana and Bushmen, whom they attempted to reduce to servile status as laborers. Traill (2002:35) believes that this could have attenuated the language of the Korana even further. Today Kora and Gri are extinct, not without passing over remnants to the Orange River Afrikaans that replaced it. In 2002, I encountered a young Colored female in Durban who was able to produce some remnant phrases remembered from her grandmother of Griqua extraction. Menan du Plessis (personal communication, 2007) informs me that scholars at the University of the Orange Free State have come across about a hundred descendants of !Ora extraction who remember the language to varying degrees and have expressed keenness to resuscitate it.

Shift from a Khoekhoe variety to Afrikaans in the north-western Cape occurred at a slower rate, and did not affect all areas. Nama survives till today in the Richtersveld area of the Northern Cape (just outside the Cape Colony), 'where no missionary ever achieved political power' (Carstens 1966:208, cited by Traill 2002:33). Speakers were in fact monolingual up to the 1950s, the time of the compulsory introduction of Afrikaans in the schools (Traill 2002:334). Nama remains in this community as the sole surviving Khoekhoe language of South Africa.

One notably different pattern of language shift in Khoekhoe concerns the Gonaqua (or Gona) in the Eastern Cape frontier of the early nineteenth century. The Eastern Cape Khoekhoe were caught between the struggle for supremacy over the frontier between the Boers and the Xhosa. Some of them were absorbed into the Boer and English missionary sphere of influence, shifting to Afrikaans and becoming Christians. Many Gonaqua remained with the Xhosa and were incorporated into Xhosa clans, shifting to the Xhosa language in the process around 1800 (Mesthrie 1998; Sales 1975).

Turning to the San languages of South Africa, the picture is no better. The largest and most extensive of the Bushman languages was /Xam (or Cape Bushman), which has been well recorded by Wilhelm Bleek and Lucy Lloyd in the mid-nineteenth century. A rich collection of linguistic and folklore materials exists, but no speaker of /Xam can be found today. The more recent history of its speakers involves 'their societies shattered by warfare, starvation and disease; the women and children enslaved; the men all but exterminated by the genocidal hatred of their enemies' (Penn 1991, cited by Traill 2002:37). Those enemies included just about everyone: Boers, Griqua, Xhosa and Koranna (Marais 1968:28, cited by Traill 1996:165). Apart from enslavement, this history is not very different from the colonial ravages happening in North America, the Caribbean and Australia at the same time. This can be seen from Traill's (1996) detailed study of /Xam, which reached a point of 'irreversible' decline by the mid-eighteenth century, within four generations of colonial contact. However, as with the Khoekhoe, some speakers of San languages shifted to a Bantu language (Tswana, Xhosa, Swati, Zulu or Sotho to varying degrees) over time, rather than Afrikaans. This applied, for example, to Seroa (or Sarwa), whose speakers in East Griqualand (and the neighboring country, Lesotho) were bilingual in Seroa and in Nguni (Traill 2002:40–41), and their surviving descendants shifted to the latter. San languages survive in Botswana and Namibia (Batibo 2005); and they are all but extinct in South Africa. Nigel Crawhall (2004) found twelve speakers of N/u, a Southern Bushman language believed to have been extinct; and linguists such as Crawhall and Tom Güldemann are involved in salvage work of a linguistic and cultural nature with the last surviving elderly speakers in the Northern Cape.

2.4 Immigrant Languages

In this section I briefly examine the fate of languages from outside Africa in South African history. Rather obviously, English has never faced endangerment, since its inception as a language of a settled civilian population in 1820. Even though the number of English settlers in that year was relatively small (four thousand–five thousand according to Lanham and Macdonald 1979:9) and their position on the eastern frontier of the Cape Colony was a vulnerable one, English survived because the backing of empire and colony made it and its speakers secure. From an 'ecology of language' perspective, English speakers had the resources, recourse to colonial forces and viable, though small, social networks that enabled them a relative degree of control of their environment. Their position of control and superiority should not be exaggerated: Lanham and Macdonald (1979:9), for example, invoke 'a hostile and unfamiliar environment' to highlight their settler vulnerability. An index of this unfamiliarity can be seen in the immense number of loanwords passing from Afrikaans into English in the semantic fields of the landscape and new local customs. English speakers' learning of African languages was slower; though many children learnt Xhosa from childhood friendships (Wilson 1972). The existence of institutionalized schooling, especially the boarding school, caused many of these children to lose active control over the Xhosa. Still, it must be acknowledged that the learning of an indigenous language by English speakers is more common in South African rural areas than in North America and Australia. (This is probably true of European settlers in other parts of Africa.)

From the viewpoint of the superstrata, South Africa is interesting insofar as another language, Dutch, survived and for a time and rivalled English in the local language ecology. How different Afrikaans is from Dutch has been an 'enduring crux' in sociohistorical linguistics of the language (Roberge 2002). Despite the politicization of the more formal aspects of language, including choice of name, orthographic conventions and variety to be codified in the late eighteenth and early nineteenth centuries, there is no evidence of a sharp break in speech norms from a European-based variety to a totally new system (Deumert 2003). In the case of new learners of slave and Khoikhoi descent, questions about the nature of their initial learner varieties and their role in establishing a distinct form later to be called 'Kaaps' are crucial (Roberge 2002). It also seems likely that Afrikaans has seen a greater convergence of the European-based and the slave/indigenous-based varieties than English has in South Africa or anywhere else in the world. Why the Dutch did not shift to English or vice versa are interesting questions for political sociology. Traditional views are that Afrikaners in early-nineteenth-century Cape were becoming Anglicized in more formal domains (all the more striking in view of the small size of the English community). However, this did not apply to religion or the homes, except in some isolated cases. According to Lanham and Macdonald (1979:10–11), bilingualism in English carried overtones of *geleerdheid* 'good education'. However, political antagonisms between Afrikaner and English over the right to slaves, the imposition of English as an official language and, no doubt, the very act of conquest by the English led to Afrikaner migrations away from the Cape into the interior in search of political sovereignty. Language became an essential part of this distillation of identity, especially after the anti-British feeling over treatment in the Anglo-Boer wars, which were essentially about control of the newly discovered mineral fields. Afrikaans was promoted to an official state language in 1925, in addition to English and Dutch. Central to this effort was the conviction that the Afrikaner minority had sufficient control of technological and other resources to alter and control the language ecology of the region as part of political hegemony. That Afrikaans had more mother-tongue speakers than English in 1948, the year when Afrikaner rule was instituted, made this a possibility. The census figures for 1946 are as follows: Afrikaans as home language – 1,280,285; English as home language – 923,223; both as home languages – 31,340.[2]

The collapse of apartheid and arrival of a new democracy in 1994 changed that ecology dramatically. Afrikaans has been reduced to being one of eleven official languages, nine of them more indigenous to Africa. These days there is some talk of Afrikaans as an endangered language. This alarmist discourse is a reflection of intense loyalty to the language, rather than an indication of any real language shift. In key informal domains Afrikaans continues to have millions of speakers from different backgrounds. Many of them are bilingual or multilingual. However, change has occurred in the use of Afrikaans as a dominant language of public life and institutions. There has been loss of national airtime and viewing time in the media, and a necessary compromise over Afrikaans as sole medium of instruction at institutions of higher learning. All of these are subject to intense debate in South Africa, especially in the light of constitutional backing for multiculturalism and multilingualism. What is clear is that while Afrikaans is receding in formal domains, it continues to enjoy the support base of mother-tongue speakers, many of whom are highly literate in both English and Afrikaans. Using the statistics of the 2001 census, Mesthrie (2006:539–551) shows that Afrikaans remains the most widely spread L1 in South Africa. It is a majority language of the Western Cape Province, and the mother tongue of large numbers of Colored speakers, who are not involved in processes of political control and hegemony via language or any other means.

   Other European languages such as French, German and Portuguese have not had the demographic or political presence to obtain official or other hege-monic status. The Huguenot French refugees of the late seventeenth century were not allowed to form a separate community of their own; instead, they were deliberately spread out among the Dutch of the Cape. French did not survive more than a generation in South Africa, though it is now making a reappear-ance three centuries later via Black migrants from Central and West Africa (Vigouroux 2005). German has all the hallmarks of a minority language in South Africa, with its speakers being hard pressed to resist shift to English and Afrikaans at various stages (de Kadt 2002; Franke 2007). Portuguese speakers arrived in large numbers from other parts of Africa in the post-independence era (of the 1970s), and are generally facing rapid shift to English (Barnes and McDuling 1995). In their case, the shift has been driven primarily by the pres-tige of English in urban centers, where the youth have been changing their social networks.

   Two large-scale labor movements brought slaves and indentured workers to South Africa. Ironically, at the very time when the Americas were stocking up on slaves from Africa to build new economies, within the southern tip of Africa the Dutch were looking for slaves from their East Indian holdings. The slave population of Cape Town grew steadily in relation to the declining numbers of Khoekhoe in the cities' environs. In 1798, for example, when the Khoekhoe were enumerated for the first time, there were 14,447 'Khoikhoi and Bastaards' against 25,754 slaves (Elphick and Giliomee 1989:524). Languages of the slaves included those of Indonesia and Malaysia, including Malay, Buganese and Javanese (Davids 1990), as well as of Sri Lanka and India, including Bengali, Tamil and Singhala. Two lingua francas existed in this period: a variety of Malay and Creole Portuguese developed and coexisted with the slave and Khoekhoe versions of Dutch (later identified as Afrikaans) to which they eventually gave way, by the late nineteenth century. The mid-nineteenth century was also marked by a large scale importation of Indian workers under indenture, which brought speakers of Tamil, Telugu, Bhojpuri–Hindi and Urdu into the colony of Natal. These languages were well maintained up till 1960. After that a gradual language shift set in, which is still in process today, with fluent speakers of these languages to be found mainly among the over-fifty-five age groups. Mesthrie (1992, 2007a) argues that the main motive behind the shift was not a 'straight for English' attitude. Rather, English proved a relatively neutral lingua franca among Indians of different linguistic backgrounds, together with its usefulness in education and the economy. The key to the shift lay in the choices of young people, engaged in forming new social networks that involved Indians from a diversity of backgrounds, as opposed to the relatively 'sectarian' social networks of their parental generations. The shift to English brought integration within the Indian community; there was no expectation, at the height of apartheid in the 1960s and 1970s, of integration into a broader, White-dominated, English-speaking social network. The Indian South African case shows language maintenance well beyond the three-generation pattern obtaining in the United States (Rayfield 1970), as the shift occurred in the fourth or fifth generation.

The case of shift among the one million Indians in South Africa is also interesting insofar as it raises questions about its applicability to the Black majority of the country. It is to this currently much-debated theme that I turn in the next section.

2.5 Maintenance and Shift among Bantu-Language Speakers in South Africa

This segment of the indigenous population had survived Dutch and British colonization and remained numerically dominant, despite colonial wars in the Eastern Cape and Zululand in the nineteenth century. While the gold and diamond revolution of the 1880s onwards forced Bantu speakers from all parts of southern Africa into the industrialized interior, and while urbanization was relatively rapid, bringing in degrees of cultural change, this was not to the erosion of traditional culture. Colonial policies involving segregation were made totally rigid under apartheid, thereby limiting the amount of acculturation of Black people to Western norms. Later, apartheid philosophy tried to prevent Bantu speakers from educational and economic progress (Hartshorne 1995). In the period up to the close of the twentieth century Bantu languages have never been in real danger of shift. One scholar, Jacob Nhlapo (1944), did raise questions about the future of the Bantu languages, in the subtitle of his pamphlet 'Will the Bantu languages survive?'. However, fifty years later language statistics give no clues about the possibility of language shift for these languages, as made evident by Table 2.1, based on the last three censuses of 1990,[3] 1996 and 2001.

The 'raw' figures in Table 2.1 do not suggest any endangerment for the eleven official figures. For the most part, all eleven languages show a steady growth, except for slight drops in 1995 for Ndebele, Tswana and Afrikaans. These drops

Table 2.1 Census statistics for L1 usage of the official languages[4]

Language	1990	1996	2001
Ndebele	799,216	586,961 ↓	711,818
Swati	926,094	1,013,193	1,194,428
Xhosa	6,891,358	7,196,118	7,907,154
Zulu	8,541,173	9,200,144	10,677,306 ↑↑
North Sotho/Pedi	3,437,971	3,695,846	4,208,982
South Sotho	2,652,590	3,104,197	3,555,189
Tswana	3,601,609	3,301,774 ↓	3,677,016
Tsonga	1,349,022	1,756,105	1,992,207
Venda	763,247	876,409	1,021,759
Afrikaans	6,188,981	5,811,547 ↓	5,983,426
English	3,432,042	3,457,467	3,673,197
Other	–	228,275	217,297
Unspecified	–	355,538	–
Total		40,583,573	44,819,779

↓ denotes slight drop in growth whereas ↑↑ denotes considerable growth.

Table 2.2 The four most common languages in each province of South Africa, 2001 (in millions)

Province	Most common language	Second most common language	Third most common language	Fourth most common language
Eastern Cape	Xhosa (5.4)	Afrikaans (0.6)	English (0.2)	S.Sotho (0.2)
Free State	S. Sotho (1.7)	Afrikaans (0.3)	Xhosa (0.2)	Tswana (0.2)
Gauteng	Zulu (2.0)	Afrikaans (1.3)	S. Sotho (1.2)	English (1.1)
KwaZulu-Natal	Zulu (7.6)	English (1.3)	Xhosa (0.2)	Afrikaans (0.1)
Limpopo	Pedi (2.8)	Tsonga (1.2)	Venda (0.8)	Afrikaans (0.1)
Mpumalanga	Swati (1.0)	Zulu (0.8)	Ndebele (0.4)	Pedi (0.3)
Northern Cape	Afrikaans (0.6)	Tswana (0.2)	Xhosa (0.1)	English (0.02)
North West	Tswana (2.4)	Afrikaans (0.3)	Xhosa (0.2)	Sotho (0.2)
Western Cape	Afrikaans (2.5)	Xhosa (1.1)	English (0.9)	Sotho (0.03)

do not appear significant as all three languages show recovery in 2001. In particular the gains for English show the same steady growth due to demographic growth that all the languages show. Only one language shows considerable growth of over a million L1 speakers in a ten-year period, and it is not English but Zulu. The censuses did not analyze L2 usage; here the gains for English are likely to be the most rapid. However, Afrikaans and Zulus remain significant L2s.

Geographical spread is also an indicator of language vitality, since it shows that speakers of particular languages are able to maintain them outside their traditional rural bases. Mesthrie (2006:540–541) calculated the spread of languages per province as indicated in Table 2.2.

Table 2.3 The distribution of first languages per province

Language	No. of provinces in which the language is most common	Second most common language	Third most common language	Fourth most common language
Afrikaans	2	4	–	2
Xhosa	1	1	4	–
Zulu	2	1	–	–
South Sotho	1	–	1	3
English	–	1	2	2
Tswana	1	1	–	1
Pedi	1	–	–	1
Swati	1	–	–	–
Tsonga	–	1	–	–
Ndebele	–	–	–	1
Venda	–	–	–	1

Using the information in Table 2.2, we arrive at an approximation of the distribution of the official languages of South Africa in Table 2.3, which shows the number of provinces in which each language is the most common, second most common, and so on. In arriving at a rank order, a weighting system of 4 points for the most common language, 3 for the second, 2 for the third, and 1 for the fourth was used. As can be seen from Table 2.3, all eleven languages have a sizeable geographical presence, though Swati, Tsonga, Ndebele and Venda are not as strong as the others.

Regarding geographical distribution, it is also important to keep in mind that several languages are well represented as official or national languages in neighboring countries (Sotho in Lesotho, Tswana in Botswana, Swati in Swaziland) or are languages with large numbers of speakers (Tsonga in Mozambique, Venda in Zambia and Zimbabwe, Ndebele in Zimbabwe). In this regard the indigenous Bantu languages fare much better than their counterparts in, say, Asia and South America.

Turning to the complementary measure of vitality in the number of functions a language performs and its relative status, we see a slightly different picture. English is the most visible and audible language at governmental functions, political rallies, administration, the upper echelons of business and education. These factors make English a much more important language than the tables given earlier indicate. On the other hand, African languages and Afrikaans are very much alive on individual radio stations, in music, some newspapers (chiefly Afrikaans, Zulu and Xhosa) and, to a lesser extent, on television. Where African languages could fare better (and do not perhaps compare with, say, some languages of Asia) is in the film and magazine industries. Attitudes to languages have not been studied in as much depth as they deserve. A *Sunday Times* report (Pretorius 2001) cites a *Mark Data* survey of household attitudes in the domain of education.

Of 2,160 households surveyed, 12 per cent preferred English as the only medium of instruction. A sizeable 40 per cent wanted English to be taught alongside the home language; and about 37 per cent wanted mother-tongue education in all state-funded schools and universities. The article mentions that scholars interviewed expressed doubts about the findings, saying that in terms of actual preferences, parents were increasingly opting for English: 'Black parents are lured to English-medium schools because they have better resources and their children will learn English' (Pretorius 2001).

The discrepancy between actual demographic strength and status in 'high' domains can be seen in a spate of articles prognosticating doom. The political sociologist R.W. Johnson (2006) wrote an article provocatively entitled 'Goodbye isiXhosa' in which he pointed to the difficulties of using individual African languages in domains such as higher education and government. And if one is to judge from the popular press reports of the findings and opinions of academic researchers, African languages are already under threat. A few headlines and excerpts of reports from the print media will illustrate this. In 1998 the findings of Research International were reported dramatically as follows:

> The year is 2008. You are walking down Eloff Street, Johannesburg when it suddenly hits you: there is not a single black man 'as you have always known him' in sight. If this sounds far fetched, brace yourself. According to Research International, which studied black men worldwide, the 'traditional black African man as we have known him' will have disappeared by 2008.

> But not everyone shares his [= researcher Johannes Cichorius's] views: Some black men don't think they will disappear so soon. For others it is a cause of concern. (Moya 1998)

Although the report did not include the disappearance of African languages within its (failed) ten-year prophecy, some Black leaders did make the connection. For example, Khaba Mkhize, a regional manager of the South African Broadcasting Corporation (SABC) at the time, opined that 'the findings are a wake-up call for Africans to preserve their languages' and that 'apocalypse could happen if language is neglected'. However, he conceded that 'it takes at least three generations for a language to disappear'.

The view that African languages are endangered was endorsed by President Thabo Mbeki, who called upon 'traditional leaders to stop indigenous languages from disappearing' (SABC News, April 2005). 'The president says he is very concerned that African languages and traditions are lapsing in both rural and urban areas.' Commentators would observe that the president and parliamentarians generally do not set the example themselves. Furthermore, there is more than a hint of opportunism in appealing to traditional culture when addressing traditional chiefs, who are important allies in politics.

The popular press often focuses on young women as agents of westernization and language change. An article entitled 'Death of the Mother Tongue' (*Sunday Times* 2004) claimed that 'Though there are 11 official languages in South Africa, many people are forsaking their mother tongues to speak in an American-English mode considered "cool" by their peers'. The article hinges around the tensions between a young girl's (pseudonym *Thandi*) integration into an English-dominant 'Model C' school, which does not offer Xhosa as a subject, and the more balanced bilingualism of her mother who learnt Xhosa first and then English a generation ago. The older generation frequently disapproves of the Anglicized norms of the younger middle-class children, as the article notes in connection with Thandi's mother who forces her to take Xhosa classes. ' "I mean, why?" she pouts. "Like why do I need this? If it wasn't for my mom I wouldn't bother".' The same newspaper carried an article citing a university lecture and cultural expert who says that

> smoking starts at social gatherings where women think there is glamor and status associated with it. It's like speaking English. You see them wearing pants with cigarette in hand and they seem to have the notion that they are sophisticated. It seems speaking English and smoking cigarettes go hand in hand with these modern women (. . .) (Ntshilinga 2006)

Tensions between language learning and cultural change are obvious here. The defenders of African languages are distrustful of some aspects of the modernity associated with a close-to-L1 command of English. And the threat felt to traditional gender hegemony is obvious in the previous quotation. One is reminded of Bourdieu's dictum (1977) that those who defend a language defend the whole social situation it is associated with. What is evident in the newspaper articles is a struggle between African languages and English, and the latter is not the object of unadulterated veneration.

On the whole, reports of the impending deaths of Xhosa, Zulu and the other languages are sensationalist, emotive and exaggerated. Many rural children coming to school for the first time are still monolingual; their urban counterparts are frequently multilingual, usually in more than one Bantu language. Moreover, children of the increasing number of immigrants from other African countries do acquire the local African language. Adults coming into the townships from other countries also become fluent, in a relatively short time, in the local dominant language (Jama et al. 2006).[5] None of these considerations should imply a declining trajectory for the major Bantu languages of the country.[6] So why do the headline writers thrive?

To appreciate the concern of the glotto-pessimists, we need to examine the behavior of South Africa's young middle classes and of the new political elite. Here there does seem cause for concern. Prior to the mid-1980s, the apartheid policy severely constrained the formation of nonracial social networks among young people. The apartheid policy segregated people into zoned residential areas, typically keeping Blacks and Whites the furthest apart, with Colored and Indian communities sandwiched in-between. Recreational, health and educational facilities were kept as separate as possible, as was transport and accommodation. There were separate lifts and park benches for Whites and 'Non-Whites'. Teaching staff at schools were also almost always from the same race as the students. Such rigid social streaming kept languages apart and resulted in the prolongation of the characteristic features of dialects of English and Afrikaans, the two languages that were promoted across races in the educational and economic spheres. In addition, the apartheid government hoped to promote Afrikaans more extensively than English in Black education (Hartshorne 1995).

Prior to the collapse of apartheid and the advent of democracy in 1994, 'petty apartheid' rules began to be relaxed from the 1980s onwards. In particular a small number of students from 'Non-White' groups were allowed into White private and public (or Model C) schools. This trend continued greatly with the scrapping of the apartheid laws in 1994 and free choice (depending on economics, of course) about areas of residence, choice of schools, freedom of association, use of facilities and so on. While all South Africa enjoys new freedoms, post-apartheid developments have particularly engendered a new Black middle class taking up positions in government, parastatals, private and public companies, broadcasting and so forth. The new government's policy of redress, BEE (Black Economic Empowerment), has fast-tracked the growth of a small economic elite. Seekings and Natrass (2005:309) cite studies claiming that the number of middle-class Black households rose by 78 per cent between 1991 and 1996. Seekings (p.c. 2006) has also indicated that the proportion of Blacks in South Africa's middle class has risen from close to zero in the 1980s to about 50 per cent in the early 2000s. The commercial sectors and their advertising wings have not been slow in noticing and capitalizing on this dramatic change. Where language is concerned, it seems that English is the language of 'distinction' (in the sense of Bourdieu 1984) of the new middle class. Whereas the new elite undoubtedly have attachment to their home and community languages, this is at the level of social solidarity and symbolism, rather than status. The new political leadership hardly ever delivers public speeches in an African language, even at political rallies aimed at the masses. (Some speakers at rallies do make occasional use of African languages, and songs and short slogans are often from a Sotho or Nguni language.) Reitzes and Crawhall (1998) offer an interesting Gramscian analysis of language in political change. In establishing a new hegemonic order, the first priority of the new leadership was to attempt to neutralize the bilingualism of the old order, English and Afrikaans. Factoring in the African languages reduced the significance of this old official bilingualism. Having secured political power, the new elite then consolidated its position by demarcating its difference from the Black masses, by stressing competence in

English within its own bilingualism. Occasional use of African languages for symbolic purposes (names of companies, names of towns, cities and streets, political and economic slogans) serves at once to ward off English monolinguals and give a symbolic recognition to the African languages.

The position of the young Black middle class, the true beneficiaries of change in terms of having access to quality education from an early age, is equally interesting. The first black schoolchildren in the private and Model C schools were in the minority. Given their integration into the social networks of the school, it is therefore unsurprising that they should speak English as the dominant language of socialization, with the accents common to their peer group. Detailed research concerning language change in this domain is very much in progress (e.g., Bangeni and Kapp 2007; De Klerk 2000; Mesthrie 2007b). Preliminary indications are that young people in the private schools are most susceptible not just to a shift in dominance, but to language shift. Popular acknowledgement of this phenomenon can be found in new terms such as *coconut* for the new black children who are 'dark on the outside, white on the inside'.[7] What the term suggests is that the new middle classes have gone far beyond the behavioral, cultural and linguistic boundaries once expected of young people of their background. For language it is observed that some young people are becoming monolingual (as indicated by the newspaper articles cited earlier). What is relevant to the theme of code choice, repertoire change and language shift is the extent of the coconut phenomenon and the likelihood of its triggering long-term changes among other classes. Are the young middle classes in the process of leading a linguistic revolution?

As explained earlier, the current language statistics give no indication of such a change. Moreover, in ongoing sociolinguistic work in two Cape Town townships, Imizamo Yethu and Gugulethu, led by Ana Deumert and myself, it is clear that among the working classes and under-employed people Xhosa is vibrantly alive. It is not clear if the mores of the new elite really affect the day-to-day realities of eking out a living for the large majority of urban Black residents. Moreover, large numbers of rural people migrating to the cities do not have English as part of their fluent spoken repertoire. Linguistic adaptations in the townships do initially involve learning English for work purposes. English is starting to make inroads into peer-group interaction in some working-class communities (Deumert and Mabandla forthcoming). Some migrants also learn Afrikaans in Cape Town, for employment prospects in the building and other industries (Deumert and Mabandla forthcoming). Furthermore, Tsotsitaal, an urban slang, does for township males what the most 'refined' middle-class accent does for the children of the new elite (in signalling allegiance to youth culture, albeit of radically different class bases). What I am suggesting here is that the upper-middle-class and working-class Black people of the new South Africa are worlds apart. This was explicitly noted by President Mbeki in his reference to two nations within the state (though his emphasis was implicitly more on race). In the last elections of 2003 many Cape Town township dwellers also indicated that their lives had not been touched by the political changes in South Africa. While people saw few alternatives to voting for the party that had brought in new freedoms, their lives had not been radically altered by those freedoms. The boundaries of *their* behavioral, cultural and linguistic worlds had altered but little. However, Ana Deumert (p.c. 2007) suggests that there are broad similarities in aspirations regarding consumption patterns. Friendly antagonisms (if I may be allowed an oxymoron) between the new elite students and their township counterparts can be seen at university. In my interviews of the early to mid-1990s exploring these changes, the township students who had made it to university labelled the other students *multi*s or *Model C*s, using a typical township English abbreviation with denigratory overtones for 'from a *multi-racial* school' or 'from a Model-C school'. (The *coconut* label came into being slightly later, in the same decade.) The *multi*s for their part rejected township English entirely, seeing it as deficient. Yet, given the choice, it is not unlikely that township dwellers will change in the direction of the more 'statusful' people they see on television, glossy magazine covers and so on. Such a choice is not a reality in the short to middle term, given the levels of poverty and under-employment in South Africa. On the other hand, if a language such as Xhosa is associated in the future only with the working classes and the marginalized, its position will not be as healthy as it is at present.

Turning to the Bantu languages themselves, they are continuing to undergo lexical influence from especially English in the domain of politics and technology. Where structure is concerned there might be some significant changes too, such as the adoption of the English numeral system, in colloquial as well as formal educational contexts. Other influence can be identified in the adoption of conjunctions and discourse markers from English (Deumert et al. 2006). For many speakers code-switching is a reality for communicative as well as solidarity functions (Finlayson and Slabbert 2002). Increasing urbanization is likely to bring about some dialect levelling and other changes in styles of speaking, intonation patterns and so on. While language change is definitely in the air, it is premature to talk about shift, except in the middle-class homes that exist outside the older Black residential areas. Hence *endangerment* of the major Nguni and Sotho languages is not yet on the horizon. Nor has a widespread pidgin English arisen in South Africa that might function as an urban vernacular, as appears to be the case in West Africa.[8]

2.6 Conclusion

South Africa shows a whole range of endangerment phenomena, from severe loss and death in Khoesan, to language shift in many immigrant communities. For the majority of the populace, speakers of Bantu languages, many changes in code repertoire have occurred. However, the existence of multilingualism in the townships of Gauteng, the populous area in the mining areas around Johannesburg, did not favor English as a viable community language. In this the Black communities of South Africa have shown greater resistance to shift than, say, Indian South Africans, whose settlement and living conditions were not entirely comparable. In other parts of the country individual Bantu languages still predominate demographically. The children of the new Black middle classes are the most likely to shift, as they adopt ultramodern lifestyles and find acceptance in new de-racializing social networks. But for the majority of Bantu language speakers such options are currently closed. Their languages are likely to remain an integral part of the home and community and in some public domains for some time to come. The dilemma facing these communities is to find an appropriate balance between the mother tongue and English, the language of upward mobility.

Notes

[1] Khoesan is no longer considered to be a single language family; rather it is a phylum made of three different groupings that cannot be related on current data and knowledge: Northern, Central and Southern. The Khoe languages belong to the Central family and form a unit; but the San languages of the San (Northern and Central) cannot be related to each other or to the Central group. I use the terms *Bushman* and *San* interchangeably.

[2] These figures are an aggregate for Whites, Coloreds and Indians. The census contains no listing for English and Afrikaans among Blacks. According to the same census, more Whites claimed English as a home language (833,654) than Afrikaans (821,561).

[3] In 1990 only English and Afrikaans were the official state languages. The census figures for 'South Africa' that year excluded the 'homelands' thereby giving a misleading picture about South Africa's population. Hence the statistics for this year are the adjusted figures cited in a lecture in 1990 by Gerhard Schuring of the HSRC (Human Sciences Research Council).

[4] In 1990 only English and Afrikaans were the official state languages. The census figures for 'South Africa' that year excluded the 'homelands' thereby giving a misleading picture about South Africa's population. Hence the statistics are the adjusted figures cited in a lecture in 1990 by Gerhard Schuring of the HSRC (Human Sciences Research Council).

[5] There are exceptions of course, and attitudes to immigrants are not always favorable enough to sustain such acquisition.

[6] The position might not be the same for the smaller languages such as Tsonga and Venda – an area needing research.

[7] The term is used for young, middle-class Black, Indian and 'Colored' young people, usually by other members of the same ethic group.

[8] Fanakalo, a pidgin, lexified largely by Zulu and Xhosa, has not spread throughout the country and appears to be slightly on the decline. Furthermore, it was never a viable code for use among Black South Africans.

References

Bangeni, Bongi and Rochelle Kapp. 2007. Shifting language attitudes in a linguistically diverse learning environment in South Africa. *Journal of Multilingual and Multicultural Development* 28.253–269.

Barnes, Lawrie and Allistair McDuling. 1995. The future of Portuguese in South Africa: Maintenance and shift factors. *Language Matters* 26.147–162.

Batibo, Herman, B. 2005. *Language Decline and Death in Africa – Causes, Consequences and Challenges.* Clevedon: Multilingual Matters.

Bourdieu, Pierre. 1977. The economics of linguistics exchanges. *Social Sciences Information* 16.645–658.

—1984. *Distinction – A Social Critique of the Judgement of Taste* (trans. by Richard Nice). Cambridge, MA: Harvard University Press.

Bryant, A.T. 1929. *Olden Times in Zululand and Natal.* London: Longmans.

Carstens, Peter. 1966. *The Social Structure of a Cape Colored Reserve.* Cape Town: Oxford University Press.

Crawhall, Nigel. 2004. *!Ui-Taa Language Shift in Gordonia and Postmasburg Districts, South Africa.* PhD dissertation, Dept. of Linguistics, University of Cape Town.

Davids, Achmat. 1990. Words the slaves made: A socio-historical-linguistic study. *South African Journal of Linguistics* 8.1–24.

De Kadt, Elizabeth. 2002. German speakers in South Africa. In Rajend Mesthrie (ed.), 148–160.

De Klerk, Vivian. 2000. To be Xhosa or not to be Xhosa: That is the question. *Journal of Multilingual and Multicultural Development* 21.198–215.

Deumert, Ana. 2003. *Language Standardization and Language Change: The Dynamics of Cape Dutch.* Amsterdam: Benjamins.

Deumert, Ana and N. Mabandla. Forthcoming. *I-Dollar eyi one!* Ethnolinguistic fractionalization, communication networks, and economic participation: Lessons from Cape Town, South Africa.

Deumert, Ana, Ellen Hurst, Oscar Masinyana and Rajend Mesthrie. 2006. Urbanization and language change: Logical connectors and discourse markers in urban isiXhosa. Paper presented at the Linguistics Society of Southern Africa conference, University of KwaZulu-Natal, Durban.

Elphick, Richard. 1985. *Khoikhoi and the Founding of White South Africa.* Johannesburg: Ravan Press.

Elphick, Richard and Hermann Giliomee. 1989. European dominance at the Cape, 1652 to c. 1840. In *The Shaping of South African Society 1652–1840*, ed. by Richard Elphick and Hermann Giliomee, 521–566. Cape Town: Maskew Miller Longman.

Finlayson, Rosalie and Sarah Slabbert. 2002. Code-switching in South African townships. In Rajend Mesthrie (ed.), 235–257.

Franke, Katharina. (2007). German as a contact language in South Africa: linguistic perspectives. *Monash University Linguistic Papers* 5:2. 19–31.

Hartshorne, Kenneth. 1995. Language policy in African education: A background to the future. In R. Mesthrie (ed.), 306–318.

Herbert, Robert K. 2002. The sociohistory of clicks in Southern Bantu. In R. Mesthrie (ed.), 297–315.

Herbert, Robert K. and Richard Bailey. 2002. The Bantu languages: Sociohistorical perspectives. In Rajend Mesthrie (ed.), 50–78.

Jama, Zukile, Ana Deumert and Rajend Mesthrie. 2006. The naturalistic acquisition of isiXhosa by international migrants: Lessons for linguistic theory? Paper presented at the African Languages Association Conference, University of Cape Town.

Johnson, William. 2006. Goodbye isiXhosa. *Prospect* 122. Accessed from /http://www.prospect-magazine.co.uk/article_details.php?/ in 2007.

Lanham, Leonard, W. and Carol Macdonald. 1979. *The Standard in South African History and its Social History.* Heidelberg: Julius Groos Verlag.

Marais, J.S. 1968. *The Cape Colored people 1652–1937.* Johannesburg: Witwatersrand University Press.

Mesthrie, Rajend. 1992. *English in Language Shift: The History, Structure and Sociolinguistics of South African Indian English.* Cambridge: Cambridge University Press.

—1998. Words across worlds: Aspects of language contact and language learning in the eastern Cape: 1800–1850. *African Studies* 57.5–27.

—2006. South Africa: Language situation. In *The Encyclopedia of Language and Linguistics.* Vol 11, ed. by J. Keith Brown, 539–552. Oxford: Elsevier.

—2007a. Language shift, cultural change and identity retention: Indian South Africans in the 1960s and beyond. *South African Historical Journal* 57.134–152.

—2007b. Of coconuts and kings: Accelerated change amongst young, middle-class South Africans. Paper presented at NWAVE (*New Ways of Analysing Variation in English and Other Languages*) Conference, University of Pennsylvania, Philadelphia.

Mesthrie, Rajend (ed.). 2002. *Language in South Africa.* Cambridge: Cambridge University Press.

Moya, Fikile-Ntsikelelo. 1998. No traditional black men by 2008, says study. *Cape Argus.* September 1998. p. 33.

Mufwene, Salikoko S. 2001. *The Ecology of Language Evolution.* Cambridge: Cambridge University Press.

Nhlapo, Jacob. 1944. *Bantu Babel: Will the Bantu Languages Survive?* Cape Town: The African Bookman.

Nicol, Mike. 2004. Death of the mother tongue. *Sunday Times,* 29 February 2004.

Ntshilinga, Futhi. 2006. A cultural taboo goes up in smoke. *Sunday Times,* 6 August 2006. p. 39.

Ownby, C.P. 1981. Early Nguni history: Linguistic suggestions. *South African Journal of African Languages, Supplement.* 60–81.

Penn, Nigel. 1991. The /Xam and the colony. Paper presented at the Bleek and Lloyd Conference, University of Cape Town.

Pretorius, Cornia. 2001. English versus the rest in battle for the classroom. *Sunday Times.* 22 July 2001. p. 19.

Rayfield, J.R. 1970. *The Languages of a Bilingual Community.* The Hague: Mouton.

Reitzes, M. and N. Crawhall. 1998. *Silenced by nation-building: The exclusion of African migrants in South Africa* (Occasional publication). Cape Town: South African Migration Project.

Roberge, Paul. 2002. Afrikaans: Considering origins. In Rajend Mesthrie (ed.), 79–103.

SABC News. 2005. Mbeki calls for preservation of indigenous languages. http:www.sabcnews.com/south Africa/general/0,2172,101617, 00.html.

Sales, Jane. 1975. *Mission Stations and the Colored Communities of the Eastern Cape 1800–1852.* Cape Town: Balkema.

Seekings, Jeremy and Jill Natrass. 2005. *Class, Race and Inequality in South Africa.* New Haven: Yale University Press.

Traill, Anthony. 1996. *!Khwa-ka hhouiten hhouiten* 'The rush of the storm': the linguistic death of /Xam. In *Miscast: Negotiating the Presence of the Bushmen,* ed. by Pippa Skotness, 161–183. Cape Town: University of Cape Town Press.

—2002. The Khoesan languages. In Rajend Mesthrie (ed.), 27–49.

Vigouroux, Cecile B. 2005. 'There are no Whites in Africa': Territoriality, language and identity among Francophone Africans in Cape Town. *Language and Communication* 25.237–255.

Wilson, Monica. 1972. *The Interpreters.* Grahamstown (pamphlet).

Wright, John. 1971. *Bushman Raiders of the Drakensberg 1840–1870.* Pietermaritzburg: University of Natal Press.

Chapter 3

The Circumstances of Language Shift and Death in Southern Africa

Herman M. Batibo

3.1 Introduction

As observed by Crystal (2000:68) and Mufwene (2004), languages and cultures have risen and fallen several times in human history; new ones have often emerged, as older ones vanished. Many causes have been identified for their demise, ranging from sudden ones such as genocide, devastating epidemics and coercive absorption, to more gradual ones, such as domination, stigmatization and marginalization. The general trend in most continents, particularly in Australia, East Asia and the Americas, has been that of language death being triggered by long distance migrations, especially by European conquerors and settlers, who have caused violent cultural and linguistic disruptions in the colonies. The situation in Africa has, however, been different because of the complex circumstances that have emerged with regard to the types of language contacts and the resultant dominance patterns that have evolved over many centuries (Grenoble and Whaley 1998:42). Moreover, although long distance, migrations were also involved in the colonization of Africa, what would really account for differences between, on the one hand, the fate of indigenous languages in the Americas, Australia and East Asia and, on the other, the fate of their counterparts in Africa may be related to differences in colonization style and in patterns of social interaction (Mufwene 2005).

This study examines the circumstances of language endangerment and language death in Africa by discussing historical developments on the continent from the time the autochthonous hunter–gatherer communities were overwhelmed by the agro-pastoralist communities. Its main focus will be Southern Africa where the traditional Khoesan hunter–gatherer groups were progressively dominated by the Bantu agro-pastoralists around AD 300 and then by the Dutch colonial settlers, several centuries later, followed by many waves of dominance, before the emergence of nation-states during the last forty years. The main argument in this study is that the phenomena of language endangerment and language death in Southern Africa have occurred, since the outset, in a number of complex circumstances resulting from the many types of contact, dominance patterns and relationships between the various groups. These circumstances can be divided into three phases, namely, the period of Bantu expansion and predominance in the region, that of the European colonization since the late nineteenth century, or earlier, for South Africa, and lastly that of the emergence of nation-states. Although this study will treat each of these phases separately, it must be pointed out that in some cases they overlap.

3.2 Phase of Language Contact and Dominance

3.2.1 The Bantu expansion and control of Southern Africa

The first language contacts causing group marginalization and language death in Southern Africa's prehistory were triggered by the many ethnic movements and migrations in the region. Before the last three millennia, most of Africa south of the Equator was inhabited by Khoesan and Pygmy populations scattered, almost undisturbed, in the extensive forests, woodlands and savannas as hunter–gatherers (Barnard 1992; Traill 1995). They lived mainly in small bands, with loose or no central authority, for ease of access to and sharing of the resources in their immediate environments. Their languages were also highly clustered as a result of the diverse physical locations that they inhabited. Although they lived nomadic lives, linguistic and cultural interferences between the clustered groups were rare as each band had its own ecological niche (Denbow 1986).

However, since the end of the first millennium BC, waves of other groups, namely, Southern Cushitic, Central Sudanic, Nilotic and Bantu populations, migrated in turns into many parts of East, central and Southern Africa. With their socioeconomic superiority as mainly crop-farmers and herders, they easily conquered, displaced or absorbed the former autochthonous groups in the region (Gueldemann and Vossen 2000). While the first three groups became confined to the northern part of the region, North of the Zambezi River, the last group to arrive in the region, namely, the Bantu, expanded further South. The Bantu expansion into East, Central and Southern Africa affected not only the earlier Khoesan and Pygmy groups, but also the later intruders, namely, the Southern Cushitic, Central Sudanic and Nilotic groups (Ehret 1998; Huffman 1989). The rapid Bantu spread in the Southern parts of Africa apparently owed its success not only to its demographic superiority, brought about by their rapid reproduction and the absorption of other groups, but also to their technological skills, namely, the art of iron-making (Inskeep 1979). Moreover, the Bantu spread was also facilitated by their organized social systems and centralized authority, which, according to Diamond (1993), is one of the agriculturalists' assets in their quest to expand and control the territories around them.

The early Bantu expansion and settlement in southern Africa, more than fifteen hundred years ago, was characterized by progressive contacts between the Bantu speakers and the Khoesan-speaking people. The early contacts were generally intimate and often developed into a symbiotic relationship characterized by regular interactions occasioned by inter-ethnic marriages and exchanges of commodities (Herbert 1995; Nurse et al. 1985). The two populations often would depend on each other during natural catastrophes such as drought, epidemics and animal diseases (Parsons 1993; Westphal 1963; Wilmsen 1980). However, as is frequently the case with hunter–gatherer communities that have come in contact with other populations that are demographically larger and have superior technology, many Khoesan groups in southern Africa reacted by either moving away into other uninhabited areas or allowing themselves to be absorbed by the intruders (Crawhall 2005). Moreover, the advent of agriculture and pastoralism in the area changed the physical landscapes and impacted on the movements of game on which their survival depended. Much of natural foodstuff necessary for these hunter–gatherers was also destroyed, thus gradually making them vulnerable and dependent on the newcomers.

As the Bantu communities began to settle in the many parts of Southern Africa from around AD 500, there arose a gradual need for them to control and expand in their new environments. Their agro-pastoralist practices required extensive territory to cope with their ever-increasing numbers and changes in their ecologies to fit their socioeconomic needs. Their increasing numbers and land needs would constantly drive them to expand in other territories. Due to their socioeconomic vulnerability and lack of centralized authority, the Khoesan groups were easily subjugated to the more socioeconomically sustainable and politically more organized invaders. A system of serfdom and servitude, known as *Botlhanka*, arose in which Khoesan communities were under the economic control of the Bantu (Gadibolae 1999; Silberbauer and Kuper 1996). Consequently, many Khoesan languages became stigmatized, with their speakers shying away from them (Crawhall 2005; Vossen 1997). They easily lost self-esteem and started considering themselves as inferior. Situations of 'marked' or asymmetrical bilingualism (Batibo 2005a:103) arose in which most Khoesan groups became bilingual in Bantu languages, while the Bantu remained monolingual in their own languages. Gradually, this evolved into language shift at the expense of the Khoesan languages.

The progressive language shift, marked by the disruption of intergenerational language transmission and the reduction of domains of use, was concurrent with structural simplification, including the loss of clicks. Extinct Khoesan languages now include Khakhea and Tyua (Botswana), =Khomani and !Ora (=Kora) (Namibia), //Xegwi, and Seroa (South Africa) (Traill 1995). Crawhall (2005) has listed more languages from South Africa, which include N/u, /Xam, //Ku//e, /Uingkekwi, =Unkwe, /Ga!ne, all of which belong to the San group.

In some cases, the Bantu–Khoesan interactions were so extensive that the Khoesan languages affected the Bantu languages substantially, before their extinction. This is the case of the Eastern Cape Khoe in which sociopolitically organized speakers of the Eastern Cape Khoe dialects heavily influenced not only the vocabulary but also the grammatical and phonological systems of IsiXhosa and IsiZulu (Herbert 1995; Lanham 1964; Louw 1974, 1979; Traill 1995). Also in the Okavango region of present-day Botswana, Khoesan influence has been extensive on particularly the phonological systems of several Bantu languages such as Shiyeyi, Thimbukushu and Rugciriku (Rumanyo). All these languages have clicks. In some cases, some originally Bantu speakers in the area have also shifted to Khoesan. This is the case of the //Ani, who are linguistically Khoesan but who are essentially Bantu genetically (Vossen 1997). As a matter of fact, DNA tests on some Bantu speakers in Southern Africa have revealed that they are more than 50 per cent of Khoesan stock. They include speakers of IsiXhosa, Shekgalagarhi and Setswana (Herbert 1995:57). Such revelations point to the fact that the linguistic landscape and dominance patterns were very complex in the region.

At the same time, the competition for territorial dominance took place not only between the Bantus and Khoesans but also within these populations themselves. Thus the most demographically and sociopolitically dominant groups, such as the AbaZulu, AbaXhosa, Bashona and Batswana, dominated the smaller Bantu groups, such as the Batsonga, the Bakgalagarhi, the Bayeyi, the Hambukushu, the Bekuhane (Basubiya) and the Bakalanga. Within this dominance hierarchy, a system of subjugation arose in which the most powerful Bantu languages were at the top and the most vulnerable, mainly the Khoesan languages, at the bottom. Thus, although Shekgalararhi, a Bantu language spoken in the Central Kalahari area of southern Africa, was predominant over the Khoesan speakers, such as !Xoo, /Gwi and //Gana, to which many speakers had shifted, it was itself considered inferior to Setswana, to which many Kgalagarhi speakers were progressively shifting. This dominance hierarchy was not only dependent on demographic size, but also on sociopolitical and economic factors. Table 3.1 gives a schematic scenario of this hierarchy.

3.2.2 The European colonization and settlement

3.2.2.1 The European colonization and dominance

European domination of the Southern African region started at the time of scramble for Africa by Western European powers in the 1880s. This followed the series of travels and expeditions to many parts of the Continent by individual

Table 3.1 The hierarchy of dominance among the languages of Southern Africa

1	The demographically and sociopolitically powerful Bantu languages
2	The less powerful Bantu languages
3	The Khoesan languages

adventurers, missionaries and trading agencies from those nations, who brought in their governments for protection and support. The repartition of Africa was completed in 1885, at the Berlin Conference (convened to established international guidelines for the colonization of Africa South of the Sahara), which involved mainly five European powers, namely, Britain, France, Portugal, Germany and Belgium. They came to Africa with a stereotyped attitude of superiority and sense of mission. They defined their colonies in complete disregard of traditional ethnic boundaries. The French and the Portuguese, who adopted a style of direct rule, ended up with a policy of assimilation of their African subjects to the metropolitan culture and lifestyle. (However, cf. Stroud, this volume.) The German exercised a centralized mode of administration with suppressive and harsh rule, thus giving rise to uprisings such as the German–Herero War in the German South West Africa (today's Namibia) in 1904 and the Maji Maji Uprising in the German East Africa (today's Tanzania) in 1907. The Belgians, on their part, exercised loose colonial system in which all decisions were left to King Leopard II of Belgium. However, the subjects were treated harshly and allowed only basic education that would enable them to serve the colonial system (Khapoya 1994:132). As for the British, they practised indirect rule, giving substantial power to local chiefs at the village and tribal levels. However, for the sake of efficiency, often, in this system of divide and rule, some ethnic groups were given more powers and privileges over others.

In spite of the apparent differences in the style of colonial administration, the effect was basically the same, namely, the subsequent domination and exploitation of the African subjects. The limited educational system that was introduced was mainly meant to train clerks and assistants who would serve their interests as well as provide the much needed semi-skilled labor, particularly in the factories, mines, plantations and ranches. The emergence of paid labor, based on education and skills, which were usually provided in the colonial languages, gave rise to special perspectives of the metropolitan languages, now considered as the key to white-collar jobs and Western lifestyle. Hence their status, prestige and demand increased at the expense of the indigenous languages. (However, cf. Stroud and Mc Laughlin in this volume.)

In the case of South Africa, the history of Western colonization and settlement took place in phases, starting with the Dutch settlement of the Cape area in the middle of the seventeenth century; the expansion of the burglar farmers into the rugged hinterlands (following the displacement of the original inhabitants, the Khoekhoe); and the coming of the British in the area in 1795. The Portuguese and German colonization and exploitation of the western and eastern coasts occurred in the late nineteenth century, although the Portuguese had already established trade forts on the Atlantic and Indian Ocean coasts since the fifteenth century. Eventually, Germany lost its colonies after being defeated at World War I. This complex colonial history has given rise to the predominance of English, Portuguese and to a lesser extent, German in southern Africa, and the birth of Afrikaans, as a vernacular, from Dutch. As shown by other contributions to this volume, these languages have not had much impact on the dynamics of language endangerment in the region, with the exception of Afrikaans.

3.2.2.2 The Dutch settlement of the Cape Coast

When the Dutch settlers arrived at the Cape of Good Hope, in the early seventeenth century, there were about eleven closely related Cape Khoe varieties, spoken by between one hundred thousand and two hundred thousand people (Elphick 1985). However, in the whole of Southern Africa, there were other groups, which included several San varieties and some agro-pastoral Bantu-speaking communities. The settlement of the region by the Dutch has been described as the only case in Africa where European colonization has caused devastating impact on the indigenous languages in a manner comparable to the extinction of languages in the Americas, Australia and East Asia (Marais 1968; Nienaber 1963). The Cape Khoe groups were the first to suffer under the hands of the invaders, as within sixty years of the newcomers' arrival, their indigenous economy, social structure, and political order had almost completely collapsed under the pressures of the new socioeconomic structure and due to diseases and epidemics (Elphick 1985; Traill 1995). These changes had a devastating effect on the Cape Khoe language varieties, which began to decline rapidly. They were gradually being replaced by Khoe-Dutch (Nienaber 1963:97ff). Thus, with a few cases of egalitarian coexistence between the Dutch and the Cape Khoe, the general dominance and destruction of the latter has been described as violent and intolerant (Crawhall 2005:71). One should note however that some linguistic overlays, particularly vocabulary relating to fauna and flora, were left in Khoe-Dutch, the ancestor of modern Afrikaans. According to Crawhall, the socioeconomic dynamics that caused language endangerment and language death among the Cape Khoe, and later other Khoesan groups, when the latter too came in contact with the Dutch settlers, were varied and complex. In the case of the Khoe speakers traditionally known as Hottentotts the process of rapid language shift to Khoe-Dutch was usually prompted by socioeconomic forces, such as absorption into farms as laborers, political influences, and land seizure. This reduced them to a dependent status in which marked bilingualism developed in favor of Khoe-Dutch. The other affected Khoe language varieties included Nama, Kora (!Ora) and Gri (Xri) (Traill 1995:6). In time, after the seizure of their land and being subjugated and controlled politically, the Khoe were absorbed into the agro-pastoral economy of the settlers.

The first San language to be in contact with the Dutch settlers was /Xam, a member of the !Kiri group. This was one of the many San groups that faced violent destruction, dislocation and extermination, as Dutch influence intensified in the mid-eighteenth century (Traill 1995:10). Such uncompromising aggression had linguistic repercussions that laid the seeds for the dramatic demographic reduction and death of /Xam and other San languages, such as /'Auni. Since their labor and culture were not particularly valued, the San had nothing other than the land to offer to the invaders. On the other hand, they could not easily adjust themselves to the new socioeconomic set-up. Thus, the estimated ten thousand–twenty thousand San speakers with their respective languages appear to have perished within the three hundred years of the Dutch invasion and expansion in the Cape area (Traill 1995).

From this it is clear that the Dutch settlers' contacts with the Khoe and the San caused the death of several Khoesan languages through a combination of events that ranged from genocide, relocation and absorption through pressure. Where the speakers of these languages survived, they were subjected to marked bilingualism with progressive shift to colonial Dutch. Most of all, the most distinctive force was the new language ecology caused by the advent of the settlers that triggered dramatic sociolinguistic and political changes, thus upsetting the earlier language ecology (Crawhall 2005). On the other hand, the Dutch settlers' contacts with the Bantu populations, although equally violent, did not cause devastating linguistic loss. This is presumably because of the relative demographic importance and the strong sociopolitical structures of the latter, for instance, the AbaZulu, AbaXhosa, Batswana and Basotho.

Since the recent political changes in South Africa and the adoption of a democratic constitution, the status of Afrikaans has lessened. It is now only one of the eleven official languages, together with English, IsiZulu, IsiXhosa, IsiNdebele, Tshivenda, Setswana, Sesotho, Sepedi, Siswati and Shitsonga. Although it still has an edge over the Bantu languages, due to its extensive use in socioeconomic spheres and in scientific and technical domains, Afrikaans has lost much of its political power and prestige. Consequently, fewer and fewer young non-Afrikaners have been acquiring or shifting to it.

3.2.3 The emergence of nation-states in Southern Africa and its linguistic impact

The third phase is represented by the current sociopolitical set-up in Southern Africa, in which the creation of nation-states, namely, Botswana, Lesotho, Namibia, Swaziland, Zimbabwe, and the democratization of South Africa have led to the promotion of some indigenous languages to the status of national languages. This has significantly enhanced the dominance pattern hierarchy that started during the previous phases.

The new hierarchy of language dominance has four levels – the international, the national,[1] the areal[2] and the local levels. This hierarchy, invariably referred to as quadriglossia (Batibo 2006), is shown in Table 3.2.

Table 3.2 The four-tier structure of language status and
prestige in African countries

High prestige and status	European language
	Nationally dominant
	Areally dominant
Low prestige and status	Minority language

In most Southern African countries, the official language, which is usually the ex-colonial language, is the most prestigious. However, this language often remains an elite medium that is used almost exclusively by the educated few in official and technical domains. The nationally dominant languages, which are the ones that have assumed national lingua franca status, have amassed substantial powers, prestige and extensive use as national media. They are often used in semi-official public functions. Their intense socioeconomic attraction and extensive use down to the grassroots have made them the most effective language killers, as they have every charm to attract the speakers of the other languages in their respective countries (Batibo 2005a). At the third level, we would have the areally dominant languages, which are used as inter-ethnic lingua francas by speakers of minority languages. Lastly, at the bottom we would have the minority languages, whose use is confined to family and village interactions and to practice of some specific cultural traditions. Usually, the languages in this category are spoken by groups that are not only historically underprivileged but also socioeconomically marginalized (Brenzinger et al. 1991).

The emergence of nation-states in Africa, although based on the colonial arbitrary repartition of territories, has been enhanced by the growth of nationalism and national identity in which language was seen as an important emblem. At the dawn of independence, mostly in the early 1960s, the majority of African countries became aware of the three national needs that Fishman (1971) has termed as unification, authenticity and modernity, all of which demanded supportive language policies. Although most countries of southern Africa did not put in place explicit or constitutionally enshrined language policies, the general tendency was to adopt the ex-colonial language to serve as official language. In Southern Africa, this practice gave English and Portuguese considerable status, prestige and power, particularly English. However, the roles allocated to the indigenous languages varied from country to country. Three categories can be identified.

The first category is that of countries that have one major dominant language whose status has been enhanced since independence by its promotion to national language. The countries in this category include Botswana, Lesotho, Swaziland and Zimbabwe, which have each one nationally dominant language that has been accorded certain national roles. Although in the case of Lesotho and Swaziland, the dominant languages enjoy a quasi-monolingual indigenous status, the situation is different in the case of Botswana and Zimbabwe, where there are other indigenous languages spoken by at least 20 per cent of the population. In these cases, the enhanced status of the dominant languages, namely, Setswana in Botswana and Chishona in Zimbabwe (which were already privileged under the colonial era), has increased their hegemony and therefore the pressure they exert over speakers of other languages. In both countries, these languages have been associated not only with national identity, but also with economic and sociopolitical modernity (Nyati-Ramahobo 2002).

In the case of Botswana, where there are twenty-eight languages, the inexplicit assimilating language policy has brought pressure on minority ethnic groups to use Setswana in public and adopt the Setswana culture as the sole form of national identity. It has also given rise to some destructive decisions, such as the re-allocation policy according to which the Khoesan groups in the Central Kalahari Game Reserve are being moved to settlements in other areas, apparently to integrate them with the mainstream communities and give them access to modern facilities. This move has disrupted their traditional nature-based ways of life and made them totally dependent on the state, thus leading them to language shift. In the case of Zimbabwe, where seventeen languages are spoken, the predominance of Chishona nationally and of Isindebele in the south-west of the country has given tremendous power, status and privileges to both languages, particularly the former, making them the media of public spheres, such as lower education, local administration, customary law courts and public services (Ndlovu 2007). Consequently, the smaller languages have been confined to serve only intra-ethnic communication and are therefore considerably marginalized. The highly endangered languages in Zimbabwe include Hietshware (Tshwa) and Dombe (Grimes 2000).

The second category of countries consists of those that have opted to promote all or the majority of languages as national or official languages. This is the case of Namibia and South Africa. In Namibia, in spite of having major languages such as Oshiwambo, spoken by at least 51 per cent of the population, and Afrikaans, spoken by many as second language, the language policy recognizes all the twenty-six languages spoken in the country as national languages, while English serves as the official language. In pursuance of this policy the country has endeavored to codify most of the languages and to use them in education and other public spheres. However, despite the government's efforts to promote all or most languages in the country, many Namibians are bilingual in the major languages and are gradually shifting to them. The most endangered languages in Namibia, at present, include /Aakhwe, =Kx'au//ein, Kung-Ekoka, !Kung, Hai//'om, Mashi and Shiyeyi. The languages =Khomani and !Ora (Kora) have long become extinct.

On the other hand, South African has declared eleven out of the twenty-three languages in the country as official languages. Although in practice, English remains the main official language, especially in government business, education and technology,[3] the government is making all efforts to codify and standardize the (more) indigenous official language, developing new terminology for their modern functions in technology, education and politics. Despite the genuine government efforts, the hierarchy of language status and prestige has persisted, as English and, to a certain extent, Afrikaans have remained at the top. The other (more) indigenous languages that do not have an official language status are spoken by smaller populations, are socioeconomically vulnerable and appear to be endangered, as their speakers are bilingual in the more prestigious languages. The highly endangered languages include Camtho (IsiCamtho), Sebowa, Gail and Kxoe (Mbarahuesa, Mbarakwengo). On the other hand, N/u, which has only eleven elderly people who can speak it, is a dying language, as it is no longer being transmitted intergenerationally (Crawhall 2005:71). The already extinct languages include /Xam, //Xegwi, Xiri (Criqua, Cape Hottentot, Seroa and Gemsbok Nama. Many of these languages, as we saw earlier, became extinct after the Dutch arrival in the Cape of Good Hope area in the early seventeenth century.

The last category is that of countries that have not made any conspicuous effort to promote their indigenous languages. The ex-colonial language has assumed both official and national functions. The only country in this category in southern Africa is Mozambique where, although thirty-three languages are spoken and two major indigenous languages prevail, Portuguese continues to be used extensively, even at grassroots level (however, cf. Stroud, this volume). This language situation is not at all surprising given the assimilating language policy of the Portuguese colonial system. In spite of a language situation that favors the extended use of Portuguese, the two major indigenous languages, namely, Emakhuwa and Tsonga, have considerable influence over the smaller languages, even in their non-official national status. At present the most endangered languages include Bwarwe, Dema, Chikunda, Nathembo and Phimbi. Most speakers of these languages are bilingual in one of the areally dominant ones, and their speakers are progressively shifting to them. The number of speakers in their respective communities is generally very low (Grimes 2000).

3.3 The Uniqueness of the African Continent

3.3.1 Patterns of language contact in Africa

One important question that could be asked about the circumstances of language endangerment and language death in sub-Saharan Africa (henceforth 'Africa') is why the European languages have not made any significant impact. Although European languages, such as English, French and Portuguese, have enjoyed special privileges not only as super-imposed colonial languages but also as prestigious official and elitist media, since their first use in the continent more than eighty years ago, they have not particularly endangered the indigenous languages. According to Grenoble and Whaley (1998:43) there are five interrelated extra-national variables that are relevant to describing the unique nature of endangerment patterns in Africa. These variables include the following:

1. The fact that European conquerors and settlers in Africa represented a very small proportion of the overall population. Hence the European languages, with the exception of Dutch in the Cape coast of Africa, could not make a substantial impact on the indigenous languages.
2. The language density in many parts of Africa is so high that the constant interaction between them reinforces their vitality.
3. The multilingual nature of most African communities has often created a hierarchy of language use in different social contexts, thus the languages used in one context do not form a threat to the languages used in others.
4. The special pan-African spirit that allows the shifting from one indigenous language to another while resisting the use of colonial languages or Arabic.
5. The prevailing economic disasters in most African countries that have prevented many governments from promoting a single national language to the exclusion of all others, unlike in other continents. Tanzania is cited as a potential exception.

In fact, these variables could be categorized between external and internal factors. The external factors involve the manner in which the process of colonization took place, as specified in variable 1. As shown earlier, with the exception of South Africa and to some extent Namibia and Zimbabwe, the colonial conquest of Africa was not that of settlement and domination, but that of rule and exploitation of the human and physical resources (what Mufwene 2004, 2005 identifies as 'exploitation colonization'). The internal factors would comprise the remaining variables. They are based on the complex African ecology in which the patterns of language contact and use not only are intricate but also constitute a unique sociolinguistic context. While the absence of protracted settlement colonization is important, the most relevant factor is 3. the multilingual nature of most African communities, which has often created a hierarchy of language use in different social contexts. Although the European languages did not make direct impact on the minority languages, the colonizers themselves introduced a new stratification pattern of the indigenous languages, through the urban centers they developed and the social promotion of some indigenous languages that they used to communicate with the masses of the populations. Moreover, the socioeconomic reorganization of Africa created conditions that were dangerous to the minority languages.

The European (ex-)colonial languages have operated in the African countries within the four-tier hierarchy, as described in Table 3.2. In most African countries the European languages have been confined to their status as official languages and to technical and formal domains, such as government business, science and technology, higher education, judiciary, trade and commerce, and mass media. However, they do not function as vernaculars and constitute no threat to the minority languages. (See also Mc Laughlin, this volume, about the status of French in Senegal.) This is because their primary rivals, where applicable, are not the minority languages but the nationally dominant ones. The two groups of languages usually compete in certain secondary domains, such as administration, education, parliament, judiciary, trade and commerce, social services and mass media. But because of the demographic and extended use of the nationally and areally dominant languages, language conflict does not result in any significant language shift.

On the other hand, the ex-colonial languages have not infiltrated into the grassroots where most minority languages are found. In most African countries, the process of language shift usually takes place in favor of the nationally or major areally dominant indigenous languages. This is because most minority language speakers are bilingual in one of these dominant languages for socioeconomic or wider communication purposes. The attraction is even greater in cases where these languages have been accorded public roles such as administration, education, judiciary, legislature, trade or mass media.

3.3.2 Botswana as a case study

Focusing on Botswana, one finds that with a population of only 1.7 million, it is the most linguistically diverse country in Southern Africa, as it has at least twenty-eight languages, the highest number among the Southern African countries. Like in the other multilingual African countries, the presence of so many languages has not only created a complex language situation in terms of language contact and dominance patterns, but also brought about a hierarchy of language status and roles. Thus, English, the ex-colonial language, has been accorded the official status and therefore enjoys the highest prestige as it is used in most of the formal and technical domains, such as government business, judiciary, science and technology, international relations, higher education and most of the mass media. Setswana, as the national language and main lingua franca (spoken by 78.6 per cent as first language, but by over 90 per cent of the population as either L1 or L2), also has considerable status and prestige as the inter-ethnic language, used mainly in non-formal or semi-official functions and public domains such as *Kgotla* (ward) meetings, local administration, lower education, customary law, social services and popular mass media. The other languages are not accorded any official roles in the country's constitution and are therefore confined to village and family communication as well as cultural expression. The larger ones among them, namely, Ikalanga (spoken by 11–15 per cent of the population) and Shekgalagarhi (spoken by 2–3 per cent

Table 3.3 The patterns of language use (in per cent) among the Shuakhwe and/
Xaise of northeastern Botswana

Domains of use	L1 (Shuakhwe// Xaise)	L2 (Ikalanga)	L3 (Setswana)	L4 (English)
1. With parents	38.9	6.8	54.3	0.0
2. With friends	35.8	9.0	53.2	2.0
3. In public places (shops, beer places, etc.)	19.8	7.5	67.1	5.6
4. At village gatherings	6.5	0.0	93.5	0.0
5. Most frequently used language	31.3	5.8	62.9	0.0
6. Language in which one is most proficient/ at ease	22.3	6.5	71.3	0.0

Source: Batibo 1997b.

of the population), have also attracted L2 speakers, as areally dominant languages, particularly among the Khoesans.

The rest of the languages, referred to as minority languages, are highly endangered. Most of the studies that have been carried out on them have shown that most of their speakers are progressively shifting to Setswana (Batibo 1997a, 1998; Chebanne and Nthapelelang 2000; Smieja 1998; Vossen 1997). In the areas where Ikalanga and Shekgalagarhi are spoken, some groups are also shifting to these languages. Thus the patterns of language use are gradually changing in favor of the dominant languages as shown in a study carried out by Batibo (1997b) on two Khoesan languages, namely, Shuakhwe and /Xaise in Eastern Botswana, each spoken by only a few thousands (see Table 3.3). There were more than 150 respondents between the ages of fifteen and seventy-five. The study was carried out in two mainly Khoesan villages in northeastern Botswana.

As is obvious from Table 3.3, Setswana is the most used language at both family and village levels. It is also the most frequently spoken one and that in which most Shuakhwe and /Xaise speakers are most at ease. In fact, most of those who expressed good proficiency in the two languages were in the older generation. Most of the younger speakers, particularly below thirty years of age, were more fluent in Setswana or Ikalanga. Many young people had little or no knowledge of Shuakhwe or /Xaise. On the other hand, only those who had spent several years at school had some knowledge of English, which they used only occasionally with friends.

The diminishing proficiency in the minority languages in favor of the dominant languages was compounded by the negative attitudes that have been developed towards the minority languages. As shown in Batibo (2001, 2005a), Chebanne and Nthapelelang (2000), Smieja (2003) and Sommer and Vossen

(2000), the negative attitudes are correlated with the sentiment that their languages are not socioeconomically useful. This then becomes one of the primary causes of language shift and the death of the relevant languages as they would prefer their children to be proficient in Setswana and English for reasons of education (offered in Setswana at the lower and English at the upper levels), job opportunities and communication in the wider world. As a result of the substantial proficiency in Setswana, and to a lesser extent Ikalanga or Shekgalagarhi, these groups have developed marked bilingualism in which the dominant languages are progressively monopolizing all domains of language use, even at family and cultural levels. In the case of the Khoesan languages, they have been made more vulnerable by the recent government move to relocate the Khoesan communities from the Central Kalahari Game Reserve to other settlements where they are forced to intermingle with speakers of dominant languages. The increase in such interactions eventually leads them to the frequent use of the dominant languages at the expense of their own languages (Chebanne and Monaka 2005).

3.3.3 The future of the Southern African languages in the era of globalization

Defined as the growing economic interdependence of countries worldwide through increasing volume and variety of cross-border transactions in goods and services, free international capital flows, and more rapid and widespread diffusion of technology (IMF 2006), globalization has often been considered as another critical factor in the processes of language endangerment and language death. Globalization, made possible through efficient worldwide communication networks, has been associated with English, which has emerged as the leading world language and has been claimed to be a big threat to the other languages world-wide, including those of Africa. However, as explained above, the impact of English has not been the same on the African arena, as it has depended on the levels of contact between English and the respective African language, the degree of attachment the speakers have to their cultural norms, the types of socioeconomic activities that they conduct and the type of lifestyle that the speakers have.

Since the most threatened languages in Africa tend to be located in rural and remote areas, the impact of English, or any other global language, on them would be minimal. However, the global impact of English is being felt in certain quarters, particularly in the urban areas and among the educated. A number of parents in urban areas prefer to send their children to English medium schools in the hope that they will have wider access to knowledge and work opportunities. In fact, there is a rapid mushrooming of English medium schools in many African cities, mainly for the middle-class children. Even former non-English speaking countries, such as Rwanda and Mozambique, have chosen English to be one of the official languages because of its global impact. This is evidenced by the frequent use of English in international meetings by the heads of state from these countries. At the same time, in many African countries, local varieties of English (including pidginized forms such as *Sheng* in Kenya) are fast emerging. Such varieties could penetrate into the grassroots, as it has been the case in some countries of West Africa, such as Cameroon, Nigeria, Liberia, Sierra Leone and Gambia. The question then would be whether to consider these varieties as foreign language intrusion or part of the enriched local linguistic ecosystem. Such trends have been considered elsewhere as *glocalization*, because of their localized nature (Mufwene 2005). Evidently, these new language forms can only be considered as a threat to the minority languages if they engulf local sociocultural characteristics to make them more localized and more accessible to the speakers of other languages.

3.4 Conclusion

The circumstances and processes of language shift and language death in Southern Africa over the last fifteen hundred years could be described as both complex and varied, involving cases of prolonged contacts, integration, absorption, relocation as well as progressive language shift through marked bilingualism. The hunter–gatherer Khoesan populations were the most affected as they went through several phases of domination, first by the agro-pastoralist Bantu intruders, who changed the original hunter–gathering socioeconomic lifestyle of the area by introducing a more sedentary and more intensive food production mode. Although the advent of European colonization did not affect the languages at the grassroots, settlements by the Dutch, coupled with their exploitation of certain parts of Southern Africa, were another source of language domination of the area, particularly as the indigenous populations could not adapt themselves easily to the new competitive economic and political ecology, almost in the Darwinian conception of competition and selection. As rightly remarked by Diamond (1993:29), the languages of the hunter–gatherers in Africa are generally more threatened than those of groups that are involved in other sorts of socioeconomic organization. Many of the Khoesan languages, which had survived the earlier contacts with the intruding groups, were progressively overwhelmed, except those that were insulated by barriers such as the arid land of the Kalahari, the Okavango swamps or the Springbok woodlands. Moreover, following the formation of nation-states in Southern Africa, the process of language shift and language death was accelerated by the promotion of some major languages , which have been spreading through individual bilingualism, as national ones. Overall, the languages with the most utilitarian value or public functions, such as the ones accorded official, national or provincial lingua franca roles, have become more devastating killers than the ex-colonial languages, as they have gained greater socioeconomic charm and attraction.

Although the circumstances and processes of language shift and language death in the three phases look different and distinct, in many respects, they have many common features. In all three cases, the process of language shift and language death has been motivated by a state of marked bilingualism produced by contact in which speakers of the socioeconomically weaker languages have been shifting to those associated with modernity and socioeconomic advancement, provided they are accessible to them. What can be observed from the discussion in this chapter is that the process of language death in most Southern African countries is being triggered, not by the ex-colonial languages, but by the major indigenous languages, particularly those that have been elevated to official or national status. Such languages have developed charms and attractions in their new roles as media of education, administration, social services, trade, modern jobs and wider communication. Consequently, parents, who see their languages as socioeconomically valueless, have developed negative attitudes towards them and have been encouraging their children to be more proficient in the publicly used languages.

Notes

[1] Of course not all countries have nationally dominant languages. Countries such as Namibia, Mozambique and South Africa have major areally dominant languages predominating in specific parts of the respective countries.
[2] The term *areal* is used to refer to an area or territory in which a major language predominates within a given country (Batibo 2005a).
[3] Afrikaans competes with English only to a limited extent, in business and in the industry.

References

Barnard, Alan. 1992. *Hunters and Herders of Southern Africa: A Comparative Ethnography of the Khoisan Peoples*. Cambridge: Cambridge University Press.
Batibo, Herman M. 1997a. The fate of the minority languages in Botswana. In *Human Contact through Language and Linguistics*, ed. by B. Smieja and M. Tasch, 243–252. Essen: Peter Lang.
—1997b. Patterns of language use among the Shuakhwe and /Xaise of north-east Botswana. A Paper presented at a Staff/Student Seminar, held on 15th March 1997. University of Botswana.
—1998. The fate of the Khoesan language of Botswana. In *The Endangered Languages of Africa*, ed. by Matthias Brenzinger, 267–284. Cologne: Ruediger Koeppe Verlag.
—2001. The unlamentable loss: The role of attitude in language shift and death. In *Language and Democratization*, ed. by K. Legère and D. Akindele, 197–209. Windhoek: Gamsberg MacMillan.

—2005a. *Language Decline and Death in Africa: Causes, Consequences and Challenges.* Clevedon: Multilingual Matters.

—2006. The imposition of English on the triglossic structure of language use in Africa. In: Arna, E. Arua, Mompoloki M. Bagwasi, Tiro Sebina and Barolong Seboni (eds) *The Study and use of English in Africa,* 76–88. Cambridge: Cambridge Scholars Publishing.

Brenzinger, Matthias, Bernd Heine and Gabrielle Sommer. 1991. Language death in Africa. *In Endangered Languages,* ed. by R.H. Robins and E.M. Uhlenbeck, 19–44. Oxford/New York: BERG.

Chebanne, Anderson and Kemonye Monaka. 2005. San relocation: Endangerment through development in Botswana. In *Creating Outsiders: Endangered Languages, Migration and Marginalization,* ed. by N. Crawhall and N. Ostler, 101–106. Bath: Foundation for Endangered Languages.

Chebanne, Anderson and Moemedi Nthapelelang. 2000. The sociolinguistic survey of the Eastern Khoe in the Boteti and Makgadikgadi Pans areas of Botswana. In *Botswana: The Future of the Minority Languages,* ed. by Herman M. Batibo and Birgit Smieja, 79–94. Frankfurt: Peter Lang.

Crawhall, Nigel. 2005. The story of !Hi: Causality and language shift in Africa. In *Creating Outsiders: Endangered Languages, Migration and Marginalization,* ed. by Nigel Crawhall and Nicholas Ostler, 71–81. Bath: Foundation for Endangered Languages.

Crystal, David. 2000. *Language Death.* Cambridge: Cambridge University Press.

Denbow, James R. 1986. A new look at late pre-history of the Kalahari. *Journal of African History* 27.3–28.

Diamond, Jared. 1993. Speaking with a single tongue. *Discover* (February) 78–85.

Ehret, Christopher. 1998. *An Africa Classical Age: Eastern and Southern Africa in World History, 1000 BC to AD 400.* Oxford: J. Currey.

Elphick, Richard. 1985. *Khoikhoi and the Founding of White South Africa.* Johannesburg: Ravan Press.

Fishman, Joshua. 1971. The impact of nationalism in language planning. In J. Rubin and B. Jernudd (eds) *Can Language be Planned? Sociolinguistic Theory and Practice for Developing Nations,* 3–20. Hawaii: University Press of Hawaii.

Gadibolae, Mabunga N. 1999. *Selfdom (Bolata) in the Nata Area (1929–1960).* MA thesis, University of Botswana.

Grenoble, Lindsay A. and Lenore J. Whaley. 1998. Towards a typology of language endangerment. In *Endangered Languages: Current Issues and Future Prospects,* ed. by Leonore A. Grenoble and Lindsay J. Whales, 22–54. Cambridge: Cambridge University Press.

Grimes, Barbara. 2000. *Ethnologue.* Dallas: Summer Institute of Linguistics.

Gueldemann, Tom and Rainer Vossen. 2000. The Khoisan languages. In *African Languages: An Introduction,* ed. by Bernd Heine and Derek Nurse, 99–122. Cambridge: Cambridge University Press.

Herbert, Robert K. 1995. The socio-history of clicks in Southern Bantu. In *Language and Social History: Studies in South African Sociolinguistics,* ed. by Rajend Mesthrie, 51–67. Claremont: David Philip Publishers.

Huffman, Thomas N. 1989. Ceramic settlements and Late Iron Age Migrations. *African Archaeological Review* 7.155–182.

IMF (International Monetary Fund). 2006. *Globalization.* http://en.winipedia.org.

Inskeep, Ray R. 1979. *The Peopling of Southern Africa.* Cape Town: David Philip.

Khapoya, Vincent B. 1994. *The African Experience: An Introduction.* Englewood Cliff, NJ: Prentice Hall.

Lanham, Len W. 1964. The proliferation and extension of Bantu phonemic systems influenced by Bushman and Hottentots. In *Proceedings of the Ninth International Congress of Linguists,* ed. by H.F. Lunt, 55–76. The Hague: Mouton.

Louw, Jacobus A. 1974. The influence of Khoi on the Xhosa language. *Limi* 2. 43–93.

—1979. A preliminary survey of Khoi and San influence in Zulu. In *Khoisan Linguistics Studies* 8.8–21.

Marais, Johannes S. 1968. *The Cape Coloured People 1652–1937.* Johannesburg: Witwatersrand University Press.

Mufwene, Salikoko S. 2004. Language birth and death. *Annual Review of Anthropology* 33.201–222.

—2005. Globalization and the myth of killer languages: What's really going on? In *Perspectives on Endangerment,* ed. by Graham Huggan and Stephan Klasen, 19–48. Hildesheim/New York: Georg Olms Verlag.

Ndlovu, Finex. 2007. *Nationalism/Hegemony, Language Politics and Language Marginalization in Post-Colonial Zimbabwe.* PhD Thesis, presented to Monash University, Australia. July 2007.

Nienaber, Gabriel S. 1963. *Hottentotts.* Pretoria: Van Schaik.

Nurse, George T., Joseph S. Weiner and Trefor Jenkins. 1985. *The Peoples of Southern Africa and their Affiliations.* Oxford: Clarendon Press.

Nyati-Ramahobo, Lydia. 2002. Ethnic identity and nationhood in Botswana. In *Minorities in the Millennium: Perspective from Botswana,* ed. by Isaac N. Mazonde, 17–28. Gaborone: Light Books.

Parsons, Neil. 1993. *A New History of Southern Africa,* second edition. Gaborone: Macmillan.

Silberbauer, George and Adam Kuper. 1996. Kgalagadi masters and Bushmen serfs: Some observations. *African Studies* 25.171–179.

Smieja, Birgit. 1998. Language Shift and its impact for minority languages in Botswana. A Paper presented on the 16 September 1998 at the Institute of Research for Development, University of Botswana.

—2003. *Language Pluralism in Botswana: Hope or Hurdle.* Berlin: Peter Lang.

Sommer, Gabrielle and Rainer Vossen. 2000. Language gain and language loss: The spread of Setswana in Ngamiland. In *Botswana the Future of the Minority Languages,* ed. by H.M. Batibo and B. Smieja, 129–146. Frankfurt: Peter Lang.

Traill, Antony. 1995. The Khoesan languages of South Africa. In *Language and Social History: Studies in South African Sociolinguistics,* ed. by Rajend Mesthrie, 1–18. Cape Town: David Phillip.

Vossen, Rainer. 1997. What click sounds got to do in Bantu: Reconstructing the history of language contacts in Southern Africa. In *Human Contact through Language and Linguistics,* ed. by B. Smieja and M. Tasch, 353–368. Frankfurt: Peter Lang.

Westphal, Ernst O.J. 1963. The linguistic prehistory of Southern Africa: Bush, Kwadi, Hottentots, and Bantu linguistic relationships. *Africa* 33.237–265.

Wilmsen, Edwin. 1980. Exchanges, interaction, and settlement in northwestern Botswana: Past and present perspectives. *Working Papers*, No. 39. African Studies Center, Boston University.

Chapter 4

African Modernity, Transnationalism and Language Vitality: Portuguese in Multilingual Mozambique

Christopher Stroud

4.1 Introduction

In this chapter, I argue that questions of language vitality in Mozambique are best understood in relation to the (complex) notion of *modernity*, here taken to refer to how 'different societies and cultures change as they come into contact with one another, with the spirit of capitalism and an ever-encroaching scientific rationality' (Wittrock, cited in Macamo 2005), or how different societies manage the transition from traditional society (Giddens 1990, 1991). In modern society, the conduct of individuals and populations is the outcome of a plethora of heterogeneous factors in the workings of state and non-state institutions, political rationalities, systems of expert knowledge, technologies (in the Foucauldian sense of 'techniques' – editors) of governance and notions of subjectivity and agency. The structuring of modernity in different nation-states is also determined by transnational economic, demographic and cultural processes, such as the expansion of multinational capitalist corporations, transnational labor migrations and global media, which are themselves labels for complex and contradictory sociopolitical dynamics. These multinational flows are filtered through local modi operandi of class and state formation, as well as the workings of state and non-state institutional bodies; and they are transformed into (new) structures of economic and demographic organization, cultural practices and modes of decision-making. Given such a heterogeneous assemblage of forces that make up modern life, it should come as no surprise that modernity is far from being a uniform experience across contexts, leading to the coinage of expressions such as *vernacular modernities* or *alternative modernities* to make reference to the multiplicity of local manifestations of the modern.

An essential means whereby individuals and groups negotiate, manage and experience modernity is through linguistic practices and perceptions of different languages and their associated capital values. In multilingual ecologies, the extent to which a community of speakers maintains a language as a primary language, adopts it as a lingua franca, appropriates it as a second language or gradually abandons it in favor of alternative modes of communication reflects the perceived value of that language on capital markets of modernity. Speakers strive to appropriate languages associated with economic value, social mobility and educational and cultural advancement, and to pass on this linguistic capital to the next generation. I argue here that the way multilingualism is practised and perceived in the Mozambican context differs from what we find in center economies such as the American or European precisely because the forms that modernity takes in Africa differ from those commonly found in the industrialized North. In many African contexts, although colonial projects of state formation were predicated on the *promise* of modernity, in practice states were built on the edifice of its very *denial* to the majority of the colonial population (Macamo 2005). Postcolonial developments are no exception. Marginalized and globally peripheral African states have increasingly been forced to relinquish state functions to an assemblage of civil society and transnational organizations (NGOs, Churches) and to institutions outside the state proper (e.g., IMF, GATT). This shift has implications for language relationships and linguistic practices, as well as ramifications for the theoretical presuppositions and concepts used in standard accounts of language vitality that do not easily apply to multilingualism in contexts of African social transformation. In particular, I argue that the notions of *local* and *global* applied to language, and the link between tradition and local language, on the one hand, and modernity and metropolitan language, on the other, requires revision. Also in need of a critical revisit are received models of language shift and vitality, particularly with respect to how an approach to *shift* and *vitality* in spatial terms can complement a traditional bias towards phrasing accounts of language shift in temporal terms alone. Finally, I submit that the current dystopian over-reliance on transnational and global processes as instigators of shift to 'world languages' needs rethinking in contexts where global processes are (re)localizing international languages and transforming indigenous African languages into languages of global modernity.

Viewing language vitality as a reflex of a complex and heterogeneous modernity where the state is but 'one element in a multiple network of actors, organizations and entities' (Inda 2005) requires an analytical framework capable of capturing

> how and in what ways, and to what extent the rationales, devices and authorities for the government of conduct [including linguistic conduct] in the multitude of bedrooms, factories, shopping malls, children's home, kitchens, cinemas, operating theaters, classrooms and so forth have become linked up to a 'political apparatus?' (Rose 1996:38)

Given the changing fortunes of the State in Africa, such an approach should also be able to problematize the notion of *state*, particularly in terms of the pluralization and mélange of diverse orders of organization (Pieterse 1995), both local and transnational, that work in parallel to, or in conjuncture with, it. Foucault's (1991) approach to modern government, articulated principally in the notion of *governmentality*, is precisely such an approach. Governmentality refers to the complex assemblages of 'persons, forms of knowledge, technical procedures and modes of judgment and sanction – a machine for government' that 'shape and manage individual and collective conduct in relation to norms and objectives that are considered non-political' (Rose 1996:38). Studies of governmentality have developed along three analytical foci, namely that of *political rationality, technologies of governmentality and subjects of governmentality*. *Political rationalities* refer to the 'regimes of truth' or the 'epistemological regimes of intelligibility' (Inda 2005:8) and the problem-oriented nature of governmentality that formulate the problem of government, the nature of those governed and the solutions and programs of efficacious government, as 'in order to govern well, it is necessary to know' (8). *Technologies of government*, on the other hand, refer to the 'strategies, techniques and procedures through which different authorities seek to enact programs of government' as manifested in the 'complex assemblage of diverse forces (legal, architectural, financial, judgmental), techniques (notation, evaluation), devices (surveys and charts) that promise to regulate decisions and actions of groups, organizations, etc' (Rose 1996:42). Finally, the *subjects of governmentality* refer to 'the diverse types of subjects, persons, actors, agents, identities that arise from and influence government activity,' to the extent that government practices and policies seek to cultivate particular types of individual and collective identity, forms of agency and subjectivity (such as citizens, consumers, etc.).

Ferguson and Gupta (2002) remark on how governmentality is essential to the forms that the imagination of the state takes, as the state is 'a resultant, not a cause, an outcome of the composition and assembling of actors, flows, buildings, relations of authority into relatively durable associations mobilized to a greater or lesser extent, towards the achievement of particular objectives by particular means' (43).[1] They also note how contemporary figurations of states are *transnational* or global in character.

Applied to language, the notion of *governmentality* opens up an approach to language issues that goes beyond a politics of the state and the constraining dichotomies of civil *society/state, public/private, national/transnational* that much traditional politics of language and multilingualism has relied upon. Instead, it encourages attention to the multiple organizations, institutions and individuals behind the economies and rationalities of language, highlighting how multilingualism is an accidental and historically arbitrary outcome of a heterogeneous assemblage of different contingent forms of power and their realization in diverse local technologies.

   The argument in this chapter is based on a case study of language shift and vitality in Mozambique. Like many colonial constructs, Mozambique was a product of modernity; and as elsewhere in Africa, the plethora of processes involved in its colonial and postcolonial (re)construction have produced deeply ambivalent and contradictory experiences of modernity (cf. Macamo 2005) that bear significantly on patterns of language diversity. In Section 4.2, I first detail some characteristics of the Mozambican sociolinguistics of multilingualism, raising some specific issues on language vitality and shift that need to be addressed in relation to the structuring of Mozambican modernity. Section 4.3 contains the body of the analysis, where I discuss the processes and dynamics of linguistic governmentality that have shaped the Mozambican state from colonial times to the present. I explore in detail how these processes resonate with the linguistic vitality of Mozambican indigenous languages and Portuguese. This leads to a concluding discussion on the nature of Mozambican multilingual dynamics in Section 4.4, which critically revisits some conceptual issues in language vitality research in light of the current data.

4.2 Multilingualism in Mozambique

Despite many years of colonial and postcolonial disregard and at times outright marginalization of African languages, the Mozambican language ecology shows very little evidence of wholesale shift towards Portuguese, and shifts across African languages are also minimal (1997 Census).[2] In fact, in recent years, the status of Mozambican languages has changed from 'patrimonial' acknowledgement to a more substantial recognition, including their use in official contexts, such as political debates and education. With respect to Portuguese, no significant local or indigenized variety of the language has evolved during its five-hundred-year presence in the territory, and there is no consensus around any identifiable norm of Portuguese other than that of the European norm spoken by the elite. In practice, the majority of those who speak Portuguese produce a range of hybridized varieties that can be distinguished by age, gender, occupation and education.[3]

4.2.1 Demographics of multilingualism

At independence, in 1976, a population of fourteen million people spoke an estimated twenty Bantu languages (NELIMO 1989),[4] a handful of Indian languages and Portuguese as the official language (Lopes 1999). According to the latest census conducted in 1997, the distribution and use of languages have changed little since the first mapping in 1980. Then, the number of speakers who claimed Portuguese as their mother tongue was around 1 per cent as opposed to 3 per cent in 1997, with 25 per cent speaking it as a second language in 1980 increasing to 40 per cent of the population in 1997. Portuguese has remained a predominantly urban language with over 90 per cent of its speakers found in the few major cities: Maputo, Beira, Quelimane and Nampula. It is the language of the young, spoken predominantly by people in the age group of fifteen–thirty-nine, and more by men than by women.

Bantu languages, spoken predominantly in the rural regions of Mozambique, are still the mother tongues of the majority (about 75 per cent) of the population. The largest Bantu language, Emakua, is spoken by approximately 25 per cent of the population in the north of the country, on the border with Tanzania. Many Mozambican languages share with Emakua the status of cross-border languages, for example, CiChewa (also spoken in Malawi), XiShona and Ndebele (Zimbabwe) and Tsonga (South Africa). Many speakers of Xironga, the original language of the capital Maputo, have shifted to XiChangana/Tsonga, a language virtually identical to Xironga. A variety of other languages, such as Hindi, Punjabi, Gujarati and Chinese languages, are spoken in small numbers principally among trades-people throughout the country, although the majority of them live in urban areas.[5] A wide range of Bantu languages are spoken in the urban metropolises, in contrast with the rural areas, where the number of languages spoken locally is generally very small (Firmino 1995, 2000, 2002).

A significant fact about Mozambique is that patterns of multilingualism vary from one region to another, and also differ across urban and rural contexts.[6] For example, in the northern province of Cabo Delgado, where the city of Nampula is situated, speakers of every age claim to use Portuguese in formal meetings, when issues relating to politics and administration are discussed. In other contexts and for other functions, such as interactions around sports, and for use with intimate friends and colleagues, the older population tends to use Emakua, whereas the younger generation reports more frequent use of Portuguese. In Vilanculos, a much smaller metropolis in the south of the country barely six hundred kilometers from Maputo, Portuguese is also used mainly in formal meetings. However, in contradistinction to Nampula, the local language Citswa is used across *all* age groups for all other functions, and in all other situations. Furthermore, urban/suburban differences in language use interact with age and gender differently for different languages. In both Nampula and Vilanculos, Portuguese is more often a second language for women than for men. The number of languages mastered by speakers in urban areas is greater than in rural areas; men in all age groups report knowing more African languages than women, and younger speakers know more languages than older ones. In other words, the *urban/rural* split in multilingualism figures differently depending upon region, and interacts with social variables such as *gender* and *age*, as well as *function/register* and *context* of language use. It would thus appear that urbanity and mobility translate into a gendered and age-differentiated access to linguistic resources, introducing social stratifications around multilingualism that do not appear to be the case in the rural areas (Stroud Ms).

4.2.2 Perceptions and discourses on Portuguese and African languages

The prevailing ideology generally rates Portuguese over the indigenous languages. Portuguese *voices* are judged as formal, urban, cultivated and modern. Local discourse on Mozambican languages considers them informal, local, traditional or rural. The ideological division of labor is remarkably reminiscent of how the languages were perceived and ranked at certain times during the colonial period, although this may change, with the increasing use of African languages in the government and public institutions. Furthermore, whereas large segments of the population of Maputo agree that there is a 'correct', standard way of speaking Portuguese, namely, the European norm, Mozambican languages are clearly represented as polycentric, with speakers conceding that one and the same language may be spoken in different ways.

Particularly relevant to the urban framing of Portuguese is the interaction of age, education and employment in the *formal* economy for level of proficiency attained in Portuguese. It would appear that an important factor determining whether or not a speaker uses the European norm is whether or not s/he has *employment.* This is especially the case for those who are less educated (Stroud 1996:201). In fact, among speakers with the same level of education (year 5), those who were in gainful employment were generally considered to be more proficient speakers of EP on an attitude test.[7] This might suggest that speakers with a prior, good, knowledge of Portuguese gain easier access to the formal market (as has been shown to be the case for other African contexts, cf. Deumert 2005 for South Africa). However, it is also quite likely that access to the formal market on grounds other than linguistic (such as family contacts, residential availability) helps provide the necessary social networks and institutions to sustain and develop the rudimentary Portuguese skills of fifth graders.

4.2.3 Varieties of Portuguese

Portuguese in Mozambique covers a range of (L2) varieties that are determined by age, education, occupation and gender (Firmino 1995, 2000, 2002; Gonçalves 1996; Stroud and Gonçalves 1997). They are marked by borrowings and mixing of materials from indigenous languages, as well as appropriations of materials from one local variety to another that reflect the dynamics of shifting conditions of modernity. It is not uncommon to find contest and debate among speakers over the provenance of specific structures, for example, whether the lexical item *machibombo* 'local bus' is of Portuguese or Bantu origin. There is no attested Portuguese-based pidgin or creole (unlike in Cabo Verde) and no new generally accepted emerging standard L1 Portuguese (unlike in Brazil).

The best-documented local variety, or set of practices, of Portuguese is that spoken in the capital city of Maputo, comprehensive overviews of which are provided by Gonçalves (1996, 2001, 2002) and from which all of the following examples adduced later are taken. Predominant *lexical characteristics* comprise new word coinages and borrowings from primarily Bantu languages and English with European Portuguese (EP) inflections or derivations, for instance, *maçala;* 'apple'; *machamba;* 'cultivated ground'. These borrowings are only partially integrated, as they may be assigned *gender* but not *number.* With respect to the morphological treatment of Portuguese lexical items, it is not clear what forms are the most productive. The majority of lexical innovations involve either (i) alterations in the basic meanings of Portuguese lexical items (such as the verb *apanhar* to mean *receive* in *Nas escolas não apanham boa educação* 'In the schools, they do not *receive* a good education') or (ii) a change in their semantic and syntactic selection restrictions. One common alteration is the transitiviza-tion of intransitive verbs (such as *Aquele rapaz estava sempre disposto a evoluir a sua aldeia* 'That boy was always disposed to evolve his farm', where *evoluir* is an intransitive verb in EP) and verbs that take either an indirect or oblique com-plement (as in *Niguém protestou a iniativa – contra a iniciativa* in EP – 'Nobody protested [against] the initiative'; and *Chegou na sala, entregou o emissário –* EP: ao emissário – '[He/She] arrived in the room and gave [it to] the emissary'). The transitivization of intransitive verbs allows forms of passives that do not occur in EP, such as *Os rapazes foram sexualmente abusados por padres,* (*abuser de* in EP) 'The boys were sexually abused by the priests'.

Mozambican Portuguese *syntax* is noted for (i) its different order in clitic placement and (ii) different mechanisms for forming relative clauses and reporting speech. Clitics appear affixed to the right of the inflected verb, as illustrated by the following example: *Há pessoas que opõem-se à religão* (EP: *que se-opõem*) 'There are people who are opposed to religion'. A common strategy in the formation of relative clauses is to use a resumptive pronoun, as in *O apaga-dor que apagamos o quadro com ele* (EP: *com que apagamos o quadro*) / . . .

With respect to morphosyntax, some predominant traits of Mozambican Portuguese are the following:

1. The regularization in the expression of the imperative. Mozambican Portuguese makes consistent use of present conjunctive morphology for all persons, including *tu* where EP requires an indicative form, such as *Queres ganhar um fato de treino? Vá agora* (EP *Vai*) 'Do you want to win training shorts? – Go now'.
2. The use of the 'inflected infinitive' where EP uses the bare infinitive form, for instance, *Chefes deviam criarem condicoés* (EP *criar*), 'Bosses should create conditions'.
3. The use of the indicative mood in contexts where EP requires the conjunctive, such as (i) in phrases introduced with *talvez* 'perhaps', for instance in *Talvez eu tenho vocação* (EP: *tenha*) 'Perhaps I'll have a vocation'; (ii) in concessives, as in *Embora que eu sou mais novo, posso dar uma opinão* (EP: *embora seja*) 'Even though I am the youngest, I can give an opinion'; and (iii) in relative clauses

with negated antecedents, as in *Não há ninguém que fica satisfeito* (EP: *fique*) 'There is nobody who is satisfied'.

4.2.4 Multilingualism and language vitality in Mozambique

Clearly, there are some significant characteristics of language vitality in Mozambique that need accounting for. First of all, how have the Bantu languages managed to remain the mother tongues of the majority of the population and to 'survive' colonial and postcolonial impositions relatively intact, with only minimal influence from Portuguese? And why didn't any Bantu-based pidgins or creoles, or major Bantu language lingua francas, develop during this time? Second, what explains the regionally distinct patterns of multilingualism that can be found in urban and rural areas throughout the territory? And third, how is it that the transplanted norm of EP appears to have retained relative integrity, with only selective and limited Bantu substrate influence? Just as importantly, what accounts for the developmental trajectory of 'popular' Mozambican Portuguese in terms of the range of hybrid practices manifest in predominantly unstable, sociolinguistically patterned and distributed, second language forms?

The analysis submitted Section 4.3 suggests that any account of the sociolinguistics of Mozambican modernity needs to refer to the historically contingent political rationalities behind different orders of indexicality, to the nature and role of shifting and competing techniques of governmentality (such as what norms are enforced, through education, or in the formal market) and to emerging and variable conceptualizations of the subject of governmentality (*indigine* 'Native'). In this context, it is useful to take the notion of *linguistic governmentality* to refer to a regime of governance, a regulatory mechanism that targets the form that (public) voice may take (cf. Bourdieu's 1991 notion of 'legitimate speaker'). Linguistic governmentality may take the form of a political rationality (as when a nation-state is imagined as necessarily monolingual or when minority languages are seen as nationally divisive) or technological rationalities (through the definition of a 'language' embedded in school curricula, tests and exams, and language censuses). It may also pertain to the subject of governmentality (e.g., when citizens are stipulated or hailed into existence of speakers of a particular language).

4.3 Governmentality and Multilingualism in Colonial and Postcolonial Mozambique

4.3.1 Colonial governmentality

The Mozambican colonial state was only really firmly established through concerted military pacification in 1918, four hundred years after the first colonial contact. Before this time, Mozambique was a stop-over point en route to the prized colony of India, and, later, a source of slave labor (a cruel distinction it shared with the Congo–Angola region) for the Brazilian plantations. The loss of Brazil in the late nineteenth century coincided with the search for a new Portuguese identity in Europe, at the time when other Western European powers were carving up Africa among themselves. In many respects, Portuguese colonial acquisitions were the result of political machinations on behalf of the other colonial powers to limit each others' territorial ambitions.[8]

Mainly two transnational processes were at play in the formation of the Mozambican colonial state: on the one hand, Portuguese imperial ambitions to create a Catholic and moral state, and, on the other, the Protestant mission's alternative figuration of Mozambique in its quest for a New Jerusalem (Macamo 2005). These two distinct political rationalities worked in tandem with precolonial structures of authority, technologies of demography, and migration and subject characteristics (particularly gender roles) to create two very different structures of modernity that would come to bear on multilingual practices. The early Portuguese colonial state, built on an elaborate system for the regulation of labor (Macamo 2005), was characterized by ambivalence and exclusion. It implemented ingenious methods and strategies designed to control the mobility and orderliness of the indigenous population with the purpose of limiting access to the privileges of colonial modernity. These strategies were various: all Mozambicans were required to carry a pass-book, the *Cadeneta*, at all times; urban planning (spatial governmentality) permitted only domestic workers and 'civilized natives' to live in the 'concrete city'; local structures of authority were created that corresponded to arbitrarily delimited tribes led by customary chiefs (so-called *regulos* who were appointed by the Portuguese colonialists); the 'native' Mozambican was governed according to customary law through the medium of African languages; and rural structures of (gendered) social reproduction were put in place. There were few schools available to Black Mozambicans (*indigines*). In 1890, there was only one primary school in Mozambique, and, in 1915, only sixty-eight in the whole country (Gonçalves 1996). Only Catholic schools were sanctioned by the government, as Catholicism was a core component of a colonial doctrine that felt it was its moral task to discipline and provide salvation to the 'lazy' Native through compulsory labor.[9] Official knowledge production was similarly subordinated to the (re-)production of indigenous labor. Thus, for example, the Geographical Society had the expressed purpose of contributing to a body of knowledge that would guide the 'judicious management of the colony' (Junod 1905, 1946).

A second phase of colonial structuring (1918–1975) brought a change in Mozambican colonial policy from emphasis on the extraction of labor to the first halting steps towards the creation of a settlement colony. The government in Lisbon had long harboredplans to transform the colony into a Portuguese 'overseas' province. To this end, agricultural reforms and an expanded urban development of the center and south of the country were put in place, at the same time as the influx of Portuguese colonists was almost doubled in a ten-year period, from fifty thousand in 1950 to ninety thousand in 1960 (Gonçalves 1996). A significant political contribution to the building of this new Portuguese province was the attempt to incorporate the Native Mozambican more firmly into the colonial social fabric by creating a special form of citizenship, namely the *assimilado*, important requirements of which were mastery of Portuguese, a commitment to monogamy, evidence of employment and true Catholic faith. As part of this strategy, schooling for a broader 'Native' population was begun in 1930. These technologies contributed to a 'variegated citizenship' where different technologies of governmentality were defined for distinct segments of the population.

The Protestant missions, which comprised a number of different churches,[10] took an entirely different approach to their transnational ambition. In their desire to win converts and build communities of faith, the Protestant missions actively encouraged a broad popular participation, and to this end they deployed techniques of linguistic delimitation and codification to create constituencies of speakers who would have access to religious teachings in Mozambican languages. The missions thus came to provide a resource for the native Mozambican to appropriate the fruits of modernity otherwise denied them by the Portuguese state. Many middle-class, relatively well-born Mozambicans, or migrant (mine) workers who found it increasingly difficult to return to rural life, found refuge in the Protestant Christian community. As the Protestant communities worked with Mozambican languages, these languages became valuable local resources in the construction of an alternative colonial modernity (Alfredsson and Linha 1999; Cruz E Silva 1996; Helgesson 1991).

The sociolinguistic situation that confronted the early missionaries was confusing in the extreme. Harries (2007:156) remarks on how the missionaries quickly realized that the community in which they found themselves in the south of the country comprised a veritable '*pot pourri* of refugees drawn from the length and breadth of coastal Southeast Africa'. These people lived in scattered villages independent of each other, with no shared language between them. What had appeared to be a vehicular language, namely, Gwamba, was characterized by the Swiss missionary Berthout as 'a fruit-salad of Hlengwe, of Djonga, of Boer, of English, of Nwaloungou, of Hlavi, of Venda, of Sotho' and as 'barely comprehensible' (quoted in Harries 2007:160). The situation was similar for the peoples of the coastal plain, where languages such as Zulu, Swati and Gaza had all contributed linguistic forms to the local vernaculars. Unperturbed by the challenges posed by such linguistic diversity, the missionaries set about designing a religious lingua franca. Eight territorially based dialects of Gwamba, which were thought to correspond to the different origins and ancestral identities of the speakers, were 'isolated'. Having thus determined what they considered to be the authentic core of the language, the missionaries set about standardizing and cultivating Gwamba for use in religious contexts primarily.

The vitality of Portuguese and African languages was thus a direct consequence of the competing rationalities of government on behalf of the Portuguese
colonists and the Protestant missions, the technologies employed to realize
these rationalities and the construction of a fitting subject/citizen. A number of
structures, policies and principles of Portuguese colonial governmentality
directly involved language. The (gendered) structure of labor and its reproduction privileged the use of African languages and African traditional structures
of government. Strict management of the urban environment privileged Portuguese literacy, also reinforced through education and Catholic ethics. It also
created a fertile soil for the germination of transient and rudimentary Portuguese varieties, called 'kitchen Portuguese'. Colonial policies of indigenous
citizenship made Portuguese a requirement. On the other hand, Protestant
governmentality implicated indigenous languages in a central way, specifically
through the selection and codification of African language literacy for religious
uses (Makoni 1998).

4.3.2 Governmentality in the postcolonial state

4.3.2.1 *Towards a post-independence nation-state*

The first years of Mozambican independence were characterized by ambitious
attempts at modernization, in accordance with the political rationalities of a
modern nation-state striving towards clearly demarcated, linguistically and culturally delimited, geopolitical boundaries, the construction of a modern
hierarchical administration, adherence to the rule of the law and access to full
citizenship for all Mozambicans. The state sought to attain these goals through
the formation of a disciplined population of modern Mozambicans, the *novo
homen,* 'new man', with a clear moral commitment to the new state and its security and welfare, and through a planned and centrally managed economy.

Through a variety of ordinary and everyday sociopolitical practices of governmentality, the state was figured and enacted as hierarchically 'above' local and
civil society and as encompassing the regional and the local (cf. Ferguson and
Gupta 2002, who use the scalar and spatial metaphors of verticality and encom-
passment to talk about nation-states). The image of the Mozambican state as
vertical and encompassing was partially constituted out of the decision to designate Portuguese as the official language, symbolically equating it with the
Mozambican territory, as opposed to local, vernacular or regional languages,
with a more limited provenance and less esteemed position on the sociolinguistic hierarchy. These types of spatial and scalar sociolinguistic hierarchies are
reproduced through a variety of mundane, everyday, practices. In the early days
of the new government, for example, all traditional and local structures of
decision-making were dismantled and replaced by new structures managed
by FRELIMO cadres in the Portuguese language. New forms of workers'

management units took over the running of nationalized industries, agri-cooperatives, nationalized housing boards, and other spheres of society, such as local councils and citizens' watch committees, which were run in Portuguese. State machinery in the form of censuses, registers, protocols and so on worked only through Portuguese, and the use of Portuguese in public space was even made mandatory. In fact, a particular kind of moral subjectivity (the good citizen) was explicitly linked to correct usage of Portuguese (Stroud 1999). At the same time, Portuguese was spread throughout the territory in the wake of the expansion of institutions such as schools, clinics and maternity wards, an infrastructure that, like the new administrative structures, was associated with use of Portuguese. Education, for example, was conducted solely in Portuguese, and school personnel were transferred to parts of the country whose local language they did not know, to ensure that only Portuguese would be used in the classroom. Portuguese usage was strictly regimented in teacher method handbooks, especially in extensive model exercises, classroom dialogues and drill patterns that dictated every classroom session in detail. Furthermore, language use in exams was monitored by all institutions in the hierarchy, including the local education offices, the provincial education directorates and the Ministry of Education.

These quotidian sociopolitical processes did not just create a state, they also simultaneously configured Portuguese and the indigenous Mozambican languages, as well as their relationships in the image of the state, typically projecting ideas of hierarchy to the relation between local and metropolitan languages. Language ideological debates construed Portuguese as a language of consensus, the language of the territory and the state, and co-terminus with the governing party, FRELIMO, whereas the indigenous languages were ideologically construed as ethnically divisive and as vestiges of colonial structures of management of patrimonial interest only.[11] Official concerns about the use of 'broken varieties' of Portuguese introduced new structures of iconicity and indexicality based on social class and education that had not existed in the same form previously. In general, the policies had the effect of incorporating traditional Mozambican languages and Portuguese into identical systems of indexical value, reinforcing the perception that the indigenous languages were *dialectos*, whereas Portuguese was a 'language'.

However, the new forms of authority, modernity and urbanity that the FRELIMO government promoted created dissatisfaction and unrest among many segments of the population, particularly those living in rural areas. One expression this took was a devastating civil war led by the guerilla organization RENAMO (National Mozambican Resistance), founded in the then Rhodesia (now Zimbabwe) and financed later by South Africa. The war resulted in wanton destruction of infrastructure, hospitals and schools, the pillaging and burning of rural areas and general disruption to industrial production. This led to rural stagnation and increasing migration to urban areas, as populations fled the ravages of war, under-development and unemployment in search of safety and security. The result of this massive rural exodus was that in the mid-1980s the capital Maputo became an assemblage of different contingent technologies of governmentality, sedimented political rationalities and traces of different subject populations, thus a highly hybrid context in terms of spatial and temporal organization. Colonial spatial politics had built new functional suburbs for the Mozambican *assimilado,* such as the *bairro* of Chamanculo, meant for functionaries in the lower administration, such as teachers and clerks. This now became populated by a variety of people. The *bairro* of *Polana Cimento* saw a radical switch in population at independence, as new groups, principally the new political and administrative elite, but also local and foreign NGOs and diplomatic representatives, took the place of the previous White inhabitants who had moved to other countries. The extensive migration from rural Mozambique due to unrest created areas such as Maxaquene, where newly arrived migrants, either as displaced refugees or as labor migrants, settled into neighborhoods where other members of their various ethnic groupings lived (Firmino 2002).

The significance of this urban mélange is reflected in speakers' frequency of use and knowledge of Portuguese and traditional Mozambican languages, as well as in the ideologies attached to different languages. With respect to Portuguese, the different residential groupings show clearly different patterns of acquisition and use of Portuguese with varying degrees of Bantu substrate influence (Stroud 1996; Firmino 2002; Gonçalves 2001, 2002). In Table 4.1, the proportion of utterances produced per neighbourhood is displayed.[12]

The proportion of EP utterances is considerably higher among speakers from Polana Cimento (PC) than in the other neighborhoods, and significantly higher than among speakers from Maxaquene (MX), with every second utterance among MX speakers comprising a non-EP utterance, as compared to every fourth utterance from speakers in PC. Given the demographic composition of residents in PC, who were generally better educated and made up of more white-collar professionals, this might not be surprising. In Table 4.2, we note further that men in urban neighborhoods have significantly more EP utterances than women in urban zones on one hand, and than both men and women in suburban areas on the other.

Table 4.1　Average percentages of EP utterances correlated with neighborhoods

MX	CH	AM	PC
49.27	50.40	55.27	73.10

MX, Maxaquene; CH, Chamanculo; AM, Alto Mãe; PC, Polana Cimento.
Difference between PC and MX significant at the 0.05 level.

Table 4.2   Average percentages of
EP utterances correlated with
neighborhood and gender

Gender	Neighbourhood	
	Suburban	Urban
Male	49.11	82.09
Female	50.33	43.60

Difference between urban males and other
groups significant at the 0.001 level.

Table 4.3   Average number of non-European
Portuguese structures per neighborhood

MF*	MX	CH	AM	PC
5.6	18.3	3.9	4.3	8.1

*Mafalane

Again, given the gendered history of access to Portuguese in colonial times, such a distributional pattern could be expected.

A finding of interest can be observed in Table 4.3, where the proportions of non-EP structures are indicated for twenty speakers evenly distributed among the four residential groupings.

First, as could be expected, non-EP structures are more frequent in Max-aquene, where speakers have three–four times more non-EP structures than speakers from other neighborhoods. However, interestingly, speakers from PC also exhibit a high proportion of non-EP structures, despite the fact that they also display a significantly higher proportion of EP utterances, as noted in Table 4.1.

The explanation for these patterns of Portuguese practices lies partly in the importance of the formal market, which is linguistically regulated in terms of the EP norm and the differential access of the different residential groupings to this market. It also lies in the nature of the local, non-urban social networks that PC speakers cultivate. With respect to this latter dimension, PC residents have more dispersed networks than those of AM and CH, as they have ties with speakers outside the immediate neighbourhood. This pattern is tantamount to relatively loose knit networks, which create conditions for 'innovations' to spread over long distances (Milroy and Milroy 1992). In this case, the Bantu substrate is part of a refiguring of linguistic repertoires that came about through social exchanges in the contact zone between the formal and informal economy, as PC residents rely on the informal market for vital economic supplies in the form of material goods and non-material benefits, such as contracts and

Table 4.4 Proportions of non-EP forms for certain structures according to neighbourhood

	MF	MX	CH	AM	PC
Categorical selection	20	38	11	14	32
Semantic selection	7	32	5	20	37
Conj	11	42	13	13	22
Embedding	18	50	7	8	17
Reflexive pronoun	17	45	12	17	10
El	3	49	21	18	10
Agreement	9	73	9	3	6

land tenure deeds. MX residents, on the other hand, have compact local networks, compared to other residential groupings.

In general, the more established pre-independence residents in Maputo tend invariably to show less Bantu substrate influence and speak a more European-normed Portuguese than the migrant groups or the residents of PC (Table 4.4).

Many of the older residents would have acquired Portuguese in colonial times as a prerequisite to becoming *assimilados*, a resource that they would have passed on to their children. The in-migrant residents in the MX neighbourhood, on the other hand, exhibit typical across-the-board Bantu influence in their varieties of Portuguese and span a wide range of proficiencies. What is of interest here is the extent to which Bantu substrate influence, comprising fairly low-level morphological 'errors' in this case, is stigmatized and perceived to be indicative of bad education and uncultivated habits. This contrasts with the Bantu substrate influence in the speech of PC residents, which is not only free from stigma, but widely believed, on indicators of attitude tests, to comprise core features of Portuguese.[13]

4.3.2.2 Degovernmentalization of the state: Privatization, decentralization and new forms of governmentality

The rapid disintegration of the socialist Eastern bloc countries, which had provided the primary economic (and ideological) support to Mozambique, had deleterious implications for the country. As in many African nations, it opened a space for the gradual disengagement of Western support for an Africa, since it had lost its strategic importance. Together with civil unrest and the violence of the civil war, these developments outside of the rigorous mandate of the state forced the government to begin redefining the pressing issues of governance. In the period immediately prior to and following Samora Machels' death and in conjunction with the first democratic elections, a new blueprint for Mozambican governance was taking shape. During the 1990s, the bulk of economic growth took place in the informal sector, while the formal sectors were subject to massive privatization (Pitcher 2002). A new entrepreneurial state had emerged that was set on privatizing key sectors of the industry. Peace accords and international aid to develop the infrastructure opened up rural space for the expansion of the state. Citizens became 'voters' and sometimes consumers, which created new political and socioeconomic spaces for governance. The formation of the Mozambican state in this period increasingly took place under the influence of transnational institutions, such as the IMF, USAID, SIL and Gulbenkan, which affected multiple economic, political and cultural realms simultaneously.[14] A diminished role for the state as an economic actor, as an employer and as the provider of goods and services was accompanied by a mushrooming of foreign-funded NGOs, many of which began to address the pressing need for reforms in public sector services such as transportation, health and education (Fauvet 2000; Nugent 2004:366). This evolution gave rise to competing foci of power and legitimacy. The increase in available forms of organization, through what Ferguson and Gupta (2002) call the 'transnationalized local' (i.e., fusion of the local and the global), created the contingent conditions for very diverse experiences and manifestations of modernity (Pieterse 1995). As these authors note, organizations such as these have provided alternative forms of governmentality that are not necessarily part of the nation-building logic per se.

The state was forced to accommodate these new autonomous structures of governmentality, evident in the advent of multiparty politics in the early 1990s and the vernacularization of Mozambican politics. Decentralization of political power to more traditional structures of governance and local decision-making (Buur and Kyed 2003)[15] has also been part of this process (Chabal and Daloz 1991; West 2003). State institutions have also increasingly embraced linguistic diversity; Radio Mozambique now transmits in twelve Mozambican languages, and more and more community radios are in the pipeline (Lopes 1999). To a large extent, these processes have involved the deconstruction of the vertical and encompassing Mozambican state, as conceived of by the FRELIMO party, into a more horizontal, permeable and multilayered state.

The transformation of the Mozambican state has simultaneously rearticulated the roles of Portuguese and Mozambican languages, with the latter reframed as languages of (local) politics (Liphola 1996). The extended civil society role taken up by religious institutions also carried implications for language. Churches have historically been important institutions in the development of prestigious forms of African languages. As the various denominations employ distinct languages (Cruz E Silva 1996), including in some cases Portuguese, these have come to play an important part in disseminating alternative discourses and practices of language, sometimes in conflict with official state's perceptions of local languages. Finally, NGO activities are also ushering in more frequent use of African languages, in attempts to better engage the community in processes of development, especially in the education sector, where one of the predominant activities has been the promotion, evaluation and design of mother tongue programs in African languages for elementary-level schooling and adult literacy. The use of indigenous Mozambican languages in education has brought with it the beginnings of a development of technical and metalinguistic registers in Mozambican languages, and the development of assessment and evaluation instruments for Mozambican languages.

Although religious organizations and NGOs appear to be local, they are transnational in that their financing, technologies and mandates emanate from powerful mother organizations that are globally active. The pervasiveness of these organizations in this period stands in marked contrast to the time of Samora Machel and the early post-independence nation-state, when the majority of such organizations stood under strict government control and their influence was severely curtailed. Ironically, it is precisely these transnational but seemingly local institutions that most actively promote the use and vitality of African languages. Transnational processes have also been instrumental in the development of pan-African markets, providing the resources for Mozambicans to engage with the global market 'on their own ground'. The resultant hybridization in the political economy is finding reflexes in new forms of multilingualism in regional and cross-border languages, such as Tsonga and Zulu in South Africa, facilitated by the more permeable territorial borders between South Africa and Mozambique, and the increasing market opportunities for informal trade in Malawi and a Zimbabwe in disarray.

Just as the vitality of Mozambican languages has benefited from both transnational and local processes of governmentality, so too has that of Portuguese. In the main, however, influences on Portuguese have come from economic developments in the formal sector. The establishment of Portuguese-speaking television stations, the growth of the hotel and tourist industries and increased trade with Lusophone organizations has ushered into Mozambique a range of non-Mozambican varieties of Portuguese. Although Brazilian soap operas are highly popular, their influence on viewers' language is predominantly confined to the incorporation of lexical items. The biggest impact of external norms of Portuguese can be found among members of the Brazilian *Igreja National* 'national church' who are moved to speak by the Holy Spirit in fluent Brazilian-sounding Portuguese.[16]

4.3.2.3 *Regovernmentalization: Reinscribing alternative governmentalities into the state apparatus*

Contemporary Mozambique continues to recognize diversity in competing processes of governmentality. However, there are also clear attempts on behalf of the state to appropriate contemporary techniques and forms of expertise, and to re-inscribe (Barry et al. 1996) these technologies into a new and more dominant state apparatus. Strategies to 'de-autonomize' the Mozambican 'civil society' by means of a range of new state-driven technologies that implant state-run institutions at local levels is also a pervasive feature of modern Mozambican politics. For example, sectors that have long been run on a private basis (such as much of the functioning health care) or that have simply fallen into some disarray (such as higher education) are being 'regovernmentalized'. An example of this is the recent closing, by the minister of health, of private clinics housed in the public hospital system on the grounds that such an arrangement benefits only those who can afford to pay for special medical services. Coming from a government that openly seeks productive alliances with the private and corporate sectors, this is clearly no new socialist welfare program in the unfolding. Rather, it is an attempt to reestablish state authority in an affluent and expanding sector through a merger of corporate interests with those of the state. Another example of the same process is the recent strengthening of links between local agriculture in the Gaza province with the University of Pedagogy in the province, and the creation of a new public university in the province of Nampula.

Sociolinguistic correlates of the re-inscription of vernacular governmentality can be found in the re-articulation or semiotic incorporation of political messages into official public discourse. Translation specifically (but also code-switching) is a technique often employed to re-appropriate and elevate communication in African languages back into the sphere of public transparency. A recent example of this is when President Guebuza delivered an Easter speech in Portuguese to an audience of Changana/Tsonga-speaking women, despite the fact that he is a fluent and native speaker of this language himself. The occasion was in honor of a Mozambican feminist organization, and the speech was translated, as well as subsequent interactions, on the spot by a Portuguese–Changana/Tsonga translator. The performance of this event enacted and underscored the link between modernity and feminism (in Portuguese), on the one hand, with tradition and womanhood (in Changana), on the other.

These attempts to reinscribe erstwhile non-state forms of governmentality into the state apparatus has also meant trying to recapture those segments of civil society that found 'patronage' and voice in alternative modes of governance rooted in traditional forms of authority and claims to authenticity. Today, in official ceremonial contexts (such as when buildings are inaugurated or bridges built), traditional leaders are invited to attend and officiate, and traditional ceremonies are being reinstated, for example, *festa maio* and 23 September music festival or choral song ceremonies (all common ceremonies in the first years of independence but then scrapped under the Samora Machel government's later years because of their associations with reactionary tribalism). The political rationale here is the incorporation of forms of tradition in the modern symbolic management of Mozambique. Not surprisingly, all this is accomplished in Mozambican languages.

In conjunction with this emerging statal (re)appropriation of traditions, much contemporary political debate has been concerned with the search for a true Mozambican identity. In this outreach for authenticity, the southern Mozambican dance and music form *Marabenta* has been promoted as a true representation of Mozambicanness, while rap music in Mozambican languages was recently hailed as unequivocally 'Mozambican' in a recent televised debate between Mozambican youth and representatives from the art world. In southern Mozambique, it is now possible to purchase 'fake' Makonde masks, originally of the Makonde wood carvers in the North, as preeminent icons of authentic Mozambicanness. What is interesting in this search for, and appropriation of, tradition and authenticity through aspects of culture is its very obvious link with transnational discourses of *consumption*. The commercial value and recognition that an artifact, a dance form or a musical register receives on local and international markets (especially) would appear to be the prime source of its license or legitimacy as authentically Mozambican. In other words, what has come to be counted as *bona fide* traditional is that which can be marketed on global arenas in consumerist discourses. What is especially interesting, however, is the hybrid process of collapsing of scales: the global consumerist framing of local customs into a mélange of translocal and vernacular meanings. It is surely also no coincidence that the traditions, artifacts and languages of music that are embraced as authentically (and globally consumerist) Mozambican are predominantly from the southern part of the country, the region from which the majority of the political leaders come.

One language ideological implication of this is the redrawing of boundaries between Mozambican languages and Portuguese with respect to notions such as *traditional* and *modern*. Changana (Tsonga) is a pre-eminently traditional language of Mozambican authenticity in that it has a capital value in modern consumerist discourses.

4.4 Discussion and Conclusion

The earlier sections suggest that the historical and contemporary diversity in processes of colonization and globalization preclude any uniform account of language vitality across contexts. Rather, language shift is one manifestation of how speakers manage their economies in contact and how they participate in the formation, transformation and reproduction of locally constituted *alternative* and *vernacular modernities*. The linguistic and cultural realities lived by the speakers are mediated by interactions between, on the one hand, global, macrostructural, political and economic institutions, and, on the other, the local structures of state and civil society, as well as their ideologies and practices of government. Language vitality reflects the position of the nation-state in this fundamentally uneven and fragmentary facet of the world system, as well as the specific cultural and historical resources, in the form of institutions, agencies and actors that inhabit the nation-state (Stroud 2007a,b).

In this chapter, the interplay between *state, market, language,* and *forms of life* has been captured by the notion of *governmentality,* which has been extended to *linguistic governmentality,* that is, language as a political rationality and technology of government and as a technology of subjectivity. More specifically, the notion of *governmentality* has opened a window onto language practices as an assemblage of technologies for the reproduction and change of the social order and for the figuration of the nation-state. By providing an account of the contingent way in which African and ex-colonial languages are tied to changing formations of the (global) nation-state, it also throws light on how specific developments in the structure and register of these languages are tied to a wide range of transnational and local sociopolitical processes.

Within this framework, I have attempted to capture some of the potentially significant variation in the coexistence of Portuguese and indigenous Mozambican languages across space and time by appealing to the historical and contemporary assemblage of contingent rationalities, technologies and resultant subjectivities of Mozambican government from colonial times to the present. The rationalities of the early colonial state created an ambivalence in the experience of modernity, also with respect to language, which were resolved through speakers either deploying available African language resources in contexts of a benevolent Protestant mission or through abandoning their African languages in favor of Portuguese and the status of *assimilado*. In postcolonial Mozambique, earlier technologies of governmentality implicated in the semiotization of the vertical and encompassing nation-state were gradually superceded by subnational and transnational rationalities and technologies of government that rested upon a multiplicity of newly available local resources. The attempt by the government of Samora Machel at independence to create a strong, centralized nation-state built on the principles of modern socialism had at one level significant negative implications for the vitality of Mozambican languages vis-à-vis *Portuguese*. The subsequent re-figuration of the Mozambican state into a weaker assemblage of institutions and procedures for engagement with diversity not only forced it to recognize entities of government outside the state proper such as traditional authorities and informal, associative economic networks, but also obliged it to accommodate forms of engagement with global and transnational processes through the medium of independent, non-governmental regional African markets. The result was a highly polycentric and linguistically heterogeneous community characterized by competing norms and conceptions of linguistic legitimacy with respect to both Portuguese and African languages. Today, the Mozambican state is actively embracing diversity and autonomy in governance and economy, language and lifestyle, by entering into new alliances with the non-state sector and re-inscribing institutional and organizational, economic and cultural diversity into new technologies of governmentality. There has been a significant shift in the visibility and importance of indigenous languages and Portuguese as languages for the local management of globalization and the state with concomitant implications for language vitality.

These contingent developments can account for the specific patterning of language vitalities noted in the introduction to this chapter. The polycentric and varied nature of African languages, together with the lack of a Bantu-based lingua franca, is one outcome of an ambivalent colonial modernity, where social reproduction took place through Mozambican languages, and where Protestant missionary communities cultivated a handful of these languages for Biblical use. At this time, the politics and economics of settlement patterns meant that groups speaking widely divergent languages lived in neighboring hamlets with little mutual contact between them. Harries (2007:163) quotes the American Board linguist Erwin Richards as claiming that 'it sometimes happens that there is a Babel of tongues in a single kraal', stating that there were no geographical borders separating people who spoke Tswa, Tonga and Chopi. It was also commonly the case that young male speakers, especially, speakers of Chopi, Zulu and the Ngoni languages, would easily give up their languages for the language of a more powerful group, whereas women would continue to socialize their younger children in their original language – a gendered practice that still holds true today in Mozambique (cf. Stroud 2007a).

In postcolonial time, developments fuelled by unrest and civil war in tandem with the weak institutions of support for Portuguese have served to limit the territorial spread of this language to mainly urban centers, allowing Mozambican languages subsequently to retain a certain degree of vitality.[17] The shift in the location of the political power base from urban metropoles in the center and north of the country, hosting Portuguese-speaking garrisons, to the Changana-speaking south of the country is also a factor in the relative weakening of Portuguese. Subsequent national developments in decentralization and enhancement of diversity in conjunction with the influence of foreign NGOs (principally in the education sector) have also contributed to the vitality of Mozambican languages. The most recent phase in Mozambican state building is clearly shifting the linguistic balance of power in favor of Changana, particularly under the impact of ongoing localizations of transnational developments.

Similar processes underlie regionally distinct patterns of multilingualism. The uneven spread of NGOs and churches in different areas of Mozambique during the colonial and postcolonial times and the migrations and urban spatial policies of later years have undoubtedly contributed to contemporary profiles of multilingual social structure. The political rationalities of Portuguese colonial citizenship (as expressed in the idea of *assimilado*) might well have contributed to the non-existence of an earlier Portuguese pidgin or creole.

And finally, the characteristic type of Bantu imports found in present-day Mozambican Portuguese could typically have evolved under particular forms of governmentality in urban contexts, namely in cases of contact between Mozambican Portuguese L1 and Bantu L1 speaking migrants from rural areas, and through 'low-level' schooling and restricted access to L2 learning in highly monitored, controlled and regulated teaching environments. This outcome could be particularly expected in a context of a poor spread of institutions and 'weak' governmentality in predominantly Bantu-speaking environments.

The broad approach to the organization of multilingualism illustrated here potentially carries a number of implications for understanding language vitality and shift. First of all, transparent cases of language shift seem to occur almost consistently when there is an identifiable 'language of the State', and when the 'position of interest' found in the state is part of a unified market in Bourdieu's sense. In cases where the institutions of the state (in particular education) are in tune with the requirements, demands, practices and ideologies of the employment (and other) sectors, then shift will occur to that language. This is why a shift to Portuguese was underway nominally in Mozambique during the time of Samora Machel immediately after independence, and why an increasing orientation to Changana is evident in the Mozambican state of today. This could also provide an explanation for why the period of Chissano, from the mid-1980s to the end of the 1990s, after Machel's death and before the advent of Guebuza, stimulated the maintenance of more linguistic diversity. It was a period characterized by a weaker state.

Second, the linkage of African languages with *tradition* and of metropolitan language with *modernity* (as in many models of language shift and vitality) make little sense in the Mozambican context (as in many other contexts), where African languages were part of an assemblage of strategies for locking into modernity. A related point is that notions of *local* and *global* need to be re-conceptualized. It is clear that Mozambican languages, *local* in one popular sense, are locked into new metropolitan modes of representation and discourse through transnational processes of consumerism, just like Portuguese has been refigured in some contexts as a 'local' language. In both cases, we are confronted with 'collapsed scales' or a 'jumping of scales', thus with the 'active social and political connectedness of apparently different scales' (Smith 1992:66), where local and 'authentic' semiotic organization is the outcome of decisions and outcomes at different scalar levels (such as global organizations) and vice versa. The notion of *translocal* (Clifford 1997) captures this well, where in order to understand 'local/global historical encounters, co-productions, dominations and resistances, one needs to focus on hybrid, cosmopolitan experiences, as much as on rooted, native ones' (24). Pratt's (1992) notion of *transculturation*, where 'subordinated or marginal groups select and invent from materials transmitted to them by a dominant or metropolitan culture' (6) is also well suited to understanding the sociolinguistic structuring of the 'contact zone', 'the space of colonial encounters, the space in which people geographically and historically separated come into contact with each other and establish ongoing relations, usually involving conditions of coercion, radical inequality and intractable conflict' (6).

The arguments, analyses and historiographies detailed in this chapter suggests that an emphasis on how space and place are organized from the point of view of governmentality can provide an important complementary perspective to predominantly temporal accounts of language shift in a sociolinguistics of contact. This is because the notion of governmentality allows precise insights into the sociopolitical situation underlying much language shift and vitality, namely, the 'randomness and disorder of the flows of people, knowledge, texts and objects across social and geographical space in the boundaries of inclusion and exclusion, and in fragmentation, indeterminacy and ambivalence' (Rampton 2000:32).

Notes

This research has been supported by a generous SAREC grant, SWE-2005-493.

[1] Another way of phrasing this is to see the unified state as a series of locales/sites/arenas, a historical collection of practices and discourses, where particular interests are constituted.

[2] I am aware of the contentious nature of the notion of 'language' and the need to critically deconstruct this notion (Makoni and Pennycook 2007), especially bearing in mind the history of linguistic appropriation in colonial times (Errington 2001; Stroud 2007b). However, I employ it here merely as a convenient shorthand for practices.

[3] There are some suggestions in the literature on what could comprise a Mozambican Portuguese norm (cf. e.g., Lopes 1999), as well as discussions on the difficulties of actually practically determining such a norm.

[4] *Ethnologue*, SIL, suggests there may be as many as forty-eight different languages spoken. Cf. Lopes (1999) for alternative estimates.

[5] Lopes (1999) claims that Mozambique is among the fifteen most linguistically diverse countries in the world, where 'linguistic diversity' is 'a situation where no more than 50 per cent of the population speak the same language' (Robinson 1993:52).

[6] What follows is based on preliminary analysis of answers to a questionnaire on multilingualism distributed to a small population of twenty-five hundred subjects in different parts of the country. National Census provides no information on multilingualism that is based on age, gender or urbanity. The census did contain one question of interest, in this respect, namely P17B asking what languages other than their vernaculars Mozambicans speak, but the information remains to be processed.

[7] The instrument was administered to 250 informants selected from different social backgrounds and 'bairros' (residential neighborhoods) of Maputo as part of a larger study on developing varieties of Portuguese.

[8] Even at the height of colonial rule, Portuguese control of the territory covered only pockets of urban development spread unevenly across the nation, mainly in

the center and north of the country, including Tete, Queliman and Ilsa de Mozambique (cf. Gonçalves, 1996).

[9] There was also a gender rationale. As they did not understand the system of male labor, the Portuguese colonists viewed the male *indigine* as parasitical upon the labor of women and therefore wanted to change the tradition.

[10] A number of different churches were at work in Mozambique at this time, the most important being the Swiss mission.

[11] For a more extensive review of Portuguese as a modernist project in postcolonial Mozambique, see Stroud (1999). This does not mean there was a complete consensus on this issue; much debate in the 1980s regretted the marginalization of the indigenous languages (and with it the marginalization of large parts of the population from civil and political society) (see Stroud 1999 and references therein).

[12] The data for the following are taken from forty-two informants (and twenty-five hundred utterances) evenly distributed among four neighborhoods in Maputo (Stroud 1996).

[13] In this latter case, many of the Bantu-influenced variants found in Portuguese are in some sense expanding the expressive repertoire of the EP lexicon, for instance, the 'transitivization' of certain verbs to allow passive forms. Also, the fact that different indexical meanings are attributed to different types of substrata suggests that proficiency is a situated notion, which is ideologized differently, in ways that may provide a linguistic rationale for the organization of social inequality and linguistic vitality.

[14] Even seemingly indigenous organizations, such as RENAMO, and local NGOs, such as GTZ, have typically been financed and controlled from outside Mozambique.

[15] A recent USAID project supported an African American Institutes Project called 'Democratic Development in Mozambique' built on traditional authority (Fry 1997).

[16] Recent increase in regional and global trade has enhanced the role of English, which has further complexified the dimensions of multilingualism in Mozambique (Matusse 1997).

[17] Note, however, the possible 'erasure' of specific registers (especially in southern Mozambican languages that are more familiar to government members) due to the removal of structures of local government.

References

Alfredsson, Ulla and Carlisto Linha. 1999. *Onde dues vive. Introduçao um estudo en Igrecia Independente em Maputo* [Where God lives. Introduction to a study of the Independent Church in Maputo]. Maputo: INDE.

Barry, Andrew, Thomas Osborne and Nicholas Rose (eds). 1996. *Foucault and Political Reason: Liberalism, Neoliberalism and Rationalities of Government.* Chicago: University of Chicago Press.

Bourdieu, Pierre. 1991. *Language and Symbolic Power.* Cambridge, MA: Harvard University Press.

Buur, Lars and Helene Kyed. 2003. Implementation of Decree 15/2000 in Mozambique: The consequences of state recognition of traditional authority in Sussundenga. Copenhagen: Centre for Development Research.

Chabal, Patrick and J.-P. Daloz. 1991. *Africa Works: Disorder as Political Instrument.* Oxford: James Curry Press.

Clifford, James. 1997. *Routes: Travel and Translation in the Late Twentieth Century.* Cambridge, MA: Harvard University Press.

Cruz E Silva, Teresa. 1996. *Protestant Churches and the Formation of Political Consciousness in Southern Mozambique (1930–1974).* PhD thesis. Department of Social and Economics Studies, University of Bradford.

Deumert, Ana. 2005. Language, informal networks and social protection. Evidence from a sample of migrants in Cape Town, South Africa. *Journal of Global Social Policy* 5(3).303–328.

Errington, Joseph. 2001. Colonial linguistics. *Annual Review of Anthropology* 30. 19–39.

Fauvet, Paul. 2000. Mozambique: Growth with poverty. A difficult transition from prolonged war to peace and development. *Africa Recovery* 14(3).12–19.

Ferguson, James and Akhil Gupta. 2002. Spatializing states: Toward an ethnography of neoliberal democracy. *American Ethnologist* 29(4).981–1002.

Firmino, Gregorio. 1995. O caso do Portugues e das Linguas Indigenas de Mocambique. *Revista International de Lingua Portuguesa* 13.33 –43.

—2000. Siutação Linguística de Moçambique [Linguistic situation in Mozambique]. Maputo: Instituto National de Estatística.

—2002. *A Questão Linguística na Africa Pós-colonial: O Caso do Português e das Linguas Autoctones em Moçambique* [The language question in postcolonial Africa: The case of Portuguese and the indigenous languages of Mozambique]. Maputo: Promedia.

Foucault, Michel. 1991. Governmentality. In *The Foucault Effect: Studies in Governmentality*, ed. by Burchell Graham, Colin Gordon and Peter Miller. 87–104. Chicago: Chicago University Press.

Fry, Peter. 1997. Final Evaluation of the Decentralization/Traditional Authority Component of the African American Institute Project 'Democratic Development in Mozambique' (Cooperative Agreement #656-A-00-4029-00). Maputo: USAID.

Giddens, Anthony. 1990. *The Consequences of Modernity.* Stanford: Stanford University Press.

—1991. *Modernity and Self-Identity.* London: Polity.

Gonçalves, Perpetua. 1996. Português em Moçambique: Uma Variedade em Formação. [Portguese in Mozambique: A variety in formation]. Maputo: Livraria Universitária & Faculdade de Letras da UEM.

—2001. Panorama geral do Português de Moçambique. *Revue Belge de Philologie et D'Histoire* 79.977–990.

—2002. A Nativização da lingua Portuguesa em sociedades Africanas póscoloniais: O caso de Moçambique. In *Actas dos IX Cursos Internacionais de Verão de Cascais (1 a 6 de Julho de 2002).* Cascais: Câmara Municipal de Cascais, 2003 (2).47–58.

Harries, Patrick. 2007. *Butterflies and Barbarians: Swiss Missionaries and Systems of Knowledge in South-East Africa.* Oxford: James Currey.

Helgesson, Alf. 1991. Catholics and Protestants in a clash of interests in Southern Mozambique. In *Religion and Politics in Southern Africa,* ed. by Carl F. Hallencreutz and Mai Palmberg 194–206. Uppsala: Scandinavian Institute of African Studies.

Inda, Jonathan Xavier (ed.). 2005. *The Anthropology of Modernity: Foucault, Power and Ethnographic Subject.* Oxford: Blackwell Publishing.

Junod, Henri. 1905. What Should be the Place of the Native Language in Native Education. Morija: Sesuto Book Depot.

—1946. *Usos e costumes dos Bantos. A vida duma tribo Sul-Africana. Tomos 1 e 2.* [Habits and traditions of the Bantus. Life in a South African tribe. Vols 1 & 2]. Imprensa Nacional de Moçambique, Lourenço Marques.

Liphola, Marcelino. 1996. The use of Mozambican languages in the elections. In *Mozambique: Elections, Democracy and Development,* ed. by B. Mazula. 265–282. Maputo: Inter-Africa Group.

Lopes, Armando J. 1999. The language situation in Mozambique. In *Language Planning in Malawi, Mozambique and the Philippines,* ed. by Robert B Kaplan and Richard Baldauf Jr. 86–132. Clevedon: Multilingual Matters.

Macamo, Elisio Salvado (ed.). 2005. *Negotiating Modernity: Africa's Ambivalent Experience.* Dakar: Codesria.

Makoni, Sinfree. 1998. In the beginning was the missionaries' word: The European invention of an African language. The case of Shona in Zimbabwe. In *Between Distinction and Extinction: The Harmonization and Standardization of Languages,* ed. by Kwesi Prah, 157–164. Johannesburg: University of Witwaterstrand Press.

Makoni, Sinfree and Alistair Pennycook (eds). 2007. *Disinventing and Reconstituting Languages.* London: Multilingual Matters.

Matusse, Renalto. 1997. The future of Portuguese in Mozambique. In *African Linguistics at the Crossroads,* ed. by Robert K Herbert. 541–554. Cologne: Rudiger Koppe Verlag.

Milroy, Lesley and Milroy, James. 1992. Social network and social class: Toward an integrated sociolinguistic model. *Language in Society* 21.1–27.

Nederveen Pieterse, J. 1995. Globalization and hybridization. In M. Featherstone, S. Lash and R. Roberrtson (eds). *Global Modernities.* London: Sage. pp. 45–68.

NELIMO. 1989. 1 seminario sobre a Padronizão da Ortografia de Linguas Moçambicanas. Univesidade Eduardo Mondlane: Faculdade de Letras.

Nugent, Paul. 2004. *Africa since Independence.* London: Palgrave Macmillan.

Pitcher, Anne M. 2002. *Transforming Mozambique: The Politics of Privatization, 1975–2000.* Cambridge: CUP.

Pratt, Marie Louise. 1992. *Imperial Eyes.* New York: Routledge.

Rampton, Ben. 2000. Speech Community. In *Handbook of Pragmatics,* ed. by Jef Verschueren, Jan-Ola östman, Jan Blommaert and Chris Bulcaen, 1–34. Amsterdam: John Benjamins.

Robinson, Clinton D. W. 1993. Where minorities are in the majority: Language dynamics amidst high linguistic diversity. In AILA Review, 10.52–70.

Rose, Nicholas. 1996. Governing 'advanced liberal' democracies. In Andrew Barry, Thomas Osborne and Nicholas Rose (eds).

Smith, N. 1992. Contours of a spatialized politics: Homeless vehicles and the production of geographical scale. *Social Text* 33. 54–81.

Stroud, Christopher. 1996. The development of metropolitan languages in postcolonial contexts: Language contact and language change and the case of Portuguese in Maputo. *Nordic Journal of Linguistics* 19(2).183–213.

—1999. Portuguese as ideology and politics in Mozambique: Semiotic (re)constructions of a postcolony. In *Language Ideological Debates*, ed. by Jan Blommaert, 343–380. Berlin/New York: Mouton de Gruyter.

—Ms. A sociolinguistic survey of Mozambican languages. SAREC (Swedish International Agency for Research and Development Cooperation) Report.

—2007a. Bilingualism: Colonialism and postcolonialism. In *Bilingualism: A Social Approach*, ed. by Monica Heller, 25–49. New York. Palgrave Macmillan.

—2007b. Multilingualism in excolonial countries. In *Handbook of Multilingualism and Multilingual Communication,* ed. by Auer Peter and Li Wei, 509–558. Amsterdam: Mouton de Gruyter.

Stroud, Christopher and Perpetua Gonçalves. 1997. (orgs). *Panorama do Português Oral de Maputo. Vol 1: Objectivos e Métodos* [Panorama of oral Portuguese in Maputo. Vol. 1: Objectives and methods]. Maputo: INDE.

West, Harry G. 2003. 'Who rules us now?': Identity tokens, sorcery and other metaphors in the 1994. Mozambican elections. In *Transparency and Conspiracy: Ethnographies of Suspicion in the New World Order,* ed. by Harry G. West and T. Sanders, 92–124. Durham: Duke University Press.

West, Harry G. and Scott Kloeck-Jenson. 1999. Betwixt and between: 'Traditional authority' and the democratic decentralization in post-war Mozambique. *African Affairs* 98(393).445–484.

Wittrock, B. 2000. Modernity: One, none or many? European origins and modernity as a global condition. *Daedalus* 129(11).31–60.

Chapter 5

The Lives of Local and Regional Congolese Languages in Globalized Linguistic Markets

Eyamba G. Bokamba

5.1 Introduction

5.1.1 The issues

The passionate and extensive debate on language endangerment or death that started with the publication of Nancy Dorian's *Investigating Obsolescence: Studies in Language Contraction and Death* (1989) shows no sign of abatement. There has been a proliferation of books and articles that dramatize this new 'cause célèbre' in linguistics and 'cultural studies'. The explicit linking of the new technico-economic phenomenon of globalization with colonization and hegemonic language domination, as exemplified in numerous titles such as *Languages in a Globalising World* (Maurais and Morris 2003), 'Colonization, globalization and the plight of "weak" languages' (Mufwene 2002a) and 'The search for a global linguistic strategy' (Tonkin 2003), leave no doubt whatsoever that we are now facing a new and serious threat to our most functional form of communication that has defined us as human societies. The dramatization of the situation with predictions such as '[t]he world's languages are dying. Ninety per cent of them are expected to disappear in the next one hundred years' (Nettle and Romaine 2000, cover page) and with the following kind of statistics, exacerbate the threat of the problem:

- 90 per cent of the world's population speak the 100 most-used languages out of the estimated 6,600;
- there are at least 6,000 languages spoken by about 10 per cent of the people on earth;
- based on languages that have more than 100,000 speakers, there may be only as few as 600 'safe' languages;
- the overwhelming majority of the world's languages may be in danger of extinction;
- 80 per cent (149 out of 187) of native Indian languages [in the United States] are no longer being learned by children;

- only 4 of the at least 60 Native American languages spoken in Canada 'are truly viable';
- 'only five of the native languages of what is now the US have as many as 10,000 to 20,000 speakers, and only two have as many as 40,000 to 50,000 [speakers]';
- '17 per cent (50 out of 300)' and '27 per cent (110 out of 400)' of, respectively, Central and South American indigenous languages 'are no longer viable' – the reason for this state of affairs lies partly in the decimation of their speakers;
- '90 per cent of [the] estimated 250 Aboriginal languages [of Australia are] near extinction';
- and 54 [of the estimated 2035 African] languages were already extinct, and another 116 were in the process of extinction.' (8–9)

Similar predictions are made in Crystal (2000). Yamamoto and Zepeda (2004), in their discussion of Native American languages, highlight similar losses when they report that of the estimated 300–600 native American languages in the United States and Canada only about 211 had survived as of 1997, 'although not necessarily as a major means of communication' (174). What is dramatized by all these data is not only the mere death of ethnic languages and the respective cultures they encode, but also, by implication, the potential destruction of the diversity of the socioeconomic structures that exist today and their replacement by one or a few new hegemonic world systems that are implemented through dominant languages such as English, French, Spanish, Chinese and Arabic (for the latter see, e.g., Ennaji and Sadiqi (2007) and James (2007), about the Arabization of Morocco and Sudan, respectively).

This issue of language endangerment clearly transcends the bounds of linguistics as it embraces simultaneously the fields of anthropology, economics, education, history, political science and cultural studies generally. While the ostensible concern that has energized so many linguists of various persuasions is language extinction, presumably via language shift and attrition, the associated issues that 'conspire', as it were, to contribute to this outcome and the potential remedies to it are certainly interdisciplinary. Specifically, language endangerment in general is blamed on colonization, globalization and the spread of European languages, especially English, French, Portuguese and Spanish, through Western education systems, trade, the media, including the Internet in urban centers wherever such conditions hold (Maurais 2003; Nettle and Romaine 2000). Language endangerment, as understood in this area of research, is associated with two basic conditions: (i) the severe decline in the vitality of a particular language as a result of language shift by its speakers in domains in which the heritage vernacular was dominant (e.g., family, friendship, inter- and intra-regional trade); and (ii) failure to transmit the heritage language inter-generationally such that increasingly larger and larger numbers of children and grandchildren have no knowledge of it. Therefore, it becomes necessary to investigate in a detailed fashion the particular ecological conditions that bring about these changes in communicative practices.

5.1.2 Questions addressed

As Mufwene (2002a,b, 2004, 2005) aptly observes in his critique of the state of the art, the effects of language endangerment are too often treated as if they applied uniformly across all languages and cultures. Although many of the facts presented in studies of language endangerment are real and eloquent, it is not evident that the root causes of the outcomes are the same everywhere. For example, do the different language ecologies, including failed states, educational systems and economies affect the rate of the spread of hegemonic colonial languages uniformly in all former colonies? Are all former colonized populations under identical socioeconomic pressures to abandon their ancestral vernaculars? These are some of the fundamental questions that research on this topic is called to answer eventually if it is to shed light on the differential experience of language endangerment throughout the world, and thereby offer possible realistic pre-emptive solutions to counter or slow it down.

In the case of sub-Saharan Africa (SSA), language endangerment has often been blamed on the same agents as elsewhere: the on-going, extensive spread of major European languages through colonization, education, trade and the media in urban centers (Brenzinger 1992, 1998; Breton 2003). This development has allegedly been exacerbated in the postcolonial era largely by the expansion of educational systems, the opening of African markets to non-former colonial powers such as the United States, Japan and now China, as well as the exclusion of most indigenous languages from public domains (Bamgbose 2000; Bokamba 2007b; Webb 2002). But is this characterization accurate, or simply a hasty extrapolation to Africa of situations observed especially in North America and Australia?

5.1.3 Objectives

Focusing on the Democratic Republic of the Congo (DRC), this chapter addresses the following major questions: (i) To what extent are these claims and concerns realistically applicable to the African 'linguistic markets'? (ii) Are European languages really threats to the vitality of local and regional African languages? (iii) If they are not, what other real and potential threats exist in such linguistic markets, especially in urban centers? And (iv) in what respects might these factors impact on the development, functionality and vitality of the relevant African languages?

This chapter attempts to answer these questions, among others, by examining critically samples of inter-generational 'language loss' data collected in 2004 and 2005 via participant-observation and face-to-face interviews conducted in twelve different households in two major contact settings, namely, Mbandaka, the capital city of the Equateur Province, and Kinshasa, the capital city of DRC. The focus is on the interaction and competition between the following languages: *French*, the official language; *Lingala*, the dominant lingua franca of the Congolese popular music and the dominant vernacular of the two cities; and four sub-regional languages spoken predominantly in the Equateur Province: *Dzamba, Libinza, Likila* and *Lomongo.* Agreeing with Mufwene (2002a, 2005) that situations of language shift and potential endangerment are much more complex than has been generally acknowledged in the literature, I adduce historical socioeconomic facts and recent data on language use to demonstrate that the putative cross-regional process of economic globalization, which facilitates the spread of so-called Western 'killer languages' and the endangerment of indigenous ones is not evident in DRC. What has been observed is, instead, a locally based language endangerment vector that is fostered and yet constrained largely by endogenous conditions. I also conclude that while language shift and eventually language loss are inevitable developments in pervasively multilingual Africa, they can still be managed carefully and successfully with committed planning at different levels of the society concerned (Bokamba 2007a,b).

5.2 Current Language Practices and Their Markets

In order to address the questions raised earlier and understand the contextual settings that inform the observed changes, one must examine, first, what Abdulaziz (1980) and Mufwene (2001) refer to as the 'ecological conditions' in which the relevant languages function. This section accordingly summarizes, with particular attention to the pervasiveness of multilingualism in DRC, the language policies and practices specific to this polity, as well as the failure of the state relative to the education system and its impact on the evolution of the local linguistic markets. I begin with the facets of multilingualism.

5.2.1 Pervasive multilingualism

With its estimated 214 languages, consisting mainly of Bantu and a small number of Nilo-Saharan languages in the North, DRC is the third most pervasively multilingual nation in Africa after Nigeria, with 521 languages, and Cameroon, with 286 languages (Gordon 2005). As observed in Bokamba (2007a), this multiplicity of languages and related cultures 'naturally raise[s] a number of fundamental questions from a Western perspective, including the basis, if any, upon which nationalism is defined and achieved, how inter-ethnic communication is conducted, and how discourse in public domains is carried out' (6).

Congolese multilingualism resulted from King Leopold II's creation in the nineteenth century of his personal fiefdom called the Congo Free State (CFS) from a variety of kingdoms, empires and chieftaincies. Contact in different spheres of activities within and across ethnic boundaries from that time (1885–1908) and through the colonial period under Belgium (1908–1960) facilitated the spread of selected indigenous languages as 'regional' or 'trade languages'. Thanks largely to inter-ethnic trade and missionary work, the following six indigenous languages emerged as the leading linguae francae: *Kikongo, Kiswahili, Lingala, Lomongo, Tshiluba* and *Zande. French* has since then also served as the official language of the colonial administration and as the exclusive medium of communication in 'higher domains' of education, politics and the business sector. It has likewise been associated with the social elite.

Language policies formulated in the 1920s and subsequently revised in 1948 by Christian missions, which then dominated the education sector (with the acquiescence of the colonial administration), firmly established these languages as linguae francae in different provinces and districts (Bokamba 1976; Ndoma 1977; Polomé 1968). Revisions of the policies in the late 1950s and then after the decolonization on 30 June 1960 promoted Kikongo, Kiswahili, Lingala and Tshiluba to the rank of 'national languages', while maintaining French, still a minority language in DRC, as the exclusive official language, in principle, for administration, post-primary education, diplomacy and international trade, and the higher courts.

5.2.2 The ecologies of the national and official languages

As elsewhere in colonial Africa, where similar conditions arose (e.g., Nigeria, Ghana, Kenya, Uganda, South Africa), the linguae francae have competed, on the one hand, among themselves in their respective regions and domains of contact, and, on the other, with French for legitimacy in non-official public domains, for example, worship services, upscale shopping centers, hospitals and transport hubs (namely, train stations, shipping ports and airports) in major urban centers. The competition has increased gradually over the years and was heightened during President Mobutu's regime (1965–1997) by population exoduses from rural communities and small towns to major urban centers in search of employment in factories, transportation companies and various public sectors. I summarize here the different national languages' ecologies, including their distribution in DRC, particularly since independence, providing the backdrop against which the intergenerational language loss is discussed in Section 5.3.

5.2.2.1 National languages

Since their establishment and evolution as linguae francae during the colonial era, the national languages have enjoyed a remarkable degree of functionality in the country that is unparalleled by their counterparts elsewhere in Africa, except perhaps in Nigeria, Ghana and South Africa. Specifically, Kikongo, Kiswahili, Lingala and Tshiluba are each used in their respective regions of dominance or competition (see Bokamba 2007a for a detailed discussion of this distribution) in the family domain, in inter-ethnic communication with or between speakers of other languages, in selected worship services, in local and sub-regional marketplaces and in various public administrative domains (Bokamba 2007a; Nyembwe 1986; Nzeza 1987). During the Second Republic (i.e., Mobutu's era) they also served as the media of communication for selected educational programs (e.g., agriculture, family hygiene and childcare) on the regional and national radio and TV programs (*La Voix du Zaire*), and in selected political rallies in the multi-parties election campaigns in 1965 and 2006. Further, per the 1974 DRC language policy and a recent government's decree, all four national languages also serve as media of instruction in the lower primary education (at least up to third grade) and as a subject of instruction in secondary and tertiary education in their regions, and in theory, beyond.

Over and above these functions, all four national languages serve as the media of Africa's most popular music that is known variously as 'Congolese rumba' or 'Soukous', although Lingala is by far the dominant medium (estimated at 70 per cent) in this function (Dzokanga 1979; Stewart 2000). Since the 'liberation' of Congolese churches in the early 1990s from the strictures of their Western founders, the national languages have increasingly become the media of contemporary religious music, which is performed on Congolese popular music beat and rhythm.

While all the national languages are now firmly established as important and vital linguae francae, it also appears that Lingala is the most important one, assuming many nationwide functions that far exceed even those of French. Many of these evolved from the colonial era. They include its roles as the official language of the Congolese armed forces since 1930 (Bokamba 1976; Polomé 1968); the official language of the Catholic clergy and worship services in the Diocese of Kinshasa, the largest diocese in DRC, since 1966; the dominant lingua franca in urban marketplaces along the Congo River and many of its tributaries in the western part of DRC up to Kisangani in the Orientale Province; and, as noted earlier, the dominant language of at least 70 per cent of the Congolese popular music productions. This is especially true of the urban varieties known as 'Spoken Lingala' and 'Kinshasa Lingala'[1] (Bokamba 1976, 2007a,b; Epanga et al. 1992; Kazadi and Otom'si Ebok 1992; Mumbanza 1973; Ntita and Nanzanza 1992; Sesep 1986, 1987).

Lingala's roles as the language of the Congolese national police and army and as the dominant language of Congolese music make it a nationwide medium, used and heard practically everywhere in DRC among almost all segments of the population. The colonial and postcolonial tradition of stationing battalions of soldiers of the Congolese National Army (ANC) in each province have facilitated and privileged the spread of Lingala in all the provinces to the disadvantage of its primary competitor, Kiswahili. The publication in 2004 of the Protestant Bible in the Kinshasa Lingala dialect, long stigmatized as 'corrupted Lingala', not only sanctions this variety, but will undoubtedly increase its popularity among younger generations of speakers.

5.2.2.2 *French*

French, the exclusive official language of DRC since the advent of political independence, is the medium of official communication for all aspects of administration at the provincial and national levels (governance, legislative, judiciary, education, business reports), for mass media, and for international communication. It also serves as a language of selected worship services in major urban centers where there is a significant body of Congolese intellectuals and international worshipers, of some contemporary religious and popular music and as the official language of white-collar sectors of major companies (e.g., telecommunication, international mining trade, international shipping, international banking, etc.).

While the percentage of French speakers as 'a second' language in DRC may be significant (estimated to be between 12 and 15 per cent) and its role in higher public domains critical, it is actually a minority language whose daily use even in official contexts is mainly limited to the educated elite: secondary school- and university-educated Congolese. It is the language of elite official discourse, but not a lingua franca or a vernacular for daily communication among the average citizens, unlike in Côte d'Ivoire, where 'a popular French' variety has emerged (see, e.g., Kube 2005 and Moseng Knutsen 2007). Interestingly, in spite of the late president Mobutu's implementation of the doctrine of 'Return to Authenticity', according to which things Congolese were re-valorized (including the re-officializing of indigenous city names such as *Kinshasa* instead of *Léopoldville*, *Lubumbashi* instead of *Elizabethville*, *Kisangani* instead of *Stanleyville* and *Mbandaka* instead of *Coquilhatville*), French has remained firmly the sole language of the print media for major Congolese newspapers and journal publications. It competes in print with the four national languages only in the publication of popular materials (e.g., fiction, the Bible and some monthly magazines wherever these still appear).

Further, unlike the national and sub-regional languages, which are learned informally on the street, French is mainly learned formally as a second/foreign language in school. The segment of the Congolese population that can claim to use it comfortably is essentially co-terminus with the recipients of four or six years of secondary and tertiary education. Consequently, its poor mastery by elementary school pupils and teachers has often been viewed as the major cause for the high attrition, wastage rates and poor academic performance observed in the schools and universities since independence (Bokamba 1986; Ndoma 1977).

5.2.3 DRC's language policy

To understand the complexity of the language situation in DRC and the potential barriers, at least for the next decade, that globalization will likely encounter in the spread of Western languages, it is necessary to examine briefly the evolution of the country's language policy vis-à-vis public domains. In particular, the language ecologies described earlier developed initially over many decades of evangelization and provision of Western-type education by various Christian missionaries (Bokamba 1976; Ndoma 1977; Polomé 1968; Yates 1981). They were eventually re-enforced de jure by a series of educational language policies, especially that of 1948, which accompanied the curriculum reform launched that same year, and by subsequent post-independence reformulations of that policy. The 1948 policy advocated the use of regional Congolese languages as media of instruction in lower primary school (first–third grades), the obligatory teaching of French as a subject from the second grade and its use as the medium of instruction from the fourth grade through university (Bokamba 1976; Ndoma 1977; Polomé 1968; Yates 1981). Until around the 1957–1958 academic year, this policy applied to all church-operated schools, the majority in the Congolese education system and the ones best subsidized by the colonial government, but not in the state-sponsored urban schools called 'écoles laïques', which operated under 'le système métropolitain' where French was the exclusive medium of instruction from the first grade onwards, starting around 1957 in Kinshasa and 1958 in other cities. The implementation of the general policy was very sporadic, however, largely due to the lack of qualified Congolese teachers, especially in small towns and rural communities. Hence, the regional and national languages continued to be used for most subjects up to, and some times through, the fifth grade.[2]

The 1948 policy was slightly modified by the education reform of 1958 that called for the use of French as the medium of education in all schools; but it was not feasible to apply it across the board due to the lack of qualified personnel. Still, the policy was retained until 1974, when the first national conference of Congolese linguists, meeting at the *Université Nationale du Zaire* (UNAZA) at Lubumbashi, on 22–26 May, essentially proposed its abrogation. Influenced by Mobutu's doctrine of authenticity,[3] the conference proposed a language policy that advocated strongly the promotion of the four national languages (namely, Kikongo, Kiswahili, Lingala and Tshiluba), while recognizing and yet subordinating the role of French in education. As discussed in Faik-Nzuzi (1974), Bokamba (1976, 2007a) and Sesep (1987), the new policy called for the promotion in the teaching and use of the national languages as media of instruction for all subjects up to the eighth grade (namely, middle school) in the school system, for the extension of this function in teaching social sciences and humanities beyond the eighth grade, and for delaying the teaching of French as a subject until the third grade and for the restriction of the use of French as a medium of instruction to the upper secondary school level (i.e., ninth grade). Interestingly, the 1974 policy recommendations, which were eventually implemented selectively (Nzeza 1987), also called for the teaching of English as a foreign language in secondary schools from the fourth year onwards.[4]

If the dominant literature on language endangerment were correct, the predominance of French, an almost exclusionary privilege, since at least 1958 as the official language of administration, education and international business in DRC should have been leading to massive language shift to it from the national, sub-regional and local/ethnic languages because of the centrality of these agencies, especially education. But this has not occurred for the reasons discussed in Section 5.2.4.[5] As is argued, a number of factors have militated against such an evolution. However, the threat from the linguae francae to local/ethnic languages brought to major urban centers remains a serious reality, just as it is elsewhere in Africa (Blench 2000; Brenzinger 2000b,c).

5.2.4 State failure and dysfunctionality of the educational system

Pursuant to Mufwene (2001), it is important to point out here that the functional allocation, de facto or de jure, of languages in a society does not by itself account for the vitality or lack thereof that they exhibit. One must also take into consideration socioeconomic factors such as patterns of colonization (exploitation versus settlement), population structure, communicative interactions between the populations in contact and the patterns of settlements that can affect contact between the languages concerned (Mufwene 2001:145ff). A critical language ecological factor that has retained my attention in Mufwene (2002b, 2005) is the population structure of a given territory, colonial or post-colonial. It can be related to the role the government plays in bringing this about. With this in mind, I turn here to a brief discussion of the state and educational failure in DRC from the early 1990s to the present in order to better contextualize some of the conditions that have contributed to a redefinition of linguistic markets and to language shifts in urban centers in DRC.

That pervasive societal and, by implication, individual multilingualism is a fact of life in DRC that dates back to the creation of CFS and is a well-known reality (Ndaywel è Nziem 1998; Vansina 1966). The spontaneous and planned spread of regional and sub-regional Congolese linguae francae by missionaries during the colonial era was intended to facilitate inter-ethnic communication in different life spheres and proselytizing by the different Christian denominations. Further, the adoption of educational language policies prior and subsequent to independence was envisaged as a response to societal multilingualism. Incidentally, it also modified the structure of local linguistic markets à la Bourdieu (1991).

The emergence of modern economic markets pre-supposes a functioning nation-state with at least a functional economic and educational system. These conditions were met during the Belgian colonial period, despite the restricted access to secondary and university education to Congolese. They were maintained and expanded to a significant extent during the first nineteen years or so of decolonization (1960–1979) in spite of the civil wars and coups d'état that characterized much of that period. This was undoubtedly the best era in DRC for the spread of French and the national languages in urban centers. On the one hand, the completion of secondary and university education during this period, with the presumed good command of French for the fortunate few graduates, practically guaranteed a white-collar position in the public and private sectors to any graduate. On the other hand, migrations to urban centers from the rural communities, combined with a demonstrated command of the appropriate national language (namely, Lingala in Kinshasa, the Equateur Province and part of Bandundu; Kikongo in part of Bandundu and in Bas-Zaire; Tshiluba in Kasai and Shaba; and Kiswahili in the Orientale, Nord Kivu, Sud Kivu and Maniema provinces), offered high probability for employment to the migrants. There were, therefore, considerable motivations for parents in any social stratum to not only encourage their children to acquire French, the official language, but also to acquire and shift to the relevant regional language. While the 1960–1979 era was not the first time that Congolese experienced economic growth and educational expansion that triggered migrations to the city, it was certainly the most effervescent in these activities, unleashing in the process the power of urbanization. This power included the tendency to language shift, expansion of Lingala as a potential pan-Congolese language and the increased subordination of the national languages in education to French, which the first congress of Congolese linguists in Lubumbashi attempted to redress (Bokamba 1986; Nzeza 1987; Sesep 1987).

Unfortunately this most momentous period of the expansion of official and national languages was subsequently undermined by President Mobutu's authoritarian regime, which was characterized by ostentatious state spending, endemic kleptocracy, mismanagement of state resources, Zairianization and retrocession of private companies, all of which ended in what is referred to in political science as 'state failure'. While all these changes were occurring (1979–1990), the pressing social needs of the citizens were left unattended (Afoaku 2005; Maractho and Trefon 2004; Nzongola-Ntalaja 2002; Persyn and Ladrière 2004; Tollens 2004), including especially education (at all levels) and economic development. This failure contributed to the erosion of the value of French as the official medium of communication whose knowledge via formal education, as stated earlier, served as a critical linguistic capital à la Bourdieu (1991) for job opportunities. Hence, the traditional agents of the spread of legitimate languages, namely, education and government employment, seem to be no longer as influential in potentiating the expansion of the symbolic power that characterized linguistic markets in the immediately preceding era (1960–1979).

As the papers in Trefon's edited book vividly demonstrate about this era, the state collapse forced the inhabitants to 'reinvent order in the Congo', by responding in their own ways to the 'State Failure in Kinshasa' and elsewhere in the country. In many cases they 'did without' basic life amenities, including food, public transportation, free access to elementary and secondary education, health care facilities and so on (Trefon 2004). In a word, the scandalously endowed state of DRC experienced scandalous abject poverty (Afoaku 2005; Nzongola 2002) resulting not only in high unemployment (estimated at as high as 80 per cent) in all formal economic sectors, but also causing changes in the dynamics of the linguistic markets. Two examples will suffice to illustrate these conditions. First, the Mobutu regime's kleptocratic practices and economic mismanagement generally deprived civil servants, including teachers at all levels, of their salaries for months, and thus made such jobs unattractive and forced those who could find employment elsewhere in Africa to emigrate. A consequence of this situation was the devaluation of French as a linguistic capital. A second example is the introduction of an English-speaking community in DRC after the proxy war of its natural resources sponsored through Rwanda and Uganda (1996–2001). This invasion brought to the country Ugandans and Rwandese Tutsi who had grown up in Uganda, and injected a second globalizing language in an already pervasive multilingual nation where the marginalization of the national languages in official functions in favor of French had become an impediment to the expansion of their functional loads. In spite of these conditions, however, the vitality of the national languages has remained unaffected by these so-called killer languages. Nonetheless, as will be shown later, ethnic languages experienced some degree of endangerment by the national languages.

5.2.5 Real and imagined linguistic markets

As stated earlier, the successful completion of secondary and university education in DRC used to be generally viewed not only as an intellectual achievement of the highest order, but also as a ticket to a white-collar or professional employment. One's linguistic assets, combined with their intellectual accomplishments, determined their chances to secure a job. In reality, however, these options have evaporated in DRC during the last thirty years (Tsakala and Bongo-Pasi 2004) as unemployment, irrespective of educational achievements, has in effect devalued to a significant extent the knowledge of French as a linguistic capital.

5.3 Language Shift and Endangerment: A Case Study

Clearly, under these circumstances of state failure one cannot realistically view the official language, French, and much less the ethnic languages, as invaluable linguistic capitals in the existing linguistic markets. The questions then become, which language does one learn in a pervasively multilingual society such as

DRC, and for what purpose(s)? Further, and to return to the fundamental questions raised in Section 5.1, to what extent are claims of 'the killer languages' as negative side effects of globalization applicable to DRC? More specifically, is French a threat to the vitality of the national languages and of the sub-regional or ethnic languages? If so, in what respects is it? If not, why? How about Lingala: is it a threat to the vitality of local languages such as Dzamba, Likila, Libinza and Lomongo? If so, under what conditions does this threat occur?

I turn to these questions by examining the interaction of French and Lingala, on the one hand, in their (potentially) overlapping linguistic markets in Kinshasa and Mbandaka. I then consider the interaction of Lingala, the apparent pan-Congolese lingua franca, and the four ethnic languages mentioned earlier under similar communicative conditions. The analysis, as stated earlier, is based partly on my personal knowledge of these language ecologies, and partly on a preliminary survey of a total of twelve families residing in Kinshasa and Mbandaka.

5.3.1 Preliminary case study

Most studies on the apparent language shift and the ensuing endangerment of especially minority languages ascribe these processes to globalization, with which they associate the expansion of Western languages, namely, English, French, Portuguese, Spanish and major non-Western languages such as Arabic and Chinese. The studies are based largely on census data wherever they are available, some field work and on oral reports from speakers of such languages (including Ethnologue's surveys by SIL). This is the case for several of the major studies on the subject matter, for instance, Dorian (1989), Fishman (1991), Brenzinger (1992, 1998, 2000a), Crystal (2000), Nettle and Romaine (2000), and Maurais and Morris (2003). The conclusions they present are, accordingly, based on the statistical information that do not in and of themselves account for the reported cases of language shift and endangerment. Except for Muaka (2006) and Marongiu (2007), few studies are informed by empirical investigations involving actual language use patterns by the targeted language speakers. Such investigations, when conducted via a survey questionnaire followed by face-to-face interviews with the speakers to ascertain further their language attitudes, would offer data that are not only more reliable but are also explanatory of the observed changes in language functional loads. Language attitudes are relevant because they account for the frequent uses and maintenance of certain languages, and the reasons why speakers shift from their mothers' or fathers' languages to others.

It is the lack of such information that led Mufwene (2002a,b, 2005) to question, quite correctly, the speculative nature of the conclusions presented in the literature on the impact of colonization, globalization and Western education, which are blamed for spreading economically powerful languages at the expense of both local and regional indigenous languages even in developing regions. This study attempts to redress this weakness by drawing on a preliminary investigation of language uses to supplement the researcher's personal knowledge of the targeted languages' ecologies. I consider, first, the competition between French and Lingala in Kinshasa.

5.3.1.1 French versus Lingala in Kinshasa

Kinshasa, the capital city of DRC and its leading megapolis with an estimated population of over eight millions (Wikipedia 2008), is home to dozens of Congolese linguae francae (including Kikongo, Kiswahili, Lingala, Tshiluba), and several ethnic languages (e.g., Dzamba, Lokele, Kitetela, Kiyansi, Lomongo, Ngbandi, Ngbaka, Kiyombe, Kimanyanga and Kiteke). In this pervasive societal multilingualism, Lingala functions as the dominant lingua franca, and French as the official language. As discussed in Section 5.2, these two languages have some domains that are almost in complementary distribution (i.e., mutually exclusive), and others in which they are in an overlapping relationship. For example, French in Kinshasa is the official language for instruction from fourth grade through the university; it is the official/formal medium of all higher administration (legislative, judiciary, executive), diplomacy and international commerce.

Just as Lingala encroaches in domains formerly reserved to French, so does the latter penetrate domains formerly associated with the former. However, there is often a price to pay for such cross-overs. For example, asking to buy, or offering a Congolese, some goods in French at a marketplace in Kinshasa is perceived as educational arrogance. Such a behavior can cost a buyer a higher price, more typical of an expatriate, or can lead the potential buyer to decline the transaction. Using French to ask a taxi driver for a ride also places the prospective passenger in the 'foreigner' category or that of an arrogant 'je le connais' ('I know it'), a derisive phrase used during Mobutu's regime to portray highly educated people. The response from taxi drivers was/is most likely to refuse transporting such passengers, especially since such customers were then stereotyped as unable to pay the required fare because they were too poorly paid as civil servants and/or would prefer to bargain the fare down. Similar cases can be described for violating the expected Lingala use in some of these domains, but what is worth noting here is that Lingala, not French, is the unmarked people's vernacular and lingua franca for daily interactions. Communication with Europeans and other conspicuous foreigners (e.g., Lebanese, Senegalese, Arabs) is often initiated in French, unless the interlocutor shows knowledge of Lingala or another Congolese lingua franca. Public domains in which the two languages overlap include worship services involving international attendees, interactions at international ports (airports and Congo River ports), up-scale restaurants, shops, movie theaters, night clubs, postal and telephone services, major hospitals, lower judicial courts and state-owned companies involved in international business.

During the vibrant postcolonial economic times (1960–1979), these domains of language interactions represented linguistic markets in which French and Lingala competed in Kinshasa. As noted earlier, their availability constituted the strongest motivations for educated parents to master and maintain both languages and for their children to learn not only French well, but also to be able to alternate between the parents' vernaculars and Lingala. While many in-migrants who had spoken other languages were under ecological pressure to learn Lingala, those who had spoken standard Lingala did their very best to develop some competence in the urban variety, although this is derided by some purists as too code-mixed with or corrupted by French. It is marked by 'nonce borrowings' from French and contracted forms such as *nazokenda* < *nazalí kokenda* 'I am going/leaving'; *ngáí naza kuna te*< *ngáí nazalí kuna te* 'I am not here/I am not in it', among other features (Bokamba 2007a,b,c).

Since nongovernmental employment has become increasingly scarce in Kinshasa, as evidenced by the unemployed thousands of university and post-university educated Congolese (Tsakala and Bongo-Pasi 2004), French and Lingala have lost the strong symbolic power with which they were associated in the formal job markets before the Congolese state failure, but they remain an imaginary insurance for potential future opportunities of sorts. For example, during Mobutu's thirty-two-year rule, Lingala, which he spoke natively, was a highly valued asset in his patron–client system of employment (Afoaku 2005; Nzongola-Ntalaja 2002; Schatzberg 1980). While many of his acolytes were ethno-linguistically mixed, Lingala was generally, correctly or not, viewed as the inside track language. And certainly young men and women who aspired to a music career saw it, the dominant medium of this creative art, as a passport to the profession. Accordingly, prospective second-generation speakers of other national linguae francae (namely, Kikongo, Kiswahili and Tshiluba) often found it necessary to shift either partially or completely to Lingala. This behavior accounts, to a large extent, for the increased spread of this lingua franca in a city in which Kikongo once dominated, and in which it still maintained a competitive momentum until the end of the First Republic (ca. 1967).

The competition for legitimacy between Lingala, French and Kikongo then appears to have been driven not only by the Africanization of Congolese education and Mobutism (the culture of accessing jobs based on what Afoaku terms 'internal colonization' rather than on one's merits/qualifications), but also by connections to the pervasive patron–client system established by Mobutu and his cronies (Afoaku 2005; Nzongola-Ntalaja 2002; Schatzberg 1980). The six families in our survey originated in the Equateur Province, and are all middle class with each parent holding at least a secondary education diploma. More specifically, five of the mothers are recipients of 'Diplôme d'état' ('High school diploma') and one holds a 'Graduat' (certification after the first cycle of college that consists of three years), while one father was a 'diplômé d'école moyenne', and the remaining fathers hold a 'licence' (BA) in different fields. All six families have resided in Kinshasa since the early 1970s. Four of the six parents took their elementary-school-age children to the nation's capital city and two either gave birth to some or all of them there. Our major and not so surprising findings are summarized as follows:

1. There is no intergenerational shift from Lingala to French even in cases where one or both parents often spoke French in the family domain with the child(ren).
2. The children acquired French as an additional language (namely, L2 or L3) through formal education in school.
3. Lingala was learned naturalistically at home and on the street.
4. The children use French largely in its official domains and the friendship domain, rarely with their parents, but to a limited extent with their siblings.

An initial conclusion that can be drawn at this juncture is that French, even in the country's capital city, is not a threat to at least Lingala, in spite of the 'prestige' associated with it as the official language. Second, Lingala seems to be a strong competitor to French for legitimacy in a number of public domains, even though, unlike French, it is not obligatorily taught throughout the school system.

5.3.1.2 *Lingala versus sub-regional and local languages in Kinshasa*

The findings presented earlier raise an interesting question: Since, in Kinshasa, French is somewhat favored over Lingala with regard to government jobs, why is there not an observable shift to it in the sampled families? The answer to this question is not evident from the responses to the French versus Lingala part of the survey, but one emerges from part on the coexistence of Lingala and the local and sub-regional languages, namely,

5. The first generation of children whose parents migrated to Kinshasa from Mbandaka and who had mastered their mother's or father's ethnic language have maintained it and their regional Lingala variety (namely, Standard or Spoken), and have learned French and Kinshasa Lingala.
6. Their siblings who had not yet mastered their mother's or father's ethnic language (MEL/FEL) at the time of their family migration became tri-lingual in French, Lingala and the MEL/FEL.
7. The children of these second-generation in-city migrants, namely, the third generation, who were born in Kinshasa, were predominantly bilingual in French and Kinshasa Lingala, with passive knowledge of standard Lingala.

While generally speaking the elder child in the families surveyed have considerable passive knowledge of MEL/FEL, the younger siblings generally reported no such knowledge. They had some smattering knowledge of its vocabulary due to the close genetic affinity between Lingala, Dzamba, Likila, Libinza and Lomongo, but they were much more comfortable in French and Kinshasa Lingala. Interestingly and not surprisingly, the children in these families who moved to Kinshasa with their parents as pre-schoolers and those who were born in Kinshasa have no productive mastery of standard Lingala, which almost all the parents know and use with friends at home.

Metaphorically speaking, the third generation of these migrants to the city 'lost' or failed to learn their MEL/FEL for one reason or another. Explanations for the parents' failure to transmit their language to the children or for the children to learn the parents' language(s) ranged from (i) the children showed no interest in the MEL/FEL, preferring instead to learn and speak Lingala; (ii) the parents never really pushed or insisted on the children to speak the languages to them; (iii) from the children's perspectives, there was no real, tangible incentive to acquire one's parents' languages; and (iv) the local and/or sub-regional language was seen as a marker of ethnic membership, whereas Lingala offered ethnic neutrality, music entertainment and opportunities for developing needed friendship at school or at the university. The desire and pressure to integrate in the capital city's culture as a 'Kinois' ('resident of Kinshasa'; Trefon 2004), rather than being seen as an outsider who came from the province and a particular ethno-linguistic group also seems to be a strong motivating force to 'melt' by not learning the ethnic language. This response to urban life is consistent with findings in other countries, including the case of Spanish in the northeast and southwest of the United States (Silva-Corvalán 2004; Zentella 2004), Luhya in western Kenya (Muaka 2006), Sardinian in Cagliari, Italy (Marongiu 2007), Wolof in Senegal (Mc Laughlin 2007) and Kiswahili in Tanzania (Topan 2007).

5.3.1.3 French versus Lingala in Mbandaka

The ecology of French and Lingala in Mbandaka, the capital city of the Equateur Province, located some 730 km northeast of Kinshasa and the urban hub of Lomongo, Dzamba, Libinza, Likila, Mungbandi, Ngbaka, Ngombe and numerous other sub-regional and local languages, is significantly different from that in Kinshasa. While French is very much omnipresent in public domains in Kinshasa, especially in government offices and in over a dozen of universities and technical colleges, it is much less used in Mbandaka, for a number of reasons. First, while there are several secondary schools in this city of over 729,000 inhabitants, there are only two functioning community colleges, a much smaller government apparatus, practically no state-owned companies in the past twenty-seven years, and therefore few opportunities that require the intensive use of French. Further and because of these conditions, Lingala, the dominant urban vernacular and lingua franca, competes with French as the language of oral communication in government offices, the radio and TV station. French is used in more formal occasions, including instruction in primary and post-primary education, provincial assembly debates, high provincial courts and public speeches by provincial officials. Outside of these contexts, Lingala claims every space in the public domain. Initiating a conversation in French with a Congolese in Mbandaka, unless one knows the interlocutor personally, is generally viewed not only as arrogant, pedantic, but also in very bad taste. Our survey of six families in Mbandaka reveals that there is, generally speaking, little evidence and incentive to shift to French. The language is mainly used as an additional medium of communication for the specific public domains in which it is a necessary tool for employment in the provincial government controlled sectors: education and government administration. This observation is consistent with findings elsewhere in SSA as reported, for example, in the studies by Blench (2000), Connell (2000) and Brenzinger (2000b,c) on West Africa, Central Africa and Southern and Eastern Africa, respectively.

5.3.1.4 *Lingala versus Dzámba, Libinza, Likila and Lomongo*

Mbandaka, as the largest city and potentially the economic engine of the Equateur Province, is inhabited by a variety of ethnic groups largely from within the region, although a few are from elsewhere in DRC, notwithstanding some war refugees from Rwanda and Chad. As stated earlier, Lomongo is the dominant sub-regional language that had served as the default language of the city until Lingala prevailed in the late 1920s. It is the competitor to Lingala for communication spaces in some marketplaces, worship services, river ports in nearby surrounding suburbs and in family domains involving couples who are both Mongo. The competition, in all these domains, however, weighs heavily in favor of Lingala, which is viewed as a non-ethnic language, and the language of wider communication, even in lower primary education and employment in the greater Mbandaka city. For example, when the provincial radio and TV stations, affiliates of RTNC, were operating regularly, French and Lingala were used as the broadcast media, with the latter being given more airtime. Neither Lomongo nor the other ethnic languages were used for broadcasting. Academically, Lingala was required as a subject of instruction and testable in all elementary and secondary schools (i.e., government- and church missions-operated), but Lomongo was only required before independence in church mission schools.

The different enclaves of ethnic groups that live in the city, in some cases in specific neighborhoods such as Basoko (considered the fishermen's enclave) for Libinza speakers, and Bongonzo and Marché de Mbandaka for Dzamba,

Likila, and Ngombe speakers, offer weak competition to Lomongo. While the speakers of these languages in such neighborhoods do form important communicative networks, their overall population in the city in each case is smaller than that of the Mongo. Particularly significant in these cases, however, is the fact that unlike in Kinshasa, the presence of these ethno-linguistic communities re-enforces a sense of ethnic loyalty. The periodic contacts their residents have with travelling merchants of local products from rural areas (selling, for instance, palm oil, dried fish, game meats of various sorts, plantains and dried cassava) who stay with them provide an additional stronger motivation for maintaining the ethnic languages in the family and other social domains. There is also the reverse traffic, from Mbandaka to the rural communities, for example, of upper elementary and secondary school students returning home for vacation, various individuals going to visit their extended families or to join them in fishing trips on the Congo River and its tributaries in the Equateur Province. These sustained contacts appear to reduce the pressure for the Mbandaka residents to shift from their ethnic languages to Lingala. Instead, they maintain both languages, while some of these acquire at least some passive knowledge of Lomongo to participate in conversations as listeners.

These linguistic behaviors were confirmed by our participant–observer survey and were followed-up with face-to-face interviews with the families in Mbandaka that consisted of two Dzamba-, one Likila-, one Libinza- and two Mongo-speaking households. One of the Dzamba couples and the Libinza couple have no post-elementary education, while all the remaining couples have university degrees. The finding summarized here is not surprising as speakers of these languages also speak Lingala (both Standard and Spoken varieties) as their second native language.

It is worthwhile pointing out here, however, that unlike in the rural communities where Dzamba, Libinza, Likila and Lomongo dominate their respective discourse spaces as the daily vernaculars, Lingala serves this role in most domains outside the family and intimate friendship in our sampled families. In the interest of maintaining traditional family respect at home and in the neighborhood, children in these families tend to use their MEL/FEL whenever they are addressed in them; but they often code-switch between Lingala and these languages. When they initiate a conversation with their Dzamba-, Libinza-, Likila- or Lomongo-speaking peers in Mbandaka, however, they generally do so in Lingala, their dominant language.

So, in contrast to the ecologies of French, Lingala, and the four ethnic languages under consideration in the context of Kinshasa versus Mbandaka, what emerges here are rather typical differences and similarities that characterize language use in what Brenzinger (2000c) refers to as 'established context of nation-states' versus 'traditional sub-national context' (i.e., national and subregional, respectively, in our terminology). In Kinshasa, with its estimated population of over eight million people, humongous state and commercial infrastructure, international missions, and incredibly diverse ethnic/national groupings make the pervasiveness of Lingala as a vernacular a necessity. French functions primarily as the official language in high domains. As such, both languages have acquired 'added values' as linguistic capitals, which require an investment of time and effort to acquire them. Failure to do so leads one to be labeled as 'uneducated' in reference to French, and, at best, as *moútá* 'outsider' or *campagnard* 'rural inhabitant'. To be seen as a *Kinois* 'inhabitant of Kinshasa', one must at least be able to communicate in Lingala; similarly, to be perceived as 'educated' one must show fluency in French. The use of ethnic languages in Kinshasa appears to stigmatize the user as a 'tribal', a label that many Kinois try to avoid via all sorts of acts of neutrality. These considerations favor the acquisition and use of French and Lingala in Kinshasa, militating against that the maintenance of ethnic languages.

In contrast, knowledge and use of French and Lingala in Mbandaka, a city of approximately 729,257 inhabitants (Wikipedia 2004), with a very small state apparatus and a totally bankrupted modern economic sector, are generally seen as communicative options. While proficiency in French indexes the speaker as an educated person, it is not a necessity for communication in the city, although it is a requirement for a white-collar job in the provincial government. On the other hand, knowledge of Lingala as a first or additional language is a necessary requirement for inter-ethnic communication. However, unlike in Kinshasa, this knowledge does not seem to award anyone a status as a 'Mbandakais', irrespective of the dialect he/she speaks. Similarly, ethnic languages and their utilization in family as well as in certain public domains (e.g., marketplaces, restaurants, night clubs) are not stigmatized. They, like Lingala, are simply seen as part of one's linguistic repertoire to be used appropriately and as necessary. Ethnicity co-habits happily with regionalism and nationalism due largely to the constant contacts between rural and urban dwellers within and outside of Mbandaka.

5.4 Conclusions

This chapter had two goals: (i) to ascertain the conditions under which language endangerment in DRC occurs; and (ii) to assess the extent to which the state of the art on the subject matter applies to and accounts for the situation in DRC, focusing on French, Lingala and four sub-regional languages. The earlier discussion indicates that Lingala, Lomongo, Dzamba, Libinza and Likila in DRC are not as much endangered by French as, for example, Native American and Aboriginal Australian languages are by English. I wish now to address the question of what are the specific ecological conditions that set the situation in DRC and apparently elsewhere in SSA (see, e.g., Blench 2000; Brenzinger 2000b,c; and Connell 2000) apart from North America and Australia. I begin with what has emerged thus far as cases of competing language legitimacies (Bourdieu 1991; Stroud 2002; Swigart 2001).

5.4.1 Competing language legitimacies

Individual and societal multilingualism are common Congolese realities: Congolese are strongly attached to their languages and their respective cultures. The production of Congolese music, predominantly in Lingala, is not only a dominant form of entertainment appreciated throughout the country irrespective of mother tongue loyalties, but also the leading agent of the spread of Lingala. When this factor is added to the use of the language as a lingua franca in urban contact settings, personal identity as a Kinois and/or an urban dweller, and acts of neutrality vis-à-vis ethnic languages, Lingala becomes, at least in Western DRC, the vernacular or lingua franca of choice for enter-ethnic communication to compete against the legitimacy of French, the official language, in a number of major domains. A consequence of this competition, which has been exacerbated by the Congolese state failure and the ensuing collapse of DRC's modern economy, is that French cannot be viewed as a threat to Lingala. Instead, it simply serves as an additional language in the educated language repertoires of the Congolese, to be used in specific communicative settings. This particular kind of (post-) colonial language evolution is evident in other SSA nations (e.g., Senegal, Mozambique and South Africa) (Mc Laughlin 2007, this volume; Mesthrie, this volume; Mufwene 2008; Stroud, this volume; Topan 2007). While optimism suggests that the Congolese state, with its immense natural and human resources, will rise again and that the level of urbanization will surpass the current 52 per cent and thereby expose more people to Lingala, other national languages, and the globalized economy, the ecological factors of rural life, continuing significant illiteracy (ca. 27 per cent), bankrupted modern economy and loyalties to the national languages will undoubtedly continue to prevent the endangerment of the Congolese languages by French or English (Bokamba 2007b). A second set of potential deterrents against the endangerment of Congolese languages by French, as documented in West Africa, Central Africa and Southern and Eastern Africa (Blench 2000; Brenzinger 2000c; and Connell 2000), is the on-going stable multilingualism involving the use of three or more languages as dictated by the contexts of situation, and the perception that French or English are additional languages for communication in their respective domains. The globalizing socioeconomic conditions that have facilitated shifts to these languages in Western countries simply do not yet obtain in DRC. Thus, one need not fear, unjustifiably, that imperial Western languages are endangering the indigenous languages of DRC and the rest of SSA, at least for the near future (Blench 2000; Brenzinger 2000; Connell 2000; Mufwene 2002ff).

In contrast, as we have seen, the spread of Lingala and apparently of the other national languages in DRC's major urban centers not only deters the spread of sub-regional and local/ethnic languages, but also seriously threatens their long-term viability, as third-generation and subsequent prospective speakers of these languages shift to them under the pressures of their current linguistic markets (Bokamba 2007a; Epanga et al. 1992; Kazadi and Otom'si Ebok 1992; Nyembwe et al. 1992). Shifts from ethnic or minority languages to urban vernaculars or regional linguae francae, even in some rural communities, have been amply documented in SSA (e.g., Blench 2000; Brenzinger 1998, 2000b,c; and Connell 2000). DRC will undoubtedly not be an exception to this evolution; it is in fact likely to increase in the near future with migrations to the city.

There is another factor that militates against the endangerment of Congolese languages by languages of wider communication (LWC): Congolese's pride vis-à-vis their own languages and cultures. To be sure, over the past three decades or so, the emergence of linguistic markets driven by pressures of modern economy have influenced the linguistic behaviors of urban Congolese in particular, and they have largely viewed French, rather than any of the national languages, as the best investment for post-primary education. However, there is very little evidence, generally speaking, that the Congolese in the post-independence era who do not speak French or any other LWC feel linguistically inferior or ashamed. The Congolese typically learn to speak a language, in any form, when they find it necessary to their communicative needs; consequently, they are highly multilingual, often commanding three–four languages. Also, as argued in Bokamba (2007a), they often learn and speak languages in code-mixed varieties: either one Congolese language mixed with another, or a Congolese language mixed with French (Bokamba 1988; Sesep 1978).

The introduction of English as an obligatory foreign language in secondary schools in the 1960s, and recently as a required subject for one year at the university level, has expanded the range of contact further between the Congolese and Western LWCs. This development has resulted not only in a diminution in the perceived symbolic power of French as the defining language of high social standing and education, but also in injecting English significantly as a competitor to French in at least international commerce and scholarly research domains. Hence, English has increasingly become part of the language repertoires of several Congolese, especially with the increasing opportunities to work in local branches of American businesses and to emigrate and find employment in the United States.

5.4.2 Multiple sources of language endangerment

As discussed in Section 5.3, however, DRC's stable multilingualism, the Congolese acceptance of French and English as LWCs and their positive attitudes towards their national, sub-regional and local languages camouflage two emergent problems: language shift and what is generally termed as inter-generational language loss, which I prefer to refer to as L1 non-transmission, in urban settings and possibly major rural communities (cf., e.g., Blench 2000; and Brenzinger 2000b,c). Also as observed elsewhere in Africa, both of these phenomena have been occurring for decades presumably since at least the establishment of urban centers during the colonial period, although they have not been documented. My personal experience growing up in DRC in the 1950s and in observing the occurrence of language shift in the patterns of language use among extended family members in Kinshasa and Mbandaka represent only the tip of the iceberg. While the description offered earlier is limited to the languages discussed here, the phenomenon has been observed and discussed about other languages in DRC (see, e.g., Bokamba 2002; Mumbanza 1973; Nyembwe 1986; Polomé 1968) and elsewhere in Africa with respect to the spread of national official languages and linguae francae (Blench 2000; Brenzinger 2000b,c; Calvet 1992; Heine 1970; Topan 2007). The entrenchment of urban vernaculars as lucrative necessities and useful linguae francae has triggered gradual shifts from ethnic languages. Thus, it appears that Congolese linguae francae, but not the LWCs, are the primary threats to ethnic languages (Mufwene 2004, 2005) – an echo of findings elsewhere in Africa as noted earlier. There are multiple sources of such language endangerment. They include not only urbanization (a locus of globalization) that nurtures the spread of linguae francae, but also language policies, and failed states.

5.4.3 Potential corrective measures

From the perspective of national integration, shift from and loss of ethnic/local languages are not in and of themselves bad developments. The reduction of such languages from any country's repertoire potentiates an increase in nationalism against ethnic loyalties. Contrary to the popular view advanced in the literature, the solution to language shift, inter-generational L1 non-transmission and language loss or death is not simply to codify and teach them to future generations, but more importantly, to also advocate and actually work with interested state authorities and scholars to (a) develop realistic language policies that will permit them to flourish, (b) to create, in light of (a), adequate socioeconomic conditions for them to thrive and (c) to increase infrastructures at the local levels/communities, including literacy programs and publication of at least elementary school level textbooks that can serve as vehicles for the production and reproduction of local knowledge that is being lost with each passing older generation in rural communities. I concur with Mufwene's (2002a, 2005) arguments that language codification and eventually elaboration by themselves will not revitalize any language, nor prevent its eventual demise. The great efforts devoted to the revival of Gaelic and Irish have not succeeded in revitalizing them against the onslaught of English since they do not serve any perceived socioeconomic markets for the younger generations. The proposals made in (a)–(c) earlier must be pursued vigorously so as to make such languages invaluable linguistic capitals.

5.4.4 Directions for future research

Language shift, the onset of the so-called inter-generational language loss, in multilingual societies is as inevitable as language variation in the sense that it is an expected occurrence when languages compete for functional allocations. As argued in several of Mufwene's studies (2002ff) and in Blench (2000), certain ecological conditions facilitate language shift and eventually language loss, while others prevent these processes. The cases of language endangerment in West and Eastern Africa, according to Blench (2000) and Brenzinger (2000c), are quite illustrative in this respect. According to Blench (2000:141), in West Africa 'the most common causes of language endangerment are rather patterns of cultural and economic dominance', but not 'the constant shifting of subsistence strategy and thereby ethnic identity characteristic of small East African groups'. Such conditions cannot be determined a priori, especially not by extrapolation from Western experience. They have to be discovered empirically, on a case-by-case basis. Accordingly, what linguists can pursue profitably at this juncture in the study of language endangerment are the following:

1. To conduct empirical research, including participant-observation, to document more adequately patterns of language shift, intergenerational L1 non-transmission and perhaps language death.
2. To develop realistic language policies; establish and create socioeconomic infrastructures that are conducive to strengthening, rather than weakening, the existing linguistic markets.
3. To increase infrastructural facilities and programs at the local communities, including literacy programs and publication of at least elementary school level textbooks that can serve as vehicles for the production and reproduction of local knowledge that is being lost with each passing generation in rural communities where ethnic languages prevail as the media of daily discourse.

It is important to point out here that linguists, in their attempt to focus on language form and function, often fail to realize the intricate relationship that obtains between languages, which Mufwene (2001) characterizes as 'parasites', and their speakers, whom he views as 'hosts' (to the parasites). In this nexus, solutions to language endangerment can logically target either the parasites themselves or their hosts, but the most effective target is clearly the host (namely, speaker) in whom the parasite (language) resides. As demonstrated, for example, in Marongiu (2007) with regard to the on-going shift of Sardinian to Italian in Sardinia and the endangerment that this process potentiates for Sardinian, changes in economy under globalization and language policies can result in the diminution and eventual loss of a language's vitality and reversing the process is very difficult. A preliminary analysis of field data collected by Muaka (2006) for his forthcoming PhD dissertation on the utilization of Luhya, Kiswahili and English among Kenyan youths reached a similar conclusion with regard to the role of Kenyan language policies and the habitus that they have entailed on the teachers and the school youths. Thus language shift, inter-generational L1 non-transmission and actual death at the speech community level do not result merely from the spread of globalizing languages via global capitalism, but also via a number of other factors, including what has been characterized as predatory economic practices that are often achieved under created crises such as the recent resource wars in Angola, DRC, Sierra Leone and Sudan, to name but a few.

If researchers on language endangerment are serious about saving and revitalizing indigenous languages, the proposals specified in (1)–(3) earlier must be given serious attention in view of the perceived threats of economic globalization as seen by some social scientists. Specifically and in our case here, while Congolese languages and their counterparts elsewhere in the continent may not be under threat in the near future, the socioeconomic viability and national autonomy of their speakers are clearly under imminent danger as '[g]lobalization views the world as a single entity [, and considers] [t]erritorial demarcations . . . [as] impediments to its full realization' (Ferraro 2007:4). The reason for this, as Ferraro convincingly argues, is that the interests of the rich who own and operate multinational companies are very clear:

> Their perceived interests are served by the universal harmonization of regu-
> lations and policies governing trade, investment, environmental protection,
> worker protection, and tax policies, all at levels consistent with their desire to
> maximize profits. In this strategy, states are nothing more than useful bar-
> gaining chips to extract concessions from other states. In a fully globalized
> world, there is absolutely no reason at all for private interests to have any
> primary loyalty whatsoever to any state. (4)

These rich's interests are in direct conflict with those of the exploited 'poor' who need 'decent incomes, medical care, education for their children, and economic assistance for retirement' (ibid.).

It is my hope that this preliminary study, with all its limitations, can be extended and replicated on other speech communities in DRC to enable us to contribute eventually to an assessment of language vitality (including cases of endangerment) in the country. Future research must take into consideration all the major ecological conditions under which indigenous languages function.

Notes

I am greatly indebted to the editors for their encouragements during the writing of this chapter, and particularly for their questions and constructive comments that forced me to revisit some of my explanations in order to improve the quality of the study. Any remaining errors of analysis or interpretation are solely my responsibility.

[1] Lingala consists of several varieties or dialects, including, in DRC, the following: (i) Standard, also known as Mankandza or literary Lingala; (ii) Spoken Lingala; (iii) Kinshasa Lingala; (iv) Indoubil Lingala; and (v) Mangala. Varieties (ii)–(iv) represent the continuum referred to as 'urban Lingala'. I have adopted this terminology here, unless otherwise specified.

[2] The present writer experienced both aspects of this policy when he underwent his first five years of primary school in a rural community, and then in an 'école laïque' and 'Athenée royale' in Mbandaka, the capital city of the Equateur Province.

[3] [Authenticity is] the awakening of political consciousness on the part of the Zairian ['Congolese'] people to return to their own roots, to seek the value systems of their ancestors in order to select judiciously those values that contribute to their harmonious and natural development. It is the refusal of the Zairian people to espouse blindly imported ideologies. It is the affirmation of the Zairian man or of man in short, where he is, and how he is made with his own mental capabilities and social structures.

[4] For a more detailed statement of the most relevant clauses of the 1974 policy recommendations, see Bokamba (2007a) and other references cited there.

[5] For a related discussion of this topic, see also Chaudenson (this volume).

References

Abdulaziz, Mohammed M. 1980. The ecology of Tanzanian national language policy. In *Language in Tanzania,* ed. by Edgar Polomé and Clifford Hill, 139–175. Oxford; Oxford University Press.

Afoaku, Osita G. 2005. *Explaining the Failure of Democracy in the Democratic Republic of Congo: Autocracy and Dissent in an Ambivalent World.* Lewiston, NY: The Edwin Mellen Press.

Bamgbose, Ayo. 2000. *Language and Exclusion: The Consequences of Language Policies in Africa.* Hamburg: LIT Verlag Münster.

Blench, Roger. 2000. Endangered languages in West Africa. In *Language Diversity Endangered,* ed. by Matthias Brenzinger, 140–162.

Bokamba, Eyamba G. 1976. Authenticity and the choice of a national language: The case of Zaire. *Présence Africaine* 99/100.104–143.

—1986. Education and development in Zaire. In *The Crisis in Zaire: Myths and Realities,* ed. by Georges Nzongola-Ntalaja, 191–218. Trenton, NJ: Africa World Press.

—1988. Code-mixing, language variation, and linguistic theory: Evidence from Bantu languages. *Lingua: International Review of General Linguistics* 71.21 –62.

— 2002. [The spread of] Lingala. In *Encyclopedia of Twentieth-Century African History,* Vol. 1, Part 13, ed, by Dickson Eyoh and Paul T. Zeleza, 328–330. London: Routledge.

—2007a. Arguments for multilingual policies in public domains in Africa. In *Linguistic Identity in Postcolonial multilingual Spaces,* ed. by Eric A. Anchimbe, 27–65. London: Cambridge Scholars Press.

—2007b. D. R. Congo: Language and 'authentic nationalism'. In Andrew Simpson (ed.), 214–234.

—2007c. Urban Lingala: The metamorphosis of a lingua franca. Paper presented at the 38th ACAL, University of Florida at Gainesville; 23–25 March. To appear in Fiona Mc Laughlin (ed.), *Languages of Urban Africa.* London: Continuum.

Bourdieu, Pierre. 1991. *Language and Symbolic Power.* Cambridge, MA: Harvard University Press.

Brenzinger, Matthias (ed.). 1992. *Language Death: Factual and Theoretical Explorations with Special Reference to East Africa.* Berlin and New York: Mouton de Gruyter.

—1998. *Endangered Languages in Africa.* Cologne, Germany: Rüdiger Köper Verlag.

—2000a. *Language Diversity Endangered.* Berlin/New York: Mouton de Gruyter.

Brenzinger, Matthias. 2000b. Language endangerment in Northern Africa. In Brenzinger (ed.), 123–139.

—2000c. Language endangerment in Southern and Eastern Africa. In Brenzinger (ed.), 179–204.

Breton, Roland J.-L. 2003. Sub-Saharan Africa. In *Languages in a Globalising World,* ed. by Jacques Maurais and Michael A. Morris, 203–216. Cambridge: Cambridge University Press.

Calvet, Louis-Jean (ed.). 1992. *Les langues des marches en Afrique.* Aix-en-Provence: Institut d'Etudes Créoles et Francophones.

Connell, Bruce. 2000. Endangered languages in Central Africa. In Brenzinger (ed.), 163–178.

Crystal, David. 2000. *Language Death.* Cambridge: Cambridge University Press.

Dorian, Nancy (ed.). 1989. *Investigating Obsolescence: Studies in Language Contraction and Death.* Cambridge: Cambridge University Press.

Dzokanga, Adolphe. 1979. *Dictionnaire lingála-français, suivi d'une grammaire lingála.* Leipzig: VEB Verlag Enzykolpadie Leipzig.

Ennaji, Moha and Fatima Sadiqi. 2007. Morocco: Language, nationalism and gender. In Andrew Simpson (ed.), 44–60.

Epanga, P., Nzanza Makokila, Otom'si Mundekeand Ntita Nyembwe. 1992. Les langues des marches au Zaire. Première partie: Monographie sur la ville de Kinshasa. In Louis-Jean Calvet (ed.), 273–290.

Faik-Nzuji, M.C. 1974. Premier seminaire national des linguistes du Zaire. *Habari* 2(7).22–25.

Ferraro, Vincent. 2007. A new conflict. In *Courting Africa.* Special issue, *Harvard International Review* 29(2).4–5.

Finegan, Edward and John R. Rickford. 2004. *Language in the USA: Themes for the Twenty-First Century.* Cambridge: Cambridge University Press.

Fishman, Joshua A. 1991. *Reversing Language Shift: Theoretical and Empirical Foundations of Assistance to Threatened Languages.* Clevedon: Multilingual Matters.

Gordon, Raymond G., Jr. (ed.). 2005. *Ethnologue: Languages of the World,* fifteenth edition. Dallas, TX: SIL International online version.

Heine, Bernd. 1970. *Status and Use of African Lingua Francas.* Munich: Weltforum.

James, Wendy. 2007. The Sudan: Majorities, minorities, and language interactions. In Andrew Simpson (ed.), 61–78.

Kazadi, Ntole and Mundeke Otom'si Ebok. 1992. Les langues des marchés au Zaire: Le cas de Kikwit. In Louis-Jean Calvet (ed.), 343–350.

Kube, Sabine. 2005. *La francophonie vécue en Côte d'Ivoire.* Paris: L'Harmattan.

Maractho Mudzo Mwacan, Angéline and Theodore Trefon. 2004. The tap is on strike: Water distribution and supply strategies. In Theodore Trefon (ed.), 33–46.

Marongiu, Antonietta M. 2007. *Language Maintenance and Shift in Sardinia: A Case Study of Sardinian and Italian in Cagliari.* PhD thesis, Department of Spanish, Italian and Portuguese, University of Illinois at Urbana–Champaign.

Maurais, Jacques. 2003. Towards a new linguistic world order. In Jacques Maurais and Michael A. Morris (eds), 13–36.

Maurais, Jacques and Michael A. Morris (eds). 2003. *Languages in a Globalising World.* Cambridge: Cambridge University Press.

Mc Laughlin, Fiona. 2007. Senegal: The emergence of a national lingua franca. In Andrew Simpson (ed.), 79–97.

Moseng Knutsen, Anne. 2007. Ivory Coast: The supremacy of French. In Andrew Simpson (ed.), 158–172.

Muaka, Leonard. 2006. Linguistic practices and attitudes of the rural multilingual speakers: Evidence from language practices of Luhya speakers of western Kenya. Department of Linguistics, University of Illinois at Urbana–Champaign, Ms.

Mufwene, Salikoko S. 2001. *The Ecology of Language Evolution.* Cambridge: Cambridge University Press.

—2002a. Colonization, globalization and the plight of 'weak' languages. Review article. *Journal of Linguistics* 38.375–395.

—2002b. Colonization, globalization, and the future of languages in the twenty-first century. *International Journal on Multicultural Societies* 4(2).162–193.

—2004. Language birth and death. *Annual Review of Anthropology* 33.201–222.

—2005. Globalization and the myth of killer languages: What's really going on? In *Perspectives on Endangerment,* ed. by Graham Huggan and Stephen Klasen, 18–46. Hildesheim, NY: Georg Olms Verlag.

—2008. *Language Evolution: Contact, Competition, and Change.* London and New York: Continuum.

Mumbanza, mwa Bawele. 1973. Y a-t-il des Bangála? Origine et extension du terme. *Zaire-Afrique* 13.471–483.

Ndaywel è Nziem, Isidore. 1998. *Histoire générale du Congo: De l'héritage ancien à la République Démocratique.* Paris: De Boeck & Larcier, S.A.

Ndoma, Ungina. 1977. *Some Aspects of Planning Language Policy in Education in the Belgian Congo:* 1906–1960. PhD dissertation, Northwestern University, Evanston, Illinois.

Nettle, Daniel and Suzanne Romaine. 2000. *Vanishing Voices: The Extinction of the World's Languages.* Oxford: Oxford University Press.

Nyembwe, Ntita. 1986. Fonction véhiculaire et expansion linguistique. *Linguistique et Sciences Humaines* 27.49 –68.

Nyembwe, Ntita and Nanzanza Makokila. 1992. Les langues des marchés au Zaire: le cas de Matadi. In Louis-Jean Calvet (ed.), 351–358.

Nyembwe, Ntita, Nanzanza Makokila and Otom'si Mundeke. 1992. Les langues des marchés au Zaire. Deuxième partie. Enquête sur les marchés: le cas de Kinshasa. In Louis-Jean Calvet (ed.), 291–342.

Nzeza, Lufuma. 1987. L'utilisation des langues nationales dans l'enseignement primaire – Bilan d'une décennie 1974–1984. In *Linguistique et Sciences Humaines,*

Volume 27, No. Spécial: *Utilisation des Langues Nationales: Actes du colloque sur les langues nationales*; Kinshasa, 11–16 March 1985, ed. by Ntole Kazadi and Ntita T. Nyembwe, 18–36. Kinshasa, CELTA.

Nzongola-Ntalaja, Georges. 2002. *The Congo, From Leopold to Kabila: A People's History.* London: Zed Books.

Persyn, Peter and Fabienne Ladrière. 2004. The miracle of life in Kinshasa: New approaches to public health. In Theodore Trefon (ed.), 65–81.

Polomé, Edgar. 1968. The choice of official languages in the Democratic Republic of the Congo. In *Language Problems of Developing Nations*, ed. by Joshua A. Fishman, Charles A. Ferguson and J. Das Gupta, 295–312. New York: John Wiley and Sons.

République du Zaire. 1973. *Discours du Président de la République à l'Assemblée Générale des Nations Unies, New York, le 4 octobre 1973.* Kinshasa: Département de l'orientation nationale.

Schatzberg, Michael. 1980. *Politics and Class in Zaire: Bureaucracy, Business, and Beer in Lisala.* New York: Africana Publishing.

Sesep, Nsial B. 1978. *Le métissage français-lingala au Zaire: essai d'analyse différentielle et sociolinguistique de la communication bilingue.* Thèse de doctorat de 3ème cycle, Université de Nice, France.

—1986. L'expansion du Lingala. *Linguistique et Sciences Humaines* 27.19 –48.

—1987. Planification et utilisation des langues zaïroises dans l'éducation et l'administration. In *Linguistique et Sciences Humaines*, Volume 27, No. Spécial: *Utilisation des Langues Nationales: Actes du colloque sur les langues nationales*; Kinshasa, 11–16 March 1985, ed. by Ntole Kazadi et Ntita T. Nyembwe, 108–119.

Silva-Corvalán, Carmen. 2004. Spanish in the Southwest. In Edward Finegan and John R. Rickford (eds), 205–229.

Simpson, Andrew (ed.). 2007. *Language and National Identity in Africa.* Oxford: Oxford University Press.

Stewart, Gary. 2000. *Rumba on the River: A History of the Popular Music of the Two Congos.* London: Verso.

Stroud, Christopher. 2002. Framing Bourdieu socioculturally: Alternative forms of linguistic legitimacy in postcolonial Mozambique. *Multilingua* 21.247–273.

Swigart, Leigh. 2001. The limits of legitimacy: Language ideology and shift in contemporary Senegal. *Journal of Linguistic Anthropology* 10.90–130.

Tollens, Éric. 2004. Food security in Kinshasa: Copying with adversity. In Theodore Trefon (ed.), 47–64.

Tonkin, Humphrey. 2003. The search for a global linguistic strategy. In Jacques Maurais and Michael A. Morris (eds), 319–333.

Topan, Farouk. 2007. Tanzania: The development of Swahili as a national and official language. In Andrew Simpson (ed.), 252–266.

Trefon, Theodore (ed.). 2004. *Reinventing Order in the Congo: How People Respond to State Failure in Kinshasa.* London & New York: Zed Books.

Tsakala Munikengi, Télésphore and Willy Bongo-Pasi. 2004. The diploma paradox: University of Kinshasa between crisis and salvation. In Theodore Trefon (ed.), 82–98.

Vansina, Jan. 1966. *Kingdoms of the Savanna.* Madison, WI: University of Wisconsin Press.

Webb, Vic C. 2002. *Language in South Africa: The Role of Language in National Transformation, Reconstruction and Development.* Philadelphia: John Benjamins.

Yamamoto, Akira Y. and Ofelia Zepeda. 2004. Native American languages. In Edward Finegan and John R. Rickford (eds), 153–181.

Yates, Barbara. 1981. Educating Congolese abroad: A historical note on an African elite. *The International Journal of African Historical Studies* 14.34–64.

Zentella, Ana C. 2004. Spanish in the Northeast. In Edward Finegan and John R, Rickford (eds), 182–204.

Chapter 6

Globalization and Sociolinguistic Stratification in North Africa: The Case of Morocco

Ahmed Boukous

6.1 Introduction

North Africa has been a land of confluence between culturally diverse communities since Antiquity. In fact, the languages and cultures of communities around the Mediterranean have at various times come in contact with those of the indigenous populations in North Africa. This analysis will focus mainly on the Amazigh (or Berber) language and culture, which, over the years, have successively been influenced by those of the Phoenicians, the Greeks, the Arabs, the Spaniards, the Portuguese and the French (Julien 1994). This situation of successive contacts has resulted in various substrate and superstrate phenomena, which continue to bear on the Amazigh language and culture today. While it appears that globalization has always played some role in the history of certain communities, the phenomenon has intensified during the recent period of our modern age. The language market is thus marked by the diversity of languages, of interactions and of conflicts, which have in turn contributed variably to the loss of minority languages (see Skutnabb-Kangas 2000).

In this chapter, I focus on the current sociolinguistic situation in the Maghreb, more specifically in Morocco, where the sociolinguistic issue is undeniably representative of those prevalent in other countries of the region. What is particularly relevant to the analysis of such situations is the ways in which globalization triggers new dynamics of political, economic and cultural transformations that influence language practice in the whole region. The issues that will be examined herein are, in order, the widespread multilingualism that characterizes the region, the revitalization of indigenous language (*autochthophony*) embodied by the use of Amazigh, the strategies of ideological legitimization of Arabic, the economic power of French and the emergence of Anglophony in the realm of technology. The discussion of these questions will lead us to address the crucial issue of how languages are managed politically within the context of glocalization.

6.2 Linguistic Strata

Large-scale sociolinguistic analysis of the current situation in the Maghreb reveals not only linguistic diversity, but a peculiar linguistic dynamic, which manifests itself in the ways languages coexist and compete with each other, often outside of their usual domains. Foreign languages, most notably French but also Spanish and, to some extent, English, coexist alongside national languages, namely, various dialects of Arabic and Amazigh. These languages differ somewhat regarding their prestige, social role and overall patterns of usage. As such this de facto multilingualism bears on such important domains as education, administration, the cultural sphere and the economy. A major issue in tomorrow's Maghreb will therefore be whether this plurality of languages and cultures is managed rationally, functionally and harmoniously (Boukous 1995).

Demographic data provide an important indicator of the 'weight' or market value of various languages; unfortunately, we do not have any reliable data available. The results of the population census carried out in 2004 are given in Tables 6.1 and 6.2.

An examination of these two tables reveals that the language market splits into two categories. The first includes the mother tongues, namely, Amazigh and Moroccan Arabic, which constitute a weak social and symbolic capital; whereas the second consists most notably of Standard Arabic and French, which are the institutional languages and have strong social capital. It can further be concluded that there exists as much competition between languages within the same category as between the two separate categories. Sociolinguistically, the

Table 6.1 Arabic- and Amazigh-speaking population (in per cent) in 2004

Language	Amazigh	Moroccan Arabic	Total
Urban	21	79	100
Rural	34	66	100
Ensemble	28	72	100

Table 6.2 Percentage of literates (ten or more years of age) in Arabic, French and other languages

Languages written and spoken	1994	2004
None	52.7	43.0
Arabic	14.7	17.3
Arabic + French	23.8	30.3
Arabic + French + another language	5.6	9.1
Arabic + another language (-French)	0.1	0.1
None of the above	3.1	0.2

languages compete both for *social capital*, in the form of distinction and recognition, and for *material capital*, in the form of material profits and privileges. As the languages have neither the same symbolic value nor the same social functions, they occupy different places in the speakers' linguistic *habitus*. This reliance of the speakers on the practices of bilingualism and diglossia constitutes one of the peculiarities of the linguistic environment of the Maghreb. Perhaps, the situation can more aptly be described as a form of instable diglossia, in which the positions of the various languages are not fixed but evolve as a function of the power struggle between their respective users, the attitudes and motives of those users and their symbolic representations.

This conflict manifests itself most visibly in the area of public education. Here, French is alternately incorporated, marginalized, worshipped and even reviled, depending upon the situation. The attitudes reflect the dynamics of the power struggle between policy makers who advocate Arabization and the language users themselves. The term *linguistic conflict* is used here in reference to the power struggle between languages in contact, a relationship that reflects, at a symbolic level, the antagonism, manifest or latent, between social groups that identify with them and invoke them as capital for material or symbolic gain (Bourdieu 1982).

Research on multilingualism in the Maghreb reveals that the nature of individual bilingualism varies depending on the speaker's situation (Boukous 1995; Gravel 1976; Moâtassime 1992). In general, speakers whose first language is Amazigh tend to practice diglossia insomuch as they alternate, at the very least, between their native language and Colloquial Arabic. Moreover, literate speakers may also employ Standard Arabic, and sometimes French. Those whose first language is Arabic may be monolingual if they have not been formally educated; otherwise they are subject to diglossia, using both Colloquial and Standard Arabic, or triglossia, if they are capable of communicating in French or Spanish.

The linguistic dynamics are characterized by concurrent changes in language practice. The four most significant trends are:

(i)   the progressive recognition for Amazigh as a legitimate language after years of marginalization;

(ii) the emergence of a variety of Arabic, characterized as *Arabe médian* 'Median Arabic', which establishes a continuum from Standard to Colloquial Arabic, the principal effect of which is a renewal of sociolinguistic vitality for Arabic;

(iii) the social marking of the use of French, which, in light of Arab patrimonialist ideology, threatens to create a cultural and sociolinguistic rift between the Arabophone and Francophone camps; and last,

(iv) the emergence of English in the wake of economic globalization, and the imposition of its role as a universal language in the expanding service sector.

6.3 Amazighophony: The Local Stratum

Amazigh has undergone a process of institutional marginalization, which has contributed largely to the precariousness of its current situation. The process of linguistic and cultural assimilation, extending throughout the history of North Africa, has led to an attrition of the Amazighophone population. Amazigh is the earliest attested language in the region. Thanks to archaeological evidence from Ancient Egypt, it is possible to reconstruct its written history over at least the past five thousand years. Protohistorians estimate that the Amazigh settled North Africa during the Neolithic age. Some consider them autochthonous, others as originating from the northern coast of the Mediterranean, while still others place their origins in the southern part of the Arabian Peninsula. The question of origin remains laden with the ideological presuppositions of numerous groups, the Amazigh population itself being no exception. The Amazigh language is currently divided into dialect groups. It is used chiefly across rural, mountain and desert regions; however, its use in cities has increased due to in-migration from rural areas, and to the urbanization of Amazigh-speaking regions.

Until recently, the Amazigh language was in decline, both because it was excluded from participation in institutions, and because the number of its speakers was declining due to migrations and assimilation. To combat this loss, a fraction of the Amazighophone elite have initiated strategies of extra-institutional development, based on individual actions at the level of associations. Their actions have focused mainly on fostering a modern consciousness of Amazigh identity, on demands for linguistic and cultural rights and on the conditions conducive to maintaining cultural and artistic terms through language modernization, music and access to other forms of expression, such as press materials, audio-visual media, movies and theaters. The work that has been done in these areas, often under difficult political and ideological conditions, has enabled substantial progress both at the level of resolving the general issue facing Amazigh, and at the level of operationalizing certain actions. It is thus that usage of written Amazigh has made considerable progress, most notably in the domains of printing and publishing. There are several works of literature written in Amazigh, of which most are collections of poems, short stories and translations. To this may be added numerous periodicals composed entirely or partially in Amazigh. The oral repertoire of the language has been equally enriched by its use in theater and film, and in certain formal contexts, such as lectures and gatherings pertaining to Amazigh language and culture. Amazigh is also used in political discourse, and in administrative meetings in some Amazighophone regions. Nevertheless, the range of these extra-institutional actions is limited by the narrow scope if its component associations and by lack of finances, materials and logistics.

There was a qualitative change in the situation of the Amazigh language at the beginning of the second half of the twentieth century. The creation of institutions dedicated to the preservation and promotion of Amazigh language and culture, namely, *Le Haut Commissariat à l'Amazighité* (HCA) 'the High Commission to the Amazigh Community' in Algeria and *L'Institut Royal de la Culture Amazigh au Maroc* (IRCAM) 'the Royal Institute of Amazigh Culture' in Morocco had a positive effect on the status of Amazigh. A new strategy was initiated in the domain of cultural and linguistic politics. This strategy is best analysed in light of its two main goals: the assessment of the linguistic and cultural plurality within the society, and the development of an Amazigh national character. Accordingly, six main arguments form the basis of Amazigh community's claims to legitimacy:

   (i) they are the historical entity most deeply rooted in the history of civilization in the Maghreb,
  (ii) they constitute an essential element of the Moroccan cultural heritage shared by all members of the national community, without exception,
 (iii) they represent one of the linguistic and cultural symbols of the national character,
  (iv) the promotion of Amazigh culture represents an important step in the path to the democratic and modernist society to which the Maghreb aspires,
   (v) the management of Amazigh issues is a matter of national responsibility,
  (vi) and, last, the Amazigh community must open itself to the modern world in order to prosper and endure.

   The ultimate goal of the proposed course of action is to set the stage for the revitalization of Amazigh language and culture, which suffer dramatically from a need for renewal after centuries of marginalization and underdevelopment. The expressed mission of this institution is therefore to contribute to the preservation and promotion of Amazigh culture, especially in the areas of public education, information and public life in general, at the national, regional and local levels. From this perspective, it is undeniable that the exploitation of new technologies developed in the wake of recent economic globalization has equipped the Amazigh with such advances as a numeric keyboard, a codified writing system, tifinagh-unicode and the multimedia support that enables the virtual transmission of Amazigh language and culture on an international scale.

   As a part of the movement's political agenda, civil society has demanded a constitutional status for Amazigh in order to guarantee the effectiveness of measures taken at the institutional level. This demand is founded on the fact that Amazigh is the autochthonous language of the Maghreb. It is claimed that the culture that it conveys constitutes central values of the system of symbolic representations of large sections of the national community. Likewise, it is believed that the enjoyment of linguistic and cultural rights is a part of the inalienable human rights of the Amazigh people. It follows from this that the language should be accorded de jure status at the constitutional level, and not simply de facto status as the native vernacular. It would no longer function simply as an ethnolinguistic marker of Amazigh identity but as an official language of the institution. This process of language revitalization is, however, still in its infancy, and both the overall strategy and specific methods of revitalization require that numerous factors be taken into account, especially socializing proximity, politicized self-determination, institutional involvement, ideological legitimacy, synergetic collaboration, and teleological subordination and asymmetry (Landry et al. 2005).

6.4 Arabophony: The Supralocal Stratum

The Arabic language established a footing in the Maghreb during the late seventh century CE. Today, the issue of Arabic is approached with great care, due in part to the intricacy of the Standard Arabic–Colloquial Arabic diglossia, and in part to the nature of the political ideology of Arabization. The question of Arabic has become a recurrent theme both in the general debate on language policy and in the domain of public education (Boukous 1996; Grandguillaume 1983).

The aim of the Arabization policy is to impose Standard Arabic as the language of operation in all public institutions, ideally occupying all domains of communication and monopolizing both oral and written language, notwithstanding the fact that Colloquial Arabic has quasi-monopoly on oral communication and that French is a serious competitor in the domain of written communication. Its stated objective is to eliminate the use of French, at least in pubic institutions, and to transform French from a medium of instruction into an object of instruction. Standard Arabic and French are the only codes in the language market endowed with the highest value indices, but their values are neither equal nor constant. Indeed, their market values are a function of the sphere in which they are employed by social agents. For example, mastery of Standard Arabic grants access to a certain number of professions associated with domains that bear on religious matters, such as traditional education and religious affairs and law, or with domains regard the teaching of Arabic literature, Islamic studies and the humanities. On the other hand, French acts as the key to modern economics, especially in the service sector. Thus, for example, a candidate for a management position within a company has a better chance of being recruited if he has a firm command of the French language. The acquisition of this capital occurs mostly within the framework of the school system. Here we see again the well-known role of school as a place of production and reproduction of dominant languages and cultures (Bourdieu and Passeron 1970).

The value of the *symbolic capital* is determined by the nature and status of the institution that grants it. Although Standard Arabic is used as the medium of instruction in public schools and the level of competence in French attained by students in the same institutions remains rudimentary, it is not exaggerating to say that Standard Arabic represents only a subsistence-level linguistic capital for mostly children of the working class. Excluded from technological and scientific instruction at the university level, Standard Arabic has become the de facto language of the Arabo-Muslim tradition. That is, in order to maintain footing in both the language and the job markets (associated with the expression of modernity), Arabic itself is in need of modernization and revitalization.

Assuming that language is an essential tool for human development, it is obvious that in order for Moroccan society to achieve endogenous social and economic development, Arabic must, as the official language, respond to the demands of modernity; consequently it must also modernize. It is for this reason that the various countries within the Maghreb have opted for a policy of Arabizing institutions in the public sector, albeit with varying degrees of success. The Arabization policy was therefore planned with the intent of imposing, sometimes through draconian methods, the exclusive use of Arabic within public administration. For example, in 1960 the Moroccan government created *L'Institut d'Etudes et de Recherches pour l'Arabization* (IERA) 'the Institute for the Study of and Research on Arabization', whose mission was to promote the Arabic language and to implement the Arabization policy in both education and administration.

To be sure, the term *Arabization* is not optimal, as it lends itself to ambiguity (Boukous 1996). It may be interpreted ethnically as the assimilation of non-Arabophone populations, especially the Amazighophones; just as can be interpreted an applied process of linguistic normalization. Arabization was intended as a process of recovering national cultural identity. It is viewed by all – intellectuals, unions, political and cultural organization alike – as a political decision intended to minimize the importance of la Francophonie, which is seen as encroaching upon the educational, administrative and formal economic sectors. It is for this reason that the state seeks to establish the historical, political and religious legitimacy of the Arabic language; it promotes Arabic against French, thus exercising a state monopoly on the language market.

Among those participating in the Arabizationist discourse are graduates of such institutions of traditional education as the University of the Qaraouiyine at Fez, Zeytouna University in Tunisia and Ibn Badis College in Algeria. Also among the supporters are the graduates of Arabized public education, and the Arabist and fundamentalist elite. Nevertheless, it would be erroneous to suppose that the pro-Arabization discourse conforms entirely to the convictions of the traditionalist elite. There is no official anti-Arabization discourse; in fact, one might even go so far as to say that there is near-unanimity as to the need for Arabization in public institutions, and for the systematic substitution of French with Standard Arabic. The modernist elite, therefore, generally construct the same discourse, even if the conditions and methods of Arabization are interpreted differently. For some modernist intellectuals, Arabization is necessary to pave the way for the country's cultural development and independence. They are quick to add, however, that the goal is not to impose the fixed and archaic Classical Arabic of pre-Islamic poetry, but to create a new, modern Arabic language, an Arabic that has been updated both in grammar and orthography and facilitates the transmission of science and technology. In short, a statement that calls into question Arabization is judged politically and ideologically incorrect (Chikh et al. 1988).

The ultimate goal of the discourse on Arabization is undoubtedly the legitimization of Arabic as a language of modernity, competitive with French. Attempts at legitimization have relied on several arguments:

(i) The religious argument: The Arabic language is the language of Islam, and therefore sacred; it is also the language that unites the Islamic community.
(ii) The historical argument: Arabic is the language of the State.
(iii) The cultural argument: Arabic is the vehicle of Arabo-Muslim heritage.
(iv) Last, the ideological argument: Arabic is the glue that holds the Arab Nation together.

If this is the case made in favor of Arabic in the prevailing discourse, it remains necessary to compare this with the reality as observed in the examination of the linguistic interactions between speakers, and with their attitudes and opinions regarding Arabization. Understanding the way in which the issue of Arabization is perceived and experienced by the social agents implicated in the process provides precious insights into those factors that both favor and hinder the process. In other words, the success or failure of Arabization does not depend solely on the utopian ideals of ideologues, the methodological strategies employed by its creators or the choices of its executors, but also on the participants in the process itself through their language behavior (Boukous 1995; Elbiad 1991; Elgherbi 1993; Gravel 1976).

In short, the stated goal of the Arabization policy is to help Standard Arabic regain its legitimacy by modernizing it and revitalizing it as the national language. However, the reality is that while the process aims to Arabize large sectors of the educational and administrative systems, it has neither given sufficient consideration to the various mother tongues of its intended users nor adequately assessed the position held by French. A radical analysis of Arabization in the Maghreb would suggest that this policy is simply a political subterfuge concocted by the upper class to provide to children of the working class a sort of third-rate Arabized education, an education that would not permit access to those areas granting socioeconomic power; while the upper class entrusts the education and upbringing of their own progeny in foreign schools. This is a clear example of a strategy of social reproduction.

6.5 La Francophonie: The Colonial Stratum

The presence of French in the Maghrebi language market began with the French colonization of the region: Algeria in 1830, Tunisia in 1885 and Morocco in 1912. By all accounts, its presence weighs quite heavily on the language market for reasons of logistic leverage, from which the French benefit both economically and politically. We must bear in mind that France is the principal economic partner of all the Maghrebi countries; often, it is the primary supplier, purchaser and foreign investor. France is also the residence of choice for most North Africans living abroad. The largest Maghrebi community outside the region is to be found in France. Conversely, the largest French community outside of continental France resides in the Maghreb. Such facts shed light on the privileged position of French in North Africa.

The relatively high position of French in the market of symbolic goods is not so much indicative of a strong dependence on France as it is of the privileged relationship between France and the Maghreb, a testament to a bilateral agreement of economic, technical, cultural and strategic cooperation. Furthermore, the countries of the Maghreb participate in conferences of *L'Organisation Intergouvernementale de la Francophonie* (OIF), which rallies governments and heads of states of countries that are fully or partly Francophone. France is also bound to these countries both by shared cultural conventions, and by agreements between French and Maghrebi universities.

The importance of French in the media is strengthened by radio broadcasts, such as *Radio France Internationale*, and on the local level by *Radio Méditerranée Internationale* (*Médi 1*), 'the radio of the Maghreb', as well as a number of television and radio stations operating partially in French. Regarding the print media, we notice that while the Maghreb is opened to press materials from around the world, the Francophone press, especially the French press, predominates. The local press within the Maghreb is also largely Francophone. Major political organizations publish one journal in Arabic and another in French; likewise, local publishing houses publish works written both in Arabic and in French. French TV channels are the most watched, most notably *TV5*, probably the largest audiovisual disseminator of French culture and la Francophonie.

The considerable role that French plays in the Maghreb is the result of the power associated with the French language and culture in general. It is not, therefore, an inherent property of the system, but a consequence of a situation of dependency, the sort of 'dependency within interdependence' espoused by the Francophonie movement, described by the Québec Summit (1987:5) as 'a common space, in which the objectives are cooperation, exchange, development, and political discussion, which (the member states) propose to attain through mutual support and solidarity'. La Francophonie is also frequently interpreted as a token of sorts, allowing poorer Francophone countries to benefit from the aid provided by richer Francophone countries in the form of economic, cultural and strategic assistance. The implications of la Francophonie are therefore political, economic and cultural; it is no longer simply a linguistic matter (Calvet 2004; Chaudenson 2000; Hagège 1996). This is why certain nationalist factions suggest that French has evolved from a language of colonialism to a language of imperialism (Chikh et al. 1988).

Social actors are conscious of the value of French on the job market. Hence the social demand for French remains strong, despite the fact that, in the realm of public education, French is no longer the medium of instruction. Indeed, a public high school graduate attains only an elementary level of competence in French, which limits his chances for academic advancement, since French is the exclusive language of higher education in science and technology, and the only language that grants access to the most lucrative professions, such as engineering, medicine, pharmacy, architecture and business management. In such a system, the children of the upper class have a clear advantage. They include the children of the traditionalist elite who nurture the ideological discourse in favor of Arabization.

Another indicator of the importance of French in the Maghreb is its dominance in the service sector. We know that, for about two decades, a large number of graduates of higher education in literature, science and technology have been hit hard by an unemployment crisis, largely because of their poor command of French. The state, in turn, is attempting to diagnose what structural readjustments might be necessary in order to respond to the demands of the changing job market. The realization that university training has been unable to address the current demands of the job market has raised the need for educational reforms that place greater emphasis on the teaching of French, on the introduction of applied fields conducive to the production of a functional working class and favoring the creation of private institutions. Studies on the question of demand within the language market suggest that one's qualifications are directly correlated with mastery of French. Moreover, private companies often require knowledge of English. These demands are a reality that no discourse for monolingualism, regardless of the best of its nationalistic motivations, can bypass (cf. Boukous 1995; Sadiqi 1991).

It appears, therefore, that the historical gravity of the colonial era, made explicit in the nationalist discourse, has less and less of a hold on the public conscience. Five decades since independence, it seems that the ideological function of this discourse has been to reserve access to modernity, top management and decision-making power for the elite graduates of French education. It is an indication of the fragility of a utopia based on social mobility through education. It becomes clear, then, that in the Maghreb, as in all former colonies, the primary function of French schools is the production and repro- duction of a local elite within a particular social stratum. La Francophonie no longer concerns the masses of the educated population but the urban elite and their descendants, who are most certainly a strategic asset in the appropriation of symbolic power.

6.6 Anglophony: The Imperial Stratum

The position of English in the Moroccan language market is still weak, though its presence is not entirely negligible. English tends to play the role of the out- sider in the local language competition, acting as a vehicle for the transfer of technology, and as a tool for the acquisition of modernity. As is well known, accepting modernity is accepting the cultural universe that generated it. Thus, modernity contributes partially to the reorganization of the cultural model that integrates it. It is often said that 'all technology carries with it its own metaphys- ics' (cf. Heidegger 1954); in this case, it is an Anglo-Saxon metaphysics, just as the French language would reflect the French cultural universe.

Individuals or groups educated in the Anglo-Saxon school, or receptive to the dominant international culture, believe that access to modernity is not a special privilege of the French language, and that the granting of such access should not be the monopoly of the French education system. In defence of their material and symbolic interests, they accuse la Francophonie of giving way to Francophilia. For them, English, in its de facto role as the universal language of communication and the language of high technology – in short, the language of the age of globalization – represents a more competitive, more substantial and more credible capital than does French. The symbolic power of English is the result of its dynamic use in the international arena, where it has become the undisputed universal language, relegating French to a secondary position. English is the primary working language of the United Nations, with UNESCO being the only UN organization in which French still predominates. Actually, 65 per cent of all scientific publications appear in English, compared to 9.8 per cent in French. Even in Europe, 73–98 per cent of high-schoolers choose English as their primary second language, compared to 17–30 per cent who choose French. Such facts suggest that opting for la Francophonie is simply an uphill battle (Moâtassime 1992).

A quick analysis of the power struggle between English and French in the media reveals the undeniable superiority of the former. This superiority has a definite effect on the linguistic situation in the Maghreb, where English is slowly developing a position in the market parallel to that of French. English is making its mark in a number of strategically important areas, most notably education and the media. In reality English is present in both public and private education. In the public education system, it is part of the middle school curriculum; at higher levels, it is taught as the language of specialization in the English Language and Literature departments of the Faculties of Letters at major universities. It is also taught as a second language in most institutes of higher education, professional schools and university faculties. In the private education sector, English is taught at the preschool level in some institutions, at the primary school level in others and generally at the high school level. There are also some private institutions in which English functions as the general language of instruction, especially those that have adopted the Anglo-Saxon system of education. The founding of the English-language Al-Akhawayn University in Morocco confirms that the Anglo-Saxon educational system is already operating at a significantly high level. In addition, organizations such as the British Council and the American Language Center offer language courses for both children and adults seeking linguistic proficiency. English books can be found in any university town, and are available at bookstores affiliated with American or British cultural center, or at specialty bookstores. These books are sought after by those in the sciences, medicine, technology and the humanities.

In the mass media, English is found largely in written materials and foreign television broadcasts, mostly from the United States and the United Kingdom. Periodicals available on the market are also imported from those countries, in addition to a few local publications. English is used in everyday radio broadcasts. In addition, listeners can also receive broadcasts in English from foreign radio stations such as the *BBC World Service* or *Voice of America.* Last, Anglo-American language and culture are disseminated across Morocco via satellite, through broadcasts such as *World Net, CNN, Eurosport, Super Channel* and *Sky One.* English is also regularly heard in radio and television advertisements. In large cities, a number of signs are written in English.

The competition between French and English is therefore quite real, and English is winning domains that have hitherto been the monopoly of French, which implies that the two languages are (at least potentially) in competition. The next few decades may see the position of English strengthened by the opening of the Maghrebi market to foreign products, thanks to new free trade agreements.

6.7 Globalization, Glocalization and Stratification

'Think globally, act locally' is the strategic equation to be solved by every state and society in the world. The solution is even more crucial in the countries of the Southern Hemisphere, insomuch as they have felt most acutely the effects, both positive and negative, of globalization. The question becomes, then: By what means can globalization be directed towards local interests?

For language, the solution must be found in the framework of language policy, directed by the state and defined at the constitutional level, and implemented at the institutional level. The ultimate goal of a language policy is the management of the linguistic resources of the national community. As such, the nature and quality of this management directly impacts human development (cf. Weinstein 1990). In the case of the Maghreb, states have opted for a language policy that generally consists of allowing the natural course of language competition to play out on its own. For this reason, an understanding of the rules of this competition is in part a matter of understanding the centripetal forces of globalization and the centrifugal forces of localization, those that begin with the state and with individual social agents. The solution to the whole problem rests, therefore, in the equitable management of the globalization/glolocalization dichotomy by both states and societies.

The type of multilingualism we see in the Maghreb, especially in the practice of diglossia and transitional bilingualism, represents a sociolinguistic phenomenon typical of social groups that experience multilingualism as the simultaneous product of localization and globalization. This phenomenon is best explained in terms of a competition between linguistic products, and the consequent dominance of one or more stronger linguistic products over the weaker local ones. Through their everyday linguistic practice, people interact with the languages in question in accordance with the laws of the market, contingent upon the value of the languages, and the relative 'weight' and value that they carry. Hence subjects are in a way condemned to diglossia; that is to say, condemned to communicate in such a way that the distinction between the social uses of various languages leads to their classification as either strong or weak, depending on whether the language yields symbolic or material profit, or is confined to its own small sphere of influence. The implication is that the language market evolves based on two criteria: pragmatic utility and an attachment to a sense of identity, corresponding to external and internal motivation, respectively.

Within the framework of a usually favorable macro-environment, the Maghrebi populations are entering a new stage of sociopolitical development. They envision a society founded on pluralist democracy, full-fledged modernity and human development. From the point of view of competition within the language market, the users of 'strong' languages – Standard Arabic, French and to a lesser extent English – employ strategies aimed at strengthening their linguistic capital, imposing their language as the sole tool for the appropriation of power. The legitimization strategies employed differ from one language to another. Standard Arabic relies on such major assets as religion, the constitution, public institutions and Arabo-Muslim heritage, while French benefits from the systems set in place during the colonial period, strengthened by the post-colonial relationship between France and the Maghreb. The situation may lead to an official endorsement of a certain type of diglossia in the domain of education, a linguistic division of labor whereby subjects dealing with matters of

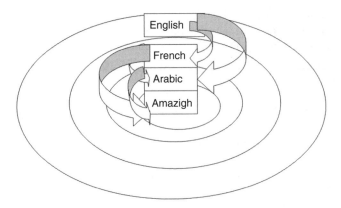

FIGURE 6.1   Language interaction.

identity are taught in Standard Arabic, while subjects that grant entry into the world of science and technology are generally taught in French. This strengthens the integration of the Maghreb into France's economic, cultural and strategic sphere of influence. However, in nationalist, traditionalist and Islamicist circles, French is still perceived as a legacy of colonization. Thus, it is viewed negatively in these circles, where colonization has a negative ideological connotation. As for English, it is progressively gaining more ground in the language market, where it enjoys prestige as the dominant language at the international level, and as a vehicle of high technology and international culture. A representation of the interaction between these various languages is given in Figure 6.1.

This figure illustrates how the languages in contact are ranked in relation to each other. English appears not to be influenced by the other languages and stands as the 'supercentral language' (in Swaan's 2001 and Calvet's 2006 metalanguage), whereas French ranks higher than both Arabic and Amazigh, and Arabic in turn prevails on Amazigh. Affected by all the other languages, the latter is ranked the lowest.

Insomuch as languages are in fact social products, the power struggle between them necessarily depends upon the state of the relationship between the countries and social groups that support and identify with them. In general, it seems that groups that support communitarianism identify with Amazighophony; those who support a patrimonialism anchored in Arabo-Islamism support Arabophony; while those in favor of liberalism are more open to bilingualism, which, given the current situation, will most certainly be Standard Arabic–French bilingualism. This does, however, lead one to wonder whether, in the future, French – being increasingly marginalized on the world stage – might still be considered a valuable gateway for entry into the international scene, and into the universal culture of the modern age. In other respects, we must also ask ourselves to what extent the restriction of access to post-colonial and imperial languages – currently monopolized by the upper classes and used as a barrier to elite circles – is a form of social discrimination (cf. Myers-Scotton 1990).

To sum up, an analysis of the current sociolinguistic situation in North Africa reveals how languages are hierarchized according to a number of ecological factors, most notably the economy, politics and technology. The history of the region is a huge burden for the various communities, and for the institutions who must manage the political, economic, social, cultural and linguistic situations in which various endogenous and exogenous elements intertwine; hence the struggle between tradition and modernity, and between the search for a communitarianist ideal and forced extraversion. Such are the issues and challenges of globalization and glocalization facing this region of the world.

References

Boukous, Ahmed. 1995. *Société, langues et cultures au Maroc*. Rabat: Publications de la Faculté des Lettres.

—1996. La politique linguistique au Maroc: enjeux et ambivalences. In *Les politiques linguistiques, mythes et réalités*, ed. by Caroline Juillard and Louis-Jean Calvet, 73–82. Beyrouth: AUPELF-UREF.

Bourdieu, Pierre. 1982. *Ce que parler veut dire: l'économie des échanges linguistiques*. Paris: Fayard.

Bourdieu, Pierre and Jean-Claude Passeron. 1970. *La reproduction: éléments pour une théorie du système d'enseignement*. Paris: Editions de Minuit.

Calvet, Louise-Jean. 2004. La diversité linguistique: enjeux pour la francophonie. *Hermès* 40.287–293.

—2006. *Towards an Ecology of World Languages*. Malden, MA: Polity Press.

Chaudenson, Robert. 2000. *Vers une révolution francophone*. Paris: L'Harmattan.

Chikh, Slimane, Mehdi Elmandjra and Béchir Touzani. 1988. *Maghreb et francophonie*. Paris: Economica.

Elbiad, Mohamed. 1991. The role of some population sectors in the progress of Arabization in Morocco. *International Journal of Sociology of Language* 8.22–44.

Elgherbi, El-Mostafa. 1993. *Aménagement linguistique et enseignement du français au Maroc*. Meknès: La Voix de Meknès.

Grandguillaume, Gilbert. 1983. *Arabisation et politique linguistique au Maghreb*. Paris: Maisonneuve et Larose.

Gravel, Louis-André. 1976. *Sociolinguistic Investigation of Multilingualism in Morocco*. PhD dissertation, Columbia University.

Hagège, Claude. 1996. *Le français, histoire d'un combat*. Paris: Odile Jacob.

Heidegger, Martin. 1954. *La question de la technique*. Trad. André Préau. Paris: Gallimard.

Julien, Charles-André. 1994. *Histoire de l'Afrique du Nord*. Paris: Payot et Rivages.

Landry, Rodrigue, Kenneth Deveau and Réal Allard. 2005. Au-delà de la résistance: principes de la revitalisation ethnolangagière. Papier présenté au 73ᵉ Congrès de l'ACFAS, Université du Quebec à Chicoutimi.

Moâtassime, Ahmed. 1992. *Arabisation, langue française et pluralité au Maghreb.* Paris: Presses Universitaires de France.

Myers-Scotton, Carol. 1990. Elite closure as boundary maintenance: The case of Africa. In *Language Policy and Political Development,* ed. by Brian Weinstein, 25–42. Norwood, NJ: Ablex.

Québec. 1987. *Organisation Internationale de la Francophonie.* Second Sommet de la Francophonie.

Sadiqi, Fatima. 1991. The Spread of English in Morocco. *International Journal of Sociology of Language* 87.99–114.

Skutnabb-Kangas, Tove. 2000. *Linguistic Genocide in Education, or Worldwide Diversity and Human Rights.* Mahwah, NJ: Lawrence Earlbaum.

Swaan, Abram de. 2001. *Words of the World.* Malden, MA: Polity Press.

Weinstein, Brian. 1990. Language policy and political development. In *Language Policy and Political Development,* ed. by Brian Weinstein, 1–21. Norwood, NJ: Ablex.

Chapter 7

The Ascent of Wolof as an Urban Vernacular and National Lingua Franca in Senegal

Fiona Mc Laughlin

7.1 Introduction

In Africa today there are certain dominant languages such as Swahili, Hausa and Maninka that serve as urban vernaculars and/or regional, national or even international lingua francas. Their domain of use is expanding as speakers of other languages seek to acquire them for a variety of reasons, not least of which is their association with modernity and urban life. In some cases those speakers, or their children, turn away from their ancestral languages and the process of language shift at the population level begins; in other cases, speakers maintain their ancestral languages even as they acquire a new one. These urban vernaculars and lingua francas play a seminal role in the language ecology of the continent and are deeply implicated in issues of language endangerment and language vitality. In this chapter, I discuss the ascent of one such language, Wolof, from its origins in the heartland of Senegal to the status of urban vernacular and national lingua franca. I also examine how the dominant position of this language has affected other languages that share the same linguistic space.

7.1.1 Africa in the master narratives of globalization and language endangerment

Language death has been predicted to occur on an unprecedented scale during the course of this century. Since Krauss' (1992) alert, many linguists and funding agencies have put their energies and resources into documenting and attempting to revitalize or preserve endangered languages. The current state of language endangerment is frequently attributed either explicitly or implicitly to the effects of globalization (Crystal 2000; Nettle and Romaine 2000), although globalization remains a poorly understood phenomenon, especially when discussed within the context of Africa. Contemporary theories of globalization purport to explain the consequences of increasing interconnectedness and interdependence between communities and cultures on all parts of the planet, but they are far from being global in scope, especially when it comes to Africa. Seminal volumes on globalization such as Sassen (1998) and Giddens (2002) have, as Ferguson (2006:25–27) points out, almost nothing to say about Africa, despite the fact that they claim to shed light on a planet-wide phenomenon. Although studies on globalization that focus specifically on Africa, such as Piot (1999) and Ferguson (2006), have indeed started to emerge, it is clear that the master narrative of globalization has largely been constructed without factoring Africa in.

Much of the master narrative of language endangerment and death has been constructed on a North American and Australian model, where Native populations in recent times have engaged in large scale societal shift to English. This model has fed a widespread popular belief that the spread of colonial languages such as English and French spells the demise of indigenous languages in all corners of the globe. Against these narratives, linguists who study Africa have often pointed out that the languages of the former colonial powers, namely, English, French and Portuguese, are not normally the targets of language shift, although they continue to serve as official languages (e.g., Batibo 2005; Brenzinger 2007; Mufwene 2001). When African languages are endangered or lost, it is usually because their speakers have shifted to another more widely spoken African language such as Swahili, Hausa or Maninka. The master narrative of language endangerment, informed as it is by the Australian and North American situations, has also been implicitly predicated on monolingualism as a norm: as a new language is acquired, the old one is lost. Again, Africa provides an important counterexample to this model, since speakers frequently acquire a new language without losing their ancestral language.

But despite compelling evidence to the contrary, the master narrative persists. Consider the following statement from Crystal's volume, *Language Death* (2000): 'And in parts of West Africa, where English and French creoles in particular are attracting huge numbers of new speakers, many local languages are felt to be endangered (13). Apart from the fact that there are no French creoles spoken in West Africa,[1] the acquisition of a widely spoken European language derivative such as Nigerian Pidgin English, an extended pidgin, does not necessarily trigger language shift (Deuber 2005) but adds to the speaker's repertoire. In the wake of statements such as Crystal's, it becomes clear that there is much work to do just to get the facts right about Africa.

Remarking on the fact that we know so little about globalization in Africa and that the little we do know 'looks so unlike what most global theories lead us to expect' Ferguson (2006) provides an accurate assessment of our state of knowledge: 'Above all, what the inconvenient questions coming out of Africa show us is how much more thinking, and how much more empirical social research, remains to be done before we can really understand a globalization that divides the planet as much as it unites it' (49).

Similar observations can be made about language endangerment. Considering the fact that Africa is home to approximately one-third of the world's six thousand or so languages, it would be bad science if the continent were not to play a central role in informing our understanding of language vitality and language endangerment. I would argue that we do not yet have a good understanding of what the effects of globalization are on language vitality in Africa, mainly because globalization is experienced in very local ways on the continent. On the Senegalese coast, for example, large industrial Japanese fishing boats have depleted the waters of fish, prompting thousands of Lebu fishermen to attempt clandestine migration to the Canary Islands in artisanal dugout boats in search of work. While these events are in a very real sense the result of globalization, it is very difficult to know what kind of effect, if any, they and other similar sequences of events are having on language practice.

This chapter is a first step in attempting to understand the linguistic ecology of Senegal, a multilingual West African country where a single language, Wolof, has emerged as an urban vernacular and national lingua franca. Used already as a lingua franca in Northern Senegal during the precolonial period, Wolof was spoken in areas of the country where Africans first came in contact with Europeans and where Senegal's first cities were established. Thus, it became an urban language at an early point in its colonial history. It is now spoken in urban areas throughout the country and is known informally as the national language. In this chapter I consider the ascent of Wolof as an urban vernacular and national lingua franca and its relationship to other languages spoken in Senegal in terms of their ongoing vitality and robustness or their attrition.

Although there is much work to be done in order to understand the impact of Wolofization ('the spread of Wolof') at a microlevel in communities all over Senegal, certain preliminary conclusions are reached in this chapter. They include the following:

1. Globalization does not threaten minority languages in Senegal; its influence is felt only on French and Wolof.
2. Urbanization is the greatest threat to minority languages in Senegal because it often precipitates generational language (or dialect) shift to urban Wolof.
3. Minority languages are maintained in rural and urban areas if their domains of use do not overlap with those of Wolof.
4. Many of Senegal's languages are undergoing substantial change as the result of contact with Wolof even as they are being maintained.
5. Wolof is encroaching on areas such as the governmental and white-collar sectors that were once reserved for French and still are in many francophone countries in Africa.

If we are to draw conclusions about the linguistic ecology of Africa and the attendant issues of language vitality and endangerment, we must understand the individual cases first. As we will see, although the linguistic ecology of Senegal has many parallels to situations elsewhere on the continent, it also has its own unique history, which this chapter attempts to elucidate.

7.1.2 Senegal's contemporary linguistic landscape

Senegal consists of two distinct linguistic eco-zones: the northern part of the country, between the Senegal River, which forms the border with Mauritania and Gambia, is dominated by the three languages, Wolof, Pulaar and Seereer-Siin, with the largest numbers of speakers, while the southern part of the country, south of Gambia in Casamance, is characterized by much more linguistic fragmentation and higher degrees of multilingualism. This chapter concentrates on the northern linguistic eco-zone, the main area in which Wolof is spoken. According to the most recent edition of *Ethnologue* (2005), there are thirty-five African languages currently spoken in Senegal, of which three, Wolof, Pulaar and Seereer-Siin have more than a million speakers each.[2] The *Ethnologue* estimate for the number of Wolof speakers is low, numbering only three-and-a-half million, when in reality, the number is more likely to be double that and even more when those who speak Wolof in addition to their native language are considered. Pulaar has close to two-and-a-half million speakers in Senegal while Seereer has approximately one-and-a-half million. Most of the other languages have fewer than fifteen thousand speakers, and several have no more than two or three thousand. Despite these smaller numbers of speakers for most of Senegal's languages, almost all of which are members of either the Atlantic or Mande branches of Niger-Congo, their relative robustness confirms for Senegal Blench's (2007) statement that '[i]n general, West African languages are in a healthy state' (150). To understand the vitality enjoyed by most of Senegal's languages, it is necessary to examine the linguistic repertoires of Senegalese speakers, many of whom speak one or more languages in addition to their native language(s), and to understand the domains in which those languages are used. As Mufwene (2001:173) emphasizes, languages only compete for speakers within the same domain of use. In the case of Senegal, Wolof has nudged Casamançais Portuguese Creole out of its niche as the lingua franca of the city of Ziguinchor (Juillard 1995) only because it too is an urban lingua franca, but it has not replaced Saafen or Ndut as the home language of villagers in the Cangin-speaking areas around the city of Thiès, because, although adults almost universally master it, Wolof is not spoken at home and is therefore not in competition with Saafen or Ndut.

Of the Senegalese population, which totals slightly over eleven million people, approximately 44 per cent are ethnically Wolof, yet close to 90 per cent speak Wolof as a first or second language, a situation that has led to the informal dubbing of Wolof as the national language. Senegal's official language is French, a consequence of French colonial expansionism and rule in West and

Central Africa during the nineteenth and first part of the twentieth centuries, up until independence, which came for most countries in the early 1960s. Despite a number of historical circumstances discussed later, which might otherwise point to a favorable environment for the French language, a 1990 report from the *Haut Conseil de la Francophonie* puts the number of real Francophones in Senegal at a mere 10 per cent of the population and occasional Francophones at the slightly higher figure of 14 per cent (Cissé 2005:272). Wolof, rather than French, is the most desirable language available in the Senegalese linguistic marketplace, but the dual questions of how and why it has achieved this status have not been fully addressed.

The remainder of this chapter, which addresses the reasons why Wolof has become Senegal's dominant language and how its position of dominance affects other languages, is organized more or less chronologically with a focus on the nature of the linguistic space occupied by Wolof speakers in each period. In cases where past events have had direct bearing on contemporary linguistic dynamics, I discuss the contemporary situation, breaking with any strict chronological sequence. In Section 7.2, I discuss the precolonial period from the founding of the first Wolof kingdom in the thirteenth century up to early European contact in the fifteenth century, a period during which Wolof

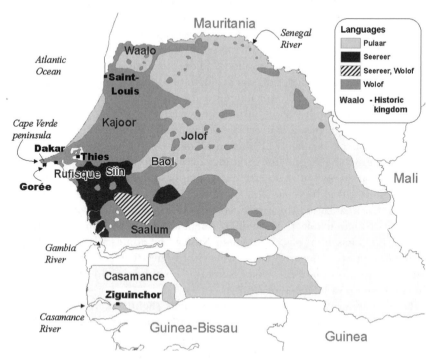

MAP 7.1   Map of the northern Senegalese languages.

became the lingua franca of Northern Senegal. In Section 7.3 I focus on the period of European contact from the founding of the earliest trading posts on the Atlantic coast up to Senegalese independence in 1960. Senegal's first cities were established during this period and Wolof became an urban language. In Section 7.4 I discuss Wolofization and its social and linguistic consequences. In Section 7.5 I examine the situation of other Senegalese languages vis-à-vis the further expansion of Wolof in the postcolonial period from independence to the present, and in Section 7.6 I look at the impact of globalization on Senegal's languages.

7.2 The Foundations of Wolofization in the Precolonial Period

Senegal is a predominantly Sahelian country located just south of the Sahara desert on the Atlantic littoral, whose history and patterns of human settlement have been radically affected by both ecological factors and human agency. The major populations of Senegal north of Gambia include the Wolof, the Seereer and the Haalpulaar, all of whose histories point to previous occupation of the Senegal River valley, somewhat north of where the Wolof and Seereer home-lands are now located, and where the Haalpulaar still live. Other northern populations include the smaller groups of speakers of five Cangin languages (Noon, Ndut, Palor, Saafen and Lehar) who also call themselves Seereer, as well as the Lebu, a Wolof-speaking people who settled on the Cape Verde peninsula in the area that now comprises greater Dakar. Although they call their language Lebu, it is essentially a dialect of Wolof. To the east of these areas are populations of Mande speakers including Soose (Maninka) and Saraxole (Soninke) speakers. The early history of these peoples and the interaction between them sheds light on how Wolof came to be the lingua franca of the area in precolonial times.

7.2.1 The early history of the Wolof

The ancestors of the Wolof people originated in the northeast of the middle Senegal River valley. Before their migration southwards, they must have come within the sphere of influence of the Ghana Empire (750–1076 AD), especially under its Soninke rulers. The Wolof, as well as the Haalpulaar and the Seereer, have a hierarchical social structure (Diop 1981) comprised of (a) various noble classes, *géer* in Wolof; (b) endogamous artisanal castes such as blacksmiths, musicians, leatherworkers and griots who are verbal artists and genealogists, *ñeeño* in Wolof; and (c), at least in the past, slaves, *jaam* in Wolof. Some version of this hierarchical system is shared by several other ethnic groups of the Western Sahel, many of which are ethnically unrelated to the Wolof. Although its origins are not entirely clear, it appears to have emerged close to the beginning of the second millennium (Tamari 1997:18), suggesting an early origin, possibly under the influence of the Ghana Empire.

Migrations of populations out of the Senegal River valley were precipitated by the emergence of the state of Takrur in the tenth century, and by important ecological transformations. Both the Sahara Desert and the Western Sahel were once much greener and biologically diverse than they are now, but desertification and the changing natural landscape put pressure on populations to migrate southwards, and myths of origin among the peoples of Northern Senegal often trace the consolidation of their societies to these migrations (Searing 1993: 2–3). The mythical founder of Jolof, the first Wolof Empire (1200–1550), was Njaajaan Njaay, born purportedly of a Berber father and a Haalpulaar or Tukuloor[3] woman, whose first words to those who were to become the Wolof people were uttered in Pulaar (Fula).[4] In conjunction with the myth of Njaajaan Njaay, it is worth noting that today, many expressions associated with what is known as 'deep Wolof', a conservative and erudite form of the language typical of griots' speech, are actually Pulaar in origin, corroborating historical evidence of long-standing contact between the two languages and their speakers.

Since their consolidation as a distinct ethnic group, the Wolof have inhabited a harsh ecological zone characterized by little rainfall, sparse vegetation and sandy soil suitable only for a small number of crops such as millet and peanuts. Their social hierarchy was efficient in mobilizing labor for, among other things, the digging of wells, and it also produced military expertise to defend people from attacks originating in the Sahara. In addition to Jolof, three other Wolof kingdoms, Waalo, Kajoor and Baol, came into being and were unified, according to oral tradition, under Njaajaan Njaay. The Wolof kingdoms were centralized, militarily strong and located in a region that was beyond the domain of the tsetse fly, which allowed for widespread use of horses by the military aristocracy (Searing 1993:3). They dominated the region of Northern Senegal westward to the Atlantic and southward to the frontier with the Seereer kingdoms of Siin and Saalum, while the area along the Senegal River was, and still is, occupied by Haalpulaar or Pulaar speakers, namely Fulɓe and Tukuloor people.

7.2.2 The linguistic landscape of Northern Senegal in the precolonial period

Wolof, Seereer, Pulaar and the Cangin languages all belong to the Atlantic branch of Niger-Congo. The Atlantic branch is considered to be a typological grouping rather than a genetic unit by most linguists who work on the languages (Childs 2007) since there is no shared innovation that distinguishes them within the Niger-Congo phylum. Based on linguistic evidence such as the nature of the noun classes and the structure of the verb, however, the northern

Senegal languages are clearly related, although a comparison of their respective lexicons, which show relatively low rates of cognacy overall (Sapir 1971), suggests a considerable time depth for their differentiation.

To the east of the Atlantic-speaking area of Northern Senegal lies the Mande-speaking region. The Mande languages represent an early branching of Niger-Congo and have influenced many of the Atlantic languages via the mixing of Mande and Atlantic-speaking populations. Evidence of cultural exchange between these two groups is abundant throughout the Senegambian area in a multiplicity of practices such as drumming traditions (Charry 2000; Tang 2007) and political institutions, but less so in the linguistic arena.

The northern extreme of the Atlantic-speaking area was abutted by a Berber-speaking area of which the main ethnolinguistic group were the Zenaga whose name is most probably the origin of the word Senegal.[5] Several Wolof words for Muslim religious practices and celebrations, such as *tisbaar* and *tàkkusaan* (both denoting prayer times) and *tabaski* (the major Muslim holiday, *Eid al-Kebir*), are from Zenaga (Kossmann 2007). The fact that the Zenaga did not use the Arabic terms for these observances, in spite of the hegemonic role the Arabic language has played in the spread of Islam, suggests that at the time of these conversions they were not yet Arabized and their knowledge of Islam was still superficial, a hypothesis that is supported by accounts of early conversions in the tenth and eleventh centuries (Robinson 2004:39). Today Zenaga is an endangered language with only a couple of hundred speakers at most, located in the south-west corner of Mauritania near the Senegalese border, and they, like most of the Berber populations of Mauritania, have been Arabized. Their role in bringing Islam to Senegal is highlighted in the Wolof oral tradition by the belief that Njaajaan Njaay's father was allegedly a Berber Muslim.

The linguistic landscape of Northern Senegal in the precolonial period after the migrations of populations from the Senegal River valley and at a point where Wolof emerges as a regional lingua franca was thus as follows: the Atlantic-speaking area was bounded on the east and south by Mande-speaking peoples and to the north by Berber-speaking peoples. Within the Atlantic-speaking area, Pulaar speakers settled the northern inland area all along the Senegal River towards the east while their pastoralist counterparts moved around a greater area to the south. The central area was settled primarily by Wolof speakers in the kingdoms of Waalo, Kajoor and Baol, which extended to the Atlantic coast, and Jolof, which was further inland. Dotted among this area were smaller enclaves of Seereer and Cangin speakers, the latter concentrated in hilly areas around Thiès and towards the Atlantic, and to the south were the Seereer kingdoms of Siin and Saalum, where fair numbers of Wolof also lived. The Lebu inhabited the westernmost point of the continent, having migrated all the way to the coast, and associate their myths of origin and identity as an ethnic group distinct from the Wolof with their encounter with the sea (Searing 1993:2).

7.2.3 The emergence of Wolof as a lingua franca

Two major factors led to the emergence of Wolof as a lingua franca in Northrn Senegal during the precolonial period. The first of these is the fact that the Wolof occupied an extensive area at the center, rather than the periphery, of the ethnolinguistic territory of Northern Senegal described in Section 7.2.2; and second, they wielded considerable military power and dominated the region politically. Although it is difficult to know exactly when Wolof emerged as a lingua franca in this area, it may have been as early as the thirteenth or fourteenth century and certainly no later than the sixteenth (Klein 1968). While the Haalpulaar occupied the area to the north of the Wolof kingdoms and the Seereer for the most part occupied the kingdoms of Siin and Saalum to the south of the Wolof kingdoms, several small communities of Seereer lived within Wolof territory. Looking at what has happened to those communities today, we see two distinct linguistic outcomes, both of which are the result of Wolof dominance. The first can be seen in villages where the minority Cangin languages are spoken. Here, people retain a strong ethnic identity, and are bilingual in their own vernaculars, which they use at home and for communication in the village, and Wolof, which they use as a lingua franca, in communications outside the village and with speakers of other Cangin languages. Children up to school age are monolingual in the Cangin languages in a great number of these villages, a robust sign of linguistic vitality, and it is only recently that their languages have started to be affected by contact with Wolof, as will be shown in Section 7.5.3. Myths of the origins of the Cangin-speaking peoples are about seeking refuge, ostensibly from being enslaved, and the areas they inhabit are hilly and remote and used to be heavily forested (Searing 1993:2).

A different picture appears to emerge in the non-Cangin-speaking, Seereer villages. Note, incidentally, that their linguistic situation as described here is based on anecdotes rather than on scientific linguistic evidence. Almost no studies have been carried out in these locales. Although people from the relevant villages identify themselves ethnically as Seereer, their language has been mixed with Wolof for so long that they cannot understand speakers of Seereer-Siin. What exactly this means in linguistic terms needs investigating, but the anecdotal evidence suggests a much less closed society than those of Cangin speakers, and one that interacted freely, and often intermarried, with Wolof speakers in the region.

With regard to Pulaar, spoken to the north of the Wolof-speaking region, there are many lexical items in both languages that come from the other, although expressions associated with 'deep' forms of language, as mentioned earlier, come from Pulaar into Wolof and not the other way around, suggesting a position of cultural superiority for the Haalpulaar. Seereer-Siin, too, spoken to the south of the Wolof-speaking area, has borrowed a great number of lexical items from Wolof, but Wolof has borrowed little from Seereer.

7.2.4 A note on Arabic

As the language of Islam, Arabic occupies an important place in Senegal, whose population is over 90 per cent Muslim. Although the Zenaga Berbers may have been responsible for early conversions to the religion among Atlantic speakers, it was not until much later, well into the colonial period, that the majority of the Wolof population converted. The history of the Islamization of Senegal is one of neighboring peoples converting each other (Robinson 2004). Subsequent to initial conversions by the Zenaga and later the Almoravids, the Haalpulaar (Tukuloor) population of the Senegal River valley converted to Islam and they in turn converted their southern neighbors. An Islamic theocracy was to emerge in the Senegal River valley in the eighteenth century and many West African jihadist movements originated there. The Tukuloor continued to proselytize among the Seerer in Siin and Saalum up until the 1960s.

As a consequence of the adoption of Islam, many Arabic words and expressions have been borrowed into Senegalese languages. Many of these involve religious terms, but also words in other domains such as greetings, time units, including days of the week, and legal terms. Although most Senegalese Muslims go to Qur'anic school and learn how to write and recite verses from the Qur'an, very few actually master the language. However, those who have not attended state schools and do not know any French often use the Arabic script to write their own language. This form of *ajami* writing for Wolof is known as *wolofal*.

7.3 European Contact with Wolof

With the advent of European maritime exploration along the West African coast, Wolof speakers came in contact first, although sporadically, with the Portuguese and the Dutch, and eventually with the French and the English. The most significant European contact was with the French, beginning in the early 1600s and lasting until independence in 1960 and beyond.

7.3.1 From *comptoir* to city

In 1638, the French staked a claim on the West African coast by establishing a *comptoir* 'commercial outpost' on Bocos Island near the mouth of the Senegal River. The outpost was moved to the larger uninhabited island of Ndar in the Senegal River in 1659. The French renamed the island Saint-Louis after King Louis IX of France, and built a fort there. By 1678 they had also established an outpost on the island of Gorée, just off the Cape Verde peninsula where Dakar is located today. The establishment of these two *comptoirs* on the Northern Senegalese coast marked the beginning of a significant shift in trade away from the trans-Saharan routes in the interior westward towards the Atlantic; and the Wolof became the primary trading partners of the French on both islands.

By the middle of the eighteenth century a group of influential slaveholding Wolof women known as *signares,* from the Portuguese *senhora* 'lady', started to settle on the island and engaged in business with the French. The *signares* formed mutually beneficial alliances with French traders and sailors and often entered into both business arrangements and personal relationships with them. Starting with these unions, a complex Afro-European *métis* society emerged on the islands. Although many of them spoke French, their main language was Wolof (Searing 2005).

As the French became more interested in the exploitation of resources towards the interior of the territory, they used Saint-Louis as a base for expeditions up the Senegal River. The towns of Saint-Louis and Gorée, and a third, Rufisque, grew and prospered as the result of Atlantic commerce, including trade in human cargo. Located on the southern part of the Cape Verde peninsula, Rufisque had long served as a stopping point for boats, because of its fresh water source. The societies that emerged in what could now, in the late eighteenth and early nineteenth centuries, be considered cities were cosmopolitan. They included a general Wolof population, people of other Senegalese ethnicities who had been attracted to opportunities in the coastal cities, French and other Europeans, and a small but politically and commercially influential population of *métis*. Wolof was the dominant language of these societies, and no French-lexified creole developed in these first cities along the Senegalese coast. As European trade interests expanded and their boats ventured up the Senegal River, *laptots* 'interpreters' became essential to the smooth functioning of such ventures. Most of the *laptots* would have been Wolof speakers and it is probable that they further encouraged the use of Wolof as a lingua franca along the river. Wolof was also used on boats and in ports further down the West African coast, and up into Mauritania, which was at that point also under French control and was a major supplier of gum arabic.

In a preface to a vocabulary list he authored in 1864, Louis Faidherbe, the governor general of French West Africa, comments on the geographical extent of Wolof as a lingua franca:

> The Wolof language is spoken in Saint-Louis, in Gorée, in Saint-Mary of Gambia, in the Waalo, in Kajoor, in Jolof. It is understood by half the inhabitants of Baol, Siin, and Saalum. It is the commercial language of all Senegal; half of the Trarza [a Mauritanian group] speak it. It is also known along the African coast to Sierra Leone. (Faidherbe 1864:4; my translation)

In the same document Faidherbe also points to the emergence of an urban variety of Wolof spoken in Saint-Louis, marked by French borrowings:

> Many objects introduced by us [the French] in the country are designated, in Wolof, by the mangled French name, and naturally have no name in the languages of the interior. (Faidherbe 1864:3; my translation)

It is the Wolof of Saint-Louis that we present here; it is not the purest, but it is the one that is most useful to know. (Faidherbe 1864:4; my translation)

These observations on the nature of urban Wolof are extremely pertinent today, since the defining characteristic of the urban dialect, and the one that distinguishes it from its rural counterparts in contemporary Senegal, is the significant number of lexical borrowings from French.

7.3.2 The peanut trade and the new city of Dakar

The tip of the Cape Verde peninsula where Dakar is located was until the second half of the nineteenth century sparsely populated and consisted of small villages inhabited by Wolof-speaking Lebu fishermen. The urban centers of Senegal were Saint-Louis and Gorée, where Wolof was the lingua franca, but at times, when epidemics broke out on Gorée, the European population moved temporarily to the mainland. As the scale of French operations increased, the island of Gorée became an increasingly inconvenient site, not least because there was no fresh water source on the island and water and other provisions had to be brought in by ship from elsewhere. Saint-Louis' location in the Senegal River had served it well as a protection, but it too was inconvenient as a port because ships had to make their way several miles up from the mouth of the Senegal River before they could dock. Dakar was thus founded as a naval and maritime post by French decree in 1857, because of its proximity to Gorée and its potential as a harbor for seafaring ships.

By the middle of the nineteenth century France was fully engaged in the exploitation of the peasantry and extraction of resources from the Senegalese interior. These came in the form of peanuts, which were highly valued for their oil, used in France to make soap. Largely in order to transport peanuts to the coast, the French built a railway system. This was begun in 1880 and the first route went from Saint-Louis along the coast to the new city of Dakar. At the beginning of the twentieth century the railway was expanded into the interior as part of the Dakar–Niger railroad project, but was only built as far as Bamako in present day Mali. The headquarters of railroad construction was the town of Thiès, to the east of Dakar. Thiès, and other towns on the railway lines, such as Diourbel and Tivaouane to the north and Kaolack to the south, prospered and grew as commercial centers during the height of the peanut trade. These towns were in predominantly Wolof-speaking areas. So, when non-Wolof speakers migrated there either as laborers or to participate in other commercial activities, they also had to learn Wolof.

Dakar was founded as a European post with only a small number of African inhabitants, but when peanut exportation from Rufisque was halted, after the railroad connecting Dakar to the interior had been built, this town rapidly developed into a city. From the end of the nineteenth to the middle of the twentieth centuries the new city grew rapidly, while the French built a substantial urban infrastructure of buildings, roads and public works. Consequently, Dakar became a pole of economic attraction and brought in a labor force from all over West Africa. The multiethnic, and hence multilingual, nature of Dakar was remarked on by researchers already in mid-century. Despite a certain amount of initial ethnic segregation, there was progressive mixing, especially in the Medina, the African quarter that had been laid out in 1914 by the French, largely as a response to outbreaks of bubonic plague in the misguided belief that separating African from European populations would protect the latter. In a 1954 study, conducted only six years before independence, forty-three African ethnic groups were documented in Dakar, with 60 per cent of the African population of the city belonging to the three largest ethnic groups: Wolof, Haalpulaar and Seereer. Of those interviewed, only 22 per cent had been born in Dakar (Mercier 1954). Within this multilingual setting, an urban variety of Wolof became well established as a lingua franca and urban vernacular.

7.4 Wolofization and Its Consequences in the Urban Environment

The history of Senegal since independence has been one of increasing urbanization, which has in turn contributed to increasing Wolofization. With the rise of Dakar as the capital city, Saint-Louis and Gorée declined in status. Dakar became the main economic pole, attracting people, both professionals and unskilled laborers, from other cities and from rural areas. As the dominant language of this multilingual city, Wolof became a useful lingua franca for speakers of other languages to acquire. Cissé (2005) claims that 96 per cent of the Dakar population speaks Wolof, so it is important to understand what happens to other languages in the Dakar context.

There are certain neighborhoods in Dakar and its sprawling suburbs where people from specific ethno-linguistic groups tend to group and settle, but they are never entirely homogeneous. These ethnic neighborhoods may help speakers maintain languages other than Wolof, but because the spheres of their social interactions expand beyond the individual neighborhood, speakers use Wolof as much as, if not more than, the home or neighborhood vernacular. These neighborhoods are also characterized by high rates of code-switching and code-mixing between their native languages and Wolof (Dreyfus and Juillard 2005). Thus, Wolof features are spreading into the neighborhood languages, as illustrated in Section 7.6.2 with Pulaar.

In addition to speaking a language other than Wolof within a specific ethno-linguistic neighborhood, some speakers maintain their native language through extensive social networks. In general, these are people who have recently moved to Dakar from an environment where their native language dominated locally, and it is doubtful whether their children will eventually maintain that language.

Despite these enclaves, languages other than Wolof are threatened in urban areas because urbanization almost always results in generational language shift. Surveys carried out in the mid-1960s among primary school children show that in Senegalese households where one parent speaks Wolof as a native language and the other a different language, the language of the household is almost always Wolof (Wioland 1965; Wioland and Calvet 1967). Consequently those children grow up with very little knowledge of the language of the non-Wolof parent. Today, primarily in urban areas, it is also common to find the parents speaking a language other than Wolof to each other, but using Wolof with their children. A case in point involves a prominent Seereer family that lives in Dakar. The parents, who are first in their respective families to move to Dakar, speak Seereer to each other and the now grown children speak Wolof among themselves. Intergenerational conversations are sometimes bilingual, where the parents speak Seereer to the children and the children answer in Wolof, but more often they are completely in Wolof. In one generation in an urban context, the family has gone from having Seereer as L1 and Wolof as L2 to being Wolof-dominant and only passively bilingual in Seereer. It is not surprising that the new generation of grandchildren in the same family do not even understand Seereer at this point. Urbanization can thus be seen as the greatest threat to languages other than Wolof in Senegal because it motivates language shift to Wolof.[6]

7.4.1 Wolofization and ethnicity

The consequences of Wolofization are not just linguistic. The process has also had a profound effect on the notion of 'ethnicity' in Senegal, contributing to the emergence of a de-ethnicized (Mc Laughlin 2001; Ngom 2004) or post-ethnic (Eisenlohr 2007) identity, according to which people no longer identify with a specific ethnic group. The fluidity of ethnic identity is revealed in the words of a Pulaar-speaking elementary school teacher who reported, 'When I'm at home I'm Haalpulaar, when I'm in Dakar I'm Wolof' (Mc Laughlin 1995:156), an utterance that suggests a new, urban identity rather than a switch in ethnicity. Tellingly, a worker for the 1988 Senegalese census reported that the category of ethnicity was problematic in the context of Dakar because when questioned, people frequently hesitated and told him to mark Wolof because that was the only language they spoke (Swigart 1990:4). The conflation of ethnicity and language in this context suggests the emergence of a new, urban identity that often goes by the cover name of Wolof (Mc Laughlin 2001). More recently, however, even this term is being abandoned as a small group of urban dwellers reject any ethnolinguistic term and simply say they are from Dakar. In 2000, for example, a professor at the Université Gaston Berger in Saint-Louis asked another with a decidedly Seereer name whether he was Seereer, to which the latter replied 'No, I'm from Dakar'. The first professor then commented 'That's the new ethnicity now in Senegal, to be from Dakar!' And a 2000 newspaper article on a group of young urban artists based in Dakar reported on one of them, 'Il peint la nouvelle ethnie sénégalaise, l'ethnie urbaine qui vit dans les cars' ('He paints the new Senegalese ethnic group, the urban ethnic group that lives on the buses'). Although certain individuals have started to abandon the ethnic term *Wolof* to describe themselves, the emergence of an *ethnie urbaine* in Senegal is directly related to the dominance of Wolof as an urban vernacular. Urban vernaculars can, then, have a profound effect on core notions of identity, and thus have the potential to fundamentally change urban societies (Mc Laughlin 2001).

7.4.2 Attitudes towards urban Wolof

As noted earlier, urban Wolof has borrowed extensively from French. Attitudes towards it, revealed in frequent metalinguistic commentary on the topic, are complex and often contradictory. A frequent criticism is that urban Wolof is a corrupt form of Wolof, that Wolof speakers have lost their roots in the city, have forgotten how to speak their ancestral language correctly and have to substitute French words because they do not know the right Wolof word. These criticisms are often levelled at urban Wolof by speakers of other Senegalese languages, but it is equally true that urban varieties of many other languages such as Pulaar and Seereer have also borrowed from French. The negative attitudes towards urban Wolof can also be read as a critique of the difficulties of urban life in general, which is contrasted with a romantic view of a more authentic, purer culture. Urban dwellers often joke that they are *gàlli*, a word meaning deracinated, inauthentic and cut off from one's culture and language, which is perceived as an inevitable consequence of moving to the city. People express admiration for what is known as *olof piir* 'pure Wolof', meaning a Wolof free of French borrowings, which is almost non-existent in Dakar and other urban areas. At the same time, knowing how to speak in the city is extremely important to avoid appearing rustic, and speaking urban Wolof in Dakar constitutes an essential part of what Mbembe (1997:153) terms 'urban knowledge' (Mc Laughlin 2001:156). (See also Bokamba, this volume, about urban Lingala in the Democratic Republic of Congo.)

Urban Wolof carries a covert prestige despite the overtly negative attitudes towards it. Interestingly, it is the younger generation that has the most negative attitudes towards it, while those who are older are generally much more tolerant. This unexpected discrepancy can be attributed to the history of Wolof as an urban language in Saint-Louis and Gorée, where the French borrowings were considered as characteristic of an urbane variety, an attitude that still exists among older speakers. These attitudes towards urban Wolof, while complex and even contradictory, merely reflect ambivalent attitudes towards urban life in general.

7.5 Wolof and Other Senegalese Languages

Despite the dominance of Wolof in the Senegalese linguistic landscape, Senegal remains a highly multilingual society in which many people who use Wolof on a daily basis speak other languages at home. As evidence of Wolof's hegemony, however, native Wolof speakers rarely speak another of Senegal's indigenous languages since there is little need to do so. At the village level and in rural areas, there are certain ecological factors that contribute to continued language vitality in the face of Wolofization. The most salient factor is the fact that Wolof does not compete as a home or village vernacular in these areas, but rather as a lingua franca. Similar niches are to be found in ethno-linguistic neighborhoods in Dakar, but this environment is unstable because the neighborhoods are never completely homogeneous and are susceptible to constant change in their ethno-linguistic makeup.

In urban areas, reactions to the dominance of Wolof are also varied. There is plenty of ideological resistance among speakers of other Senegalese languages, which can translate into practices of resistance when circumstances justify it. However, just how efficacious these practices are in protecting languages is debatable. This section provides a small set of case studies that examine the ways in which Wolof has affected various speech communities.

7.5.1 Wolof and speakers of Pulaar

Among the linguistic groups that are most vigilant against Wolof hegemony are the Haalpulaar or speakers of Pulaar. As noted earlier, they go by several different ethnic names in Senegal, including Fulɓe (sg. Pullo), Tukuloor and Haalpulaar, the main group. Because the Fulɓe were originally a pastoralist, cattle-herding people, Fula is a widely dispersed language spoken from Mauritania, Senegal and Guinea in the west to Nigeria, Cameroon and Chad in the east, forming what Boutrais (1994) has called the 'Fula archipelago', with a population that some estimate at twelve million. Even though it is a major language in West Africa overall, Fula remains a minority language in every one of the relevant countries except Guinea. It is thus particularly vulnerable to the effects of urban vernaculars or of national or regional lingua francas such as Wolof, Bambara and Hausa. Senegalese Pulaar speakers constitute about 23 per cent of the population, making them the largest minority language group in the country. However, their sense of belonging to a wider international community of Fula speakers and their strong sense of the role of language as a central marker of ethnic identity have led them to be quite vigilant in maintaining and transmitting their own language and keeping at bay the encroachment of Wolof in their communities. Within urban areas such as Dakar and Saint-Louis, there are Pulaar-speaking neighborhoods, and it is only here that Wolof and Pulaar compete for dominance. Outside urban areas, and especially in the Pulaar-speaking region of the Senegal River valley, Wolof is an additive rather than a replacive language. In 1989, as a consequence of tensions between Senegal and Mauritania, the Hassaniyya Arabic-speaking Moors, who had been small shopkeepers in villages all over the country, were expatriated to Mauritania. Along the main road in the Pulaar-speaking areas of Northern Senegal, many Wolof shopkeepers moved in to replace them, bringing Wolof with them to villages where it had been spoken only by a very few people before. Although this by no means puts Pulaar at risk in these locales, the Haalpulaar view it nonetheless as a potential threat to their language. As a footnote to the events of 1989, Blench (2007:141) reports that they resulted in the permanent departure of the Moorish ethno-linguistic group, but in fact many Moors have returned to Senegal; and Hassaniyya now has the official status of national language in Senegal.

Attempts among Haalpulaar intellectuals to counter the cultural and linguistic hegemony of Wolof have taken a variety of shapes. One of these is the emergence of Kawral, a Haalpulaar movement originally founded as a support organization at the Université Gaston Berger in Saint-Louis, in the early 1990s, for Pulaar-speaking students from Fouta Toro who did not have scholarships. In addition to undertaking activities such as collecting extra meal tickets for students who needed them, they organized cultural activities and invited Pulaar-speaking activists to the campus. Kawral has since evolved into a much more militant Haalpulaar movement with a strong emphasis on speaking Pulaar and not Wolof.[7] There is also a popular Pulaar-speaking radio personality nick-named Murtuɗo 'the passionate one' whose radical pro-Pulaar and anti-Wolof views have attracted some criticism from more moderate Pulaar speakers, one of whom dubbed him an *intégriste de la langue Pulaar* ('Pulaar fundamentalist'). On a visit to France in 2006, President Abdoulaye Wade was strongly criticized by Pulaar speakers living there for addressing a group of Senegalese émigrés in Wolof rather than French, the official language. What these efforts and reactions show is a great reluctance on the part of Pulaar speakers to recognize Wolof, even informally, as a national-cum-nationwide language.

There is a long tradition of out-migration of labor from Senegal's Pulaar-speaking heartland, the Fouta Toro, towards Europe and more recently the United States. These communities of expatriate Pulaar speakers have started overseas branches of the Pulaar-speaking organizations that function as burial societies but also have additional cultural functions. They bring speakers such as Murtuɗo from Senegal to instill in members the importance of the Pulaar language, and they also teach literacy in Pulaar and sell Pulaar books.

Pulaar speakers' attitudes towards Wolof are varied, but in general they consider it an inferior language to Pulaar, an attitude that stems partly from the hybrid nature of urban Wolof. They also consider the Wolof to be linguistic imperialists and frequently point out that while they have to learn Wolof, Wolof speakers generally do not speak another Senegalese language. But the reality of the situation is that these attitudes, no matter how militant, rarely stop Pulaar speakers from learning Wolof when it is to their advantage.

7.5.2 Wolof in Casamance

Casamance, the more tropical region of Senegal, between Gambia and Guinea Bissau, has been a challenge to national integration since independence, and harbors fairly widespread popular resentment against the domination of the north. This is due in part to cultural differences between northern and southern Senegal. Societies in the north have a typically Sahelian, highly stratified social structure that is not shared by their compatriots in the south. Casamançais groups such as the Joola and Bainunk share many more cultural traits with their neighbors in Guinea-Bissau than they do with Northern Senegalese. Additionally, the population of Lower Casamance, the westernmost area abutting the Atlantic, is more heavily Catholic than the rest of the predominantly Muslim country, and until fairly recently, Portuguese Creole served as the lingua franca of Ziguinchor, the regional capital. These factors, in tandem with a sense of neglect by the centralized state whose capital, Dakar, is located in the north, have contributed to the formation of a regional separatist movement founded in the early 1980s, spawning periodic bouts of violence that escalated into war in the 1980s and 1990s. These problems between Casamance and the rest of the country, however, have rarely been cast in terms of ethnic differences.

Casamance is the most linguistically diverse region of Senegal and has the highest rates of individual multilingualism. Mirroring their discontent with the north, the Casamançais are quite vocal in their resistance to Wolof and Wolofization and, especially among more educated urban populations; they prefer to use French as a lingua franca rather than Wolof. This is not true anywhere else in the country. The Joola people, who comprise between 5 and 6 per cent of the Senegalese population, are speakers of a cluster of languages and dialects of varying degrees of mutual intelligibility. Joola Foñi or Kujamaat Joola serves as the lingua franca among Joola speakers.[8] In other areas of Casamance, Maninka is used as a lingua franca as well. Among speakers of Badiaranke, an endangered language, language shift is occurring in the direction of Pulaar and Maninka, and Wolof plays little or no role in its endangerment (Rebecca Cover, personal communication, 24 October 2007). Wolof is only an urban lingua franca in Casamance. Although it has recently displaced Portuguese Creole as the lingua franca of the city of Ziguinchor, it is having little effect on the vitality of other languages spoken in the villages of the region.

At this point, it seems fairly certain that Wolof will continue to make inroads in smaller urban areas in Casamance, but because of the high incidence of multilingualism and the existence of other more local lingua francas, it is not certain that language shift and the abandonment of minority languages will actually occur in the foreseeable future. Only Portuguese Creole seems at this point to be in danger of being replaced in its functions by Wolof.

7.5.3 Wolof and Seereer

As noted in Section 7.2, the Seereer, including speakers of Seereer-Siin and the Cangin languages, have been the closest neighbors of the Wolof for centuries and have long spoken Wolof. Unlike the Haalpulaar who consider their language to be a central element in ethnic identity, Seereer speakers do not hold the same, often militant, prejudices against Wolof, although they are generally proud of their various languages (Drolc 2007). Possibly because they have been bilingual in various Seereer languages and Wolof for many centuries, compounded by the fact that they do not form a coherent linguistic group, the Seereer's concept of ethnic identity is not as centrally linked to language as it is for the Haalpulaar. Census figures for 1988 show that there are more people who consider themselves ethnically Seereer than there are Seereer speakers, thus one can ostensibly be Seereer without speaking a Seereer language.

Notwithstanding the high rates of bilingualism in Seereer and Wolof, the Seereer languages in rural communities appear to be quite healthy. In 2000, in the small village of Bandia, for example, most of the children under seven years of age spoke only Saafen, while anyone older was also able to speak Wolof. The fact that children are learning Saafen as their first language and are using it exclusively until school-age suggests that the language is healthy, although, as we shall see in Section 7.6.3, the Cangin languages are often quite heavily Wolofized. Drolc (2007:4) describes a similar situation for Lehar (a.k.a. KiLaala)-speaking villages, adding that they are endogamous and that intermarriage among second cousins is common. These kinds of ethnically and linguistically homogeneous villages are, in a sense, ideal environments for the maintenance and vitality of minority languages. However, as Drolc (2007:14) intimates, if more and more people are forced to leave their villages for economic reasons and migrate to cities, conditions could change quite rapidly for both the villages and for the languages involved, especially since adult speakers are already bilingual. (See also Mufwene [2004, 2008] for a more general discussion about Africa.)

7.5.4 Urban Wolof and rural Wolof

As noted earlier, a major characteristic of urban Wolof is its extensive borrowings from French, a feature that applies much less to rural varieties. As Wolof gains speakers in urban areas it is the urban variety of Wolof that expands as a vernacular and lingua franca. What this means is that speakers of rural Wolof who move to Dakar often engage in dialect shift, which causes this variety to lose speakers in urban areas. The urban/rural distinction is thus a very important one, since the two varieties have different domains of use: rural Wolof is used only as a vernacular and at a village level, while urban Wolof also functions as a nationwide lingua franca, despite the existence of some regional pockets where it is not much in currency. Although no in-depth studies have been conducted on this phenomenon, many Wolof speakers from rural areas have mentioned to me that they switch dialects between village and city in order to fit in. The switch generally involves an increased use of the default noun class and of French borrowings.

Patterns of language alternation in various communicative settings need more investigation, since they probably have a bearing on the vitality of Seereer and other minority languages. Urban Wolof speakers often joke that the Seereer speak better Wolof than they do, meaning that they speak the rural dialect. This evokes the earlier wave of Wolofization, when (rural) Wolof emerged as a lingua franca in the precolonial period, a point at which Seereer-speaking communities within Wolof territory became bilingual. An important question that arises, then, is whether it is only urban Wolof that has the potential to trigger language shift in Seereer villages, or is it both varieties? I suspect the former but thus far have little evidence on which to base such a claim. A second question is whether urban Wolof has the potential to trigger large-scale dialect shift. If this were to be the case it would mark a turning point in the history of Wolof since it would become a contact language.

7.5.5 Wolof and French

At independence, in 1960, Léopold Sédar Senghor, poet and philosopher, became president of Senegal. He was subsequently elected to the *Académie Française*, the watchdog institution of the French language, as its first Black member. His immediate successor to the Senegalese presidency, Abdou Diouf, is the current secretary general of the *Organisation Internationale de la Francophonie*. Although we would not necessarily expect French to become widely spoken as a vernacular, it is not unjustified to expect it to be more widely spoken among the elite than it is, given this close relationship of Senegal's political elite to the French language. However, spoken French is no longer used as much among the elite in Senegal as it is in other Francophone African countries; Wolof, spoken by almost all the elite, continues to encroach on domains once reserved for French. This is in spite of the fact that the state educational system is entirely in French and knowledge of French is increasing among the general population. French speakers still prefer to speak Wolof.

Liberalization of the media, a process that was already underway during Abdou Diouf's presidency, has played a significant role in eroding certain bastions of French usage. Although French is still the language of written media such as newspapers, the proliferation of private radio stations in particular has contributed to its erosion as the main language of non-print media. The stations broadcast programs of broad popular interest, including call-in programs on controversial topics such the popular *Wax sa xalaat* 'Speak your mind'.[9]

Upon his election in 2000, President Abdoulaye Wade adopted a pro-Wolof stance by issuing statements to the press and making public addresses in both Wolof and French, a practice that other officials soon adopted. Today it is not uncommon to hear a television or radio interview with a government official conducted in Wolof, a situation that ten years ago would have been almost unthinkable. Given these changes, Wolof has now become just as much a norm in radio broadcasting as French. Programming in other indigenous languages is still quite limited, especially on the national scene, but there are nonetheless weekly programs in Pulaar, Seereer and a few other languages.

7.6 Language Contact in Senegal

Thus far, this chapter has dealt with the sociohistorical factors that have contributed to the ascent of Wolof and with the reasons why it has nonetheless not displaced many minority languages that the dominant literature on language endangerment would lead us to consider as threatened or being at risk. In order to more fully understand the consequences of Wolofization for other languages, I turn now to some of the concrete details of language contact in Senegal to show how they are shaping language practice. The three examples I have chosen are: (i) the relationship between French and Wolof in urban settings; (ii) the diffusion of Wolof structural features into Pulaar; and (iii) lexical borrowing and code-mixing between Lehar and Wolof.

7.6.1 French and Wolof in urban settings

The situation that exists in Dakar between French as the official language and Wolof as the urban vernacular opens up a vast space of language contact that has resulted in a variety of contact phenomena. These include an indigenized variety of French (subsumed in the category of *français africains* in Francophone linguistics) that exhibits phonological, morphological, syntactic and prosodic features from Wolof as well as lexical innovations that combine Wolof and French morphemes. Also noteworthy are code-mixing and code-switching between Wolof and French among the more educated classes. But the most significant and widespread phenomenon is the extensive borrowings from French that make urban Wolof so distinctive and are the focus of this section.

Depending on their knowledge of French, urban Wolof speakers may or may not be aware of the specific French borrowings in their language. Although this is not the venue for undertaking a thorough discussion of this contact phenomenon, the example in (1), part of a personal narrative by a man in his early forties, gives some idea of the nature of urban Wolof. French borrowings are in italics.[10]

(1) *En faite*, dégg naa ko daal, Yàlla mey na ba dégg naa ko, *mais* musuma dugg *école*. Def naa *école arabe mais* defuma *école français, non. Mais* sama *papa aussi*, Yàlla meyoon na ko loolu, *parce que* moom *commerçant* la woon, *en même temps* dafa nekkoon, mujóon nekk *peseur* ci *coopératif quoi*, kon bi ñu *récolter* gerte bi *bon* ñoo koy jënd ci . . . ñuy jëndal *gouvernement* bi *quoi*, mu jëndal . . . nekk *peseur, quoi.*

Translation:

Well, I do understand it (French), God gave me the ability to understand it, *but* I've never gone to *school*. I went to *Arabic school but* I didn't go to *French school, no. But* my *father too*, God gave that to him too, *because* he was a *businessman, at the same time* he was, he ended up being a *weigher* in a *cooperative you see*, so when they *harvested* peanuts, *well* they would buy them . . . they would buy them for the *government you see*, he bought . . . was a *weigher, you see.*

Borrowing is frequently the first step in opening the door to other, structural changes in a language. Although urban Wolof has typically been described as a variety that has undergone little structural influence from French despite more than three hundred years of contact, there are nonetheless some subtle changes that are taking place. These include changes in the use of verbal extensions and the use of double complementizers.

7.6.2 Structural diffusion in Pulaar

Pulaar and Wolof have borrowed back and forth from one another for quite a long time. In a sense, the prestige of Wolof as a lingua franca was counterbalanced by the prestige of Pulaar as the language of Senegal's first converts to Islam, who in turn converted the Wolof to the religion. Consequently, many Arabic borrowings in Wolof came into the language via Pulaar. As mentioned earlier, many fixed expressions such as praise formulas used by Wolof griots also come from Pulaar although their origins are not always recognized as such by Wolof speakers who consider them to be characteristic of 'deep' Wolof. Other everyday borrowings such as *galle* 'house' are, however, typical of urban speech.

Today there is probably a higher percentage of Pulaar–Wolof bilinguals than at any time in the history of the languages, and almost all urban Pulaar speakers, as well as many others, speak Wolof. Because Wolof is the urban vernacular and Pulaar speakers use the language extensively, they have also borrowed some of Wolof's syntactic structures into their Pulaar. One such example, the NP 'one house', is given in (2), where the cardinal number, which normally follows the noun in Pulaar, precedes it in urban Pulaar, as in Wolof.

(2)	Pulaar	*galle*	*gooto*
		house	one
	Wolof	*benn*	*kër*
		one	house
	Urban Pulaar	*gooto*	*galle*
		one	house

A second example is the loss of the inclusive/exclusive distinction in the first-person plural pronouns in Pulaar, a distinction that does not exist in Wolof. Here, a girl speaking to her father about her school refers to it as *ekol-men* (school-1pl.inclusive.possessive) 'our school', using the inclusive form where the exclusive form should have been used since it is not also her father's school. And finally, a third example consists of the substitution of a third-person plural active voice construction for a passive sentence in Pulaar as in (3), in line with the absence of a true passive in Wolof.

(3)	Pulaar	*ko*	*mi*	*nulaaɗo*	'I am who is sent'
		FOC	1sg.SUBJ	REL.CLAUSE:who is sent	
	Wolof	*dañu ma*		*yónni*	'They sent me'
		3pl.	1sg.OBJ	V:send	
	Urban Pulaar	*ɓe*	*nul*	*kam*	'They sent me'
		3pl.	V:send	1sg.OBJ	

This type of Pulaar merits more research, since it signals the emergence of a more divergent urban dialect via contact with both Wolof and French.

7.6.3 The 'dangers' of bilingualism

The discussion now turns to what is perhaps the most critical aspect of language endangerment as a consequence of Wolofization. This example, taken from Drolc (2007), involves a small minority Cangin language, Lehar (KiLaala), spoken in several small villages near Thiès. There are no reliable figures on how many speakers it has, but estimates range from two to ten thousand. In Section 7.2.3 the small Seereer village was described as an ideal environment for language maintenance, but it was also noted that Seereer speakers who are school-aged or above are universally bilingual in Seereer and Wolof. Such is the case with KiLaala speakers who engage in extensive borrowings and occasional code-switching between the two. There are many French borrowings in KiLaala as well, which may come directly from speakers who have knowledge of French, or by way of urban Wolof. In a recent study, Drolc (2007) provides the data in (4) from KiLaala narratives, uttered by an elderly woman who is commenting on rampant unemployment in Senegal. Wolof words are in boldface, while French words are in italics.[11]

(4)   ɛn-an   ɗ aa ɓi   **matal nɔppɛ** lɛɛx-xa
       be-FUT   like that until finish finish

      ŋgɪr ka-waa? ka-teki? **waaye** *jusqu'à présent* **dara**
      because INF-want INF-be useful but up until now nothing

      waayɛ ɓi ɗɛn fi ɗɛn **dara**
      but up until now nothing
      'Because everybody wants to be useful, but up to now there is nothing, but up to now there is nothing.' (13)

Bilinguals are primary agents of linguistic change, and it is very likely that speakers younger than this woman incorporate even more Wolof into their Lehar. The 'danger' of bilingualism for minority languages, then, is twofold. First, the type of borrowing from a dominant language could become so rampant that much of the lexicon could potentially be replaced. Already, according to Drolc (8), only a few older people remember the Lehar word *cuurun* 'fish' although there is frequent talk of fish, a dietary staple; instead, the Wolof word *jën* has almost completely replaced it. Although pre-school age children may be learning Lehar as a first language without knowing Wolof, the Lehar they learn may be a highly Wolofized form of the language. Second, since their speakers are already fluent in the potential target of language shift, should there be a significant change in the linguistic ecology of the speech community, abandonment of the ancestral language could occur extremely rapidly.

7.7 Language and Globalization in Senegal

We have seen in the previous sections how Wolofization in the colonial and postcolonial periods is primarily an urban phenomenon and that urbanization is the greatest threat to Senegal's minority languages because it results in language shift towards Wolof. But what role, if any, does globalization play in the Senegalese linguistic arena? This is a question that demands, as Ferguson (2006:49) phrases it, 'much more empirical social research' before it can be answered in full, but there are nonetheless some preliminary conclusions that can be reached.

    Returning to the idea of globalization as the increasing interconnectedness and interdependence between communities and cultures on all parts of the planet, two areas of relevance to Wolofization come to mind. The first of these is Senegal's changing economy and the second is migration (see Vigouroux, this volume), both of which are related.

During the early post-independence period, from around 1960 to the1980s, knowledge of French was an extremely important asset for economic advancement in Senegal. It played a gate-keeping role in maintaining the privileges of an educated elite in a process that Myers-Scotton (1993) calls 'elite closure'. The children of the elite, by virtue of their education, social networks and ability to speak French, could look for employment in lucrative sectors that were closed to the non-French speaking masses. Although knowledge of French during this recent period was not a guarantee for social and economic advancement, the door to such opportunities was closed to those who did not master the language.

Although a number of migrant workers had been going to France and other European countries to work as unskilled laborers since the colonial period, an important shift took place in the late 1980s, as many Senegalese started to explore new trade and other business opportunities, first in other African countries such as Gabon and Côte d'Ivoire, and then further afield in Asia, the Middle East and the United States. Many, but not all, of these international traders came originally from the Wolof heartlands of Baol and Kajoor and many were members of the Mouride Sufi order, an indigenous Muslim brotherhood founded by Cheikh Amadou Bamba Mbacke in the 1920s. The migration of many Mourides to the cities has resulted in Dakar's main market, Sandaga Market, being dominated by Mourides. A second wave of migrations, this time out of the country, has resulted in widespread international networks of primarily Mouride traders, with interests from Cape Town to Abu Dhabi and to New York and Atlanta, all of whom send significant remittances back to Senegal.

The opening up of such new opportunities as those that have been exploited by emigrants has offered important alternatives to French-language education as the means for improving one's economic conditions. As Senegalese become more involved in these globalized trade networks, English becomes a much more important and attractive language for them to learn. French is still useful, however, for Senegalese migrants to other parts of Francophone Africa, or to places where they come in frequent contact with other Francophone Africans. In these cases French is still often used as a lingua franca. But it should also be mentioned that Wolof, too, has benefited from its migration into the world because it has become the lingua franca of multilingual Senegalese communities abroad, and some Senegalese have even learned Wolof or substantially improved their Wolof abroad. The linguistic consequences of globalization are thus experienced primarily by Senegalese abroad. Globalization, insofar as it is currently understood for the Senegalese context, has generally not threatened languages in Senegal.

At present, and with the exception of generational language shift in the cities, which is in itself a more complex phenomenon, most speech communities in Senegal have managed to maintain a more or less stable bilingualism or multilingualism. How long this will last is unclear, and will depend primarily on extra-linguistic factors, including, most importantly, the economic well-being of Senegal's citizens.

7.8 Conclusion

The dual questions of language vitality and language endangerment in Africa are much more complex than most studies would imply. Senegal is not unique in this respect, and studies based on the high rates of multilingualism and complex linguistic repertoires encountered continent-wide are contributing to an emerging counter-narrative of language endangerment that does not place English or other colonial languages at the center (Batibo 2005; Brenzinger 2007; Mazrui and Mazrui 1998; Mufwene 2001ff). The effects of globalization, the oft-cited culprit in language endangerment, do not seem to have endangered languages in Africa, but the local dynamics of population movements sometimes have. Although there are certainly groups of languages such as the Khoisan languages of Southern Africa that are quite threatened, the overall picture of language endangerment in Africa is not as dire as Krauss' (1992) predictions would suggest. As linguists and others attempt to understand the dynamics of language vitality, endangerment and death, they have much to learn from the African context.

Notes

I am grateful to the editors, Cécile Vigouroux and Salikoko Mufwene, for challenging me to think about language vitality in Senegal in new ways, and to James Essegbey for our many discussions on language endangerment in West Africa. I would also like to acknowledge the generosity of the late Uschi Drolc in sharing, as she always did, her data and observations on Lehar with me: *Xalam demoon na bay neex buum ga dagg* ('In mid-melody the cord of the xalam has snapped').

[1] The closest language to anything resembling a French creole in West Africa would be a now most likely extinct French Pidgin of Guinea (Chaudenson 2001:15).

[2] *Ethnologue* data are always somewhat problematic and their contributors have a reputation as 'splitters' rather than 'lumpers', so the actual number of languages may well be lower than this, in keeping with other estimates of numbers of Senegalese languages that put their number in the mid- to upper-twenties. For other problems and issues concerning *Ethnologue* data see Blench (2007:141–142).

[3] *Tukuloor* is the name given to the settled Pulaar-speaking people of the Senegal River valley, and is no doubt derived from Takrur. They call themselves *Haalpulaar'en* 'speakers of Pulaar'.

[4] Fula, also known as Pular, Pulaar and Fulfulde, is spoken by various ethnic groups all across West Africa from Mauritania, Senegal and Guinea in the West to Nigeria, Cameroon, Chad and Sudan in the East. Speakers, variously called *Haalpulaar'en*, *Peul* (from Wolof) and *Fulani* (from Hausa), also include smaller groups such as the still semi-nomadic Wodaabe in Niger. They are traditionally cattle-herding pastoralists whose origins are in the Fuuta Tooro region of the Senegal River valley. The direction of their original migrations is thus from west to east. Fula's closest sister language is Seereer.

[5] For a position that disputes this widespread assumption among Africanists see Kandji (2006).

[6] See Mufwene (2004, 2008) for a general discussion of shifts from ethnic languages to urban vernaculars in cities of Black Africa.

[7] Information on Kawral comes from an interview with Abdoulaye Kane, one of its founders, on 7 June 2007.

[8] Joola (often written as Diola) is an Atlantic language, not to be confused with Jula (Dyula), a Mande language that serves as a trade language in parts of West Africa. These two languages are not closely related, and they come from two distinct branches of the Niger–Congo phylum, Atlantic and Mande, respectively.

[9] Readers more curious about this division of labor may also be interested in Chaudenson's arguments, in this volume, for using audiovisual media to nurture the coexistence of French and indigenous languages in Francophone Africa (the editors).

[10] This example, from my fieldwork in Dakar in 2005, could also be described as code-mixing or even unmarked code-switching, but it is not my goal here to classify it as one type of contact phenomenon or another, since it is often hard to define the boundaries between different types of bilingual speech. Besides, the presupposition of language purity that underlies the scholarship on code-switching and code-mixing can easily be questioned (Mufwene 2008, Chapter 6). Taken as a whole, urban Wolof is highly variable, but is always characterized by borrowing from French. In this example, the speaker believes that he is speaking Wolof.

[11] The difference between my transcription of Wolf in (1) and Drolc's in (3) stems from the fact that I have used the official Wolof orthography while she has preferred to use a more broadly phonetic transcription.

References

Batibo, Herman M. 2005. *Language Decline and Death in Africa: Causes, Consequences and Challenges.* Clevedon, UK: Multilingual Matters.

Blench, Roger. 2007. Endangered languages in West Africa. In Matthias Brenzinger (ed.), 140–162.

Boutrais, Jean. 1994. Pour une nouvelle cartographie des Peuls. *Cahiers d'Etudes Africaines* 133–135,137–146.

Brenzinger, Matthias (ed.). 2007. *Language Diversity Endangered.* Berlin: Mouton de Gruyter.

Charry, Eric. 2000. *Mande Music.* Chicago: University of Chicago Press.

Chaudenson, Robert. 2001. *Creolization of Language and Culture.* London: Routledge.

Childs, G. Tucker. 2007. Suprasegmentals in Atlantic. Paper presented at the workshop Atlantic: Genetic or Typological Unity? University of Hamburg, 17–18 February.

Cissé, Mamadou. 2005. Les politiques linguistiques au Sénégal: entre attentisme et interventionnisme. *Kotoba to Shakai* [special issue of *Language and Society* on Post-empire and multilingual societies in Asia and Africa], 266–313.

Crystal, David. 2000. *Language Death.* Cambridge: Cambridge University Press.

Deuber, Dagmar. 2005. *Nigerian Pidgin in Lagos: Language Contact, Variation and Change in an African Urban Setting.* London: Battlebridge.

Diop, Abdoulaye-Bara. 1981. *La société wolof, tradition et changement: les systèmes d'inégalité et de domination.* Paris: Karthala.

Dreyfus, Martine and Caroline Juillard. 2005. *Le plurilinguisme au Sénégal: langues et identités en devenir.* Paris: Karthala.

Drolc, Ursula. 2007. Response to wolofisation: The case of the Seereer-Leexar. Ms. University of Cologne.

Eisenlohr, Patrick. 2007. *Little India: Diaspora, Time, and Ethnolinguistic Belonging in Hindu Mauritius.* Berkeley: University of California Press.

Faidherbe, Louis. 1864. *Vocabulaire d'environ 1.500 mots français avec leurs correspondants en ouolof de Saint-Louis, en poular (toucouleur) du fouta, en soninké (sarakhollé) de Bakel.* Saint-Louis du Sénégal: Imprimerie du Gouvernement.

Ferguson, James. 2006. *Global Shadows: Africa in the Neoliberal World Order.* Durham: Duke University Press.

Giddens, Anthony. 2002. *Runaway World: How Globalization is Reshaping our Lives.* New York: Routledge.

Juillard, Caroline. 1995. *Sociolinguistique urbaine: la vie des langues à Ziguinchor (Sénégal).* Paris: CNRS Editions.

Kandji, Saliou. 2006. *Sénégal n'est pas Sunugaal ou de l'etymologie du toponyme Sénégal.* Dakar: Presses Universitaires de Dakar.

Klein, Martin A. 1968. *Islam and Imperialism in Senegal: Sine-Saloum, 1847–1914.* Stanford: Stanford University Press.

Kossmann, Maarten. 2007. Islamic terminology and the reconstruction of early conversion to Islam. Paper presented at the workshop Atlantic: Genetic or Typological Unity? University of Hamburg, 17–18 February.

Krauss, Michael. 1992. The world's languages in crisis. *Language* 68.4–10.

Mazrui, Ali and Alamin Mazrui. 1998. *The Power of Babel: Language in the African Experience.* Oxford: James Currey; and Chicago: University of Chicago Press.

Mbembe, Achille. 1997. The 'thing' and its doubles in Cameroonian cartoons. In *Readings in African Popular Culture,* ed. by Karin Barber, 151–163. Bloomington, IN: Indiana University Press; and Oxford: James Currey.

Mc Laughlin, Fiona. 1995. Haalpulaar identity as a response to Wolofization. *African Languages and Cultures* 8.153 –168.

— 2001. Dakar Wolof and the configuration of an urban identity. *Journal of African Cultural Studies* 14(2).153–172.

Mercier, Paul. 1954. Aspects de la société africaine dans l'agglomeration dakaroise: groupes familieux et unités de voisinage. Dakar: Etudes Sénégalaises 5 (Institut Français de l'Afrique Noire).

Mufwene, Salikoko S. 2001. *The Ecology of Language Evolution.* Cambridge: Cambridge University Press.

—2004. Language birth and death. *Annual Review of Anthropology* 33.201–222.

—2008. *Language Evolution: Contact, Competition, and Change.* London: Continuum.

Myers-Scotton, Carol. 1993. Elite closure as a powerful language strategy: The African case. *International Journal of the Sociology of Language* 103.149–163.

Nettle, Daniel and Suzanne Romaine. 2000. *Vanishing Voices: The Extinction of the World's Languages.* New York: Oxford University Press.

Ngom, Fallou. 2004. Ethnic identity and linguistic hybridization in Senegal. *International Journal of the Sociology of Language* 170.95–111.

Piot, Charles. 1999. *Remotely Global: Village Modernity in West Africa.* Chicago: University of Chicago Press.

Robinson, David. 2004. *Muslim Societies in African History.* Cambridge: Cambridge University Press.

Sapir, J. David. 1971. West Atlantic: An inventory of the languages, their noun class systems and consonant alternation. In *Current Trends in Linguistics VII: Linguistics in Sub-Saharan Africa,* ed. by Thomas A. Sebeok, 45–112. The Hague: Mouton.

Sassen, Saskia. 1998. *Globalization and its Discontents: Essays on the New Mobility of People and Money.* New York: The New Press.

Searing, James A. 1993. *West African Slavery and Atlantic Commerce: The Senegal River Valley, 1700–1860.* Cambridge: Cambridge University Press.

—2005. Signares and sailors in Senegal's Atlantic port cities: Saint-Louis and Gorée, 1750–1850. Paper presented at the Annual Meeting of the African Studies Association. Washington D.C., 17–20 November.

Swigart, Leigh. 1990. Wolof, language or ethnic group? The development of a national identity. Paper presented at the Annual Meeting of the African Studies Association. Baltimore, MD, 1–4 November.

Tamari, Tal. 1997. *Les castes de l'Afrique occidentale: artisans et musiciens endogames.* Nanterre: Société d'Ethnologie.

Tang, Patricia. 2007. *Masters of the Sabar: Wolof Griot Percussionists of Senegal.* Philadelphia: Temple University Press.

Wioland, François. 1965. *Enquête sur les langues parlées au Sénégal.* Dakar: Centre de Linguistique Appliquée de Dakar.

Wioland, François and Maurice Calvet. 1967. L'expansion du wolof au Sénégal. *Bulletin de l'IFAN* 29(3&4).

Chapter 8

On the Futurology of Linguistic Development
Robert Chaudenson

In the past years, 'language death' has been one of the 'hot topics' favored by linguists with little public success and, consequently, by some second-rate journalists. It is the modern equivalent of '*La poésie des ruines*' in European romanticism. The success of this theme coincides with its perfect inscription into another theme, a bigger one, which is just as 'weighty': the preservation of cultural diversity. This is in and of itself a vast ideological conglomerate associated with concerns with ecology.

8.1 The Life and Death of Languages: A Case of Linguistic Futurology

To lament the death of languages is to take an advantageous position. By informing everyone that all the threats to linguistic and cultural diversity (analogous to plant and animal diversity) affect the ecological wealth and equilibrium of the world, one subscribes to an ecological trend that can do naught but inspire a sympathy that is as vague as it is general.[1]

Better yet, one often takes this position to invest oneself in the double charms of being an advocate of the Third World and scientifically current. Languages blamed for *linguicide* are, indeed, most often those associated with colonization. Not so long ago, they were denounced as 'glottophagous' or *killer languages*. Some scholars do not hesitate to give, almost with precision, the number of languages that die per day. This is a very bold move since there is no measure of how many languages there are in the world, as we lack a sure method of distinguishing between languages and dialects. To push this paradox to the extreme, one could say that just as many languages as people die in the world each day, since there are undoubtedly no two individuals who speak exactly the same language or, in any case, have the same linguistic repertoire.

The reader will forgive me more easily for this position once he/she knows that for almost four decades my research has been primarily on creole cultures and languages. While there are languages and cultures that die, there are also some that are born (see also Mufwene 2004). This is the cycle of all life on Earth that is summed up by Victor Hugo in 'A Villequier', which is surprisingly just, although terrible, especially when one imagines that he wrote it after the death of his daughter Léopoldine: *Il faut que l'herbe pousse et que des enfants meurent* 'grass must grow and children must die'.

Since this book focuses on Africa, it is logical to take as an example the way that the linguistic future of the continent was hazarded in the wake of the independences of its constituent nations, when the end of colonization seemed to entail radical changes. Authors such as Yves Person and Louis-Jean Calvet then announced the prevalence of European languages at the expense of their African counterparts, as the former were generally adopted as the official languages of the new states, contrary to what could have been expected or what had sometimes been announced. None of these states of affairs appeared to compromise, as secret agents of European colonialism, the leaders who had led these new states to independence.

Louis-Jean Calvet's book *Linguistique et colonialisme: petit traité de glottophagie* (1974), which followed that of the geographer Yves Person (1972, 1973), has the merit of presenting clearly the author's viewpoint. It is not surprising that the denunciation of the colonial linguistic oppression and the discourse on African languages about to be 'devoured' by European languages (especially French, in the Francophone world![2]) seduced the majority of young African intellectuals. Although the disappearance of African languages was certainly not explicitly proclaimed, it was unjustifiably forecast from the perspective of the linguistic history of France, thus anticipating for African vernaculars the same fatal evolution as for French *patois*.

Beyond the implications of the glottophagous character of any colonization, the factors that were admittedly taken into account to predict such an evolution were not only the complicity of the African elite (whose major figure and detestable symbol, at least for the present author, was Léopold Sédar Senghor, the agent and theoretician of the oppression) but also, and above all, the idea that the South can catch up economically with the North. This catch up had to be based, first and foremost, on education (it had indeed been decided, in Addis Ababa, in 1961, that universal education would be in place by 1980) and on a development that would be favored and accelerated by transfers of technology from the North to the South or from the part of the South that was still colonized to other parts of the South. A case in point is the transfer of sugar industry technology from Réunion to Côte d'Ivoire.

These chimerical projections were in fact founded on the idea that the part of Africa that was geopolitically Francophone would become linguistically Francophone, thanks to universal education in French. The geopolitical Francophonie was soon instituted in the very modest form of L'Agence de Coopération Culturelle et Technique ('Agency for Cultural and Technical Cooperation') in Niamey in 1970. The vast majority of states embarked on this dream, with the exception of Guinea, then ruled by Sékou Touré, and, to a lesser extent, Mali, then under Modibo Keita's rule. Thus, the denunciation of colonial 'glottophagy' could not but please, especially, young African intellectuals. One can hardly assess the impact of Louis-Jean Calvet's book more accurately than Kazadi Ntole, who undoubtedly described reactions that were then his own:

> Louis-Jean Calvet, lui, parlait vraiment le langage révolutionnaire dans lequel le jeune public universitaire africain avait le profond sentiment de se reconnaître. Il leur parlait de la langue refuge, de la langue lieu privilégié de l'authenticité refusée, de la langue dernier recours contre l'aliénation, de la langue maquis du peuple surtout, il leur disait, à la grande satisfaction de leurs propres aspirations et idéologies, qu'au vu du faible pourcentage de réels francophones « la vraie dimension de la francophonie africaine [. . .] constitue le pendant de l'économie néo-coloniale imposée aux pays présumés indépendants ». De telles prises de positions ne pouvaient que venir à la rescousse d'une contestation africaine de la francophonie. (Ntolé 1991:78)[3]

Ntolé knew better than anyone else that, in the linguistic domain, nothing had in fact been imposed on those 'presumably independent countries'; so did Louis-Jean Calvet. In the preface that Calvet wrote for Ntolé (1991), his tone had indeed changed. He cautiously refrained from invoking the very term *glottophagie*, and since then he has also avoided any implication of African political leaders as accomplices of the 'neo-colonialist' enterprise that had favored European languages over national ones. In this matter it is simpler to take note of the only two noteworthy exceptions that were Guinea's leader Sékou Touré, in Francophone Africa, and Tanzania's leader Julius Nyerere, in Anglophone Africa.

In the wake of independence, there was almost unanimous faith in a development of Africa based on universal education. For multiple reasons, leaders were determined to adopt languages alongside European educational systems, as both were taken jointly (Chaudenson 1989, 2000, 2006b). There were hardly any divergent opinions, except in the daydreams of a Cheikh Anta Diop, who wanted to see a uniquely African language adopted by his future federation of African states, or among young ideologues who refused to be the 'Senegalese skirmishers' of the French language. Certain authors already understood the difficulties of that chosen path. They were rare and, let's note in passing, Africans, not French. Thus Mudimbe (1976a,b), Nizurugero (1980) and Ki Zerbo (1980) express reservations and underscore (not without reason) the unbearable cost and maladaptation of the French schools model.

As only some enlightened minds and experts of the South had predicted, it appears today that the objectives of education have never been met and never will be. This is the consequence of both demographics and the inevitable limits of investments in education. The significance of the ravaging effects of the former has just been re-discovered, whereas in the past few years this factor was totally overlooked. Of course, contrary to the French *patois*, the African vernaculars have largely escaped the *glottophagie* that allegedly threatened them. Both national 'plurilingualism'and regional 'multilingualism' have fostered dynamics that have promoted certain languages and caused the regression of others.[4]

Confirmed in Addis-Abeba in 1961 and reformulated in a slightly different form in Jomtien in 1990, and then in Dakar in 2000 (with longer and longer, as well as extended, terms), the principle of universal education became indeed more and more utopian. The reforms were attempts to mask the evidence with diverse smoke screens articulated in the South as temporary employment in two or three schools, as multi-grade classes, as large-group pedagogy or as the development of non-state-owned systems (private and/or denominational). These methods had uncertain results. Their only merit was to give the impression that the education rates had increased, while the officials generally refrained from assessing seriously their educational and linguistic results.

The worst part is that in many cases both the states and funding agencies benefited from the complicity of quite a number of experts and institutes or study centers in the North that drew from them most of their resources and are therefore complacent to these policies. They would not be ethical enough to resist the policies or issue warnings against them (Chaudenson 2006b:162–167, 2007).

8.2 Globalization and Glocalization

Francophones and Anglophones differ in the ways they name the same phenomenon identified by the former as *mondialisation* and by the latter as *globalization*. To be sure, as observed by Mufwene (2005:174), Francophones could take advantage of a semantic distinction available in French between of the terms *globalization* and *mondialisation* 'universalization' (or 'world-wide spread'), whereas Anglophones have only the one term *globalization* for both meanings. As Mufwene (2005) observes:

> malheureusement, contrairement à ce dernier [le mot anglo-américain « *globalization* »], *mondialisation* ne fait référence qu'à la diffusion géographique de la technologie et des artefacts culturels. Elle ignore les aspects les plus importants de la globalisation, ceux qui permettent l'expansion géographique de certaines entreprises et/ou de leurs produits. (174)[5]

Consistent with the semantic clarification that Mufwene wished for, one can add the term *glocalization*, which, unless I am mistaken, Mufwene (2005) does not use and seems also to be hardly ever used in French, even though it has been used in Spanish and Anglo-American literature since the late 1990s.

It would thus be possible in French to distinguish among the following terms and meanings:

1. *Mondialisation*: worldwide expansion of exchanges of products and services (in particular those whose production and consumption embody and organize the worldwide Web and the World Trade Organization).
2. *Globalization*, which concerns in a more specific way interconnections and interdependencies in the modes of production of goods and in the management of all the large enterprises that have become multinational, thus more or less 'world-wide' or 'global'.
3. *Glocalization* (linguistically a blend from *globalization* and *glocalization*), which designates less a decentralization of powers in favor of local ones than the adaptation of globalized services and products to local conditions of production and consumption. Glocalization can be observed at the level of commercial strategies, for instance, in the phenomenon identified as *Macdonaldization* (Mufwene 2005:175), as well as in the interactions between the local cultures and the global cultural models spread by globalization as *mondialisation*, especially through the media.

I am not absolutely sure whether the adoption of such a paradigm will lead to much progress, even though, in Africa more than anywhere else, some steps have been taken towards the glocalization of French with endogenous norms and the legitimation of a number of peculiarities of 'African French'. One can find a nice illustration of glocalization but also of issues it can raise in an article by Jackie Assayag ('La glocalisation du "beau"', 1999). In it she examines, with as much erudition as finesse, in a 'glocal' perspective, the election of Miss World in Bangalore (India) in 1996. Although one could have easily anticipated, some years later, that there would be violent reactions after the election of Miss World in Nigeria (2002), a federal state where the influence of Islam is so strong that certain provinces live under the Charia regime, it is more surprising to see that Bangalore was declared a 'war zone', with incidents of extreme violence, after an election of the same type. The surprise stems from the fact that in Indian culture the image of the woman is not only very present but also appears often in representations that, outside of India, one might consider sensual and even erotic, even though this image competes with another completely different one of an Indian woman, one who is laborious and submissive (the 'goddess' and the 'female buffalo', to use Assayag's terms).

On the other hand, it is certain that the media, especially television and now the internet, play a major role in glocalization. This is particularly significant on the cultural level, because these media transmit almost instantaneously images from one part of the world to others and one may expect an evolution towards a culturally homogeneous world. However, in this domain as in others, futurology is an interminable catalogue of erroneous predictions. Note, for instance, that not too long ago almost everybody predicted that the Web would be the cornerstone of electronic domination by the English language. In reality, its place within the total traffic of electronic communication has been decreasing, since all the languages endowed with graphic systems that are fairly compatible with a standard keyboard can claim some space for themselves, as modest as this may be. Although the current obsession with the internet, stimulated and underhanded by the avid packs of computer hardware or software merchants, might suggest that the digital gap between the North and South is narrowing, just the opposite is happening (Chaudenson 2000, 2006b). Undoubtedly, the solution does not lie in the project, seemingly humanitarian but perhaps sordid in reality, of clearing out obsolete computers of the North and sending them to the South. While such donations avoid the costs of recycling discarded machines, they keep the potential users in total dependence for the software. Part of the solution lies perhaps in the predicted lowering of retail prices for the machines. Was it the Chinese (as I used to think until recently) or those designers for the Third World, living in the North, who were allegedly getting ready to put on the market of the South computers that would sell for US$100 or US$150, and would, furthermore, be equipped with free Linux software? I admit that some of this bodes poorly, but, in any case, such a hypothesis, as rich in perspectives as it may be, does not solve all the structural and economic problems of access to the Web in the South. One must also solve problems related to electricity and telephone systems, the cost of internet connections and constant renewals of hardware and software, among others.

8.3 On the Prediction of Future of Languages

Futurologists of all breeds currently predict that vernacular languages[6] are going to disappear because of globalization qua *mondialisation* and because of the combined effects of electronic communication and of television. Are they not making the same mistake as their predecessors in the early 1970s?

In fact, these new forms of communication constitute, on the contrary, the quasi-ideal modes of managing linguistic diversity and language partnership. Glocalization can thus succeed. Far from contributing to the disappearance of languages, these media give them new chances to live, develop and spread, in modes and forms that have assuredly not been anticipated. Thus creoles, which only a few hesitate to classify as moribund languages (Wurm 2001) or as endangered ones (Hazaël-Massieux 1999), are attested and used in hundreds of sites on the Web. Discussion fora have been created in these languages, as well as publications and interactive dictionaries and so on, which are sustained by internet users. No one predicted such an evolution just some years ago. (See also Mazrui, this volume.) These languages are far from being condemned to extinction by globalization and the Web. Instead, they have found new and sometimes unexpected ways of life and new usage.

The failure of futurology about language stems from the fact that these evolutions depend on numerous factors, almost none of which is in the proper domain of linguistics as traditionally practiced. How can we account for the fact that the Irish have not managed to save Gaelic whereas the Israeli have generalized usage of Hebrew over all their national territory? Mufwene (2005) submits the following explanation:

> Les efforts du gouvernement irlandais en faveur de l'irlandais face à l'anglais ont échoué tout simplement parce qu'ils n'ont pas tenu compte de cette dimension importante pour venir au secours d'une langue moribonde [mettre en œuvre une solution globale, au-delà de l'enseignement de cette langue]. L'anglais continue à fonctionner comme langue de travail et l'enseignement de l'irlandais n'a qu'une valeur idéologique et symbolique. Pour sauver une langue il faut la valoriser en l'instrumentalisant économiquement. Le manque d'utilité dans la vie économique d'un territoire est justement l'un des facteurs qui mettent en danger la vitalité des vernaculaires indigènes. (181)[7]

It may not be unnecessary to highlight the fact that in the same passage, Mufwene advocates for the adoption of a 'global solution' that can help a Quebec-style policy succeed. His three-way comparison between Ireland, Quebec and Israel is particularly informative, although I am not totally sure that French will definitely survive in Quebec.

Note also that although Mufwene privileges the economics factor in his account, he sees it only as one of many, not the only one. It is clear that the Irish population has not strongly committed itself to the rebirth of Gaelic. The involvement of the overall populations was different in Quebec and Israel, although every country's situation was fundamentally different. In the latter two cases, the promotion of French and Hebrew, respectively, has benefited from massive backing from the Québécois and Israeli populations. In Quebec, the pressure in favor of English was primarily socioeconomic, in spite of the fact that French culture was deeply entrenched and, in addition, strongly supported by the Catholic Church. Thus, paradoxically, the 'Quiet Revolution' has, since the 1960s, transformed itself into a complex evolution that has altogether reduced the influence of the Church (in the social and educational domains), promoted economic development (which of course let the American wolf back in through the revolving door) and generated autonomist and independentist movements that have sometimes taken violent forms, in spite of the reputed 'peaceful' character of the revolution. They then attempted to reduce the economic inequities that were engendered by language practice[8] with an arsenal of legal stipulations that were put in place and would eventually result in the adoption of the 1974 'Loi sur la langue officielle' ('Law on the Official Language').

This was crowned in 1977 by 'La Charte de la langue française' ('The French Language Charter'), often called 'Loi 101'.

The amplitude and constraining force of this judicial arsenal made apparent the difficulties faced by policy. The Gallicization of industries is a weapon that is difficult to wield, since industrialists can be tempted to relocate even within the Canadian borders. For instance, a company considered transferring its headquarters or its research centers to Ontario, leaving in Quebec only its production plants. An enterprise can thus be administered and managed in English from Toronto while continuing to have bolts tightened in French in Quebec. On the other hand, in a federal state such as Canada, one often faces conflicts between provincial (Quebec) and federal (Canada) legislations. Within the provincial legal system, 'La loi 101' is itself ranked lower than 'Laloi sur les droits et libertés de la personne au Québec' ('The Law on Human Rights and Liberties in Quebec'). Moreover, one can challenge the dispositions of 'La loi 101' before the federal jurisdiction, just as one can see more and more citizens in the European Union dispute the decisions of the national justice systems before the European Supreme Court. One of the more frequently contested subjects is the obligation for immigrants to enrol their children in French schools when they would rather enrol them in Anglophone schools. There are multiple arguments of this type; and Anglophone lobbyists and/or federalists are often accused of inciting or even financing such actions in the justice system.

On the other hand, the case of Israel is very different and certainly unique in the linguistic history of the world. When Israel was created, it was necessary to manage the linguistic situation of the new state, even though the Decree-Law of 1922, under the British authority, had already established English (which would be driven out of the game with the creation of the new state), Hebrew and Arabic as the official languages of Palestine. Some promoted Yiddish as the official language of Israel, a variety that Stalin had made the official language of the autonomous Jewish region of the USSR. German is also reported to have nearly taken the place of Hebrew, insofar as it was considered to be the ethnographically 'High' form of Yiddish.[9] It was primarily World War I (1914–1918) that, in addition to the militant action of partisans of Hebrew, led to the adoption of the latter as the official language. Hebrew and Arabic have, since then, been kept as the official languages, although actual bilingualism is noticeably very different from what written materials may lead one to expect.

The problem was thus not the linguistic management of Hebrew, which for a long time had essentially been a literary and liturgical language. In fact, since the late nineteenth century, militants of the Hebrew cause, whose major figure was naturally Eliezer Ben-Yehouda, had made it a language capable of meeting the communicative demands of modern life. One could thus use it without any problem in education as in the justice system and the administration of a new state. However, it was the first language of only a tiny part of the population and, most of all, it was unknown by the vast majority of immigrants who were expected to settle the new state.

In this respect, we can measure the immense difference between the situations of Quebec and Israel, which one can consider as similar only from a distance. In the first case, a province (Quebec), whose official language is French but that belongs to a bilingual federal state (Canada), finds it necessary to put in place a restrictive legislation intended for immigrants and, above all, their children to speak French. However, for pragmatic reasons, the latter most often wish that their children be taught in English, as they evolve in a national environment, and even in a continent, that is predominantly Anglophone. As noted earlier, this is one of the major reasons why the Québécois language legislation has been challenged in court.

In the second case, that of Israel, where the state is officially bilingual (in Hebrew and Arabic), it is noteworthy that when important waves of Jewish immigrants of various origins who do not speak Hebrew arrive, they learn this language in the fastest and best ways possible, so that they can speak it within their families and transmit it to their children, independent of the schooling that is provided in it. There is here an ideological and political determination, which is one of the major factors in the immigration, but that will also become one of the most essential reasons behind the rapid and complete Hebraization of Israel.

The case of Ireland, which was invoked earlier in one of the quotations from Mufwene (2005), is evidently quite different. Here, as almost anywhere, the life and death of languages depend, first and foremost, on the activities of those who speak them, although economic and social factors naturally are very relevant.

In post-independence Africa, scholars have obviously been betting on the school system. To a question on factors bearing on the development of the south, the following much-talked-about answer has alternatively been attributed to Léopold Sédar Senghor and Félix Houphouët-Boigny: 'D'abord l'éducation, ensuite l'éducation, enfin l'éducation !' ('First education, then education, and finally education!'). No one, or almost no one, then understands that universal education, be it basic or limited by literacy, is just an illusion.

The idea of education in national languages has been dismissed *a priori* in most cases, due to the fact that languages have not been planned for academic usage but often also because there are many of them, which makes the choice of one or another politically risky in those states where national cohesion is rather fragile. Interestingly, such choices have not been made even when a reform would apparently have been easy, as in Madagascar, in Cape Verde or in Guinea Bissau. This can be noticed, for example, in the correspondence between Paulo Freire and Hamilcar Cabral in *Lettres à la Guniee Bissau* (1978), where the 'colonial education model' is denounced. However, the new state will actually not abandon it at all after independence.

School systems in Africa have generally been calqued strictly on those of the North, although the new states are materially and economically incapable of facing the colossal demands that such models entail, notwithstanding the need to catch up with the education rates and the fast-growing demographics, whose rates are by far the highest in the world. In spite of the immense combined efforts of the states themselves and of international aid, the crisis of educational systems in the South has only heightened during the past decades. Repeated attempts to mask the effects failed, because their causes could not be eliminated.

8.4 School and Management of Linguistic Situations

The parallelism that Louis-Jean Calvet sketches in *Linguistique et colonialisme* (1974) between the linguistic evolution of France (especially over the last two centuries) and what he predicts for post-independence Africa is debatable, because he proceeds from a mistaken perspective. It is easy, but already point-less, to show that African languages have not at all undergone the same fate as the patois in France, where they have been 'devoured' by French (using a terminology consistent with the 'glottophagy' or 'killer language' metaphor). I will not venture into statistics, which are as complex as unfounded, to deter-mine whether, over the past forty years, French has progressed or receded in Francophone Africa. Could we seriously muse on such evaluations when, for instance, in the most populated Francophone state in Africa, the Democratic Republic of the Congo (former Zaïre), no statistics have been available for the past quarter century and, furthermore, in this case as in others, there is no definition of the level of linguistic competence at which one may be considered as a 'real Francophone', to use the most recent terminology of the late 'Haut Conseil de la Francophonie'?[10]

After independence and while the new state structures were being set up, the strongest attraction of schools was the fact that they opened the gate to jobs in the public sector. Once the schools became overabundant and, in addition, the jobs were filled, prospects of public jobs petered out. In fact, the International Monetary Fund imposed on the states massive reductions of the numbers of public servants. Suddenly both schools and the learning of French lost a good deal of their worthiness, while national languages did not necessarily increase their social value. A process of 'unschooling', sometimes latent and often masked by diverse means, was thus engaged.[11] It has naturally been aggravated by the dramatic crisis of educational systems: teachers have been recruited with lower and lower qualifications and their salaries have been decreased to worse and worse levels (especially when, in local parlance, the state or the local public administration is 'disinterested' in them);[12] their incomes have become uncer-tain; school is often closed for a whole year because teachers are on strike;

classes have become overcrowded; part-time employment in two or even three schools has become common practice, and, among other things, there are dire shortages of books and other pedagogical materials.

As noted earlier, it is also dramatic that a number of experts, primarily interested in winning favors and thus contracts from funding agencies, have often tended to mask or even approve these drifts, instead of denouncing them. If I may be allowed to cite myself here in order to avoid repetitions:

> Le *Rapport* de 1998 [du PASEC, Programme d'Analyse des Systèmes Educatifs] avance, par exemple, que la double vacation n'a pas d'effet fâcheux sur les résultats de l'éducation, alors que l'opinion inverse est à peu près générale. On comprend aisément que des maîtres, souvent mal payés, admettent difficilement, même avec une légère rémunération complémentaire, de faire un double travail ; en outre, la double vacation entraîne souvent des réductions de fait de l'horaire scolaire. Mais quelle importance de tels détails peuvent-ils avoir pour les 'experts'?[13]

I remember reading, in reports of the same kind, that the number of students per class does not bear negatively on the outcome either, in fact not any more than the scarcity or lack of books. One can thus guess that most of these experts in the econometrics of education have, no doubt, never taught in classes with many students.

Everything seems to be summed up by the following passage from the 1995 *Rapport*:

> Le PASEC fait apparaître que ces moyens classiques de réduction des coûts n'ont pas d'effets secondaires rédhibitoires sur la qualité de l'éducation. Lorsqu'on réduit le ratio maître/élèves (taille des classes, double flux), qu'on augmente la fluidité des cycles (diminution des redoublements), qu'on limite les coûts de formation et les coûts salariaux des maîtres (niveaux de recrutement, catégorie d'emploi, formation initiale ou continue), **le gain combiné peut être spectaculaire** (du double au simple) alors que **la perte sur les scores des élèves** à des épreuves standardisées **se limite à quelques points de pourcentage** » (14; emphasis mine)[14]

Under these conditions, there are no more problems! The way is made. I quote my sources in notes, as these propositions may appear incredible. It is enough:

- to further push down the teacher recruitment level (the Certificat d'Etudes Primaires (CEP) is largely sufficient and is it really necessary, after all, that the teachers know how to read?)[15];

- to lower salaries further (in Mali, the salary of a teacher paid by parents is eight times lower than that of a civil servant and apparently, according to PASEC, he is just as efficient)[16];
- to no longer train teachers at all (this does not bear noticeably on the outcome either) as quoted in note 14;
- to put more and more students in classes,[17] way above sixty, which must be the current average; this changes nothing, since, when the children can no longer move, the problems of discipline are solved[18];
- and to do away with books and all pedagogical materials (all of this only has a minimal impact[19]).

I am neither a statistician nor an economist of education, but I will indulge in a personal observation to these experts, because it is connected to the problem of evaluation of students' competence in the language that serves as the medium of education. As the reader must, no doubt, have understood already, I think that the tests used do not permit, in any way, to evaluate seriously the students' linguistic competence in French, since the levels of examination are very low. Therefore, and the 'experts' are not mistaken in this case, the knowledge acquired by the vast majority of children is so little that no factor (the much-talked-about 'variables') is of any real consequence. The remarks of the authors of these reports are not entirely irrelevant, so long as it can be added that in the contexts where children learn almost nothing in school, the results can indeed not get much worse, however much the teaching conditions deteriorate. In effect, 0-0 = 0, QED! (Chaudenson 2006b:166–167).

8.5 The Audiovisual Sphere as a Tool and Place for Language Management

I have argued for many years now that the diffusion of French in the South can in the long run happen only thanks to a global audiovisual system consisting essentially of fiction (such as cartoons and TV serials) elaborated from a foundation of linguistic didactics but made attractive, entertaining and capable of securing the loyalty of viewers. The generalized failure of the school system in the South and its anticipated degradation in the face of the demographic explosion (which has finally been acknowledged) will only precipitate an evolution towards this kind of solution, although I fear that it will be considered probably too late.

Although they do not admit it, those who announced in the 1970s that European languages were going to 'devour' African languages based their predictions on expectations for universal education, which itself was expected to give rise to and sustain development. Naturally none of this has happened. African languages have thus not evolved into what Louis-Jean Calvet characterized as 'the maquis/refuge of the people'.

When they work, schools are indeed one of the most powerful means that drive languages to extinction, by excluding them from their spheres. In this respect, I am always amused to see evoked, about colonial language teaching in Africa, the famous 'symbol' (whichever name is used for it: *sign*, '*signeur*', *symbol*, etc.) that a student caught speaking a local language had to wear, until they could pass it on to another fellow student caught in the same violation. Indeed, in the case of Francophone Africa, this custom originated directly in the old schools of the French countryside. The only difference is that in Africa the student who carried the symbol at the end of the day felt under no obligation to come to school earlier than everyone else the next morning, to start up the stove, unless they were condemned, which also often happened, to sweep the classroom.

It is somewhat surprising that no one seems to have noticed the internal contradiction between the primary objectives of La Francophonie, which are, on the one hand, universal education (expected to be done only in French), and, on the other, cultural diversity and language partnership. Except in rich countries (and even so), schools favor monolingualism. By necessity and in essence, they are therefore, inevitably, a factor of *minoration*, marginalization and even of exclusion relative to other language varieties in the same geographical area that they do not use. Not only do they tend to exclude local languages from their spheres, but even when they accommodate them with some modest space, they confine them generally to marginal activities. Moreover, if we take into account the world outside school, only the major language used in education can open up real social perspectives. It is also common knowledge that in Africa those who are the most resolutely opposed to usage of local vernaculars in schools are the students' parents themselves.

The situation that the audio-visual space can create is different in several ways. The first is that of the very usage of languages. Usage of a language as a medium of education presupposes considerable investments, as much in the planning of the language itself, especially if the primary functions of the language had been oral, as in the proper domain of education itself. In the former case, the language must be normalized (having to do with the production of norms – the editors) and standardized, while, among other things, a graphic code and both general and specialized terminologies must be developed. In the latter, grammars, dictionaries and pedagogical materials must be developed and published; and an investment must be made in teacher training, among other things.

All of this is too evident for me to elaborate. I am not even speaking of post-literacy problems and of the disappointment of all those who, made literate in a language, subsequently discover that there is little to read in that language, or, in any case, nothing interesting or useful. This sentiment of frustration explains why, most of the time, in the South, literacy campaigns in national languages incite those who have just acquired literacy in an indigenous language to request literacy in French.

On the other hand, usage of national languages in the audiovisual technology does not pose such problems, which, for the most part, are tied to writing. Creole-speakers, Haitians in particular, have for a long time found a way of sidestepping this problem. They exchange, with their family members in Canada, the United States, or elsewhere, not letters but small magnetic tapes that they remove from their casings, after recording what they wished to send to their correspondents. Once received, the recipient rewinds the strip into a cassette, and listens and replies to it on the same strip, repeating the same process, which is convenient, fast and less expensive.

Regarding the management and coexistence of languages, even their partnership, the audiovisual sphere offers even more significant advantages, which it alone can. Not only do audiovisual methods clear away all the obstacles entailed by writing down languages that are essentially oral, they offer languages opportunities to coexist in the same social and geographical space. Every language can find in it the place that is suitable to it, depending on the means available to its users, their objectives, and the conditions for the diffusion of messages.

Take, for instance, the southeastern region of Mali, where Minyanka is spoken by about seven hundred thousand Malians. This language, which is one of thirteen national languages of the country, is not counted among the three major ones, which include Bambara (spoken by 80 per cent of the population, 40 per cent of whom use it as their primary language, whereas 40 per cent speak it as L2 or L3), Fulfulde and Songhoï/Songhai. In the area where Minyanka is spoken, one could very well organize the audiovisual sphere according to the following model: a national television station that, as in the whole country, offers programs in French (the single official language of Mali), but also, for a modest enough part, broadcasts programs in the regional national language (Bambara in the present case). Television is accessible either through standard broadcasting or by satellite. Naturally, the latter offers no programs in national languages but provides French programs (especially from *TV5*). On the other hand, the national radio makes much more room for Bambara (Maïga 2004:177–178). Minyanka (and even languages spoken by far fewer speakers) can be used on regional radio and even, if desired, on regional television. A regional radio could indeed be set up, if desired, just for a few thousand listeners. There is no lack of examples of such enterprises around the world. I think in this particular case of local French television in Louisiana targeting a reduced public of Louisianan Acadians.

In an audiovisual system of this sort, all of the languages of the region (French, Bambara and especially Minyanka) occupy their spaces and functions, without anyone of them encroaching in the other's space. Members of the population can thus, at their convenience and when they wish, pass from one language to another. All the languages can exist without a problem. The audiovisual space is therefore the only one where 'language peace' can be established and can prevail.

Technical progress, in particular the invention of the DVD, illustrates how languages can share space and it provides new tools for the audiovisual management of languages. It has become customary for viewers of movies on DVDs to select the language they prefer for it to play in. We can easily imagine (in fact the possibility exists already) that TV viewers will be able to choose for themselves, in their own homes, the language in which they would like to watch a movie. In the universal audiovisual system that I propose for the diffusion of French, it will be absolutely possible to have, for the fiction that constitutes it, DVDs or multiple versions in different languages.[20] The initial French versions would certainly be the essential foundation because they would rest on embedded and invisible didactic progressions, but they could also be accompanied, for example, by versions in supra-national languages, national ones for Africa (in Hausa in the first case, in Bambara in the second, in keeping with the Malian example), or in foreign languages (for China or India, e.g.). Since this operation would have a worldwide objective, it is hard to imagine another method that could reach such diverse populations over such vast geographical areas.

8.6 Conclusion

In the domain of languages, as in the other sectors, futurology is a risky, if not a senseless, enterprise. The old predictions of the 1970s, like the more recent ones (having to do with the advent of globalization, whose symbol and major tool are the internet), prove to be equally mistaken. It is hard to predict, in a precise and concrete fashion, the future of languages, as this depends on a large number of factors: economic, social, political, psychological, technical and so on. On the other hand, it is possible to distinguish more clearly the ways and means that can be set up for managing and spreading languages.

In the current state of affairs, it is clear that if we limit ourselves to the case of French in the Francophone space of the South, and if we wish, as is constantly claimed in official proposals, to promote education, French and language partnership altogether, respecting cultural diversity, we must (using a cliché) stop putting all of our eggs in the same basket. This bottomless 'basket' is the school system, to which we persist in assigning the monopoly both for education and for the diffusion of the French and other colonial languages. I have tried for several years to make obvious this position that seems evident only to myself. I have invoked such distinguished minds as Gaston Berger and Pierre Bourdieu to support these proposals (Chaudenson 2006b:2001–2002), but apparently in vain. Perhaps the lesson to learn from these few comments on futurology, and about the planning and future of languages, is that those who make predictions are mistaken in most cases, but those who propose views that are somewhat less prophetic but are probably closer to reality are never heard, least of all, listened to!

Notes

¹ For a more serious and extensive discussion of this issue, the reader is advised to check Mufwene (2005:137–141).

² The idea that English might be less 'glottophagous' than French is one of the most common and most deeply entrenched myths in Francophone Africa, which can hardly be verified. The often-cited example of Swahili spreading at the expense of English is more complex than it seems (Chaudenson 2006b:188).

³ The translation:

> Louis-Jean Calvet spoke the truly revolutionary language which the young African collegiate public really felt they could identify with. He spoke to them about language as a refuge, about language as the privileged place where one could find denied authenticity, about language as the last recourse from alienation, [and] above all about language as the resistance tool of the people[; and] he told them, to the great satisfaction of their own aspirations and ideologies, that in light of the low percentage of real French-speakers 'the true dimension of the African Francophonie (. . .) was matched by the neo-colonial economy imposed upon the presumably independent countries'. Such positions could not but come to the rescue of the African contestation of La Francophonie.

⁴ Although some may find my choice of terms arbitrary, I propose in Chaudenson (1989:114–115) a distinction between, on the one hand, regional and/or supranational multilingualism and, on the other, national multilingualism. I use *plurilingualism* in the latter case. This distinction, which I find useful in the context of language planning, is based on the fact that the Latin etymon *plures*, which means 'more numerous' but not 'several', is the comparative of *multi* 'numerous'. The languages of national 'plurilingualisms' are naturally more numerous than those of regional 'multilingualisms' that apply to more than one state.

⁵ The translation:

> Unfortunately, contrary to the latter [the Anglo-American word *globalization*], *mondialisation* refers only to the geographic diffusion of technology and cultural artifacts. It ignores the most important aspects of globalization, those which enable the geographical expansion of some enterprises and/or their products. (Mufwene 2005:174)

⁶ It does not matter whether the languages are identified as 'vernaculars', in spite of UNESCO's diktat, or, if one prefers, as 'chtonian', 'local', 'indigenous', 'gregarious' and so on. It is the prediction that I am concerned with here.

⁷ The translation:

> The efforts of the Irish government in favor of Irish rather than English have failed simply because they did not take into account this important dimension [in their attempts] to rescue a moribund language [to institute a global solution, beyond simply teaching the language]. English continues to function as the language of work and the teaching of Irish has naught but an ideological

and symbolic value. In order to save a language it is necessary to valorize it as an economic asset. Lack of usefulness in the economic sphere of a territory is precisely one of the factors that endanger the vitality of indigenous vernaculars. (Mufwene 2005:181)

[8] When, in the early 1980s, I became interested in the connection between language and economics, the essential literature produced in this domain came from Quebec. The majority of works related the speakers' incomes with the languages they used (Chaudenson 1989).

[9] We may note *a posteriori* how ironical history would have been if German had in fact been chosen instead of Hebrew as an official language!

[10] This Coucil was phased out in 2007.

[11] Free public schools tend to be replaced by either a system that depends increasingly on the contributions of parents (which is prettily called 'partnership') or by confessional systems (in particular Muslim, with a larger and larger place for 'fundamentalist' teachers, of course to the detriment of the médersas of traditional African Islam, whose means and attraction are infinitely smaller).

[12] A public servant earns, on average, twice as much as a State-contracted worker and four times as much as parent-paid schoolmaster (PASEC, 2004:7).

[13] The 1998 PASEC *Report* states, for example, that temporary employment in two schools has had no detrimental effects on the outcome of education, whereas the opposite opinion is more or less general. It is easy to understand why teachers, who are often poorly paid, accept reluctantly to do double their work, even with complementary income. Besides, combined part-time employment often entails de facto reductions of teaching loads. But how significant are such details to the 'experts'?

[14] PASEC gives the impression that these classic cost-reduction methods do not have secondary, unacceptable effects on the quality of education. When one reduces the student/teacher ratio (size of classes, double flux), increases the flow of grade cycles (less repetitions of grades), [and] limits teachers' training and salary costs (e.g., recruitment level, employment category, initial or continuing training), **the combined gain can be spectacular** (cutting the costs by half), whereas **the loss in students' scores** in standardized tests **is limited to only a few percentage points**. (1995:14)

[15] 'Les pays qui font le choix de recruter des maîtres pour des salaires moins élevés avec des exigences de diplômes moindres sont vraisemblablement sur la bonne piste' (PASEC Programme d'Analyse des Systèmes Educatifs (Programme de la CONFEMEN) 1995:88). 'The countries that choose to recruit teachers for lower salaries and with lower levels of education are probably on the right track'.

[16] 'Un fonctionnaire coûte, en moyenne deux fois plus qu'un contractuel de l'Etat et quatre fois plus qu'un maître de parents.' 'A civil servant costs, on average, twice as much as a contractual worker of the State and four times more than a parent-paid teacher' (PASEC 2004:7). Since the recruitment of unqualified non-civil servants makes it possible to increase the education rate without any noticeable effects on the level of students' knowledge, why deprive [the system] of such an advantage?

[17] 'La taille des classes a un effet négatif sur les progrès des élèves mais cet effet est minime [. . .] L'accueil de dix élèves supplémentaires aurait un impact modéré sur la qualité de l'enseignement' (PASEC 1995:94). 'The size of classes has a negative effect on the progress of students, but this effect is minimal (. . .) Admitting ten additional students would have a moderate impact on the quality of teaching'. The French MEN should encourage the diffusion of these documents, completely written by experts, to the French syndicates of teachers.

[18] According to PASEC, 'Si les classes qui atteignent les cent élèves ne sauraient être recommandées, il semble acceptable de passer de 50 à 55 ou de 60 à 65 en moyenne, dès lors qu'il s'agit de scolariser davantage d'enfants' (1995:128). 'Although classes which reach 100 students should not be recommended, it seems acceptable to pass from 50 to 55 or from 60 to 65 on average, as long as the goal is to educate more children' (1995:128). We had well understood that the goal was not to ameliorate pedagogy!

[19] PASEC does not think that the possession of books is an important factor; the gaps are weak and, in the fifth grade of primary school, 'the effects are too weak to be significantly different from 0' (for half the countries studied; 1995:60).

[20] This proposal is to be distinguished from simple dubbing of movies, which imposes on the viewer a single language, without any possible choice. This being said, many of today's DVDs have subtitled versions, in addition to the originals produced in diverse languages.

References

Abou, Selim and Haddad Katia (eds). 1997. *La diversité linguistique et culturelle et les enjeux du développement*, Université Saint-Joseph et AUPELF-UREF; Paris: L'Harmattan.

ADEA/GTZ/UNESCO. 2005. *Optimizing Learning and Education in Africa – The Language Factor. A Stock-Taking Research on Mother Tongue and Bilingual Education in Sub-Saharian Africa*, Working document.

Alexander, Neville. 2000. *Educational Innovation in Post-Colonial Africa*. Cape Town: PRAESA.

Assayag, Jackie. 1999. La 'glocalisation' du beau. In *Le Beau. Terrain*, n° 32, March 1999.

Bernard, J.M., Beïfith Kouak Tiyab and Katia Vianou. 2004. *Profils enseignants et qualité de l'éducation primaire en Afrique subsaharienne francophone: bilan et perspectives de dix années de recherches du PASEC*. Dakar: CONFEMEN.

Bourdieu, Pierre. 1985. Propositions pour l'enseignement de l'avenir. Paris: Éditions de Minuit.

Calvet, Louis-Jean. 1974. *Linguistique et colonialisme. Petit traité de glottophagie*. Paris: Payot.

Chaudenson, Robert. 1989. *Vers une Révolution francophone?* Paris: L'Harmattan.

Chaudenson, Robert (ed.). 1993. *L'école du Sud*. Paris: Didier-Erudition.

—1997. *L'évaluation des compétences linguistiques en français. Le test d'Abidjan*. Paris: Didier-Erudition.

Chaudenson, Robert. 1997. Diffusion du français et gestion du multilinguisme dans l'espace francophone du Sud. In S. Abou and K. Haddad (eds), 307–324.

—2000. *Mondialisation. La langue française a-t-elle encore un avenir ?* Paris: L'Harmattan.

—2006a. *Vers une autre idée et pour une autre politique de la langue française.* Paris: L'Harmattan.

—2006b. *Education et langues. Français, créoles, langues africaines.* Paris: L'Harmattan.

—2007. « Plurilinguisme et développement : le cas de l'Océan Indien occidental ». Paper presented at the Colloque international de l'Ecole Normale Supérieure (ENS), Antananarivo, 29–31 September.

Chaudenson, Robert and D. Rakotomalala. 2004. *Situations linguistiques de la Francophonie, Etats des lieux,* Agence Universitaire de la Francophonie (AUF), Montreal and Paris.

Chaudenson Robert and Didier De Robillard. 1989. *Langues, économie et développement.* Vol. 1. Paris: Didier-Erudition.

Chaudenson, Robert and Calvet, Louis-Jean. 2001. *Les langues dans l'espace francophone: de la coexistence au partenariat.* Paris: L'Harmattan.

CONFEMEN (Conférence des Ministres de l'Education Nationale). 1995a. *L'éducation de base: vers une nouvelle école. Document de réflexion et d'orientation.* PASEC-CONFEMEN, STP, Ms. http://www.confemen.org/.

—1995b. *Les facteurs de l'efficacité dans l'enseignement primaire. Dakar,* PASEC-CONFEMEN, STP, Ms.

—2001. *Stratégies pour une réforme réussie des systèmes éducatifs.* Dakar.

CONFEMEN-PASEC, 1995, *Les facteurs de l'efficacité dans l'enseignement primaire,* Dakar, CONFEMEN.

CONFEMEN-PASEC, Jean-Marc Bernard, Beifith, Kouak Tiyab, Katia Vianou. 2004. *Profils enseignants et qualité de l'éducation primaire en Afrique Subsaharienne Francophone: bilan et perspectives de dix années de recherches du PASEC,* Dakar, CONFEMEN.

Freire, Paulo. 1978. *Lettres à la Guinée Bissau.* Paris: Maspero.

Halaoui, Nazzam. 2005. *Langues et systèmes éducatifs dans les Etats francophones d'Afrique subsaharienne.* Paris: Autrement.

Hazaël-Massieux, Marie-Christine. 1999. *Les créoles: l'indispensable survie.* Paris: Editions Entente.

Ki Zerbo, Joseph. 1980. De l'Afrique ustensile à l'Afrique partenaire. In Mudimbe (ed.), 42–55.

Maïga, Amidou. 2004. Le Mali. In Chaudenson and Rakotomalala, 177–178.

Mudimbe V.Y. 1976a. Langues et développement. Colloque du CILF, Dakar.

—1976b. Langues africaines et langues européennes. Problèmes de collaboration. International African Institute, Mons, Belgium.

Mudimbe, V.Y. (ed.). 1980. *La dépendance de l'Afrique et les moyens d'y remédier.* Paris: Berger-Levrault.

Mufwene, Salikoko S. 2001. *The Ecology of Language Evolution.* Cambridge: Cambridge University Press.

—2004. Language birth and death. *Annual Review of Anthropology* 33.201–222.

—2005. *Créoles, écologie sociale, évolution linguistique.* Paris: L'Harmattan.

Ndaywel, E Nziem I (ed.). *Les langues africaines et créoles face à leur avenir.* Paris: L'Harmattan.

Ndaywel, E Nziem I. and Louis-Jean Rousseau (eds). 2004. *Demain le français : vers des stratégies diversifiées de promotion et d'enseignement.* Paris : Agence Intergouvernementale de la Francophonie.

Nizurugero, Rugagi. 1980. Dépendance et créativité culturelle. In Mudimbe (ed.).

Ntolé, Kazadi. 1991. *L'Afrique afrofrancophone.* Paris: Didier-Erudition.

Person, Yves. 1972. L'Afrique Noire et ses frontières. *Revue Française d'Etudes Politiques Africaines* 80, August.

—1973. Impérialisme linguistique et colonialisme. *Temps Modernes,* August–September, 90–112.

PNUD (Programme des Nations Unies pour le Développement). 2003. *Rapport Annuel Mondial sur le Développement humain 2003.*

Rakotomalala, Dorothée. 2004. *Le partenariat des langues dans l'espace francophone: description, analyse, gestion.* Paris: L'Harmattan.

Somé, Maxime. 2003. *Politique éducative et politique linguistique en Afrique. Enseignement du français et valorisation des langues nationales: le cas du Burkina Faso.* Paris: L'Harmattan.

Wurm, Stephen A. 2001. *Atlas des langues du monde en danger d'extinction /Atlas of the world's languages in danger of disappearing.* Paris: UNESCO Publications.

Chapter 9

Globalization and the Sociolinguistics of the Internet: Between English and Kiswahili

Alamin Mazrui

9.1 Introduction

In his address to the World Economic Forum, Bill Gates, the then Microsoft chairperson and CEO, made the prediction that 'Over the next five or six years . . . you will get a very high penetration [in computer-based communication], even in Africa, where [connecting] is quite challenging' (Microsoft 1999). In fact, Africa was soon to demonstrate a higher growth rate in Internet usage than the average for the rest of the world. According to December 2005 figures provided by Internetworldstats.com, Internet users in Africa constitute only 2.2 per cent of total users the world over. On the other hand, in the five year period between 2000 and 2005, the continent showed a staggering growth rate of 403.7 per cent in Internet usage as compared to the world average of 182 per cent. The rapid Internet 'penetration' that Bill Gates predicted in 1999, then, has received its most dramatic expression in precisely that region, Africa, where 'connecting is quite challenging'.

Kenya, the research location for this study, ranks fifth among countries with the highest proportion of Internet users in Africa, constituting about 6.6 per cent of the 'African' Internet space. Until the late-1990s, Internet access in Kenya was limited to a tiny minority of the population. Since the end of the more dictatorial era of President Daniel Arap Moi, however, it has expanded rapidly, especially in response to both internal and external pressures to liberalize the cyber-space (and airwaves). In the words of Muiruri (2006):

Today the Internet touches the lives of many more people in Kenya's urban areas. Cybercafes can be found in many neighborhoods of Nairobi, secondary towns, and even small outskirts that previously had little or no access, Cybercafes are now full of patrons using the Internet for a whole range of purposes, including e-mail, searching for jobs and schools, chatting, conducting research, and enhancing awareness of HIV/AIDS. (65)

In the same period, Kenya witnessed the growth of community telecommunications access centers, mainly targeting organized women's groups in rural areas (Mudhai 2002:98). By all indication, then, the expansion of Internet access in Kenya has been a direct product of the interplay between globalization and democratization.

Yet, this phenomenal expansion in Internet usage in Africa, especially in sub-Saharan Africa, has taken place almost exclusively in the languages inherited from the colonial tradition (English, French and Portuguese). African languages have so far featured little in the Internet world of communication. However, Microsoft has recently launched a localization project that, among other things, seeks to bridge that aspect of the digital divide in Africa induced by linguistic difference. The African languages targeted initially are some of the regional ones, including Amharic, Hausa, Igbo, Kiswahili, Wolof and Yoruba.

The Kiswahili part of the project is complete and was officially launched in February 2005. Compared with the other major languages, the task was made relatively easier by the predominance of the Latin alphabet in Kiswahili writing and the fact that Kiswahili is a non-tonal language. The program's glossary is intended to cater to the entire 'Swahiliphone' region in eastern and central Africa and has received the endorsement of the National Kiswahili Council of Tanzania, the National Kiswahili Council of Zanzibar, the Makerere Institute of Languages in Uganda and Kenya's Ministry of Education, among other institutions in the region. According to Patrick Opiyo (2004), the project manager,

> [the] aim of the Kiswahili Local Language Program is strategically aligned to the Microsoft Corp Local Language Program that offers governments, institutions and local partners an opportunity to help minority language groups preserve and promote their culture and propagate the local IT economy through the provision of the Kiswahili Language Interface Pack. (2)

Though a project of Microsoft, a 'foreign' organization, Kenyan newspapers abound with voices of Kiswahili nationalists, almost all from the ranks of the educated elite, who see the localization program as a potential ally in their attempts to curb the 'uncontrolled' spread of English, allegedly at the expense of Kiswahili. The computerization of the language, then, is regarded as a way of enhancing Kiswahili's vitality and competitive potential vis-à-vis the English language. Representing the views of his *Chama cha Kiswahili cha Taifa* 'National Swahili Academy', Chairperson Kimani Njogu suggests that 'modernizing' Kiswahili by making it more compatible with the age of Information and Communication Technology is an important step within a more general strategy of counter-penetration intended to challenge English in 'its own turf', as the Internet has been perceived to be (personal communication, 16 July 2007). However, to what extent do these nationalist objectives of the Microsoft localization project, which promotes Kiswahili, in contrast to the perceived dominance of the English language, reflect the sociolinguistic trends on the 'Kenyan' Internet and the sentiments of and language choices made by Internet users themselves? And how do the Kiswahili–English Internet dynamics compare with the situation in the rest of society? These are some of the questions that will be explored in this chapter against the backdrop of contending schools of thought on the interplay between language and the Internet. For the purpose of this chapter, the Internet is regarded as one of the recent engines of globalization, of the process of rapid acceleration in the circulation of people, goods, information and images on a world scale.

9.2 Language and the Internet: Competing Schools of Thought

Since the early 1990s there has been a school of thought that has regarded the Internet as yet another instrument of English linguistic imperialism with a global reach. After all, by the mid-1990s, over 80 per cent of the Internet was in English. A survey on Internet linguistic diversity conducted by Ao Benjamin of First Byte (a speech technology company in California) and posted on a listserv entitled the *Linguist* on 14 November 1995 concludes that:

1. Linguistic diversity is greatly reduced on the Internet.
2. All but two (Russian and Bulgarian) posting languages have writing systems based on the Roman script.
3. Speakers of languages that do not have Roman alphabet-based writing systems do not bother with transliteration (with the exception of Russian and Bulgarian speakers). They simply adopt English.
4. English is by far the most popular language on the   , even if the subject matter is highly culturally and ethnically oriented.

With this linguistic trend *The Economist* was quick to conclude, in an article entitled 'The Coming Global Tongue', that 'English may now be impregnably established as the world standard language: an intrinsic part of the global communications revolution' (21 December 1996:78), a conclusion that seemed to vindicate the opponents of Internet linguistic imperialism, such as Robert Phillipson. The latter sees computer-related technology as a way of obviating 'the need for the physical presence of the exploiters', as a more effective means of stepping up 'the Centre's attempt to control people's consciousness'. And that attempt is seen to hinge primarily on 'the Centre's cultural and linguistic penetration of the Periphery' through the instrumentality of the English language (Phillipson 1992:52–53).

Within less than a decade, however, the proportion of English usage on the Internet had dropped to less than 50 per cent, as a direct result of the so-called localization industry that seeks to adapt products and services to languages and cultures of target audiences in distant lands. By the end of 2004, a little over 30 per cent of Internet usage was in English (http://www.Internetworldstats.com/stats7.htm), with two-thirds of the users being non-native speakers of the language (Crystal 2004:87). Some, like Ronald Judy (1999), have interpreted this development as a natural expression of the competitive economic and market forces. English is thus seen not as a 'property' of a particular people or culture, but as a commodity in the global marketplace with changing fortunes on the Internet as a direct response to the laws of 'consumer' demand.

Others have regarded the increasing linguistic diversification of the Internet as a locally driven, quasi-nationalistic response to an Anglo-centric cultural globalization. In the words of Warschauer et al. (2002):

> Economic and social globalization, pushed along by the rapid diffusion of the Internet, creates a strong demand for an international lingua franca, thus furthering English's presence as a global language (. . .) On the other hand, the same dynamics that gave rise to globalization, and global English, also give rise to a backlash against both, and that gets expressed, in one form, through a strengthened attachment to local dialects and languages.

The phenomenon described here by Warschauer et al. has also been noted with regard to the place of South African languages on the Internet (Wasserman 2006).

An excellent example of Internet linguistic diversification prompted by nationalism is that of Icelandic. Since the population of Icelanders worldwide is just about half a million and, furthermore, most Icelanders speak English as a second language, Microsoft did not find it imperative to translate the English version of Windows operating system into Icelandic. But Icelanders felt that Microsoft's plan would imperil their language, perhaps leading to a gradual language shift, especially among the young, to English at the expense of Icelandic. 'After the Iceland government threatened to mandate local use of different operating systems (Apple came in Icelandic), Microsoft relented and wrote an Icelandic version' (Goldsmith and Wu 2006:50). In contrast to this almost purist linguistic nationalism of the Icelanders, Warschauer et al. cite the examples of Egypt and Singapore, both ex-colonies of Britain, to demonstrate that local reactions need not always be in the direction of local languages: they could sometimes trigger a localization of what is seen as the global medium (2002). In both these countries, there emerged local varieties of English, balancing what is seen as the practical value of the language, on the one hand, and the nationalist pull of sovereignty, on the other.

Yet another school of thought is the one that regards the growing multilingualism in the Internet not as product of local resistances to globalization, but as an imposed condition by the same forces of globalization through the agenda of 'localization'. Globalization is now no longer seen to be linked to 'Englishization' as eBusiness increasingly adopts a relativist linguistic strategy. This strategy

> follows from the assumption that adapting to the local culture and language – releasing local markets from the task of translation and providing translation services as part of the product – is a necessary component in the penetration of, and competition over, local markets (. . .) Global businesses are gradually abandoning not only the attempt to 'uncover the universal predictive laws of the market' but also the utopia of an 'international lingua franca' and are looking at ways to penetrate local markets in their own languages. (Dor 2004:102)

When it comes to Internet communication, then, the forces of economic globalization are seen to have developed great interest in penetrating world markets through local languages, transforming them into commodified instruments of economic and cultural domination.

Tom Watson (1999), an ardent advocate of Internet globalization, has suggested that 'In many ways [the Internet regime] is a bit like the old East India colonial days – but without the guns and the ships and, hopefully, without the exploitation' (1). In that same colonial period in Africa, some colonial languages were privileged and selected for standardization and codification to serve imperial ends. As Johannes Fabian (1986) has argued, African languages became part of the colonial project of command and control. In this era of the new Empire, are we again witnessing a selective process, controlled from the imperial center, whereby some languages will get 'technologized' and pushed to new positions in the global constellation of languages to better feed the imperial machine, at least in the economic front? Is this relativist face of imperialism what the Microsoft African languages localization program is all about?

The preliminary survey for this study makes it clear, of course, that the Microsoft local programs in African languages are not a response to local (African) pressures of linguistic nationalism, though nationalists have been in support of the development. Apart from South Africa, where strong Afrikaner nationalism – reacting especially to the new Anglocentrism in the country – has led to wide use of Afrikaans on the Internet (Wasserman 2006:5), the situation elsewhere in Africa is such that the localization programs are 'imposed' from above, perhaps under the perception that they would better serve the market interests of neo-liberalism. On the other hand, what the study demonstrates is that far from supporting the nationalist agenda of empowering Kiswahili in its perceived competition against English through the localization program, the Internet in Kenya has generally favored the use of 'global English'.

9.3 Kenya's Language Context

Kenya has over forty ethnic languages, which are primarily known to and used by members of the respective ethnic groups. In addition, it has been fortunate to have two trans-ethnic media of communication, Kiswahili and English, which have experienced changing fortunes, sometimes conflicting and at times complementary, since the days of British colonial rule.

In terms of postcolonial language policy, the first decade of Kenya's independence witnessed little change from the old imperial pattern. The English language continued to be the primary official language, with Kiswahili declared as the language of national heritage. It was not until ten years after independence that the government took the major step of introducing Kiswahili into parliament, giving it some minimal official status. Today, even though the legislation continues to come before parliament written in English, both English and Kiswahili enjoy equal status as the languages of parliamentary debate. Parliamentary candidates are required to be proficient in both English and Kiswahili. In 1983, with the introduction of a new educational system, English continued to be the primary medium of instruction; but Kiswahili now became a compulsory and examinable subject in both primary and secondary education. Since then, every student has had to demonstrate command of both English and Kiswahili to graduate.

In spite of the new educational policy that has advanced the place of Kiswahili in society at large, English has continued to enjoy tremendous support from the government in terms of human and material resources. Kenya's language policy has put high premium on English as the language of national and individual economic and social advancement. As a result, not only has English dominated the entire educational structure, but also its use in society at large has been expanding. There is first a growing number of people whose lives are virtually dominated by the English language in meeting their communicative needs. Many members of the educated African elite have come to rely on English in public interactions as well as in their homes, especially among couples of inter-ethnic unions. There is also an increasing number of Kenyans who are growing up bilingual in English and one or more ethnic languages. And because they are exposed to the ethnic language only in the home, while they get English both at home and outside, English gains the upper hand in functional primacy. Indeed, as early as 1974, it was observed that there is a gradual shift from local languages to English in Kenya in general (Gorman 1974:361), especially among middle and upper class children in urban areas.

But the spread of English in the society as a whole is by no means limited to the urban middle and upper classes. Whiteley's study (1974) of English usage in rural Kenya, for example, is quite informative. The largest number of rural respondents who claimed competence in English was trilingual in the mother tongue, Kiswahili as a second language, and English. This group constituted an average of about 32 per cent of his (multi-ethnic) sample, a figure proportionately higher than the average percentage (of about 19) for respondents claiming competence in the mother tongue and Kiswahili alone. On the other hand, those who claimed competence in English and one or more 'vernaculars' without knowledge of Kiswahili constituted less than 6 per cent of the sample (Whiteley 1974:37–45).

If over thirty years ago the spread of English was already so extensive in the rural areas, as Whiteley's figures seem to suggest, then its impact on the urban population is likely to be even deeper. Due to the greater concentration, in the city, of schools as well as of speakers of English (as a first or additional language) and to the greater availability of radio, television, films, magazines and other entertainment in English, the urban population generally has greater access to this language than the rural population. Moreover, the international status of Kenya's capital, Nairobi, has enhanced the value of English in the country as a whole and intensified the quest for its acquisition.

There have of course been new developments since Whiteley carried out his study. For instance, every pre-university student in Kenya is now required to study Kiswahili and pass it as a subject in the national examination. This policy has been in operation for over twenty years, accompanied by a very rich and growing body of Kiswahili publications. Assessing the results of this policy, Kimani Njogu (2006), the afore-mentioned chairperson of Kenya's *Chama cha Kiswahili cha Taifa* (National Swahili Council), concludes:

> There is an aura of excitement among Kiswahili scholars because seeds planted decades ago have flowered and are beginning to bear fruit. The language is now common in offices, in the streets and homes. It is robust in the informal sector and has become an engine of economic regeneration. Official business is being transacted in the language and it is no longer viewed as 'low status' to speak it. (12)

There is evidence, however, that Njogu's views may be no more than a product of the wishful thinking of a passionate advocate of Kiswahili. In the only empirical study since Whitely, Sure (1999) demonstrates that English is indeed threatening the future of Kiswahili as well as Kenya's ethnic languages. Of his 805 (mainly educated) respondents, 71.4 per cent claimed high proficiency in English as opposed to 55 per cent for Kiswahili. And apart from the market place and the *Jua Kali* (informal) economic sector, where Kiswahili is the preferred code, English is predominant in many domains. As Sure concludes, English

> is now gradually expanding its role and functions to include those that were initially thought to be the natural domains for local languages. It is being used in the homes between siblings and to a small extent between children

and parents. It is preferred between boys and their girlfriends and between
husbands and wives. It is the language of intimacy and romance. In the public
domain it is used invariably in communication in all public institutions (. . .)
It is also preferred in dealings at banks, post office, hospitals, even though in
these institutions one has a choice between English and Kiswahili. This is
already a clear indication that 'the writing is on the wall': English may eventually replace Kiswahili and Mother tongue in all crucial areas of private and
public communication. (7)

In Sure's view, then, what began as a second language acquired mainly for purposes of economic and social mobility, is increasingly becoming the primary
language of successive generations of Kenyans.

Whatever the case, as the two trans-ethnic languages are making competing
claims on the people of Kenya, what has been their distribution in the space
of the Internet? Who uses which language, for what reasons and for what
purposes? Is the computerization of Kiswahili likely to come to the aid of
Kiswahili nationalists who seek to make the language more central and English
less central in the daily lives of the citizens? It is to these questions that we must
now turn.

9.4 The Preliminary Study

Data collection for this study ran for about three months, beginning in mid-
January 2006, approximately a year after the extensively publicized launching
of the Microsoft Kiswahili program, and ending in mid-April 2006. It was carried out among 375 randomly selected users of six cyber-cafes within the island
of Mombasa, one of Kenya's oldest towns and the country's second largest city
with a population of about a million people. Two of the cyber-cafes were located
in the Old Town area of the city, populated predominantly by Muslim native-
speakers of Kiswahili. Another two were in the city center, a more cosmopolitan
space, and the last two were situated in the Tudor/Buxton area that has increasingly come to be occupied by Kenyans from other, non-coastal parts of the
country. The survey was conducted in Kiswahili, but an English version was also
available for respondents who claimed insufficient proficiency in Kiswahili.
Answers were usually in both Kiswahili and English, often code-mixed.

The first part of the survey included seven questions related to personal information. Of the 375 people in the sample – of which 75 were native speakers
of Kiswahili and the rest non-native speakers – 225 were male and 150 female.
Because the larger portion of the survey was conducted during the hours of
9 a.m.–5 p.m., when many women were engaged in domestic chores, the
gender ratio of the sample may be deceptive: Many women may, in fact, be
making greater use of the cyber-cafés in the evening than in the morning and

afternoon. The age of the majority of the participants in the study, 265 (70.64 per cent), varied from twenty-one to thirty years; another 55 (14.66 per cent) were between fifteen and twenty years old. Clearly, then, the young generation constituted the most frequent category of cyber-café users in Mombasa (during morning and afternoon hours), a profile that probably reflects the more general global trend. In terms of religious representation, 190 participants were Christian (Catholic and Protestant), 155 Muslim and the rest followers of other faiths (Hinduism, Jainism, Atheism etc.).

Particularly significant for the study is the fact that all the 375 people in the sample had had at least eight years of elementary education, with English as the medium of instruction. In fact, the majority, 270 participants (72 per cent), were holders of post-secondary/high school credentials, including 85 (25.64 per cent) university graduates, all having been educated entirely in the English language. In a sense, then, computer and Internet usage almost implied some prior proficiency in English. Those who were attracted to the cyber-café, were so attracted partly because they already had some proficiency in English.

The sample was also mixed in terms of the professional backgrounds of the participants: The population included civil servants, elementary school teachers, traders and 'business' people, students, as well as some unemployed. Particularly under-represented were those engaged in middle level professional and management positions. These probably have their own computers at home and/or have access to computer and Internet services at work. It is still true throughout East Africa, of course, that those who own their own computers or are accorded personal computer privileges by their employers constitute a very tiny minority of citizens. That is why cyber-cafés, most of which charge less than one US dollar per hour, have been mushrooming at an alarming rate throughout the region. Though these cyber-café charges are still high for a country with an average annual income of about four hundred US dollars, there is a family-based system of money circulation that allows even unemployed Kenyans to use the Internet regularly, especially in search of job and small-business opportunities.

Finally, except for three respondents – two American study-abroad students and one Japanese visitor – all the subjects claimed speaking knowledge of both English and Kiswahili. Of course, the majority also claimed knowledge of at least one ethnic language. In other words, the largest proportion of the respondents was at least trilingual, with English and Kiswahili as the dominant trans-ethnic languages. And while the survey did not attempt to elicit information on the roles of these languages in the communicative habits of individual speakers, they most likely reflect the kind of 'triglossic' complimentary distribution originally described by Abdulaziz (1972).

The next set of questions focused on cyber-café and Internet use. The majority of the respondents (312 or 83.2 per cent) used the Internet at the cyber-cafés at least three–four times a week. The primary purpose for virtually all the respondents was e-mail communication, but 53.6 per cent (201 respondents) also engaged in chat, and 56.8 per cent (213 of the respondents) in web surfing (many of them 'window-shopping' for fashionable commodities). A tiny minority (7) used the Internet for e-commerce, and another 5 for e-education.

The common Internet medium for virtually all (374 out of 375) respondents, irrespective of level of education, was English. The single respondent who did not use English was the Japanese visitor. In addition to English, 1 respondent used French, another used the Somali language and 15 used German. The latter work intermittently as guides for German tourists, and, having informally acquired the German language in the process, they continue to communicate with some of their German clients after their return to Germany. Particularly surprising was the fact that not a single respondent claimed to use Kiswahili, even though they could easily have done so in their e-mail and chat correspondences.

Several of the respondents agreed to share with me printed copies of some of their Internet exchanges. From these print-outs it was clear that, in spite of the claim of the respondents that they used English exclusively, Kiswahili appeared quite extensively in many of the exchanges, but almost always in code-switching and code-mixing constructions with English. There was a particularly high incidence of Kiswahili slang terms associated with 'Sheng' or 'Mtaa' (neighbourhood talk) – an English–Swahili slang code that is particularly prominent among the youth, especially in urban slum areas. In spite of this significant presence of Kiswahili (words, phrases and short sentences) that constituted the 'Netspeak dialect' of several of the respondents, however, English did form the linguistic core of the texts, lending credence to the respondents' self-perception that they were, in fact, communicating in English. On the other hand, the sample of exchanges highlighted once again the extent to which Internet communication blurs the distinction between the oral and the written in the texts it produces.

In brief follow-up interviews with several of the respondents on why they preferred English to Kiswahili for their Internet needs, a number of factors were mentioned. The first is the official status of the language in the country: As indicated earlier, English is the language of governance, banking, commerce, international relations, schooling, administration of justice and of virtually every official and quasi-official domain of the society at the national level. The massive presence of expatriate workers attached to a wide range of international NGOs or business organizations has certainly consolidated the position of English in the urban society at large. And until the recent launching of Microsoft's Kiswahili Local Program, this situation was exacerbated by the lack of Kiswahili software.

Many of the participants also stressed that their computer training was entirely in English, whether in English-medium computer colleges or at their English-dominated places of work. Apart from the fact that they were not familiar with the Kiswahili computer terminology, there was a general feeling that, in any case, such a terminology would be difficult to understand. As an example, some referred to the abridged Kiswahili version of the new draft constitution of the country that, in their opinion, was virtually incomprehensible to anyone without some technical, scholarly training in the language. And for many of the young respondents, Kiswahili per se was not 'cool' enough. In the words of one of the respondents, 'If you are talking about the Kiswahili we hear on radio and television, it just does not represent *ile* spirit *ya vijana* (the spirit of the youth)'. When respondents were made aware of the fact that their Internet English was, in fact, heavily interspersed with Kiswahili, several responded that that was their way of making English cool. Paradoxically then, if Kiswahili alone was not cool enough as a marker of youth identity, it had become essential for producing a 'hip' version of a youth variety of English.

More than any other factor, however, was the issue of 'comfort'. What is sometimes at stake is not only a bilingual's comparative command of his or her two languages. It is also the comparative comfort that bilinguals may have with each language. Many of the respondents, of course, are among the small proportion of Kenyans who had studied Kiswahili as a compulsory subject throughout elementary and high school. To some it was their native tongue. At some point they were more comfortable speaking Kiswahili than speaking in English. In the written medium, however, they increasingly became more comfortable writing in the English language than writing in Kiswahili. It is true that some scored higher in Kiswahili language examinations than in English ones. But their lives were being shaped by English as an instrument rather than as an independent subject. In the process, English became the primary medium of much of their writing (and reading) activities, while Kiswahili and other African languages became oriented to the world of orality. And since the language of the computer is still overwhelmingly a written language, participants found it easier to communicate in English than in Kiswahili. Respondent after respondent emphasized that 'English is just simpler', 'It is easier to browse in English', 'I cannot write fast enough in Kiswahili', 'I am just used to English', 'I cannot read Swahili very well', 'Swahili is too difficult to understand' and so on and so forth.

The respondents have been so comfortable with English, in fact, that only 6 out of the total 375 were even aware of the Kiswahili localization program, and thus that Kiswahili is one of the languages now available for Google web searches, for example. And the 6 that were aware of this linguistic possibility did not make use of it at all – again for the reason that they are 'used' to working on the computer in English. The mere availability of a Kiswahili localization program, in other words, does not guarantee its utilization.

The 369 respondents who were learning about the Microsoft initiative for the first time were then provided with more information about the Kiswahili program, especially its features, objectives and when it was launched. Now that they had been made aware of the program, how likely were they to make use of it for their computer and Internet needs? The responses to this question were quite mixed. Of the respondents 99 indicated that they were either very likely (13.55 per cent) or somewhat likely (13.28 per cent) to make use of the Kiswahili software, especially in their communication with young relatives and friends. The majority, however, a total of 165 respondents (amounting to 44.72 per cent) – almost double the number of likely users – were either quite unlikely or very unlikely to use the program at all. The remaining 105 respondents (28.46 per cent) were non-committal, uncertain of the likelihood of ever using the Kiswahili option in their own computer and Internet work.

It was noteworthy that of the 99 respondents who indicated some likelihood of using Kiswahili, 45 (or 45.45 per cent) were university graduates. In other words, over half of those who were most exposed to English in their educational training – that is, university graduates – seemed inclined to use Kiswahili. Their reasons turned out to be primarily nationalistic, the idea that Kiswahili is our 'national language', 'a language of our cultural heritage', 'the expression of our Africanity' or 'our linguistic weapon against cultural imperialism'. After all, the African university has long been a hotbed of nationalist politics in spite of its massive cultural dependency, or perhaps because of it.

An equally interesting finding is related to the gender variable. Of the 165 respondents 91 (55.55 per cent) who indicated that they were *unlikely* to use Kiswahili were female. This means that 91 out of the 150 female respondents (60.67 per cent), in contrast to 33.79 per cent of the male respondents, showed preference for English over Kiswahili. Many of the interviewed female respondents talked of their desire to improve their English language skills as a way of increasing their opportunities in the job market. Since in policy and general practice English is the language of the professional and semi-professional workplace in Kenya, its acquisition is considered indispensable for securing a 'respectable' job and for one's professional advancement thereafter. Furthermore, as I have demonstrated elsewhere (Mazrui 2004:24–25), some women in Kenya regard the acquisition and use of English as providing a linguistic space for minimizing the effects of ethnically sanctioned cultural constraints on their lives.

An even more intriguing finding has to do with religion. Of the 165 respondents who did not believe they were likely to use Kiswahili, 89 (about 53.94 per cent) were Muslim, and the rest non-Muslim. Put in another way, 89 of the total 155 Muslim respondents (about 57.47 per cent) – several of whom were native speakers of Kiswahili – seemed to prefer English in contrast to 35.52 per cent of non-Muslim respondents.

Interviews with several Muslim users of the cyber-cafés revealed a certain interplay between language and the question of Muslim identity, on the one hand, and language and Muslim unity, on the other. In the literature on the globalization of English, the process has sometimes been problematized not only in terms of the fear that it might 'kill' the local altogether – see, for example, Day (1985) and McArthur (1999) – but also in terms of its potential, real or imagined, to erode local cultural particularities (e.g., Mazrui 1995). In many parts of the world, the language has often been seen as an instrument of cultural westernization. Yet, ironically, these nationalist sentiments of some intellectuals about English have not always led to its rejection by the population at large. On the contrary, there is an insatiable appetite for the language – even in some parts of the Muslim world where the 'danger' of westernization is regarded with greatest hostility. What has happened rather is a growing consciousness that seeks to restrict English to an 'instrumental' function as communities engage in a certain institutional revaluation of their local languages for purposes of identity affirmation. This is a dialectic that is quite evident in Mombasa, Kenya.

The demand for English in Mombasa once led Sheikh Muhammad Kasim (d. 1986), a leading Islamic reformer, to warn of the dangers of English in his Kiswahili periodical *Sauti ya Haki*, of August 1972, in the following words:

> We have no alternative but to study and know English, because today English is the language of livelihood. But we must not forget that there is also the larger world of religion and our traditions. If we are not careful the English language will swallow us completely – even our thoughts will now be cast in an English mode. The danger of English must be tempered by the wisdom encapsulated in both Arabic and Kiswahili. It is therefore imperative that our Qur'anic schools offer learning not only in Qur'anic literacy, but must also be used to teach the logic arising from Islam as well as secular subjects in our own languages, Swahili and Arabic. And this responsibility [of acquiring this integrated knowledge] is greater for women, for it is they who do much of the parenting in our homes. (My translation)

Sheikh Muhammad Kasim's relativistic thinking is clear: English is a carrier of Western values and its cognitive effects can only be counteracted by concerted efforts to re-center languages such as Kiwahili and Arabic, which he regards as the custodians of Afro-Islamic values and traditions. Though Arabic is not widely spoken in the community, it has a special place in the world of Islam as a language of religious ritual and doctrinal revelation.

Yet, as the results of this study have shown, this growing Afro-Islamic consciousness has not led to the rejection of English in Internet communication. Kiswahili, and to a lesser extent Arabic, are regarded as important media for the articulation of local Muslim identities. English, on the other hand, has the value of keeping the global Muslim *ummah* (community) better connected, its origins in the West notwithstanding. And in Islam, this global Muslim entity is given primacy over more particularistic identities. Five of the Muslim interviewees even suggested that the Kiswahili localization program is a 'conspiracy' of a sort intended to keep East African Muslims isolated from the global *ummah* at a time when their unity has become urgent as a result of what is perceived to be the growing Western hostility towards Islam.

In addition to secular functions, Muslims in Kenya use the Internet to access a wide range of Islamic materials, both visual and auditory. These include current affairs in the Muslim world, greeting cards during Islamic festivities, images of Muslim holy sites for personal or business use, purchase of Islamic books or of items from Muslim businesses, latest information on Mecca and Medina for those aspiring to go on pilgrimage, seeking answers to a variety of questions related to Muslim personal lifestyle, websites offering Islamic perspectives on HIV–AIDS prevention or management, recitations of the Qur'an by the Egyptian Shaykh Abdul-Basit Abdul-Samad, among others. A locally produced online journal in English, *Khilafah* – advocating the rejection of Western-style democracies in favor of the caliphate system practiced in the early centuries of Islam – is also visited quite frequently by Muslim Internet users.

Elsewhere we have argued that the Internet may help Islam realize some of its earliest aims more effectively. The first may be the shrinkage of sovereignty in the wake of the Internet towards a more consolidated Muslim *ummah*. The printed word may have been playing a major role in the construction of nationhood and in reinforcing national consciousness. Computer communication, on the other hand, may be contributing to the construction of other trans-ethnic communities beyond the nation, as it seems to be doing in the formation of language-based identity between Latin America and US Hispanics (Warschauer 2000:165). Islam and the information revolution may be allies in breaking down the barriers of competing national sovereignties. The new technology may give Islam a chance to realize its original aim of transnational universalism.

Linked to the shrinkage of sovereignty is the role of the Internet in the compression of distance, the perceived recession of geographical constraints (Waters 1995:3) – or what some have actually called 'the death of distance' (Wang et al. 2003). In some ways this takes Islam back to its roots. One of the most sacred cities for Islam is, of course, Jerusalem. Especially sacred to Muslims is al-Quds, focused on the Dome of the Rock. Muslims believe that on the night of *Mi'raj* distance was compressed at three levels: the Prophet Muhammad moved from Mecca to Jerusalem in a single night in the age of the camel; and he moved from earth to the Heavens during the same night, ascending from Jerusalem; and while in the Heavens the present age communicated with the ages of the past, for the Prophet was able to talk to Jesus, Moses and all the way back to Adam during the same night. The Prophet was back in Mecca before morning – breaking at least three sound barriers of cosmic experience: compressing distance between Mecca and Jerusalem; compressing distance between the earth and the Heavens; and compressing distance between the past and the present. It is in this sense that Islam prepared believers for the age of the end of distance and the age of globalized digital simultaneity. This was a prophecy of digital philoscience (Mazrui and Mazrui 2002:148–150). And for many Muslims in Kenya, the actualization of that prophecy has so far relied primarily on a 'non-Islamic' language, English. For some of the interviewees, in fact, the next linguistic challenge for the *ummah* is the Islamization of the English language and its appropriation in the service of Islam globally. Arabic can continue to be the language of Islamic ritual; but English may be the unfolding tool of an Islamic reformation.

9.5 Conclusion

As indicated earlier, the Microsoft localization project received the full support of many Kiswahili nationalists in the belief that the 'computerization' of the language will make it less vulnerable to displacement by English. This position of Kiswahili nationalists contrasts sharply with that of Muslim universalists, many native-speakers of Kiswahili, who see the use of English on the Internet as an important facilitator in the consolidation of the global *ummah*. This tension between state-nationalists and Muslim trans-nationalists on the question of the language of the Internet in Kenya is likely to remain unresolved for the foreseeable future.

On the other hand, the realization of the nationalist objective in favor of Kiswahili will ultimately depend on the extent to which the general population is aware and makes use of the Kiswahili option. For reasons discussed earlier, this has not happened in Kenya nor is it likely to happen any time soon, except among a few (especially university graduates) who are inspired by nationalist sentiments. One is bound to agree with David Crystal (2001), therefore, when he concluded that 'Until a critical mass of Internet penetration in a country builds up, and a corresponding mass of content exits in the local language, the motivation to switch from English-language sites will be limited to those for whom issues of identity outweigh issues of information' (220).

Yet the build-up of a critical mass of Internet penetration in Kiswahili cannot take place without a political paradigm shift that privileges Kiswahili over English in the economic sphere. Since independence, socio-economic advancement at the individual level and economic development at the national level have been pegged to the English language, both in policy and practice. There was a time when those aspiring to migrate from the rural to the urban area would try to acquire Kiswahili to improve their chances of employment in the urban metropolis. But as both the Whiteley (1974) and Sure (1999) studies show, there is a growing demand for English even in the rural areas and that in several parts of the country rural dwellers who are proficient in Kiswahili are also likely to have English in their repertoire. It is still true in Kenya that market forces continue to operate in two streams, favoring Kiswahili in the *Jua Kali* (low-level informal) economic activities, and English for the more formal sector of the economy. Possessing knowledge of both languages widens one's range of economic opportunities.

It is possible that, within the Swahili-speaking world, Tanzania may offer a different kind of experience from that of Kenya. The country's Swahilization program that began in the 1960s has ensured that Kiswahili will have a central role in society, and that the majority of Tanzanians will be more comfortable with Kiswahili than with English, in both the oral and written domains. On the other hand, recent events in Tanzania point to a rapidly changing situation as more and more private schools introduce English-based instruction. As the insular *Ujamaa* experiment collapsed, and socio-economic success increasingly came to be associated with the ability to connect linguistically with the outside world, the parental push for more English (from an elite already fluent in English) kept mounting. Partly as a result of this development, there has been no concerted effort to Swahilize the Internet: Indeed, by 2006, over 90 per cent of Tanzanian websites had English language content (Miller 2006:139). If the computer and the Internet have helped turn the world into a global village, the late President Julius Nyerere of Tanzania, an unrelenting advocate of Kiswahili, indirectly endorsed English as the future language of the Internet in Tanzania when he described it as 'the Swahili of the world' (quoted by Roy-Campbell 2001:100).

Yet it would be wrong, at least in the case of Kenya, to regard English exclusively as a language of the elite. It may be an additional language of a minority of the country's population, but members of that minority are not necessarily members of the elite. Indeed, the slums of Nairobi – the capital city of Kenya – where I have had the opportunity to conduct research are full of unemployed youth with an appreciable command of English. As the data on the personal background of respondents in this study indicates, the most frequent users of Internet cafés are, in fact, not from the ranks of the elite at all. They include low-level professionals, small-scale businessmen and women, students and the unemployed. In one case, the Internet user was representing a rural women's group seeking to market its basketry products internationally. The common denominator for all these Internet users was their proficiency in English: The Internet was an asset to them because they already possessed knowledge of English to some degree or other. While many of them were also competent in Kiswahili, nothing in the nation's socioeconomic system encouraged them to choose Kiswahili over English for their Internet needs.

In acquiring the English language, the respondents had also acquired the literacy skills in the language. Much of the reading and writing in the secular sphere in Kenya takes place in English. While there is an obvious overlap between the two languages, English is the primary language of the written word; Kiswahili, on the other hand, still displays its greatest vibrancy in oral communication. Developments in the print media are particularly instructive in this regard. While the expansion of television and cable network has affected newspaper readership generally, the drop in readership of the only Kenyan Kiswahili daily, *Taifa Leo*, which has always been less that 20 per cent of the readership of its English counterpart, the *Daily Nation*, has dropped at an alarming rate. On the other hand, concurrently, the audience for the Kiswahili national radio programs of the Kenya Broadcasting Corporation (KBC) has been on the rise (Matili 2001). These observations partly help to explain why the Internet, as a space of the written word, is likely to continue to be English-dominated. Internet texts may blur the distinction between the oral and the written, but the process of producing those texts is still seen essentially in terms of the basic skills of writing and reading by Internet users.

The Microsoft Kiswahili project is sometimes undermined by its own internal limitations. The Google search engine, for example, now has a Kiswahili option. Yet, that option seems to operate only at the surface level: When one clicks the icon on 'Kila Kitu Kuhusu Google' (About Google), for example, the information that follows is presented entirely in English. The icon on 'Vikundi' (Groups), leads to a bilingual page, with some items appearing in Kiswahili and others in English. Wasserman (2006) comes to a similar conclusion with regard to South African languages:

> searches on the Internet lead one to conclude that there is little available in these languages. Where these inquiries into these languages do produce results, it is mostly in references to sites which provide information on these languages (in English) rather than information in indigenous languages. (6–7)

The Kiswahili Google program, in other words, has more of a symbolic function and presupposes knowledge of English to access the more substantive information that one is searching for.

On the other hand, the failure of Kiswahili to counter-penetrate an English language domain of the Internet does not imply that the consolidation of English that Sure (1999) has described is taking place at the expense of Kiswahili. If anything, and in spite of himself, Sure's data seems to support Gorman's conclusion (1974) that English may be more of a threat to ethnic-bound languages rather than to Kiswahili, especially in its seeming invasion of domains of personal and familial intimacy. Kiswahili is clearly vibrant as the most important language of mass politicking. However, a presidential candidate who is not proficient in English is highly unlikely to be elected. Still, Kiswahili is a language of daily business transaction at the urban markets, of *jua kali* trade, of the church and the mosque, and of compulsory study at the elementary and high school levels. More significantly, there are regions of the country, such as the Trans-Nzoia district, where Kiswahili is increasingly becoming the primary language of children not only in homes of inter-ethnic marriages, but also in those where the two parents are speakers of the same language (Luyia). The children of several relatives of Ken Walibora, the distinguished Kenyan TV anchor and creative writer, are part of this new generation of Kenyans who are growing up with Kiswahili as their first language in spite of the ethnic background of their parents. In fact, according to Walibora, this pattern of language shift towards Kiswahili is quite widespread in the region (Ken Walibora, personal communication, 27 September 2007). In the final analysis, then, if Kiswahili has failed to counter-penetrate the 'space of English' in Kenya, it seems to have the potential of displacing the more local ethnic languages in parts of Kenya. The dynamics of English on the Internet seems to pose no direct and immediate danger to Kiswahili (or to the country's ethnic languages, for that matter). But in its own momentum towards national and regional consolidation, Kiswahili is certainly (re)configuring the linguistic space in East Africa in new ways.

References

Abdulaziz, Mkilifi M.H. 1972. Triglossia and Swahili-English bilingualism in Tanzania. *Language in Society* 1.197–213.

Crystal, David. 2001. *Language and the Internet.* Cambridge: Cambridge University Press.

—2004. *The Language Revolution.* Cambridge: Polity Press.

Day, R. 1985. The ultimate inequality: Linguistic genocide. In *Language of Inequality*, ed. by N. Wolfson and J. Manes, 163–181. Berlin: Mouton.

Dor, Daniel. 2004. From Englishization to imposed multilingualism: Globalization, the Internet, and the political economy of the linguistic code. *Public Culture* 16(2).97–118.

Fabian, Johannes. 1986. *Language and Colonial Power: The Appropriation of Swahili in the Former Belgian Congo: 1880–1983.* Cambridge: Cambridge University Press.

Goldsmith, Jack and Tim Wu. 2006. *Who Controls the Internet?: Illusions of a Borderless World.* Oxford: Oxford University Press.

Gorman, Thomas P. 1974. Patterns of language use among school children and their parents. In Whiteley (ed.), 351–395.

Judy, Ronald A.T. 1999. Some notes on the status of global English in Tunisia. *Boundary* 2 26(2).3–44.

Matili, Tom. 2001. Journalists' experiences can fill gaps in media culture. *The East African* (Nairobi), 17 December, 16.

Mazrui, Alamin M. 2004. *English in Africa: After the Cold War.* Clevedon: Multilingual Matters.

Mazrui, Alamin M. and Ali A. Mazrui. 2002. Islam and civilization. In *Dialogue of Civilizations: A New Peace Agenda for a New Millennium*, ed. by Majid Tehranian and David W. Chappell, 139–160. London: I. B. Tauris Publishers.

Mazrui, Ali A. 1995. The 'other' and the 'self' under cultural dependency. In *Encountering the Other(s): Studies in Literature, History and Culture*, ed. by Gisela Brinker-Gabler, 333–362. Albany, NY: University of New York Press.

McArthur, Tom. 1999. English in the world, in Africa and in South Africa. *English Today* 15(1).11–16.

Microsoft News. 1999. Gates talks about PCs, Internet and globalization at the World Economic Forum, at www.microsoft.com/presspass/features/1999/02-01davos. asp. 1999.

Miller, Jonathan. 2006. Tanzania: From padlocks to payments. In Wilson and Wong (eds), 137–151.

Mudhai, Okoth F. 2002. The Internet: Triumphs and trials for Kenyan journalism. In *Beyond Boundaries: Cyberspace in Africa*, ed. by Melinda B. Robins and Robert L. Hilliard, 89–104. Portsmouth, NH: Heinemann.

Muiruri, Mary. 2006. Kenya: Diffusion, democracy and development. In Wilson and Wong (eds), 65-84.

Njogu, Kimani. 2006. Kiswahili comes of age as tongue for decolonisation. *Sunday Nation* (Nairobi), 2 July, 12.

Opiyo, Patrick. 2004. Microsoft Kiswahili local language program: Post implementation review. (12 November), Nairobi, Ms.

Phillipson, Robert. 1992. *Linguistic Imperialism*. Oxford: Oxford University Press.

Roy-Campbell, Zaline. 2001. *Empowerment through Language: The African Experience – Tanzania and Beyond*. Lawrenceville, NJ: Africa World Press.

Sure, Kembo. 1999. Bilingual education on an uneven playfield: The Kenyan case. *Journal of Third World Studies* Spring.1–9.

'The Coming Global Tongue', *The Economist*, 21 December 1996, p. 78.

Wang, Yong, Phillip Lai and Daniel Sui. 2003. Mapping the Internet using GIS: The death of distance hypothesis. *Journal of Geographical Systems* 5(4).381–405.

Warschauer, Mark. 2000. Language, identity and the Internet. In *Race in Cyberspace*, ed. by B. Kolko, L. Nakamura and G. Rodman, 151–170. New York: Routledge.

Warschauer, Mark, Ghada R. El Said and Ayman Zohry. 2002. Language choice online: Globalization and identity in Egypt. *Journal of Computer Mediated Communication* 7(4). (Web publication at www.ascusc.org/jcmc).

Wasserman, Herman. 2006. Between the local and the global: South African languages and the Internet. LitNet-Seminar room at http://www.litnet.co.za/seminarroom/11wasserman.asp.

Waters, Malcolm. 1995. *Globalization*. London: Routledge.

Watson, Tom. 1999. Companies redefine national borders: Why Internet globalization is local, at www.atnewyork.com/news/article.php/251451.

Whiteley, Wilfred H. 1974. Patterns of language use in rural Kenya. In Whiteley (ed.), 319–359.

Whiteley, Wilfred H. (ed.). 1974. *Language in Kenya*. Nairobi: Oxford University Press.

Wilson, Ernest J. and Kelvin R. Wong (eds). 2006. *Negotiating the Net in Africa: The Politics of Internet Diffusion*. Boulder: Lynne Rienner.

Chapter 10

Writing Locality in Globalized Swahili: Semiotizing Space in a Tanzanian Novel

Jan Blommaert

10.1 Introduction

When is a language 'vital'? One of the features we cannot possibly overlook is the way in which globalization processes affect languages, how some languages perish while others persist under the pressure of globalization, notably articulated around the dominance of English or other metropolitan European languages. This dominance is often presented as marginalizing and erasing 'indigenous' languages, of diminishing their scope and function; it is also captured in a metaphorical framework of brutal, 'linguicidal' imperialism (e.g., Phillipson 1992). While good things can be said about such a viewpoint, both its metaphorical basis and its empirical sustainability have been under attack (Blommaert 2005a; Freeland and Patrick 2004; May 2001; Mufwene 2002). Empirically, we often see that 'dominant' languages not always only exclude and oppress, but often also offer new communicative possibilities and opportunities for creating new sociolinguistic identities; metaphorically, the 'killer' image of a dominant language is therefore misleading, and new images need to be sought in order to do justice to the empirical processes we observe.

One perhaps more promising metaphorical frame is that of globalization studies. The frame emphasizes terms such as *centers* and *periphery* within the *world system, flows, scales, networks, global economy* and so forth.[1] Theoretically, the main challenge for disciplines such as anthropology, sociology and (socio)linguistics may consist in loosening the connection between *culture* and a particular fixed *territory*. Whereas more traditional approaches appeared to tacitly assume that societies and their features 'belonged' to one particular geographical area, and thus attributed an *absolute* spatiality to culture, the emphasis on situatedness emphasizes flows, trajectories, movements and thus the *relative* spatiality of culture. Hannerz (1991:116–117) summarizes this as follows: 'The connection between cultural process and territory, we should remind ourselves, is only contingent. As socially organized meaning, culture is primarily a phenomenon of interaction, and only if interactions are tied to particular spaces is culture likewise so.'

Thus, whereas according to Hannerz traditional anthropology was concerned with culture as 'a matter of flow of meaning in face-to-face relationships between people who do not move around much' (1991:117), it is one of the main assumptions of globalization studies that multiple cultures can exist in one space and that, conversely, one culture can be produced in different spaces. The thematization of space and place (the latter denoting a space made social, hence becoming a space in which humans make social, cultural, political and historical investments) is thus a crucial ingredient of the process of coming to terms with globalization (Crang 1999), of producing globalized locality, of 'vernacularizing' globalization (Appadurai 1990).

This is an elementary cultural activity that we see articulated, in very Whorfian ways, in language structure and discourse. I will argue that doing so in a particular language reveals 'vitality' in that language, in the sense that the language resources are proved to be up to the task of globalized meaning production. I will argue this with respect to Swahili. This is somewhat off-mark in the literature on globalization, which is strongly focused on 'big' globalized languages such as English, French and (increasingly) Chinese, and on communicative channels such as electronic mass media and popular culture. We should not forget that many (indeed, very many) 'smaller' languages are effectively globalized, and Swahili is one of them, as we shall see.

I will consider one particular cultural form that is rather untypical in globalization studies: written literature from the 'periphery'. I show how a novel, *Miradi Bubu ya Wazalendo* ('The invisible enterprises of the patriots'), by Gabriel Ruhumbika, carries various kinds of spatial semiotizations that point towards locally salient centers-versus-periphery models, flows and translocal transactions. These models are reminiscent of Wallerstein's (1983) World-Systems analysis, which hinges on a view of the world as divided into centers, semi-peripheries and peripheries, between which an intricate division of labor exists (which is, in Wallerstein's analysis, global capitalism). At the micro-level of the novel itself, space is used as a powerful literary–stylistic device. It attributes identities to the characters; it casts their actions and their biographies in a recognizable local social semiotic; and spatial–semiotic features organize the meta-story of Tanzanian postcolonial politics. It is a form of cultural vernacularization, of the production of locality. At a macro-level (the level of the cultural act of writing itself), the novel illustrates the deterritorialized, network and translocal nature of contemporary cultural and political processes as well as the capacity of contemporary literacy to 'repatriate' meanings (Appadurai 1990:307). This latter dimension challenges established views of African literature – here, Swahili literature – as necessarily produced in Africa and tied to a particular place. Though by now it may sound rather evident that African literature can be diasporic, the theoretical implications of this may be far-reaching. More precisely, this globalized dimension of the novel makes its strongly local flavor peculiar and demonstrates the dynamics of Swahili as a globalized, vital language.

I will start by providing some background information on the novel. Next, we will move into an analysis of spatial semiotics in the novel itself, showing how a particular social and political geography of the country dominates the framing of characters and events along a centers/periphery axis. After this, I will return to the deterritorialized nature of the act of writing itself and the effect this has on the way in which we view 'local' literatures and literary actors. We will conclude by sketching some theoretical implications.

10.2 The Invisible Enterprises of the Patriots

Miradi Bubu ya Wazalendo was written in 1992 and published by Tanzania Publishing House in Dar es Salaam, Tanzania. It is written in the national language of Tanzania, Swahili, and it adds to the impressive modern written literature in that language (see Bertoncini 1989 for a survey). Especially in the postcolonial era (and notably under Ujamaa socialism), writing in Swahili was a densely symbolic act: it carried meta-meanings that indexed patriotism, loyalty to the nation and its political doctrine, and a democratic (socialist) attitude (see Madumulla et al. 1999 and Blommaert 1999, Chapter 4). Writing a literary piece in the national language was a political statement in its own right, and those doing it performed a cultural politics as much as producing a cultural product. This intense politics of literary codes and forms undoubtedly contributed to the vitality of the language after independence: it mobilized intellectuals and artists into conscious linguistic 'development', and it gave them a voice of their own as a *national* intelligentsia, a committed vanguard of people who shaped the minds of their people by shaping their language. The author, Gabriel Ruhumbika, was very much a member of this vanguard. He was born in 1938 on Ukerewe Island in Lake Victoria, in the British Mandate of Tanganyika. Ruhumbika was a professor of literature at the University of Dar es Salaam between 1970 and 1985, and he was one of the country's leading radical intellectuals (see, e.g., Mbuguni and Ruhumbika 1974). After 1985, he moved to the United States and became a professor of English at Hampton University, Virginia, and afterwards a professor of comparative literature at the University of Georgia. *Miradi Bubu ya Wazalendo* was written in the United States but was published in Dar es Salaam.

The book is a political novel, and its title already announces this. The term *wazalendo* 'patriots' was one of the key terms in the lexicon of Tanzania's Ujamaa socialism, a particular brand of socialism developed and propagated as the state ideology by the first president of Tanzania, Julius Nyerere.[2] Ruhumbika's novel is hard to read without any knowledge of the Ujamaa socialist period in Tanzania, for it is intended as a retrospective commentary on the Ujamaa political system and what it did to the country. Tanzania emerged out of the union of Tanganyika and the former British Protectorate of Zanzibar in 1964. Tanganyika had won its independence after a period of peaceful transition in 1961 under the leadership of Nyerere's TANU (Tanganyika African National Union) party; Zanzibar became independent in 1963, but the Sultanate installed by the British was soon overthrown by a popular revolution, the leaders of which sought closer union with socialist Tanganyika. The union led to a socialist radicalization within the new Republic of Tanzania, and this radicalization was codified in 1967 in the so-called Arusha Declaration, which proclaimed *Ujamaa na Kujitegemea* 'socialism and self-reliance'. The main features of this state ideology were egalitarianism, the absence of exploitation, political and economic non-alignment, pan-Africanism and self-reliant small-scale agricultural development (in 'Ujamaa villages') as the backbone of the economy (see Pratt 1976).

Ujamaa was, certainly in the years following the Arusha Declaration, very popular with the younger intelligentsia, largely based at the University of Dar es Salaam, of which Ruhumbika was a member. The university was a centers of radical political activity, not only nationally but also internationally (Othman 1994), and many of the young intellectuals saw themselves as the leading vanguard in a socialist revolution (see Shivji 1996 for excellent examples). Consequently, many intellectuals vigorously supported TANU (which had become the single party of the country), though their emphasis on a radical socialist strategy was not always welcomed by the TANU leaders (Blommaert 1999, Chapter 2). The Tanzanian Ujamaa economy collapsed in the 1970s and the country was further impoverished by a war against Idi Amin's Uganda in the late 1970s. From that point onwards, disillusionment about TANU and socialism was great. Nyerere voluntarily stepped down as president in 1985, and his successor, Mwinyi, almost immediately signed an agreement with the IMF to restructure the system. Ujamaa was abandoned; and a new official state ideology of economic liberalism replaced Kujitegemea ('self reliance') and a multiparty system was installed.

It is against this background of general disillusionment that *Miradi Bubu* is set. Written by an erstwhile radical supporter of Ujamaa, it reflects on power-abuse, inequality, class-determinism and injustice in socialist Tanzania. It does so by telling the story of two Tanzanians, Saidi and Nzoka, the main characters. Part of Saidi's story involves two other men, Mzee Jabiri and Munubi, whose lives are subplots in the novel.

The plot of the book consists of five parts, is summarized here:

Part 1: Mzee Jabiri

Mzee Jabiri lives in Masasi, in southern Tanganyika. He has two children late in life, but his daughter and wife die of an unknown disease. He leaves Masasi with his only surviving child, the boy Saidi. They travel to Tanga in the north and get a menial job in a sisal plantation owned by a white man. Mzee Jabiri gets badly injured during work in the fields. The supervisor, Munubi, forces the white plantation owner to drive Mzee Jabiri to a hospital.

Jabiri dies before they reach the hospital. The plantation owner dumps Mzee Jabiri's body in a sewage pit.

Part 2: Supervisor Munubi

Munubi leaves the plantation with Saidi and travels to a relative's house in Mombo. There, he arranges for Saidi to be brought to relatives of his in Dar es Salaam. Munubi himself finds a job on a sisal plantation in Morogoro, central Tanzania. The plantation is owned by a white South African, and Munubi, as a supervisor, is supposed to administer corporal punishment to the workers. When he does so, however, Mzee Jabiri's ghost appears in his sleep. Munubi flees to another place and he continues to move from one place to another until Independence. After Independence, he gets a job as a supervisor in Kilosa, on a farm owned by an Englishman. Munubi marries a woman there and builds himself a house outside the farm compound. The farm owner disagrees with this and fires Munubi. Mzee Jabiri's ghost incites Munubi to correct this injustice, and Munubi kills the farmer. Munubi is tried and hanged for this murder.

Part 3: Ndugu Saidi

Saidi has found his way to Dar es Salaam, where he lives with a relative of Munubi's. He finds a job as a houseboy with an Indian family, and then works as a shopkeeper in the Indian neighborhood for nine years. In his spare time, he is a volunteer worker for TANU, the leading independence party. After some time, he gets hired by TANU as a messenger. His salary is lower than what he earned from the Indians, but he is committed to TANU's cause and accepts the bad labor conditions. Saidi lives in a one-room flat in Kariakoo, the market area of Dar es Salaam. When Nyerere becomes president in 1962, Saidi joins his personal staff as a messenger. In the meantime, he has let his friend and colleague Nzoka move into his house. Saidi marries Chiku, and, between 1962 and 1967, the couple has three children. In 1967, with the Arusha Declaration, TANU installs a number of official commissions and Nzoka becomes the leader of one of them. He appoints Saidi as a messenger to the commission. Saidi decides to build a house of his own in Manzese and the family moves into the half-finished house without electricity or running water in 1970. By 1981, Saidi has nine children and is struggling to make ends meet. The country is economically devastated, and things get worse after the 1985 and 1986 economic liberalizations. Saidi's two oldest daughters become prostitutes. His oldest daughter Idaya murders her child and is imprisoned. When Nyerere steps down in 1985, Saidi is made redundant. He receives a very small sum of money and some praise for his patriotism, but lives in abject poverty in Manzese.

Part 4: Executive Director Nzoka

Nzoka was born in the Mwanza region of northern Tanzania. He fails to qualify in a state exam and is not eligible for studies abroad. Instead, he organizes a trade union and manages to impress Nyerere with his organizational and propaganda skills. Nyerere hires him to canvass popular support. He joins the TANU headquarters in Dar es Salaam in 1956, moves into Saidi's apartment, and becomes Nyerere's personal assistant. He marries Beatrice and earns enough to move to the European quarter in Oyster Bay. Nyerere sends him to various international colleges to complete his training. He travels to Ghana and Israel, and then to Ruskin College, Oxford, Lumumba University, Moscow, and the University of Sussex. In 1967, Nzoka has five children. He becomes the executive director of the State Commission for Planning, Wealth, Savings and Progress. This ends his friendship with Saidi as well as his marriage with Beatrice. Nzoka had committed adultery. He remarries and divorces several times, including a woman called Rosemary, a German female professor, and an Indian woman (who converts him to Islam). He becomes head of the Armed Forces. He falls in love with a prostitute but marries her daughter and converts to Catholicism. By 1985, Nzoka has thirty-two children, all of whom are finishing their studies or are being taken care of by nannies. He lives in luxury while the country has become one of the poorest in the world.

Part 5: Epilogue
Saidi decides to make the injustices he has experienced public at a ceremony at which he is thanked for his years of service. He walks up to Nyerere, the farewell gifts in his hand, but the latter doesn't recognize him, despite the many years of contact. Nzoka, who is also present, senses Saidi's plan and announces to Nyerere that Saidi intends to offer him the gifts he has just received, out of gratitude for what he (Nyerere) has done for the country. Saidi is praised for his patriotism but is not given the opportunity to speak out.

10.3 The Social Semiotic of Tanzanian Space

People attribute meanings to the spaces they know and use (see e.g., Feld and Basso 1996; Low 2001). Such spaces are filled with symbols and attributes, and using them creates indexical ties to them. The symbols and attributes not only refer to the objective place, but also to a particular atmosphere associated with it, including the people living in it, as well as their class and other cultural peculiarities.[3] Thus a Cockney accent does not only identify one as being from London; it also carries class, gender and other cultural indexicalities. Code-switching may indexicalize the particular flavor of a place and may thus 'make a person speak from that place' as it were (see Blommaert 2005b, Chapter 8; Maryns and Blommaert 2001; Rampton 2001). Inhabitants of a particular place distinguish between 'good' and 'bad' neighborhoods or parts of a country, and upward social mobility is often associated with (and practically effected by) moving from a bad to a good place. Features of particular places, such as the Eiffel Tower in Paris or the Statue of Liberty in New York, 'can be used to defend local identity, sell development sites, comment ironically on local transformations, or simply situate a plot development in films' (Wong and McDonogh 2001:98). They can, consequently also be used to situate a plot development in a novel. Obviously, some of the indexicalities carried by places are meaningful only to 'locals', some are to outsiders too.

Ruhumbika uses places and spatial trajectories that are indexically highly salient to Tanzanians. Investigating them may lead us to a local perception of centers and peripheries, a world-systems model transposed to one particular area. Recall that Wallerstein's model operated at the global level; we see here a 'fractal' replication of this model at a lower, national level. This fractal phenomenon may direct us to cultural and social patterns in which social behavior appears to be organized on the basis of perceptions of opportunities (generally located in 'centers') and of social mobility and ambition. Focusing on how, for instance, opportunities and social mobility are perceived, it may also direct us to empirically graspable forms of transnational flow: Appadurai's well-known '-scapes' (1990). We will now examine the way in which such patterns are perused in *Miradi Bubu*; we will first articulate some of the widespread attributes and associations tied to particular places and regions in Tanzanian popular imagery.

Tanzania is an overwhelmingly rural country with one big urban centers: Dar es Salaam. The official state capital is Dodoma, a small city in the geographical centers of the country, but all major services are concentrated in Dar es Salaam: the harbor, the international airport, Parliament, ministries, embassies, the University, the most prestigious schools, headquarters of businesses and international organizations, big international hotels and so forth. Dar es Salaam also hosts a small international community of expatriates from the West, as well as an older population of Indian descent who have traditionally controlled retail business and parts of the local industry, international trade and banking. The city is the centers of Tanzanian cultural life and it is the home of most prominent music bands, authors and artists. Dar es Salaam is the prestige place in Tanzania: white-collar careers are invariably made there, money and opportunities for obtaining money are concentrated in Dar es Salaam. The city is associated with highlife (involving both its joys and vices), access to international contacts and power: an imagery that has deeply penetrated popular consciousness and has been articulated in songs and popular novels (Blommaert 1998, 1999, Chapter 4).

There are no other cities that can compete with Dar es Salaam. Arusha in the north is an important city, and so is Mwanza on Lake Victoria, but none of them comes close to Dar es Salaam in the terms sketched earlier. In general, the northern part of the country around Lake Victoria and the Kilimanjaro region are 'better' regions with some degree of economic prosperity. The inhabitants of these regions, notably the Chagga, the Haya and the Sukuma, are often seen in popular imagery as being shrewd businesspeople and capable organizers, very often holding positions of considerable power. The southern and central parts of the country are bad regions. People from there are economically very poor and are politically less weighty than their northern countrymen. The Makonde, Makua, Hehe, Gogo and other inhabitants of the southern and central regions are often perceived as among the poorest and most disenfranchised Tanzanians. Adopting world-systems terminology, we arrive at this pattern: Dar es Salaam is the absolute centers of the country, the northern regions are semi-peripheral, while the central and southern parts are peripheral.

Dar es Salaam is, as noted earlier, the most prestigious place in Tanzania. But it itself is divided into several areas, many of which carry the same kinds of associations that are attached to the (semi-peripheral) regions. The city is located on a lagoon with a natural harbor, and the city centers itself borders this lagoon and is quite old. It is an affluent neighborhood, dominated by multi-storey banks and hotels. It is surrounded by old, densely populated areas, and its boundary is formed by a largely dried-out river bed, Msimbazi Creek, running from north to south. The main axes of the city centers are two big roads: Ali Hassan Mwinyi Road, coming from Bagamoyo in the north and ending at the waterfront, and Morogoro Road, connecting with Ali Hassan Mwinyi Road at the waterfront and moving west in the direction of Morogoro and Tabora. The northern and western axes are the main traffic arteries, but also the main social–geographic axes of the city.

The western axis is the popular, lower-class axis of the city. Moving west from the waterfront, close to the very centers of town, is Uhindini, the Indian quarter littered with oriental-style old stone buildings, mosques, small businesses and shops. A bit further west, and separated from Uhindini by Mnazimoja Park, lies Uswahilini, the Swahili quarter, a huge collection of small houses with corrugated iron roofs populated by Africans from all over the country. The centers of this part of town is Kariakoo, the market area. It is a rather poor but very lively area, with lots of shops, bars and restaurants and with dense traffic caused by the daladala, small privately operated buses. Kariakoo is the centers of highlife and popular music. Across Msimbazi Creek, along Morogoro Road, lie a number of overcrowded popular areas: Magomeni, Manzese and Ubungo. Manzese is the poorest of them, often associated with violence, crime and abject poverty among the inhabitants of Dar es Salaam.

The northern axis is the elite, upper-class axis of the city. The most prestigious quarter is Oyster Bay, a beautiful area along the shore with a concentration of spacious, detached gated houses, embassies and fine hotels and restaurants. Oyster Bay is traditionally the home of expatriates and affluent or prominent Tanzanians. The area is somewhat sheltered and separated from downtown Dar es Salaam by Msimbazi Creek. Equally prestigious are Msasani further north, and recently also Mbezi Beach, several miles further north along

Ali Hassan Mwinyi Road. In between lies Mwenge, a popular neighborhood located at an intersection of Ali Hassan Mwinyi Road and a couple of roads connecting the former with Morogoro Road. This connection between the western and northern axes runs through Sinza, a somewhat prestigious middle-class neighborhood marked by bars, restaurants and hotels. On the other side of this connection lies the campus of the University of Dar es Salaam, again a rather prestigious area and home to the intellectual elite.

We can now turn to the way in which these local social and sociocultural semiotics of space are applied in *Miradi Bubu*. We can sketch two profiles for the main characters in the novel on the basis of spatial associations and trajectories. En route we will also see how particular activities, jobs and attributes are attached to certain places.

> *Saidi* and his father are Makonde people, from the Masasi region in southern Tanzania, thus from the periphery. Disease strikes their region, and they are forced to seek refuge elsewhere. Saidi travels to Tanga in the north (a wealthy area) as a migrant worker and finds a job on a sisal plantation, often seen as one of the 'lowest' jobs. The Tanga sisal plantation is the site of gross exploitation and abuse. In order to save Saidi, the supervisor Munubi sends him to Dar es Salaam, where he lives with a Makonde family. Munubi himself travels on to Central Tanzania, and finds poorly paid and exploitative jobs in Morogoro and Kilosa. Saidi first finds jobs with Indian employers. There is no mention of education at all, he embarks on a career of low-paid, unqualified, menial jobs. When he gets hired by TANU it is as a messenger. He then moves to an apartment in Kariakoo, and later to Manzese. All of his life is spent there, he hasn't travelled, apart from the move from the local, Tanzanian periphery to the local centers. But here, he lives in the periphery, the Manzese slum, where life is tough.

> *Nzoka* is a Sukuma, from the Mwanza region in the north, the semi-periphery. He has had some education, although he failed in a crucial state exam. He appears to be an excellent organizer, and this buys him a ticket to the centers, to Dar es Salaam. He travels extensively and to prestigious places, either politically (Ghana, Lumumba University) or academically (Oxford, Sussex University). He travels, and he acquires educational qualifications as well as, inevitably, prestige. He first lives in Kariakoo with Saidi, but then moves to Oyster Bay. Nzoka's life is spent in the centers in two ways, first as opposed to his region of origin, then as opposed to the country as a whole when he travels abroad.

We see how Saidi and Nzoka move through these spaces filled with symbols and attributes. We also see how feature clusters emerge in ways that allow informed readers to make all kinds of meaningful inferences with respect to people, places, activities and value attributions. In a very sketchy way, such inferences could be represented as follows:

Saidi:
>   Makonde, Southern Tanzania > poverty, no education, lower class
>   Sisal plantations > menial jobs
>   Dar es Salaam, Indian quarter > servant, lower employee
>   Kariakoo > lower middle class, messenger
>   Manzese > poverty, prostitution, crime

Nzoka:
>   Sukuma, Northern Tanzania > relatively prosperous, ambitious, educated
>   Political activism > power, education, skills
>   Kariakoo > lower middle class
>   Travels abroad > elite, government official, intellectual
>   Oyster Bay > upper class, government official
>   Multiple marriages (including foreign spouses) > wealth, status,
>   Cosmopolitanism

The connections that are made are between space, activities and attributes, and status or value. We can identify two directions in this set of connections, roughly definable as 'margin-directed' versus 'centers-directed':

> Margin-directed: the South, lack of education, unskilled jobs in someone's service, low wages; in Dar es Salaam: Manzese; no international contacts. Locality.
> Centre-directed: the North, education, qualified white-collar jobs, international contacts; in Dar es Salaam: Oyster Bay; abroad: intellectual and political centers of excellence. Translocality.

Two particular features stand out as critical in determining one's position either in the margin or in the centers: education and international contacts or translocality. Both are closely connected. Nzoka's success appears to lie in his articulateness, and he derives considerable prestige from his education abroad. Nzoka is capable of 'moving around', both as a professional by travelling to prestigious international places, and in his private life by crossing ethnic, racial and religious boundaries in marriage and by living among expatriates in Oyster Bay. This, however, appears not to be merely an individual accomplishment; it is *determined* by his background. Nzoka comes from a part of the country that is already close to the socioeconomic centers. As a Northerner, he seems to have been dealt the right hand of cards right from the start. Saidi, in contrast, has no education and grows up in terrible circumstances. Consequently, he spends his life in 'fixed' places: among members of his ethnic group and in the socioeconomic periphery, even in Dar es Salaam. He comes from the South, the poorest region of the country, and he appears to be destined to remain in the periphery.

The way in which, through all this, we see the emergence of centers/periphery perceptions at three levels is interesting. At each of them we see a number of attributions in action:

> **The strictly local level, in Dar es Salaam:** Manzese versus Oyster Bay. What Saidi is and what happens to his family – poverty, a perpetual struggle to survive, prostitution and murder – is presupposable from his location in Manzese; conversely, Nzoka's wealth, power and cosmopolitanism are presupposable from his location in Oyster Bay. Manzese is the periphery and Oyster Bay is the centers.
>
> **The national level:** various parts of the country and trajectories followed by people allow presupposable inferences as to status, social class and opportunities. The South is the periphery, the North is the semi-periphery, and Dar es Salaam is the centers. Education is not easily accessible in the South and more accessible in the North; these differences have an impact on the opportunities people get in Dar es Salaam.
>
> **The transnational level:** Tanzania versus the rest of the world. Prestige is derived from being able to leave Tanzania and visit prestigious spots outside Africa; poverty and failure are indexed by a life spent inside the country without opportunities to travel.

From these perspectives, we notice how strongly such centers-versus-periphery perceptions organize the description of the characters and the structure of the plot. The life histories of Saidi and Nzoka are deeply anchored in a set of meaningful spatial associations that have to do with the opportunities people have and can have in the Tanzanian world. One can become a success story because he is able to 'move out', first to the prestigious places in Dar es Salaam, then to the European and American prestigious places, and in between, as he crosses ethnic, racial and religious boundaries. Much of his ability to move regionally and socially is (pre)determined by his regional background. The other character remains a poor man because his background prevents him from 'moving out'. Saidi follows a trajectory that brings him from one periphery to another, and the low status and disenfranchisement that he carries with him from Masasi sticks with him all the way through. In a way, he never 'moves out': he doesn't move out of poverty, misery, violence, his country and his ethnic and social group. The characters evolve in one of Appadurai's 'ideoscapes': an ideology of mobility and adaptation to criteria established in the centers of the world system, Europe and North America, as the key to success. Conversely, locality and localism stand here for poverty and failure. This is a widespread social and cultural script that probably accounts for lots of social processes in contemporary Africa.[4]

These social attributions of space and spatial trajectories obviously carry deep political meanings. In effect, the kind of trajectories sketched by Ruhumbika form an important part of his critique of Ujamaa Tanzania. The promise of Ujamaa was to build a classless society in which every African would have equal opportunities and in which Uzungu ('the ways of the West') would no longer be the model for success in society. His two protagonists inscribe themselves in the Ujamaa project, both become active in the struggle for independence and both become aides to Nyerere. In spite of their very different regional origins and social trajectories, both also speak this emblem of Ujamaa: Standard Swahili. But the deep cleavages that characterized the country before independence – regional differences in wealth and opportunities, and class differences – persist afterwards. Those who previously had few opportunities for upward social mobility still remain the losers; those who were less underprivileged and fol-lowed the track of education and internationalization (i.e., went into Uzungu) are still the ones who make it. Class, as inscribed in all these cleavages, persisted throughout Ujamaa, and patriotism was not enough to attain equality as a citi-zen. So whereas Ujamaa was launched as a localizing political strategy – an *African* socialism emphasizing African roots and values – only those who got inserted in translocal, globalized trajectories of education and mobility made it. The world system won. Consequently, images of globalization and the way in which Tanzania is inserted in globalization processes are powerful organizing principles in *Miradi Bubu*.

10.4 The Repatriation of a Critique

We now move into the other aspect of our discussion: the way in which *Miradi Bubu* is itself a rather typical globalization phenomenon. We concluded our discussion in the previous section by stating that globalization was an important motif in the novel. Yet, it is hard to characterize the novel as anything other than 'local': written for Tanzanian readers in their national language, and draw-ing on contextual information much of which is only accessible to Tanzanians. We also noted earlier that Ruhumbika wrote the novel while he was a professor in the United States. So what we have on our hands is a novel produced in the centers of the world system for consumption in the periphery, Tanzania, and the choice of language as well as the cultural semiotics of space articulated in Swahili provide evidence for this.

The novel, consequently, is a typical product of contemporary globalized cultural processes, and we should heed Hannerz's advice (1991:126) to 'think about the flow between places as well as within them' when studying such prod-ucts of culture. Hannerz adds that the communities within which cultural products are produced and circulated are more and more 'ecumenical', made up by networks that are translocal and often involve deep differences in outlook and framework. Thus, 'through the operation of the varied frameworks for cultural process, and the interaction between them, some meanings and meaningful forms become much more localized, much more tied to space, than others' (ibid.).

Clearly, the community within which *Miradi Bubu* is produced and circulated is ecumenical and diasporic: we have an expatriate author writing for a readership that is, perforce, largely made up of politically and artistically sensitive intellectuals. But the ecumene is restricted. The novel is written in Swahili and it draws heavily on local Tanzanian meaningful forms, strongly 'tied to space' in Hannerz's terms. Consequently, the community can sensibly be defined as Ruhumbika on the one hand (and perhaps some students of African studies programs in the United States and Europe, ourselves included), and a small group of Tanzanian (or East-African) intellectuals on the other. In that sense, *Miradi Bubu* is a local novel destined for circulation in a network that is confined to those who are privy to the intricate local semiotics he uses in his work, as well as to the code in which it is written. It is a Tanzanian novel.

But things are obviously not that simple. We have seen in the previous section that Ruhumbika draws on local meanings against the background of globalization imagery containing centers-versus-periphery models. His local critique against Ujamaa is done by means of 'translocalization', that is, by means of arguments and tropes that define, anachronistically, the failure of Ujamaa as a failure to recognize the dynamics of the modern world system. It is a critique that is built on cosmopolitanism as a worldview, an awareness that localism in social organization is an error and that centers/periphery patterns are a reality. So in order to construct a local critique of Tanzania, Tanzania has to be lifted out of its shell, delocalized, and placed into the world system. Nzoka is the key in this: his mobility and its resulting prestige demonstrate how insertion into transnational channels of power and prestige shapes success in Tanzanian society. Thus, interestingly, we see how a novel that is hard to read if one does not have access to the local semiotics of places, people and activities at the same time translocalize this semiotics and place it in the context of Tanzania-in-the-world.

It is perhaps at this point that we can begin to understand what globalization and its reflexes on literature involve. It involves a dynamics of semiotic localization and delocalization in such a way that Hannerz's space, to which meanings are tied, can be seen as *elastic* space, a space that can be reduced and expanded almost line by line and episode by episode. Ruhumbika speaks from *within* Tanzania and from *outside* Tanzania at the same time. We get images of what it means to be from Southern Tanzania both within Tanzania *as well as* in the world: the local periphery is also a global periphery, for peripheries and centers are relatively stable while they operate at various levels of awareness and activity. Consequently, being marginal in Tanzania *is also meaningful in the world*, and this stretching of local meanings into translocal ones may offer us a better understanding of poverty and disenfranchisement in the periphery.

The message is, however, primarily for Tanzanians to pick up. Ruhumbika's diasporic act of communication should be repatriated, in Appadurai's sense, and thus recontextualized and re-entextualized in Silverstein and Urban's (1996) sense. But repatriation does not necessarily mean localization. The strength of the motif of mobility, both within and outside Tanzania, and its connection to success and failure as well as to an assessment of *Ujamaa*, make it hard to read this book as other than a translocalization of the history of Tanzania. As is perhaps the case with all diasporic literature, this may precisely be the novel's Achilles' heel. In the process of repatriation, the localization of the messages in the book may be challenged by the translocal dimension it necessarily has: that of a critique from afar by an outsider who doesn't suffer from the conditions of life he criticizes in his book. And thus, whereas the book is by all standards fully Tanzanian, its status as 'Tanzanian' may perpetually be challenged by Tanzanian critics. The repatriation of meanings produced by expatriates is always a political issue, and even at that level Hannerz's ties between cultural products and space crop up.

10.5 The Cultural Codes of Globalization

Ruhumbika's choice of Swahili (rather than English, his working language as a professor in the United States) encodes this complex semiotics. In itself, the choice to write a novel in Swahili is a highly meaningful act: it dramatically restricts the scope of the readership to the groups described earlier, and this prejudices sales figures, international acclaim and other rewards of successful authorship. To some extent, it 'hides' the novel in a corner of the world, it locks it in a narrow space of circulation and uptake. All of this is undisputable: even to many people strongly interested in African literature, this essay (written, of course, in English) will be their first encounter with Ruhumbika's novel. In that sense, the dynamics of localization and translocalization always come with a price: the choice to avoid the global linguae francae seems to immediately marginalize cultural products, and minimize the symbolic bonuses one could get from cultural production.

It is undisputable, however, to the extent that one views globalization as a process of uniformization, and to the extent that cultural globalization processes are seen as the production of a global monoculture. Things are different when we see globalization as a more 'niched' complex of processes, developing at several different scale-levels, some of them truly global, others regional, national or even sub-national (Blommaert 2007). Appadurai's 'vernacular globalization', I would suggest, is globalization at one particular scale-level, lower than the fully global one: it is the connectedness of small pockets of people located (and local) in different parts of the world, sharing cultural products and being involved in processes of joint cultural production, the 'networks' described by Castells (1996). Ruhumbika's book is globalized within such a network, it is globalized at a sub-global scale-level within the communities sketched earlier. At that scale-level, a strong articulation of locality can be expected, and the choice of Swahili as well as the strongly local social semiotics of space contribute to that. There is nothing paradoxical to that – the seemingly odd combination of outspoken locality and outspoken globalization – if one understands the nature and scope of the particular communication network for which this cultural product was designed. It was designed for a dispersed worldwide network in which this sense of locality is politically, culturally and artistically meaningful for a network that shares the indexicals that render it meaningful.

Seen from this perspective, globalization offers various kinds of new opportunities for languages often seen as marginal and in danger. We have seen how an African language such as Swahili could become the cultural code for globalized cultural production at a particular scale-level, and that it even was *the best* cultural code for this particular network. This, I would say, is an aspect of vitality: these opportunities for using such languages in globalization are relatively new (they follow the increasing connectivity in diasporic networks), there are plenty such opportunities, and a quick look at the Internet shows that they are used by many people to articulate the new cultural forms of vernacular globalization. Ruhumbika uses an 'old' format, that of the postcolonial Swahili novel, to articulate a new (translocal) critique of the (local) past. The format, thus, becomes new, and the language encodes this innovation. I find this a very hopeful sign for African languages, and see this as a necessary qualification of the more widespread views of sociolinguistic globalization, in which English is seen as a 'linguicidal' force. It no doubt is, but perhaps only at certain scale-levels, not at others, and seeing globalization as something that operates at a variety of levels can help us understand the real dynamics of vitality and endangerment of African languages (cf. Blommaert 2005a).

10.6 Conclusions

We are now in a position to bring the various aspects of our discussion together. Let us first briefly recapitulate. We started out by noting that globalization offers important empirical challenges to various social–scientific disciplines and argued that perceptions of space and spatial trajectories may offer a useful point of departure for analysis. As Crang (1999) observes, 'The world contracts, occasionally unevenly, but without thinking what such spatial changes mean' (168). We saw how Ruhumbika used an intricate local social semiotics of space, in which places, people, activities and values were closely tied, providing important batteries of indexical meanings for readers familiar with this semiotics. center-versus-periphery models appeared to operate at various levels, and mobility inside and outside Tanzania was a crucial organizing theme in the novel. We also argued that a novel such as *Miradi Bubu*, though strongly local because of the indexical complexes just mentioned, systematically translocated meanings, setting the local semiotics in a wider, globalized frame. This, I argued, made up the diasporic nature of the novel and turned it into a typical example of cultural production in a globalized world, provided we understand this globalized world as niched and consisting of various scale-levels. The choice of Swahili situated the act of cultural production at a particular scale-level, where it was a most appropriate code.

What this implies theoretically, I believe, is that *mobility* should be made a central concern of social–scientific analysis. As noted at the outset, there seems to be a strong tendency to localize interpretations of cultural practices and meanings, placing their function and value with an established sociocultural community. It seems that we have to find ways to address the fact that people use cultural instruments – language, art and music – primarily to move around, not to stay in one place. Furthermore, it may be that the value and function of cultural instruments derive precisely from their potential to allow their users to move around, to get from one geographical and/or social space to another, from one scale-level to another, and to define oneself as acting within a particular network, not in others. I submit that this capacity for mobility is a feature of what is commonly understood by language vitality. In the case of literature (but perhaps also transposable into other fields of cultural production), difficulties appear in attributing identifying labels to a novel such as *Miradi Bubu*. Is it 'African', 'Tanzanian' or 'international'? Just like language names such as *English* carry connotations of stability and spatial and historical fixedness and homogeneity, attributing such labels to literature runs the risk of 'fixing' the literature to a particular place, whereas the non-fixedness of the novel and its meanings are precisely the point.

This obviously has implications for a whole set of established categorizing concepts, descriptive as well as analytical, currently used in social–scientific analysis. Who or what is African? 'Black'? 'Male'? 'Author'? The answers to these questions, recognized long ago and never adequately answered, prove to be even more difficult to come by when globalization is taken seriously. Wallerstein (1990) formulates the problem sharply: 'Emphasizing "culture" in order to counterbalance the emphases others have put on the "economy" or the "polity" does not at all solve the problem; it in fact just makes it worse. We must surmount the terminology altogether' (65).

The best vanguard point from which to meet this challenge may be the ethnographic perspective, which aims at decoding the lived experiences of people. We have seen in *Miradi Bubu* how salient space and spatial trajectories are in perceiving and giving meaning to social and political processes. We have perhaps also seen this on a variety of other occasions in research, but failed to thematize it or accept it as a relevant ingredient of people's experience, social imagery and culture. We can now turn back to our desks and go through our old notes: space, scales and trajectories will be there, and they will be meaningful.

Notes

Research for this chapter was facilitated by a personal grant from the National Fund for Scientific Research–Flanders. Many of the insights recorded in this chapter emerged out of a series of workshops on language and globalization at Ghent University, in early 2002. I am grateful to the students participating in these workshops for valuable comments and critical input. Harri Englund also provided excellent comments on the first draft of this essay, an ancestor of which was published as Blommaert & Van der Donckt (2002). I am indebted to Lieslotte Van der Donck for allowing me this piracy of the previous version. Salikoko Mufwene and Cécile Vigouroux provided very important suggestions for revising this earlier version.

[1] The body of literature on globalization and the world system is vast and its highlights are by now sufficiently known to render comprehensive strings of references redundant. Indispensable to an understanding of the general argument presented here are the insights of Manuel Castells (1996, 1997), Immanuel Wallerstein (1974, 1983) and Arjun Appadurai (1990). The collections edited by Featherstone (1990) and King (1991) remain seminal. An excellent ethnographic example is Englund (2002).

[2] *Mzalendo*, the singular form of *wazalendo*, was also the name of a prominent government-sponsored newspaper in Ujamaa, Tanzania.

[3] One could just think of the particular ring to names such as *Paris, the Kremlin, Tien an Men Square* and *the White House*. The indexicalities tied to such places are often the basis for their metonymic usage in everyday or institutional speech. Thus *Brussels* in Eurosceptics' discourse means more than 'the capital of Belgium'.

[4] An obvious field of application is language choice. Very often, language policies seem to fail because people 'vote with their feet': members of marginalized linguistic communities prefer an education in a 'bigger' language than their own, if for nothing else because of their belief that the knowledge of, for example, English would buy them a ticket out of the periphery and towards the centers: white-collar jobs in large urban centers. See de Swaan (2002) and Blommaert (2005b) for a general discussion of this phenomenon.

References

Appadurai, Arjun. 1990. Disjuncture and difference in the global cultural economy. *Theory, Culture and Society* 7.295–310.

Bertoncini, Elena. 1989. *Outline of Swahili Literature.* Leiden: Brill.

Blommaert, Jan. 1998. English in a popular Swahili novel. In *English as a Human Language: To Honour Louis Goossens*, ed. by Johan Van der Auwera, Frank Durieux and Ludo Lejeune, 22–31. Munich: LINCOM Europa.

—1999. *State Ideology and Language in Tanzania.* Köln: Rüdiger Köppe Verlag.

—2005a. Situating language rights: English and Swahili in Tanzania revisited. *Journal of Sociolinguistics* 9(3).390–417.

—2005b. *Discourse: A Critical Introduction.* Cambridge: Cambridge University Press.

—2007. Sociolinguistic scales. *Intercultural Pragmatics* 4.1–19.

Blommaert, Jan and Lieselotte Van der Donckt. 2002. African literature and globalization: Semiotizing space in a Tanzanian novel. *Journal of African Cultural Studies* 15(2).137–148.

Castells, Manuel. 1996. *The Rise of the Network Society.* London: Blackwell.

—1997. *The Power of Identity.* London: Blackwell.

Crang, Mike. 1999. Globalization as conceived, perceived and lived spaces. *Theory, Culture & Society* 16(1).167–177.

de Swaan, Abram. 2002. *Words of the World.* Cambridge: Polity Press.

Englund, Harri. 2002. Ethnography after globalism: Migration and emplacement in Malawi. *American Ethnologist* 29(2).261–286.

Featherstone, Mike (ed.). 1990. *Global Culture: Nationalism, Globalization and Modernity* (Special issue, *Theory, Culture & Society* 7). London: Sage in association with *Theory, Culture and Society.*

Feld, Steven and Keith Basso (eds). 1996. *Senses of Place.* Santa Fe: SAR Press.

Freeland, Jane and Donna Patrick (eds). 2004. *Language Rights and Language Survival.* Manchester: St. Jerome.

Hannerz, Ulf. 1991. Scenarios for peripheral cultures. In King (ed.), 107–128.

King, Anthony (ed.). 1991. *Culture, Globalization and the World-System.* London: Macmillan.

Low, Setha (ed.). 2001. *Remapping the City: Place, Order and Ideology.* Special issue of *American Anthropologist,* 103(1).5–111.

Madumulla, Joshua, Elena Bertoncini and Jan Blommaert. 1999. Politics, ideology and poetic form: The literary debate in Tanzania. In *Language Ideological Debates,* ed. by Jan Blommaert, 307–341. Berlin: Mouton de Gruyter.

Maryns, Katrijn and Jan Blommaert. 2001. Stylistic and thematic shifting as a narrative resource: Assessing asylum seekers' repertoires. *Multilingua* 20(1).61–84.

May, Stephen. 2001. *Language and Minority Rights.* London: Longman.

Mbuguni, L.A. and Gabriel Ruhumbika. 1974. TANU and National Culture. In *Towards Ujamaa: Twenty Years of TANU Leadership,* ed. by Gabriel Ruhumbika, 275–287. Kampala: East African Literature Bureau.

Mufwene, Salikoko. 2002. Colonization, globalization and the plight of 'weak' languages. *Journal of Linguistics* 38.375–395.

Othman, Haroub. 1994. The intellectual and transformation in Southern Africa. *Dar es Salaam Alumni Newsletter* 1(1).9–10.

Phillipson, Robert. 1992. *Linguistic Imperialism.* Oxford: Oxford University Press.

Pratt, Cranford. 1976. *The Critical Phase in Tanzania: Nyerere and the Emergence of a Socialist Strategy.* Cambridge: Cambridge University Press.

Rampton, Ben. 2001. Critique in interaction. *Critique of Anthropology* 21(1).83–107.

Shivji, Issa. 1996. *Intellectuals at the Hill: Essays and Talks 1969–1993.* Dar es Salaam: Dar es Salaam University Press.

Silverstein, Michael and Greg Urban (eds). 1996. *Natural Histories of Discourse.* Chicago: University of Chicago Press.

Wallerstein, Immanuel. 1974. *The Modern World System.* New York: Academic Press.

—1983. *Historical Capitalism, with Capitalist Civilization.* London: Verso.

—1990. Culture is the world-system: A reply to Boyne. *Media, Culture and Society* 7.63–65.

Wong, Cindy Hing-Yuk and Gary McDonogh. 2001. The mediated metropolis: anthropological issues in cities and mass communication. *American Anthropologist* 130(1).96–111 (special issue on *Remapping the City*, ed. by Setha Low).

Chapter 11

From Africa to Africa: Globalization, Migration and Language Vitality

Cécile B. Vigouroux

11.1 Introduction

Migration has long caught linguists' attention as an ideal domain for investigating language dynamics that can shed light on especially language spread and language change. In line with the title of the present book, I wish in this chapter to address dynamics of language vitality in Africa by focusing on language practice within a diasporic population of Black African Francophones who immigrated recently to Cape Town, South Africa. Because the migration is very recent, about fifteen years, it would be premature to draw any reliable general conclusions about language maintenance and shift. However, the study sheds light on social factors that drive these phenomena. The position in this chapter is in line with Mufwene (2001), who argues that language change within a population reflects the cumulation of individuals' choices during specific communicative acts. Those choices are to be seen both as speakers' adaptive responses to the communicative events in which they engage and as shaped by the relevant macro-scale social dynamics.

The intersection of micro- and macro-scales is particularly significant in the context of migration, which is both a private affair and an institutional one. It can be argued that the status of migrant starts long before the relevant individual sets foot in the host land, as he/she plans the journey, saves money, applies for a visa, says goodbye to loved ones and so on. It is only ratified institutionally when he/she settles in the host country. Being a migrant is also constantly actualized at the micro-scale of interactions, as he/she is indexed as a foreigner because of his/her accent, is misunderstood or is denied a job or housing.[1] Migrating is thus more than crossing transnational boundaries; it entails entering new discursive spaces and socially stratified organizations. I submit that all this affects speakers' management of their language repertoires, as they may have to reshuffle their language resources, learn one or more of the host languages, and change language functions in the new ecology.

The title of the present book suggests language vitality be approached from the perspective of globalization. It is thus helpful to start the present discussion by articulating some points of intersection between migration and globalization. I will then provide a general description on the African Francophones' migrations to South Africa to illustrate the links that were highlighted in the previous section. Language vitality itself will be discussed in Sections 11.4 and 11.5, where I concur with Blommaert et al., (2005a:206, citing Appadurai 1996) that grassroots globalization 'results in more complex and unclear forms of locality', which, as they argue, are best revealed in interaction.

As can be inferred from this short prelude, no prediction will be made about the fates of the migrants' languages. My focus is sociolinguistic dynamics of language practice and the extent to which they can shed light on language maintenance and loss. Before turning to the next section, let me just conclude this section with a brief presentation of the ethnographic data on which my analysis rests. The data were constructed from a discontinuous ten-year (1996–2005) longitudinal field investigation in Cape Town, South Africa. In addition to observations in several settings such as Congolese Pentecostal churches, collective therapeutic sessions, flea markets, Internet cafés, semi-guided interviews were conducted with 154 migrants from twelve African Francophone countries: Benin, Cameroon, Côte d'Ivoire, Gabon, Guinea, Mali, Senegal and Togo for West Africa; the Republic of Congo (RC) and the Democratic Republic of Congo (DRC) for Central Africa; and Rwanda and Burundi for the Great Lakes area. During these interviews, people were asked to talk about their migratory journeys until their arrival in Cape Town and about their lives in the host country, commenting on their relations with other African migrants and with the local population.

11.2 The Relation between Migration and Globalization Process

Migration is both a product of globalization and part of the very process of globalization itself. By their very presence in a host land, migrants embody complex and multidimensional geographical, political, economic and historical relations between countries, although one shouldn't dissociate them too hastily from their agency and depict them as passive experiencers of broader historical dynamics. Discourse on migration has often been constructed along a number of dichotomies, including (i) duration of stay in the host country (permanent versus temporary residents), (ii) geographic roles (sending versus receiving countries), (iii) direction (migrants' point of departure versus point of arrival), (iv) types of migration (forced versus free migrants) and (v) individual- versus family-type. Such dichotomies are often unsatisfactory in part because they tend to project human migrations as organized and highly structured systems.

In reality, they are often the outcomes of ambivalent, sometimes contradictory and often unplanned, individual dynamics.[2] In linguistics, these dichotomies have long been invoked as explanatory models to account for migrants' language practice in their new ecologies, or for the vitality and maintenance of their languages. Unfortunately, they obscure the complex dynamics on the ground, as I will try to articulate now. Also, linguists have generally assumed too hastily a strict fit between mobility of speakers and mobility of language repertoires, as if moving from one sociocultural space to another necessarily entails that the relevant speakers can automatically transfer their language resources to the host locality and these can work smoothly in the new discursive spaces. According to this line of thought, an English speaker from Ghana or Nigeria will have a better chance of being integrated (whatever that means) into his/her new English-speaking host country, such as South Africa, than a Japanese with no prior knowledge of the language. I argue later that this common assumption relies heavily on a misconception of language as homogeneous and primarily denotational, overlooking its indexical role. It is misguided to assume that any semiotic practice is equivalent to any other, any speaker is comparable to another or that any language variety is equally functional across communicative contexts. As aptly suggested by Blommaert (2005:73), 'mobility is not across empty spaces, but mobility across spaces filled with codes, customs, rules, expectations and so forth'. Therefore, crossing geographic spaces amounts to crossing social, situational and ideological boundaries. Whether or not particular language resources will work is thus always tied to several layers of contexts, which is why a speaker may be acknowledged as competent in a context while deemed incompetent in another.

Western governments appear to have reduced sociocultural integration to language competence, as acknowledged by the Dutch immigration minister Rita Verdonk in her recent observation that not being able to speak 'proper' Dutch is the reason why most of the six hundred thousand immigrants in her country are unemployed. Verdonk argues that the Netherlands can no longer welcome migrants who won't integrate in mainstream society and advocates a new, restrictive visa system. No one can be granted a visa unless they have passed a civic-integration evaluation and a Dutch language test (Radio Free Europe).[3] Despite the fact that many studies have proven claims such as Verdonk's wrong (see Bitjaa Kody 2000), linguistic arguments are used as political tools for regulating population movements, as governments conflate into one category language competence of migrants and their ability to adapt to a new sociocultural ecology. In discourse such as Verdonk's, social integration is framed as a one-way process, making it essentially the migrants' problem. It thus implicitly assumes that the social space in which they are inserted remains stable, and migrants therefore have to adjust to it. However, as I show later, the insertion of the migrants in the host community also causes the latter to reorganize its own patterns of interactions.

Equally unsatisfactory has been the push–pull model that attributes migration journeys only to individual decisions and projects these as driven exclusively by economic and political factors, such as search for better job opportunities and escaping oppressive regimes. Many criticisms have voiced concerns over the fact that the push–pull approach over-emphasizes individuals' agencies. They also observe that the model inaccurately portrays the migrants 'as being in a position to choose and compare their options' (Papastergiadis 2000:31). Thus, according to the critics, the push factor fails to explain why people who are the most desperate for socioeconomic improvements are unlikely to migrate, as is evident from worldwide migration statistics. On the other hand, the pull factor cannot explain why, according to the African migrations workshop report of 2007, relatively developed African countries such as Senegal and Morocco are those that experience the highest migration rate towards Europe or why a significant emigration of highly qualified health workers is taking place in relatively well-off countries such as South Africa and Ghana.

Regardless of whether one considers globalization as a recent historical phenomenon or whether one subscribes to the position that what we are experiencing are new socioeconomic, cultural and political forms of a process that started a long time ago, links between migration and (capitalist) globalization are observable at different levels. For example, the development of new means of transportation has always favored people's mobility within longer distance. In the fifteen century, the development of carrack, a heavier boat than the caravel, made sailing along and across the Atlantic Ocean possible and therefore facilitated the Europeans' exploration of remote lands such as the African West coast and Brazil. Patterns of geographic mobility must therefore be approached in relation to ramblers' and navigational routes and, more recently, airways. It is not surprising that port cities are likely to host large numbers of migrants, even only for a transitional period of time, or that cities with international airports are the first recipients of newcomers.

The spread of a population to a territory is partly facilitated by networks of communications that have become faster and cheaper, although they still remain inaccessible for the poorest. There are obviously new patterns of migration that have emerged in modern times of globalization. They are characterized by shorter stays in foreign lands and regular return trips to home countries. The decrease of long distance travel costs has favored *circular migrations*, with migrants returning home after a certain period of residence in a foreign country before moving on to another destination. Therefore, fewer and fewer people are settling permanently in a single host country and migration trajectories appear to be more complex and diverse. One may reasonably assume that these new patterns of temporary migrations must have a different kind of impact on migrants' language repertoires, for example, in facilitating the maintenance of their vernaculars even if they acquire other languages in the host country. These new patterns of migrations should undoubtedly prompt analysts to develop alternative frameworks of analysis and, as suggested by Papastergiadis (2000), a more subtle vocabulary to account for the diversity of the migratory experiences.

New technologies such as the Internet have been perceived as one of the strongest symbols of globalization, chiefly because of the common association of globalization with the notion of 'time-space compression' (Harvey 1990). The development of broadcast networks has influenced the migratory journeys of urban and literate migrants in providing better access to information that may help their migration plans. For instance, the migrants are generally better informed about visa requirements in prospective host countries or about local job markets. On the other hand, while the flow of information prior to departure helps shape the migrants' image of the country of choice, it can also raise expectations that are hard to fulfill. The Internet has certainly helped many migrants sustain regular contacts with family members or friends left behind at low costs, but it has not guaranteed economic comfort in the host country nor fast material relief to those left behind.

The impact of new means of communication on migrants' language vitality is difficult to assess. Although new technologies are increasingly part of many Africans' modern life, they remain largely an urban phenomenon limited to young literates or educated segments of the population. Literacy highly constrains both the sending and receiving end of written communication and is therefore part of a selective mechanism that determines who can communicate with whom. In addition, individuals' written communicative acts are embedded in broader language policies that often constrain scribers' selections of their written code of interaction. For example, in the majority of former French colonies, language policies going all the way back to the colonial period sustained an education system, funded by the state, that have favored French as the main language of literacy. Thus, use of the Internet still favors French over indigenous African vernaculars and lingua francas, despite the potential it provides migrants to use the latter. It is thus reasonable to think that computer-mediated interactions help shape the migrants' varieties of French, as suggested by the literature on mono- and multilingualism on the Internet (Eisenlohr 2004; Feussi 2007; Legeden & Richards 2007; Maurais 2003a). This is certainly a dimension worth investigating in the perspective of language vitality.

Another example of how globalization and migration are interconnected can be adduced from economics. The restructuring of local economies imposed by institutions such as the International Monetary Fund and the World Bank (which are themselves symbols of globalized economic and political institutions) to Third World countries has resulted in the decline of some of the latter's economic sectors and led segments of their populations to seek better job opportunities either by relocating from rural to urban settings or by migrating trans-nationally. The Senegalese Murid trade Diaspora described by Diouf (2002) is a telling example. Murids' highly visible presence at European,

North American and African flea markets is a direct consequence of the restructuring of Senegalese local economy, which has affected negatively the cultivation
of peanut, Senegal's main export crop since the French colonial period.
According to Diouf, the Murids became the largest producers of peanuts in
their region and were extremely successful at this during the first half of the
twentieth century. However, post-Independence drops in peanut prices on the
international market not only made this economic activity less lucrative but also
prompted the Murids to abandon it and seek other more lucrative alternatives.
Thus, they relocated to urban centers, where they engaged in international
trade, which entails transnational mobility (Adejunmobi 2004).

   While the study of migration reminds us that we are not equally mobile in
this world, it also informs us that the border-free world envisioned by some
businessmen such as Jacques Maisonrouge, former president of IBM World, is
far from materializing. It is not evident that many populations will ever enjoy
the experience of living in the 'borderless states' (quoted by Sklair 1999:144)
he projects. Indeed, the question of borders has never sparked so many national
political debates as it has in recent years. As aptly noted by Papastergiadis
(2000:82), 'despite the relative free transfer of capital and ideas, there is
no nation which is encouraging mass migration'. The study of people's mobility
therefore unveils an important feature of the globalization process: inequality
among peoples that often goes hand in hand with regional disparities
(Northern versus Southern hemisphere), geographical inequities (urban
versus rural) and gender inequalities.

   The term *migrant* itself, regardless of whether it is elaborated into *immigrant*
or *emigrant*, does not just denote a state of foreignness to a land; it often indexes
social status, regional origin (Southern hemisphere) if not skin color. The evolution of the meaning of *migrant* from a neutral denotation in the eighteenth
century to a socially loaded indexicality in the twentieth century inscribes the
term in the broader timespace of historical relationships based on power
dynamics between a center (often a former colonial state) and a periphery (the
geographical dependencies of the latter). These center–periphery dynamics
often translate into a race-based discourse that organizes both local and global
relations between both individuals and states. Therefore, it would be misleading to define migrants solely in reference to their geographic mobility, without
paying close attention to the social dimension of this mobility. One must
ask how mobility is constructed and discursively articulated by people and
communities.

   Writing this, I am reminded of the term *cosmopolitan*, which has become
the new buzzword in cultural studies. *Cosmopolitanism* seeks to capture the
multiple identities and belongings of people who travel and do not just rely
on one bounded-culture or pay allegiance to one nation-state. As seducing as
it may be, the notion of 'cosmopolitanism' tends to idealize mobility as a necessary enriching experience that attunes the traveller to the diversity of the world.

By doing so, one runs the risk of overlooking the real lives of those, on the ground, who experience globalization in a harsh way, like the people on whom this chapter now focuses.

11.3 Contemporary Histories of Francophone African Immigration to South Africa

Black African immigration to South Africa dates back from the apartheid regime, which officially ended in 1994, despite the institutional racism that prevailed then. However, until the 1990s, the migrants came primarily from neighboring countries such as Mozambique, Swaziland and Zimbabwe, recruited as contractual laborers in various industries, especially mining and farms. According to Morris (1999), only a few of them were given legal residence at the completion of their contract; many of the others extended their stay in South Africa as illegal migrants and were therefore often forced to repatriate. The civil war in Mozambique in the 1980s changed the nature of Mozambican immigration to South Africa, providing many immigrants an excuse to stay as refugees. Until the 1990s, African migrants to South Africa could be qualified as predominantly poor and unqualified, originating primarily in Southern Africa. Working class Black South Africans did not feel threatened by these migrants, who, according to Morris (1999), could easily blend with them. Official figures show that, between 1986 and 1995, legal African migrants, estimated at 22,078, were half the number of legal European migrants in South Africa and more numerous than the Asians, estimated at 17,855. Although it is difficult to determine with some accuracy the present number of Black African migrants to South Africa, we know that the Francophone Africans constitute only a small fraction of this population. However, despite their small numbers, they have increasingly been visible in urban centers, as I explain later.

Francophone African migration to South Africa is a recent phenomenon. According to Bouillon (1999a), it dates back from the late 1980s. In his seminal work on the presence of Black African Francophones in Johannesburg, Bouillon distinguishes three successive waves of migration. The first (1986–1991) consists of a Congolese economic and political elite, including not only a few businessmen and politicians close to the late President Mobutu's regime who came to prospect for future investments but also a number of highly trained engineers, medical doctors and university professors who were employed in the independent Bantustans (former homelands) such as Transkei, Ciskei, Bophutha-Tswana and Venda. Through the recruitment of highly educated African foreigners, South Africa sought to establish political relationships with the rest of the continent, especially after the international community's economic sanctions that followed the Sharpville massacre in 1960.[4] Political leaders such as Houphouët Boigny of Côte d'Ivoire and Omar Bongo of Gabon (two former French colonies) sustained political relationships with the apartheid regime, contrary to the majority of the members of the Organization of African Unity (OAU). To my knowledge, no linguistic or sociological study has been conducted on this first wave of migrants, though it is reasonable to think that their immersion in the community through their professional activity may have favored migrants' acquisition of one (or more) language(s) of their host environment. Their contacts with other African immigrants, mostly Anglophones from countries such as Uganda (Bouillon 1999a) must of course have accelerated their acquisition of English. The migrants' maintenance of Congolese vernaculars must have relied only on the family-type migrations of the time, since there was no critical mass of speakers that could have favored the vitality of Congolese languages. While these are largely speculations, one can still safely conjecture that linguistically the early migrants must have acculturated more easily than the recent ones to whom I am now turning.

The second wave (1991–1993) was triggered by both South Africa's political transition, initiated by Nelson Mandela' release from prison in 1990, and the end of the country's sociopolitical instability. Official figures show a drastic increase in the total population of foreign visitors between 1991 (five hundred thousand) and 1994 (four million). This second wave of migrations differs from the first in being socially more diverse, with migrants coming from different economic sectors. Although the regional origins of the migrants also tended to be more diversified, the majority of migrants were still predominantly from the Democratic Republic of Congo (DRC, former Zaire). A combination of several factors explains the African Francophones' increasing interest in South Africa as a migratory destination. According to Kadima (1999), the end of the Congolese (Zairian) single-party regime in 1990 led the path to a major socioeconomic crisis marked by large-scale lootings and massacres that forced segments of the population to seek refuge outside their national borders. Geographically and politically, South Africa represented a good alternative, as it could be reached by those who had limited financial means or who wanted to flee rapidly. Moreover, it was open to African foreigners. People from the DRC were not required entry visas until April 1993, as long as they did not plan to extend their stay. At a broader political scale, South Africa represented an alternative to traditional migratory routes to Western Europe, especially the former colonial metropoles, which became less and less receptive to migrants from the Southern hemisphere and had hardened their immigration policies since the June 1990 Schengen Convention.

The third wave (since 1994) is acknowledged as the numerically most important influx of Francophone African migrants in South Africa. This 'rush', as Bouillon (1999a:46) describes it, was triggered by multiple factors within and outside South Africa. For many migrants, South African first democratic elections in 1994 marked the beginning of a new era with opportunities to live in peace and improve their socioeconomic conditions. The election of Nelson Mandela, the charismatic leader who, for decades, had unshakably incarnated the African struggle for sociopolitical equality, has admittedly made a strong impact on migrants' decisions to come to South Africa. Based on my own 1996 interviews with some of them, the figure of Mandela has helped shape a pan-Africanist discourse that aims at asserting migrants' legitimacy on the South African soil; they invoke the fact that they are (Black) Africans and have supported the struggle of their host country for emancipation from the apartheid rule. While all this is the migrants' rationalization of their presence in South Africa, this discourse seeks to counterbalance a widespread xenophobic discourse that they have often faced (Bouillon 1999b; Mattes et al. 1999; McDonald et al. 1998; Morris 1999). From an international perspective, the year 1994 also marked the beginning of the Rwandan genocide that led to massive emigration of Rwandans to neighboring countries such as Tanzania, the DRC and Kenya, as well as to the disintegration of the sub-region (Eastern DRC, Burundi), a few months later.

From this very brief and therefore oversimplified overview of African Francophone immigration to South Africa, three general trends can be identified. The first is the increased diversity of migrants' regions of origin as evidenced by the official figures from the Ministry of Foreign Affairs (although these are not always reliable) and my own fieldwork in Cape Town. It is not exaggerated to say that almost all the Black African Francophone countries have at least one of their nationals in South Africa. The second trend has to do with the decrease of migrants' 'economic and cultural capitals' (in Bourdieu's 1991 terminology). The recent migrants have generally been less affluent and less educated than the earlier ones, although many of them are innovative and audacious entrepreneurs and skilled traders. Nevertheless, some of them have benefited from their predecessors' social networks and longer experience and have therefore familiarized themselves quicker with their new environment. I will show how a social stratification between the first wave migrants and the more recent ones has operated along linguistic lines with the use of English as a marker of distinction.

At a broader scale, the emergence of South Africa as a new migration pole of attraction for African Francophones epitomizes the partial de- and re-centering of socioeconomic powers characteristic of globalization process. Becoming a new center, South Africa is inserted into a broader set of economic, political centers. For example, studies such as Kadima (1999), Bouillon (1996, 1999a), and Vigouroux (2003, 2008) have all shown that for African Francophones, migration to South Africa is predominantly a default choice, after several unsuccessful attempts to go to Europe or North America. In the next section, we will show how the migrants orient themselves in a set of multidimensional centers that may affect, on the ground, their language practice.

The last trend of the African Francophone migration to South Africa is characterized by a centripetal movement from the former homelands, zones of sociopolitical and linguistic relegation, to the economic heart of major city centers.[5] I argue in the next section that this has translated, over the past few years, into the increasing visibility of the migrants in Cape Town's urban fabric. Their presence at the heart of the city has manifestly been transforming the latter's linguistic landscape, thanks to a reorganization of patterns of interactions and a 'reordering of language indexicalities' (Blommaert 2005).

11.4 Polycentric Spaces and Language Practice

In an enlightening article, Blommaert et al. (2005b) invite us to rethink language practice as spatially oriented along multilayered and multi-scalar centers. They convincingly argue that each center provides regimes of interactional practice to which speakers orient or fail to orient themselves and according to which they are assessed as competent or incompetent speakers. This center–periphery framework, borrowed from Wallerstein's world-system economic model (see Blommaert this volume), makes it possible to account for sociolinguistic patterns in society that are often informed by power dynamics that constrain speakers' management of their language repertoires. This is done, for example, by imposing (*right*) *ways of speaking or* dismissing some language resources as not functional in a given setting. As we shall see, it also prompts us to articulate language practice along different timespace scales, both micro and macro.

A center–periphery approach has a particular resonance in modern South Africa. Any account of sociolinguistic dynamics in urban South Africa should take into account the geographical divisions (city-center versus townships) inherited from the apartheid era. The latter came along with social inequalities (Houssay-Holzschuch 1999; Western 1996) and specific patterns of interaction determining who can interact with whom, where and in which language. My ethnographic study showed that migrants' patterns of settlement in Cape Town were often determined by long timespace divisions. Because of their affordable housing compared to other residential zones, black townships often constituted the newcomers' first place of residence, especially for those with no social networks. However, the townships were hardly envisioned as permanent settlement. Among the social reasons often invoked by the migrants for wanting to leave them was the fact that their residents usually speak only IsiXhosa or Afrikaans, a practice that hardly enables them to learn English.

Consequently, the presence of Francophone Africans in Cape Town urban landscape is not equally felt by the local population; nor is it experienced uniformly by the migrants themselves. There are two main reasons why the presence of the Francophone African migrants is considered marginal in the 'Black' and 'Colored' townships but conspicuous in Cape Town's city-centers: The first is the migrants themselves have made conscious decisions to remain as inconspicuous as possible in Black townships in order to avoid being targeted by segments of the indigenous populations that don't appreciate their presence.[6] The migrants' strategies to blend in their local social environments range from remaining silent on the streets or in public transportation to adopting the local sartorial style. The second reason is that because jobs are scarce in the townships, migrants spend most of their days working in economically more central and promising locations such as Cape Town or adjacent neighborhoods and spend little time in their places of residence. In either case, the migrants are not sufficiently immersed in the populations that speak only IsiXhosa and therefore do not learn Cape Town's dominant indigenous language. Their feeling of insecurity has not been particularly helpful in this case. To be sure, there are a few like Aurélien, from Côte d'Ivoire, who have opened businesses in the Black Township of Langa. They resort to helpers who serve as co-workers, which makes them less conspicuous, and as interpreters. The migrants' general reluctance to learn IsiXhosa or Afrikaans reflects both their often negative experience as foreigners and Black Africans as well as the power dynamics of Cape Town's linguistic market. The cost and benefits of learning a language are carefully weighted and the migrants' choice is generally driven by economic opportunities that a language may provide to them. Based on my fieldwork, those who have learned IsiXhosa are generally people who have a positive attitude toward the Xhosa population and who have already a satisfactory functional competence in English. In this case, the order of language acquisition shows that speakers expand their 'social capital' (with IsiXhosa) only after they have already 'secured' their 'economic capital' (with English).

The migrants have generally perceived IsiXhosa and Afrikaans as functionally restrictive languages, because these have a spatial scope that is confined to the outskirt of the city, historically relegated to the periphery of the urban socioeconomic structure.[7] Both languages index, in different ways, social categories of speakers with which they are generally reluctant to identify (Vigouroux 2008). Neither of the two languages is perceived as an asset that can help them penetrate the local labor market. Neither language is associated with the economic empowerment that many of the migrants came to seek in South Africa. In a way, the two indigenous languages also index the locality of South Africa on the broader scale of the global (transnational) market, where they provide even less geographical mobility.

Bourdieu's notion of *market place* appears to provide a useful framework for understanding speakers' evaluations and uses of competing language varieties. For him, the unequal values that language varieties acquire on particular markets translate into economic values. He argues that any value assigned to a language variety depends on the actual or symbolic authority of the groups associated with it. Language commodification is intrinsically linked to the economic and/or symbolic benefits that a speaker may gain from speaking or mastering the 'right' variety, namely, social recognition, access to higher positions and so on.

A language may concurrently be assigned different symbolic and economic values on different scales, and these may not overlap. For instance, although IsiZulu does not have a functional value of any significance in Cape Town, where it is hardly spoken, it generally holds a high symbolic value among African Francophone migrants. According to fieldwork, this symbolic value was assigned before migrants arrived in South Africa, thanks to the history of Shaka, the founder of the powerful Zulu kingdom in early nineteenth century who also symbolizes resistance to colonial expansion. It is important to underscore that the indexicality of IsiZulu remains stable across geographic contexts because the language is not inserted into Cape Town's economic market. A comparative study with Durban and Johannesburg, where IsiZulu is widely spoken as a vernacular and lingua franca, could show how the latter's symbolic value may be challenged when the language gets inserted into an economy of language practice. The valorization of IsiZulu by the migrants in Cape Town highlights the fact that several language markets can co-exist (a point that Bourdieu acknowledges) at different timespace scales, that is, at the level of actual language practice and at a symbolic and transnational level.

While migrants generally tried to be inconspicuous in the black townships, they have conversely made themselves increasingly visible in Cape Town's city-center, since the late 1990s.[8] Among the people who settled in Cape Town in the mid-1990s were migrants with entrepreneurship skills and an economic capital that enabled them to start a business. West Africans, especially Senegalese, Malians, who had been traders before migrating to South Africa applied their business skills in their new ecology while others such as the DRC citizens engaged in new trading activities. Some of the early migrants capitalized on the touristy character of Cape Town enhanced by the political transition of the mid-1990s; they turned to an economic advantage the fact that the city-center was predominantly white and did not match received ideas of an African city. They opened a new economic niche by providing African crafts (statues, masks, malachite, fabrics, etc.) that, until then, had not been available, except in a few upscale stores. A handful of migrants started a business by setting up stalls at the heart (physically and symbolically speaking) of Cape Town, at Green Market Square, the oldest flea market of the city and a highlight for many Cape Townians. In a centripetal movement, the presence of migrants at Green Market Square attracted young Black South Africans from the periphery of the city, looking for new job opportunities. At a small-scale level, a new economy emerged in which migrants became employers of one and sometimes two helpers.[9] Along with this localized emergent economy came a rearticulation of the city-center's linguistic landscape. From being almost exclusively a socially and geographically peripheral language, IsiXhosa has moved to downtown linguistic market. The spatial shift brought along new indexicalities. IsiXhosa got inserted into a new economy of signs, participating in migrant traders' 'Africanization' of the city-center while functioning as a sign of distinction from African outsiders.

The migrants' helpers have since the beginning been exclusively female, partly because they do not trust male Black South Africans, whom they consider 'unreliable' and as 'crooks' (*voleurs*). In the beginning, the helpers played the interface between patrons and their employers, who spoke no, or little, English. The helpers had been trained by their bosses to conduct business by learning for instance how to save the patron's face while still making profit during a transaction. In 1996, when I conducted intensive fieldwork, interactions between the migrants and their patrons at Green Market Square often followed virtually the same script from one stall to another, such as in the following example reconstructed from field notes:

> *Patron looking at a product on a stall*
> Trader: hello may I help you/ I can give you a good price
> *Patron asking for price*
> *Trader giving price before adding*
> Trader: I can give you a discount

Ready-made interactional scripts may be explained as a strategy to compensate an approximate English competence and also as an interactional routine that had developed gradually, day by day. The script spread thanks to the fact that the stalls were close to each other and the traders spent a lot of time interacting together between customers' visits. The female helpers were the earlier traders' first linguistic models and main agents of socialization. As noted earlier, the migrants' interactions with South Africans outside the market were limited. Working long hours seven days a week, they had little spare time to socialize, aside from the fact that they did not always feel safe to venture alone in new environments.[10] Black South African helpers' influence on traders' variety of English is hard to assess since the latter were exposed, often only passively, to multiple other linguistic inputs over the years. Nonetheless, it can be assumed that these linguistic models' varieties of English may have helped shape the migrants' language attitudes to local English. Being primarily in contact with non-native varieties produced by speakers who themselves also have limited sustained contacts with native speakers, owing to the now de facto racial stratification of their society, many migrants have developed the misconception that English has no standard grammar and is less sophisticated (*raffinée*) than French, which they had learned through formal education. The traders have generally shown no interest in learning standard English because they find their competence in the language functional enough to conduct business on the market. One may also wonder to what extent the traders' approximative competence in English might not be turned into a business asset by indexing 'African authenticity' in a predominantly white city-center, at least until a very recent time.

In a multilingual society such as Cape Town, the migrants' acquisition of one (or more) of the host languages has often depended on what they think they can do with the language(s) before they realize what they can actually (not) do with them. For entrepreneurs such as the traders whose professional activity does not directly depend on the local job market, the pressure to acquire English is less strong. At the opposite end, highly educated people who had occupied influential positions in their home countries and did not intend to migrate tend to perceive the acquisition of English as a sine qua non condition for competitive insertion in the South African socioeconomic structure. At a local scale, migrations to Cape Town came along for them with social downgrading. The migrants, especially women, found themselves unemployed or working in low paid jobs, such as in the now flourishing security business. The migrants' efforts to acquire English by taking membership in a public library or joining an English-speaking church community illustrate how much they appreciate competence in the economically dominant language and their recognition that it holds a key to the improvement of their socioeconomic conditions.[11] While, on the ground, the migrants' investment in language learning is driven by potential social benefits, on a broader scale, it reflects a language ideology inherited from old colonial language policies according to which a good command of former colonial language helps climb the social ladder. Although the South African sociolinguistic situation corroborates in many ways this state of affairs, it also shows that what may work for locals, may not necessarily work for outsiders, as made evident by Mohammed, a Congolese from the Democratic Republic. When I asked him whether he thought it necessary for African Francophone migrants to know English in Cape Town, he answered:

> c'est problème ou c'est pas un problème aussi ça ne dérange pas parce que il y a pas de boulot pour les étrangers – il y a pas les avantages ici en Afrique du Sud si moi j'ai l'envie de prendre des cours d'anglais pour me faire des relations ailleurs – pour me – parce que je sais qu'ailleurs j'ai – je vais avoir des avantages ailleurs parce que je – comme j'aime la France je peux faire mes relations si j'ai déjà l'anglais – ça peut me faciliter avec des gens de francophones – je peux faire des relations avec – bon – cela veut dire que l'anglais ici en Afrique du Sud donc tu peux connaître ça comme tu peux pas aussi connaître ça __ donc comme tu veux __ si tu veux tu apprends ça si tu ne veux pas tu laisses

> it's problem or it's not a problem then it doesn't bother because there's no job for foreigners – there are no advantages here in South Africa if me I feel like taking English classes to make relations elsewhere – for me – because I know that elsewhere I – I will have advantages elsewhere because I – since I like France I can build my relationships if I already have English – it can help me with some people of Francophones – I can make relationships with [them] – so – it means that English here in South Africa hence you can know it as much as you can also not know it — so as you want — if you want you learn it if you don't want to you leave [it]

Mohammed's response highlights the fact that English has a transnational value. That is, it is considered a language for social promotion, one that remains stable across various contexts, but only at an abstract level (e.g., learning English to 'make relations elsewhere'). However, this view is disputable in the local context of Cape Town, since English has not spared the migrants from social stereotyping (e.g., being treated as foreigners).[12] Language use is tied to contexts of interaction and therefore is intrinsically indexical. As noted earlier, several orders of indexicality may co-exist at different scales, with each scale providing its sets of indexicalities. Therefore, what may work at one scale does not necessarily work at another.

In this section I have articulated the multiplicity of the social and symbolic dimensions that participate in the construction of the migrants' language practice and attitudes in the host country. I have shown how these dimensions operate at different scales, that is, the micro-scale of the interactions and the macro-scale of long-term social structures and language ideologies. A micro-scale cannot be reduced to a downsized reproduction of a broader scale. Indeed, as suggested by Howitt (1993 and 1998), scales should be understood in relations to each other. These relations do not exist outside the time-space in which they are enacted through semiotic practice. Therefore, they are always being constructed by language users, at specific times and in specific settings.

As long argued by human geographers (Lefebvre 1974; Massey 2005) social space does not exist independently of the social agents who inhabit and construct it. I show in the next section that the local social space that the migrants come to inhabit is reorganized by their very presence; therefore they play a role in its construction.

11.5 Social and Linguistic Reconfigurations in/ of the Host Environment

An understanding of language vitality in the context of migration should not solely focus on the migrants' language practices but also take into account the whole social and semiotic space in which the latter are embedded and which they help transform. Blommaert et al. (2005a:201) remind us that 'diaspora[s] are *structural* processes which develop over long spans of time and result in *lasting*, or at least more or less permanent, social reconfigurations'. The latter can amount to the introduction, to the host country, of new cultural artifacts such as music or clothing styles, culinary tastes, religious cults and so on. Some members of the host population may welcome these new 'foreign' semiotic practices as reflecting the modern age of 'melting pot', others may see them as threats to their own cultural values and social cohesion. Fear of the Other has been expressed in discourse on migrants' invasion of the locals' olfactory or auditory spaces, such when Jacques Chirac, the former president of France, complained in his 19 June 1991 speech about migrants' noise and bad smells (*mauvaises odeurs*, referring to the smell of foreign cuisine). Signs indexing foreignness in relation to local practices and to the dominant culture have usually sparked heated debates in Western European countries such as when Muslim women insist on wearing a veil on their faces or when new mosques are open.

In Cape Town's city-center, African Francophones have slowly imprinted their presence on the city walls. This is evident from a few window stores displaying distinctive names such as *Touba-Fallou African Pride, Bogolan arts market* (sic) or *MaliSouth traditional clothes* on Long Street, one of Cape Town's major streets. These window stores have become part of the textual discourse of the 'geosemiotic' (Scollon and Scollon 2003) of the cityscape and therefore of Cape Townians' daily visual space.[13] The expanding visibility of the migrants marks their deeper rootedness in the local economy, which is facilitated in part by the regularization of their administrative status. Thus, the most affluent ones, who were granted a resident status, could take out loans from banks and invest in bigger businesses. A concomitant of this expanding visibility is that the successful migrants can now assert their distinctiveness as foreigners while claiming a Black African identity to promote and legitimate their particular enterprises. On the other hand, smaller migrant-run businesses not dealing with art that directly compete on the same grounds as South African companies (such as Internet cafés and beauty salons) do not display, at least from the outside, any distinctive signs of foreignness.

Imported semiotic resources are not immutable; they are indigenized by the economy of local signs. This is the case with, for instance, *Bologan arts market* (Figure 11.1), which displays, on the one hand, foreignness (or little command

FIGURE 11.1   Bogolan Arts Market, Long Street, Cape Town.

of the local business language) with the *s* added to *art* and the approximative spelling of *brading* 'braiding', and, on the other, conformity to local norms of English advertising. The board on the storefront reflects the multifunctionality of a place that hosts several unrelated businesses, including a restaurant and a beauty salon. Incidentally, *Bogolan* is a tiny place, extending no more than sixty square meters. Migrant entrepreneurs have often shared space in order to cut down on rental costs, especially in the city-center. Such partnerships often also ignore nationality differences such as between Pakistani and Congolese traders (from the both Congos) in Bogolan Market, which illustrates the migrants' impact on their host environment, as they trigger its spatial reorganization and redefine the range of business activities. I showed in an ethnographic study in Vigouroux (to appear) how language practice helps structure businesses' spatial organization by drawing boundaries between unrelated sets of activities especially in exiguous places.

Local semiosis may also be reinterpreted in light of the imported foreign signs such as in Figure 11.2, where the Xhosa-style dresses displayed in the shop's window are inserted in a transnational African discourse under the umbrella *traditional clothing* complemented by the motto *Africa is one*, written in red lower case at the bottom of the board. On the other hand, foreignness is indexed by the name *MaliSouth*, to the left of *Traditional* and above the pictures of two West-African-style shirts flanking the colors of the Malian flag. Together, the lettering, the pictures and the store window constitute a hybrid semiosis that illustrates how black South African locality is reinterpreted as being part of a transnational African globality while, in return, it constructs African migrants as being part of the host country's national space.

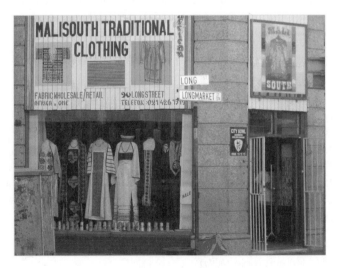

FIGURE 11.2   Clothing store on Long Street, Cape Town.

In the previous section, we saw how the restructuring of social space triggered by the African Francophones in Cape Town has led to a reorganization of the Green Market's linguistic landscape, with IsiXhosa becoming part of the interactional regime of the market. At the micro-scale, the presence of diasporic populations also affects patterns of local interactions such as in the following two sequences:

Sequence 1:

1. Store manager: hi
2. Cécile: [hi how are you/
3. Geneviève: [how are you/
4. Cécile: ça te dit une soupe/ (*you feel like a soup/*)
5. Geneviève: XX hein/ ils servent aussi des soupes ouais soupes
   [avec°°°   (*XX uhm/ they also serve soups yeah soups*
   [*with*°°°)
6. Cécile: [t'en veux une soupe/ (*you want a soup/*)
7. Store manager: this this soup is a _ lentil butternut and sweet
8. potato

This interaction occurred in a small organic café in downtown Cape Town, where Geneviève, a Congolese friend, and I went to buy carryouts. The store manager, a White South African woman, greeted us in English (line 1: *hi*). The greeting was both an acknowledgement of our presence in her store and the framing of a new space of interaction. Her turn (line 8: *this this soup is a _ lentil butternut and sweet potato*), which expanded on the topic (the soup) that Geneviève and I were discussing in French, evidenced that French had been integrated by the store manager as being part of the interactional regime of the exchange and therefore of the setting. The manager had certainly relied on the similarity of the French word *soupe* with its English counterpart as well as on our body language oriented to the soup menu.

Sequence 2:

(. . .)
9. Store manager: this is a refry bean burrito _ basil pesto pasta and
10. steak spinach pancake _ this is an ama::zing meal _ it got Danish
11. feta roasted veg _ potato and vegetables chutney/ very very nice
12. Geneviève: OK _ pancake _ _ j'ai en- j'ai mangé les mei:lleurs
13. pancakes à Bloemfontein (*OK _ pancake _ _ I ate some- I ate the be:st pancakes in Bloemfontein*)
14. Cécile: c'est vrai/ (*really/*)
15. Geneviève: oh:: _ _ molo sisi (*oh:: _ _ hello sister*)
16. Helper: molo (*hello*)
17. Geneviève: unjani/ (*how are you/*)

18. Helper: ndiphilile unjani/ *(I am fine and how are you/)*
19. Geneviève: ndikhona sisi XX ((smiles)) *(I am fine sister XX)*
20. Store manager: I like your OUTfit _ it is gor::geous
21. Geneviève: thank you [((laughs)) <thank you>
22. Cécile: [((laughs))
23. Helper: [IsiXhosa unintelligible because of noise]
24. Geneviève: uhm/
25. Helper: uyatyeba *(you are picking up weight)*
26. Geneviève: eh:/ oh sisi /uyaphosisa xe wena sisi _ mina la/ *(you are lying sister _ me here/)*
27. Helper: burst out of laughs
28. Geneviève: izimpundu zam ezingaka/ hayi sisi wena *(my bum this big/ no sister)*
29. Helper: ((laughs))
30. Cécile: ((laughs))
31. Store manager: what did she what did she say to you/
32. Geneviève: she said I I I picked [up some weights
33. Store manager: [does she know you from before/
34. Geneviève: yes she knows me before
35. Cécile: ((laughs))
36. Store manager: ah I see _ whether you picked up weight or not
37. I don't know but you look gorgeous

A few seconds elapsed between the first part of the interaction and the second. While refraining from a detailed discussion of this excerpt, I will just mention a few interesting points for my demonstration. Geneviève's change of footing in line 15 (from an exchange with the store manager to a conversation with the helper at the back of the kitchen) was accompanied by a reorganization of the interactional space, with IsiXhosa becoming part of the language repertoire of the setting. The store manager, who did not speak IsiXhosa, tried to take back the floor by reframing her previous seller–customer interaction with Geneviève (first excerpt) into a more personal relation by complimenting her on her outfit (line 20: *I like your OUTfit _ it is gor::geous*).[14] After a short exchange in English initiated by the store manager, the interaction switched back to IsiXhosa with the helper resuming her conversation with Geneviève. The manager's second attempt to take back the floor by asking for the translation of what her helper had said (line 31: *what did she say to you/*) made clear that IsiXhosa had become a meaningful language resource in the setting and that her language repertoire was no longer functional in the new linguistic reconfiguration. At a deeper level, Geneviève's interaction in IsiXhosa triggered a reorganization of the social dynamics between the helper and her manager, with the former taking the front stage. This is particularly meaningful in a sociopolitical context such as South Africa where interactions are still often shaped along racial divides.

Further research will shed light on what forms have been taken by the social and linguistic reconfigurations triggered by African Francophones' presence in Cape Town. I hope to have shown that a reflection on language vitality in territories involving migrants should take into account the whole semiotic space in which they participate and to which they contribute new meanings.

11.6 Conclusions

Diouf (2002) summarizes as follows the challenges faced by any study that must account for global dynamics without losing sight of the multiplicity of individual sociohistorical trajectories: 'The issue that continues to defy analysis is how to elaborate a single explanation of both the process of globalization and the multiplicity of individual temporalities and local rationalities that are inserted into it' (111). In this chapter, my answer to such an issue has been to favor alternative explanations, on account of the complexity of sociocultural dynamics in the field. Indeed, the study of African Francophones' language practices and attitudes in Cape Town has underscored the fact that it would be misleading to present a uniform picture not only of the migratory population and its language practices but also of its host environment. I have indeed tried to show that any language practice is produced at a given time and in a given setting by a complex intertwining of related and sometimes competing dimensions of space, namely, social, geographic and symbolic. Therefore, an accurate account of language dynamics, and thus of language vitality, should rest on fine-grained ethnographic analyses of all the different spaces in which the migrants interact and which they help construct.

By emphasizing the multiplicity of spaces to which the migrants orient, we moved away from a perspective that interprets migration solely in terms of transnational relocation. We proposed instead to focus on the migrants' mobility across discursive spaces to account for the reshuffling of their language repertoires. Thus, languages are approached from the point of view of their functions in a given interactional setting rather than as abstract codes. While the latter may remain the same across contexts (e.g., English, Bambara, French), their functions may not. For example, a host language may become some migrants' new vehicular when they interact with other migrants. This is the case for some early migrants who, despite the fact that their competence in English was still approximative, chose to interact in it with African Francophones who had just arrived in order to assert that they had arrived earlier in the host country and were established in it. Although, focusing on language codes, one may conclude that speakers switched to Cape Town's dominant language, the use of English in this context is likely indexical, suggesting some social stratification among the migrants based on the time of settlement.

A close study of language functions should thus prevent us from drawing hasty conclusions on the fate of particular languages in a given environment (cf., for instance, Mesthrie, this volume). Citing Vigouroux's (2005) discussion of African Francophones' differential language dynamics at two flea markets, Mesthrie argues that French is being revitalized in the Cape Peninsula, four centuries after its first appearance in the Cape Colony with the Huguenots. The observation is rather seductive but misleading. The fact that the Huguenots spoke French, similarly to the African migrants, should not lead us to forget that the communicative functions of this language are hardly comparable for the two populations. Whereas French was a vernacular language for the first ones and presumably did function as such in the early settlement, it is spoken only as a non-native lingua franca by the African Francophone migrants to Cape Town. Indeed, speakers tend to use French when communication cannot be carried on in one of their traditional African languages. Those migrants who constitute a critical mass of speakers of the same language, such as the DRC Lingala-speakers, and who maintain strong network ties among themselves hardly interact with each other in French. Although accounts on the Huguenots' patterns of socialization in the Cape Peninsula are not as well documented as those of African Francophones, there are reasonable doubts that they can stand comparisons with those of the Francophone migrants.

Linguistic studies of globalization such as Crystal (2000), Fishman (1998/1999) or Maurais (2003b) – to cite just a few authors of a long list – have often 'slip[ed] uneasily between description and prediction' (Cohen 1997:156), and run the risk of misrepresenting complex local linguistic dynamics. One of these misrepresentations has been the over-emphasis on the potential endangerment of local languages by European languages, especially English. The study of African Francophone migrations to South Africa should prompt more cautious assessments of the potential threat of English to the African languages spoken by the migrants. Even in this expatriate setting of Cape Town, there are no signs of English endangering their languages, as they do not use it as a vernacular. This lends support to Mufwene's (2005, 2008) position that languages compete with each other only when they also serve the same communicative functions. A shift of lingua francas can occur, however, especially among migrants speaking languages for which there is no critical mass of users in the host location. This is the case for Tshiluba or Swahili speakers who tend to switch to Lingala in order to be acknowledged as part of Cape Town's DRC community, which consists mostly of Lingala-speakers. Such language shifts prompt us to focus not only on the impact of the host language on the languages of the migrants but also on the new dynamics of coexistence and competition among those of the migrants themselves. As pointed out in this chapter, any accurate account of language vitality in the context of migrations should pay equal attention to local linguistic reconfigurations and not presume stability of the spaces crossed by the migrants. This makes the task of description and analysis more challenging but undoubtedly enlightening, as it helps us better understand both local and global language dynamics.

Notes

I would like to thank Sali Mufwene for his challenging comments on this chapter and his unshakable patience to serve as my sounding board during the writing process. Needless to say, all the remaining shortcomings are my sole responsibility.

[1] It is far from my intention to depict an overly negative image of the migratory experience. As will become apparent as the chapter progresses, the term *migrant* tends to index more than the state of 'not being native to a polity'.

[2] In the case of slavery and colonization, which obviously involve migration, it may be argued that the agency of slaves and forced laborers played only a secondary role. It was nevertheless significant in the adaptive responses of colonists, slaves and laborers alike to their new ecologies, at least at the level of spontaneous acts from which new patterns eventually emerge (Mufwene 2005, 2008).

[3] The civic-integration evaluation has aroused controversies, with opponents arguing that it is meant to exclude devout Muslims. They note that the evaluation curiously includes a movie featuring a nude beach scene and another where homosexuals are kissing. The movie is intended to determine whether the visa applicants accept these allegedly Dutch cultural values and ways of life.

[4] Sharpville is a black township in the Gauteng province (North East of the country) where sixty-nine Black South Africans were killed and more than a hundred people injured by the police during a demonstration organized against the pass law that was part of the *influx control* politics. Passes aimed at limiting Black South Africans' movements in urban white areas. After the Sharpville massacre, demonstrations sparked throughout the country leading to a state of emergency and the ban of the African National Congress (ANC) and the Pan African Congress (PAC), the organizer of the demonstration. After Sharpville, the international community condemned the apartheid regime's racist politics and organized economic sanctions against South Africa.

[5] Until the 1996 new South African constitution, any of the African languages spoken in the former homelands were given institutional legitimacy. For an informative summary of the history of language policy and politics in South Africa, see McLean (1999); and for a sociolinguistic overview of South Africa, see Mesthrie (2002).

[6] Migrants' narratives on verbal and physical threats by Black South Africans are numerous. Statistics on violence towards African migrants are worrisome. Since July 2006, around thirty Somali businessmen have been killed and more stores burned down in the townships around Cape Town. More interested readers can visit this site: http://www.mg.co.za/articlePage.aspx?articleid=284263&area=/breaking_news/breaking_news__national/.

[7] In Cape Town, Afrikaans is predominantly spoken as a first language by the so-called Colored population.

8 Unlike the townships, the city-center is primarily a workplace for the migrants. Only a small number of migrants in my field sample (9 per cent) declared that they lived downtown.

9 This goes against the common prejudice that migrants come to steal employment from South Africans (Vigouroux 2003). Regarding migrants' enterprise economy in Johannesburg, see Rogerson (1997).

10 The significance of linguistic models in the development of a (new) language variety is explained by Mufwene (1998, 2008) in the case of indigenized French in Africa and creoles and by Chaudenson (1973, 2001) for the development of French creoles.

11 It also shows how the migrants' social practice in the host country may be driven by their language-learning experience and how communicative events may be reframed by speakers in light of this experience. This was, for example, the case in the collective therapeutic sessions I attended as an English–French interpreter for three months in 1999. When I asked some of the patients why they felt the need to attend those weekly sessions designed exclusively for refugees, many of them told me that the latter were good opportunities to learn English since a simultaneous translation in French was provided.

12 A similar point is made by Urciuoli (1998) when she argues that even a standard competence in English does not guarantee social recognition of Puerto Ricans in New York.

13 It would be interesting to conduct a similar investigation to Collins and Slembrouck's (2006) on shop windows' inscriptions in Ghent (Belgium), focusing on how Cape Townians 'read' these new signs.

14 Geneviève was wearing a colorful Congolese two-piece outfit that not only attracted people's attention but also indexed her as a foreigner. Her very stylish African way of dressing hardly left people indifferent and often triggered conversations with strangers.

References

Adejunmobi, Moradewun. 2004. Polyglots, vernaculars and global markets: Variable trends in West Africa. *Language and Intercultural Communication* 4(3).159–174.

Appadurai, Arjun. 1996. *Modernity at Large*. Minneapolis: University of Minnesota Press.

Bitjaa Kody, Zachée Denis. 2000. Attitudes linguistiques et intégration socio-économique des Africains francophones à Montréal. *African Journal of Applied Linguistics* 1.58–82.

Blommaert, Jan. 2005. *Discourse: A Critical Introduction*. Cambridge: Cambridge University Press.

Blommaert, Jan, James Collins and Stef Slembrouck. 2005a. Spaces of multilingualism. *Language and Communication* 25.197–216.

—2005b. Polycentricity and interactional regimes in 'global neighborhoods'. *Ethnography* 6(2).205–235.

Bouillon, Antoine. 1999a. Migrants africains 'continentaux' et francophones en Afrique du Sud. In Antoine Bouillon (ed.), 13–74.

—1999b. Immigrés africains francophones et Sud-Africains. In Antoine Bouillon (ed.), 125–170.

Bouillon, Antoine (ed.). 1999. *Immigration africaine en Afrique du Sud*. Paris: Karthala.

Bourdieu, Pierre. 1991. *Language and Symbolic Power*. Cambridge: Polity Press.

Chaudenson, Robert. 1973. Pour une étude comparée des créoles et français d'outre-mer: Survivance et innovation. *Revue de Linguistique Romane* 37. 342–370.

—2001. *Creolization of Language and Culture*. London: Routledge.

Cohen, Robin. 1997. *Global Diasporas*. Seattle: University of Washington Press.

Collins, James and Stef Slembrouck. 2006. Reading shop windows in globalized neighborhoods: Multilingual literacy practices and indexicality. *Journal of Literacy Research* 39(3).335–356.

Crystal, David. 2000. *Language Death*. Cambridge, NY: Cambridge University Press.

Diouf, Mamadou. 2002. The Senegalese Murid trade diaspora and the making of a vernacular cosmopolitanism. In *Cosmopolitanism*, ed. by Carol A. Brechkenridge, Sheldon Pollock, Homi K. Bhabha and Dipesh Chakrabarty, 111–137. Durham and London: Duke University Press.

Eisenlohr, Patrick. 2004. Language revitalization and new technologies: Cultures of electronic mediation and the refiguring of communities. *Annual Review of Anthropology* 33.21–45.

Feussi, Valentin. 2007. À travers textos, courriels et tchats: des pratiques de français au Cameroun. Glottopol 10. http://www.univ-rouen.fr/dyalang/glottopol/numero_10.html.

Fishman, Joshua. 1998/1999. The new linguistic order. *Foreign Policy* 113.26–40.

Harvey, David. 1990. *The Condition of Post Modernity: An Enquiry into the Origins of Cultural Change*. Cambridge: Blackwell.

Houssay-Holzschuch, Myriam. 1999. *Le Cap ville sud-africaine*. Paris: L'Harmattan.

Howitt, Richard. 1993. 'A world in a grain of sand': Towards a reconceptualisation of geographical scale. *Australian Geographer* 24(1).33–44.

—1998. Scale as relation: Musical metaphors of geographical scale. *Area* 30(1).49–58.

Kadima, Denis. 1999. Motivations à l'émigration et activités économiques des immigrés congolais (RDC) en Afrique du Sud. In Antoine Bouillon (ed.), 103–123.

Lefebvre, Henri. 1974. *La Production de l'espace*. Paris: Anthropos.

Legeden, Gudrun and Mélissa Richards. 2007. 'jv me prendre un bois monumental the wood of the century g di' Langues en contact dans quatre corpus oraux et écrits 'ordinaires' à la Réunion. Glottopol 10. http://www.univ-rouen.fr/dyalang/glottopol/numero_10.html.

Massey, Doreen. 2005. *For Space*. London: Sage.

Mattes, Robert, D.M. Taylor, David McDonald, A. Poore and W. Richmond. 1999. *Still Waiting for the Barbarians: SA Attitudes to Immigrants and Immigration*. Cape Town: The Southern African Migration Project.

Maurais, Jacques. 2003a. *Analyse linguistique de 4000 courriels*. Québec: Bibliothèque nationale du Québec.

—2003b. Towards a new linguistic world order. In *Language in a Globalizing World*, ed. by Jacques Maurais and Michael A. Morris, 13–36. Cambridge: Cambridge University Press.

McDonald, David, John Gray, Lovemore Zinyama, Robert Mattes and Fion de Vletter. 1998. *Challenging Xenophobia: Myths & Realities about Cross-Border Migration in Southern Africa*. Cape Town: The Southern African Migration Project.

McLean, Daryl. 1999. Neocolonizing the mind? Emergent trends in language policy for South African education. In *Post-Apartheid South Africa*, ed. by Kay McCormick and Rajend Mesthrie. *International Journal of the Sociology of Language* 136.7–26.

Mesthrie, Rajend. 2002. South Africa: A sociolinguistic overview. In *Language in South Africa*, ed. by Rajend Mesthrie, 11–26. Cambridge: Cambridge University Press.

Morris, Alan. 1999. Xénophobie à Johannesburg. L'expérience des Congolais (RDC) et des Nigérians. In Antoine Bouillon (ed.), 75–102.

Mufwene, Salikoko S. 1998. Indigénisation, français en Afrique et normes: quelques réflexions. In *Une ou des normes? Insécurité linguistique et normes endogènes en Afrique francophone*, ed. by Louis-Jean Calvet and Marie Louise Moreau, 49–59. Paris: Didier érudition.

—2001. *The Ecology of Language Evolution*. Cambridge: Cambridge University Press.

—2005. *Créoles, écologie sociale, évolution linguistique*. Paris: L'Harmattan.

—2008. *Language Evolution. Contact, Competition and Change*. London: Continuum.

Papastergiadis, Nikos. 2000. *The Turbulence of Migration*. Cambridge: Polity Press.

Rogerson, Christian M. 1997. *International Migration, Immigrant Entrepreneurs and South Africa's Small Enterprise Economy*. Cape Town: Southern African Migration Project.

Scollon, Ron and Suzie Scollon. 2003. *Discourse in Place*. London: Routledge.

Sklair, Leslie. 1999. Competing conceptions of globalization. *Journal of World-Systems Research* 2.143–163.

Urciuoli, Bonnie. 1998. *Exposing Prejudice*. Boulder, Colorado: Westview Press.

Vigouroux, Cécile B. 2003. Réflexion méthodologique autour de la construction d'un objet de recherche: la dynamique identitaire chez les migrants africains francophones au Cap (Afrique du Sud). Unpublished doctoral thesis, University Paris X-Nanterre.

—2005. 'There are no Whites in Africa': Territoriality, language and identity among Francophone Africans in Cape Town. *Language and Communication* 25.237–255.

—2008. The 'Smuggling of la *Francophonie*': Francophone Africans in Anglophone Cape Town (South Africa). *Language in Society* 37(3):415–434.

—.(to appear). A relational understanding of language practice: Interacting times-spaces in a single ethnographic site. In *Globalization and Language Contact: Spatiotemporal Scales, Migration Flows, and Communicative Practices*, ed. by Mike Baynham, Jim Collins and Stef Slembrouck. London: Continuum.

Western, John. 1996. *Outcast Cape Town*. Berkeley: University of California Press.

Websites

http://www.mg.co.za/articlePage.aspx?articleid=284263&area=/breaking_news/ breaking_news__national/.

African Migrations Workshop. Accra, Ghana, 18–21 September 2007. http://www.imi.ox.ac.uk/pdfs/Full%20report%20African%20Migrations%20Workshop%20ghana%2007.pdf.

Radio Free Europe http://www.rferl.org/featuresarticle/2006/04/2752a95e-e5f6-4886-a65c-75618628a283.html.

Chapter 12

Creating the Conditions for a Counter-Hegemonic Strategy: African Languages in the Twenty-First Century

Neville Alexander

The idea that one day the entire world will speak English seems utopian to me; it is something that will not happen. Multi-lingualism, by definition, is an obstacle to globalization.

Hobsbawm 2000: 125

12.1 Is Language Planning Relevant to Twenty-First-Century Africa?

The ultimate subject of this chapter is to consider the most appropriate strategies for achieving one of the central goals of the African Academy of Languages (ACALAN), namely, to implement an updated version of the Language Plan of Action for Africa, which, in its original form, was adopted by the Organization of African Unity in June 1986. As such, it is based on certain assumptions about the efficacy of language planning as a scholarly and professional practice. It is necessary, therefore, to begin by referring to the current state of the debate about whether or not language planning has any relevance to initiating, sustaining or countering social change.

It ought to be immediately obvious that at the most abstract level, such a discussion is necessarily implicated in debates about the primacy of the word as opposed to the deed, debates that reach back into ancient times and that we know from texts that have come down to us from Africa, Europe and Asia. It is clearly inappropriate to canvass that metaphysical disputation in the present context. Suffice it to say that I am conscious of the fact that it is implicit in any and every proposition that is formulated in this essay.

More immediately, the discussion about the limits and possibilities of language planning has become increasingly complex and is being enriched by annual additions to the stock of case studies. This volume, too, contains such additional material. A useful, indeed excellent, recent summary and analysis of the state of play is Wright (2004), to which I shall refer presently in this introduction. Similarly, Spolsky (2006), although from a more pronounced historical angle, stresses the limits of policy and warns against the hubris of planners and policy makers.

Against this background and in the full consciousness of the secular character of the ACALAN program,[1] I shall state my approach to this central issue briefly. In my view, the question that has to be answered is not whether language policy and planning can or do 'cause' social change. In reality, the question has to be formulated much more carefully: 'under what conditions can language policy and planning influence decisively the direction and depth of social change?' Also, and as a corollary to this proposition, to those who explicitly or implicitly claim that language planning is a futile waste of time and resources, we have once again to say clearly that *laissez-faire* policy notoriously reinforces the agendas of dominant groups. To continue to believe in the twenty-first century that language planning is illusory at best and tantamount to evil social engineering at worst is, ultimately, to deny the possibility of social justice. As long as language planning proceeds in democratic consultation with the users of the respective languages, the 'danger' of social engineering can be avoided. All states, even the most 'democratic', pursue social engineering to one degree or another!

With reference to the challenges with which globalization confronts nation-states generally, and basing herself with respect to language policy on the line of argument developed by James Tollefson, among others, Wright (2004) states:

> An elite English-speaking class works in tandem with global institutions and business, aids their spread and penetration, and accrues benefits for itself. The great mass do not profit and are victims. The difficulty is to know where this leads on the language question. Can participation increase within society as English spreads vertically or should there be insistence on using the national language in institutions and business to permit greater participation? (169)

Wright tends to answer in the negative the question of whether language policy can change or influence the distribution of power that is occasioned by, for example, investment in the expansion of the use of English as an international lingua franca. However, she is well aware of the fact that in this form, it has been reduced to an unnecessary either/or dilemma. Today, most scholars know that it is not a matter of 'language planning from above' versus political and/or economic activities on the ground but rather a combination of necessary conditions, none of which by itself is 'sufficient', that is the 'cause' of social change. In her own words: 'Power relationships are constituted through force and money as well as through discourse and these three actually dovetail in a complex way' (170).

It follows that the least we can do is to follow the Polonius-type wisdom at which Spolsky (2006) arrives after consideration of various case studies: 'Not failures, then, or successes, but modifications seem to be possible results. The wise language managers will acknowledge, as Cnut did, that they cannot stop the waves, but will aim to be surfers who ride them successfully' (99).

However, in Africa, the question today is no longer whether to replace the dominant official languages of European origin with indigenous African languages, even though that question had been posed occasionally in the 1960s and 1970s under the influence of strong nationalist sentiments. The realization that the ecology of languages had changed profoundly in the last quarter of the twentieth century and that most human beings have to become proficient in their mother tongues as well as in one or more international and regional languages to one degree or another is now widespread. Especially after it became clear that the English language had in effect become the lingua franca of 'globalization', and, regardless of one's stance with respect to this phenomenon, it was inevitable that the monolingual habitus of the nationalist project would have to give way to some kind of (societal) multilingual and (individual) plurilingual norm. The matter is, of course, much more complex than this programmatic statement implies. In fact, especially in the context of the countries of the economic South, a new, much more destructive and disempowering monolingual habitus that is constituted around the aspiration to have a measure of command of the English language can be said to have become established. Even in the countries of the European Union, English is the most favored first additional language although, unlike the countries of the South and of Africa in particular, it does not necessarily threaten the national dominance of the established official languages. All supra-national state formations, because they are essentially responses to the challenges of globalization, are faced with the hegemonic position of English. In this connection, the macro-linguistic analysis, based on world systems theory, which has been put forward by Abram De Swaan (2001), even though it requires much modification at the meso- and micro-linguistic levels, is very helpful for conceptualizing the general features of societal and individual language repertoires, specifically his suggestion that individual repertoires will tend towards proficiency in two or even three languages for most people. His view that these languages would tend towards some kind of stable diglossia is more problematic.[2]

12.2 The ACALAN Program

This brings me directly to the language policy and planning aspects of ACALAN, which, it ought to be clear, is taking place in the context of debates of fundamental importance about the relationship between language policy and economic and social development, as well as debates about the rationality of language policy formulation and language planning. As the official language policy and planning agency of the African Union, ACALAN is consciously setting out to design a counter-hegemonic strategy in the domain of language policy and use. It does so because of the widespread understanding among scholars, activists and some forward-looking political leadership cadres that language policy and practice are at the heart of socioeconomic development and a kind of litmus test of the commitment to democratic governance. In addition, of course, the cultural/identity functions and effects of language policy are central to the very conception of the 'African Renaissance', which has become the lodestar of the forward-looking modern African elite, a notion that inspires their ambivalent resistance to the forces and the consequences of globalization, that is, the neo-colonial domination and exploitation of the continent.

It is, therefore, extremely important that I stress at the outset that one of the main departures from OAU theoretical and strategic positions on the language question is the proposal put forward by ACALAN (see Tadadjeu and Diakité 2005) that we accept our objective is to develop the use of African languages in high-status functions *next to*, rather than *in place of*, the current languages of European origin, specifically English, French and Portuguese. Today, in the first decade of the twenty-first century, conditions are very different from those that obtained in the last quarter of the previous century. Colonial conquest, imperialism and globalization established a hierarchy of standard languages, which mirrors power relations on the planet. The overall effect of this configuration has been to hasten the extinction of innumerable language varieties and to stigmatize and marginalize all but the most powerful languages. Above all, as intimated earlier, English, in David Crystal's coinage, is 'a global language', indeed, *the* global language.

The original proposal for Implementing the Language Plan of Action for Africa (ILPAA) was formulated self-consciously in terms of a secular strategic intervention that is cognizant of the complexity of language engineering but nonetheless has precise objectives.

> The ultimate question, for those of us who are convinced of the need to plot an alternative route for the human species is what we, as language specialists and practitioners, can do in order to strengthen those social and historical forces which are running counter to the apparently unstoppable logic of globalisation. How do we assist in the decolonisation of the mind of the billions of people who are held down by their ruling elites' de facto abandonment of the principle of equity in favor of self-aggrandizement and convenience? How can we, through language planning and other interventions, initiate or reinforce changes in the patterns of development and in the dominant social relations. These are difficult questions that go to the very heart of the politics of social transformation and that raise all the imponderables about what

factors determine, or at least influence, changes in individuals' attitudes and behavior (Alexander 2005b).

At this stage, the ILPAA program of ACALAN is setting out to establish a frame of reference within which most proposed formal state interventions and all other initiatives relating to the *language infrastructure* of the continent will be generated and formatively evaluated. It is conceived of as a kind of linguistic counterpart of the New Partnership for Africa's Development (NEPAD). It is necessary here to consider language, together with its cultural implications, as an essential dimension of the economic ('development') strategy[3] promoted under the rubric of NEPAD. This must be viewed in the light of what at this stage is seldom more than the rhetoric of the African Renaissance.

Ever since President Thabo Mbeki rather incongruously proclaimed the African Renaissance in 1998, artists, scholars and political activists have been grappling with the concept of a 'Renaissance' before the event or even before the process. Whether intended or not, in the field of linguistics and especially applied linguistics, President Mbeki's proclamation galvanized literally hundreds of scholars, writers, educators and artists into creative motion. And, even though the idea and the early genesis of ACALAN had a trajectory of its own, there can be no doubt that the consciousness that all of us in this field may well be players on a world stage on which the African Renaissance was being enacted definitely added to the intensity and the urgency with which we, in ACALAN, became engaged in the great adventure of the preservation and intellectualization of African languages. Our task, in a sentence, is to ensure that in the domain of language studies the creative momentum be turned into a purposeful pan-African language movement with a clearly determined destination of pertinent material effects for the continent as a whole.

If the Renaissance is not most relevant in the domain of language, it would have very little meaning indeed. The question asked in a somewhat naïve manner by Makgoba (1999) in the preface to their work on the African Renaissance is central to what we are trying to do in ACALAN, more specifically in the domain of education. They posed the question in the following terms:

> While most contributors in this volume are Africans who speak one African language or another, none has used an African language in their writing. We have all used the African idiom and borrowed English as a means of writing. Our nuances, impressions and interpretation of the English language are rooted in our African languages, experiences and meanings. *Can African people champion their renaissance through the medium of foreign languages?* This is perhaps one of the greatest challenges to African people. Language is culture and in language we carry our identity and culture. Through language we carry science and technology, education, political systems and economic developments. The majority of African people, about whom the rebirth or

re-awakening is about (sic), live in their indigenous languages throughout their lives. (xi)

If one of the objectives of an African Renaissance is the quest for a distinctive African position in the modern world such that all Africans can walk tall in the full knowledge that their contributions to world civilization and to the progressive development of society in general are being acknowledged and respected, then it is imperative that the languages of the people of the continent, that factor that, above all others, is a mark of their distinctiveness be 'normalized', that is, that they be used in all domains of social life. It ought not to be the case that all the important functions, 'the controlling domains of language' (Sibayan 1999), are the monopoly of the former colonial languages that, ironically, continue to be the main, if not the only, official languages of most independent African countries south of the Arabic zone. The scorching shame that is brought to the surface by the statement of fact written down by Ali and Alamin Mazrui almost a decade ago will continue if the Renaissance fails to address the language question with the necessary seriousness.

> [An] important source of intellectual dependence in Africa is the language in which African graduates and scholars are taught (. . .) [Today,] in non-Arabic speaking Africa, a modern surgeon who does not speak a European language is virtually a sociolinguistic impossibility (. . .) [A] conference of African scientists, devoted to scientific matters and conducted primarily in an African language, is not yet possible (. . .) It is because of the above considerations that intellectual and scientific dependence in Africa may be inseparable from linguistic dependence. The linguistic quest for liberation (. . .) must (. . .) seek to promote African languages, especially in academia, as one of the strategies for promoting greater intellectual and scientific independence from the West. (Mazrui and Mazrui 1998:64–65)

12.3 A Continental Language Planning Strategy

How are we approaching this question in the context of ACALAN as a specialized agency of the African Union that has been charged with monitoring the development and implementation of language policy on the continent and with advising governments in this regard? I shall summarize the relevant elements of a continental language planning strategy that will push forward our agenda by using as a template a set of very realistic and carefully considered suggestions formulated by Sibayan (1999:464–465) for the intellectualization of Filipino after many years of experience. They are not less significant for being widely known and generally accepted by language planners today.

- A core of strong 'but not offensive' advocates for the use of the local language(s) as languages of learning and teaching at all levels of education. These men and women should preferably be well known and respected scholars in their fields, researchers and, if possible, 'capable of translating and writing original research' in the relevant language(s). Some of them should be 'balanced bilinguals' in the Language of Wider Communication (usually English, French or Portuguese) and the local language(s). Most important, however:

> These advocates must have a group that will write, publish, and teach in Filipino [read local language(s), N.A.] not only from one university but a network of universities; this requires collective belief and effort and good organization; in other words, there should be a society or an association that will do translation backed up by university administrators such as university rectors/presidents, deans, heads of departments; single individuals may not succeed. (Sibayan 1999:464)

- Some employers, including the state, will use the intellectualized languages in the workplace.
- Publishers prepared to take the initial risk of publishing and marketing books and other texts written in the local languages.
- Funding sources willing to sustain the production of texts in these languages until they become self-sustaining.
- The cultural, political and economic leadership must accept and propagate among the people the acceptance of a scientific culture in the local language(s).
- An understanding that the process of intellectualization will take a long time although there may be contexts – as happened in Meiji, Japan, for example – in which the change can be effected within a single generation.
- Textbooks and other texts in the intellectualizing language(s), even if we have to begin with photocopies.

It should be noted that, according to Sibayan (1999:449), a *popularly* modernized language (used, e.g., in the electronic media and tabloid papers) is not necessarily 'intellectualized'. In order for it to become *intellectually* modernized, such that it can be used in the 'controlling domains of language', including higher education, much work (e.g., corpus development) has to be done by the universities and colleges. He suggests that it is easier to begin with L1-medium education in the primary schools, since the young in the schools are the most receptive, whereas adults who, in the controlling domains, already use the former colonial language more or less proficiently tend to be extremely resistant to a changeover towards the local language(s). 'The schools and universities play a very crucial role in the process of popular and intellectual modernization: the primary and lower secondary schools for PML development, the upper secondary schools for beginning IML development and the colleges and universities for IML development' (456).

It ought to be obvious that some, or all, of these conditions already exist in organized and institutionalized form in some, but not all, African states. One of the main tasks of ACALAN is precisely to bring about this state of affairs in all African states. In South Africa, we are very fortunate in that there are the beginnings of an adequate language infrastructure, enabling legislation for the program of modernization of the indigenous African languages and for related purposes, although budgetary provisions are inadequate. Much more can and should be done with respect to the financing of indispensable programs and of the training of the necessary language professionals that have to run the multi-lingual system. Insofar as South Africa is seen by many, including some of the best known African (applied) linguists, as an evolving model in respect to language planning and language policy formulation and policy realization (especially Bamgbose 2003), these are important starting points, even if too many of them are as yet of no more than symbolic import.

12.4 A Note on African Languages in Tertiary Education

One of the crucial issues we have to address successfully is what Sibayan (1999) raises by implication in the earlier mentioned quotation: *why bother to adapt African languages as media of instruction or languages of tuition at tertiary educational institutions, given that we have English, French, Portuguese and, albeit decreasingly so in South Africa, Afrikaans, as perfectly useable formal academic languages?* For many, including specialists in African linguistics, the demand that we do so is nothing less than a quixotic waste of money in the cause of an anachronistic and even embarrassing African nationalism. If we are unable to give a compelling answer to this question, therefore, we are unlikely to persuade anyone, least of all those whom we expect to put money on the table in order to get things moving forward, that this is one of the central questions that have to be addressed, especially by the university, if President Mbeki's 'African century' is ever to become a meaningful notion. Having due regard to the peculiarities of historical development in different parts of the world and at different times, it is essential that Africa's language scholars study with great care similar moments in the history of other social formations. In this connection, Clayton's (2000, Chapter 8) study of the Khmerization of tertiary education in Cambodia during 1979–1989 is an excellent modern example.

In terms of the profession, we have to see to it that a much greater proportion of post-graduate students take degrees and other courses in applied linguistics rather than only in the traditional domains of theoretical, descriptive and historical linguistics. It is imperative that linguists and other language professionals in Africa begin to see it as an indispensable aspect of social development rather than simply in terms of heritage.[4]

12.5 Immediate Steps: ACALAN and ILPAA

Under the joint aegis of ACALAN, the Association of African Universities (AAU), the World Congress of African Linguistics (WOCAL) and CODESRIA, as well as relevant regional and local structures and organizations, detailed implementation plans should be drawn up. These should take as their points of departure the experience of the postcolonial attempts at language planning, especially of corpus development, in the relevant African States. In this regard, Somalia, Ethiopia, Nigeria, Tanzania and, most recently, South Africa, among others, offer a lot of invaluable data. Post-graduate students in applied linguistics should be mobilized to collate, analyze and render useable all of this information rapidly. In my view, the guiding document should be the updated version of the 1986 OAU Language Plan of Action for Africa, which Professors Maurice Tadadjeu (Cameroon) and Salam Diakité (Mali) revised in late 2004 at the request of ACALAN and of the Steering Committee of ILPAA.

Outside of the immediate purview of any specific university community, the five core ILPAA projects of ACALAN have to be promoted aggressively and with the full support of the heads of state of the AU. Sonntag (2003), citing Jean Laponce's tenet that 'minority languages best able to resist the pressure of more powerful competitors [such as global English] are those having government as their champion', warns that

> (the) global politics of local languages must engage governments, individually or collectively in intergovernmental organizations, whether in regional groupings, such as the Council of Europe, or global groupings, such as the United Nations and its agencies (. . .) This is what we concluded from our case studies: the State is an important actor in linguistic globalization, be it in the local politics of global English or the global politics of local languages. (122)

Taken together, these are essentially large-scale language planning projects, calculated in principle to enhance the status, expand the corpus, and facilitate the acquisition of all African languages. These core projects are the Year of African Languages (2006–2007), the Translation Program, the closely related Terminology Development Project, the Pan-African Joint Masters and Doctoral Program in Applied Linguistics and African Languages and, last but not least, the Stories Across Africa project (Alexander 2005b). The promotion and gradual realization of these projects will assist in creating a climate favorable to the micro-planning and implementation of specific language development projects at specific universities in given countries. The synergies and economies of scale that can be anticipated will have both an exhilarating and accelerating effect on those who have to do the actual work of translating, developing specialized registers, creating innovative literature, training language professionals and so forth. For each of these constituencies, as intimated earlier, the meaningfulness of what they will be, and are already, doing will be amplified in ways that very few of them can at present anticipate. Pan-Africanism, in the context of the cultural revolutionary dimension of the African Renaissance, will assume a new meaning and a new significance (Alexander 2004). The other core project of ACALAN that requires much support and extremely dedicated focus is that which the current president and executive secretary designate Mr. Adama Samassekou has been driving with great vigor and success, namely, the quest to place as many African languages as possible in the cyberspace, so that they can become Internet languages. Generally speaking, in spite of zig-zag progress in this regard, machine assisted translation and automatic translation hold the promise of increasing 'the chances for other viable languages to function next to English' (De Swaan 2001:191). (See also Chaudenson, this volume, regarding how indigenous languages can be used in the media in Mali and the rest of Francophone Black Africa.)

12.6 The Importance of Translation

By way of example, I should like to expand on one of the core projects of ACALAN, one that is only just beginning to take shape. Scholars who have focused on the issue of intellectualization or modernization of local languages are agreed that one of the main mechanisms for bringing about and driving this process is translation of major works of literary and scientific creation that exist in the more 'developed' languages. With regards to Filipino, for example, Sibayan (1999) states unequivocally that 'Translation of important publications now available in English (the chief source language of intellectualisation) is the single most important way of intellectualising Filipino for a long time to come' (464).

Newald (1960), in an epigrammatic reference to this complex, states that the German humanists of the fifteenth and sixteenth centuries were forced through the contemplation of classically normed Latin and Greek languages to reflect on the German language and this facilitated the development of German grammar. Most recently, Eco (2003) has shown by means of practical examples how 'translation as negotiation' impacts on the target language. Citing Friedrich Schleiermacher, he refers to the strong version of the Sapir–Whorf hypothesis, according to which one's native language determines one's perceptual and conceptual possibilities but points out that Schleiermacher himself accepted that thinking people 'play their part in shaping their language' (81) and that

Wilhelm von Humboldt had been the first to remark on the fact that translations 'can augment the significance and the expressivity of the native language' (81–82).[5]

It is precisely 'this dynamic capacity of languages to evolve when exposed to a foreign challenge' (Eco 2003:82) that African university programs in applied linguistics are going to have to explore and use in innovative ways in order to initiate and sustain the rapid intellectualization of certain – in principle, all – languages of the people by agreement in the appropriate forums and constituencies. Just how difficult this task can and will be can be inferred from the tremendous investments that the Japanese intelligentsia were called upon to make over many generations. Like the Japanese and the followers of Kemal Ata Turk in the 1920s and 1930s, we will have to find the most cost-efficient ways of increasing rapidly the corpus of great works of world literature and science in the relevant African languages. It is my view that one of the most appropriate and acceptable ways of doing this is to ask all universities to consider introducing as an elective component of post-graduate assessment of course work in each discipline the translation into a relevant African language of a key text or part thereof. Very few exercises could vie with this practice in respect of gauging the grasp of a subject by an examination candidate.

The practical implementation of this crucial strategic move is completely manageable.[6] Essentially, we would need a few focus groups of people consisting of linguists, translators and subject specialists in each of the relevant languages to decide whether the document is an acceptable translation. However, above all, we need people who have the vision, the courage and the energy to do it. In this regard, the stated intention of ACALAN to launch large-scale translation programs in tandem with the appropriate terminology development project(s) is of the utmost significance, since it will serve as a compass for the individual institutions and translators of texts.

12.7 Focus on Cross-Border Languages

Hitherto, this essay has proceeded somewhat like Shakespeare's play *Hamlet*, without the Prince of Denmark, as I have not referred to any specific African languages. The reason for this omission is obvious: a grandiose strategic project such as that on which ACALAN and its related structures and associated organizations are embarking has to be justified both in terms of its political, historical and its socioeconomic necessity, as well as its technical and professional rationality and feasibility. Consequently, two important issues remain to be addressed, namely, which of the plus-minus 2000 'languages' are involved in this project and, given the putative costs of such a project, how will the political will be mobilized to realize it?

The first question can be dealt with briefly, since the ACALAN statutes, while committing the organization to the status and corpus development of all the languages of the continent, is specific about the prioritization – for the foreseeable future – of the cross-border languages.[7] At the original launching of the activities of the then 'Mission' of the African Academy of Languages on 8 September 2001, Professor Ayo Bamgbose (2002) stressed, among other things, that

> Widely spoken cross-border languages have the potential of serving as a model for empowerment, for they have a large population to back them and materials prepared in one country can be circulated and used in another. Hence to extend their use to a wider range of domains should not be problematic once the necessary language development work has been done. (25)

He goes on to cite the example of the as yet unrealized potential of Kiswahili in East Africa and states that 'one of the major objectives of ACALAN is to empower some of the more dominant vehicular languages in Africa to the extent that they can serve as working languages in the African Union and its institutions' (25).

It remains to be said that, in practice, the presence and commitment of groups of scholars and activists who are focused on the development of specific African languages for reasons of local dynamics in fact are determining which languages are actually being promoted most vigorously. ACALAN has, however, initiated a process for determining which of the vehicular languages should be given priority, for example, for the purposes of translating the major documents of the African Union into the languages of the continent. The Stories Across Africa Project has prepared, and is publishing, materials in thirteen African languages from across the continent, including Kiswahili, English, French, Arabic and Portuguese as official languages of the AU. Not all of these are cross-border languages for the reason mentioned here.

Our approach has been necessitated by the evolving success of applied linguistics and practical initiatives in the field of language planning on the continent as a whole during the past fifteen years, more or less. In that period, a few viable indigenous centers of language planning and language policy development have come into being, complementing the important work of many university departments of linguistics and of African languages and that of international institutions such as UNESCO and, in certain respects, though more controversially, that of the World Bank or of foreign-based organizations such as the Ford Foundation, the Summer Institute of Linguistics and various GTZ-supported projects. These centers have had the tacit and, in some cases, the deliberate, strategic support of their respective governments, even though they tend either to be or to behave as nongovernmental organizations. The more prominent and well-known centers of this kind are ACALAN in Mali, BAKITA in Tanzania, the National Association of Cameroonian Language

Committees (NACALCO), the Pan South African Language Board, the Centre for Advanced Studies of African Societies (CASAS), and the Project for (the Study of) Alternative Education in South Africa (PRAESA) in South Africa and the National Institute for Educational Development (INDE) in Mozambique. In other countries on the continent as well as within these four countries, there are, of course, other less well-known centers or units that specialize in one or other aspect of language planning, policy development and/or training of professionals. In addition to such units and centers, there are numerous individual scholars and activists who promote the use and development of African languages, the legitimacy of multilingualism, mother tongue-based bilingual education, creative writing in African languages and so forth.

However, the most important development in this period has been the increasing connectedness of all these various centers, units, initiatives and individuals. This has come about both as the result of the political unification of the continent and of support by foreign donor agencies. Above all, however, it has been the realization of the African intelligentsia themselves that the continent will never gain real independence until they also address what Mazrui and Mazrui (1998) call its linguistic dependence on Europe and on North America, which has driven the process of networking, especially since about 1996. We have come to a clearer understanding of the relationship between, on the one hand, language policy, language use and language practice and, on the other, the wielding of political power, economic development, social inequality and individual as well as social identities in the multilingual societies of the African continent. Today, scholars and activists in applied linguistics feel confident that they can approach governments as well as sympathetic donor agencies with specific and complementary proposals that are calculated to synchronize developments (policy and implementation) in this 'superstructural' domain with the significant moves and strategies that are being mooted and/or implemented in the obviously material domains of social life on the continent. It is our hope that the adoption of ACALAN as a specialized agency of the African Union will not only further and strengthen this networking process but also give coherence and direction to all the diverse initiatives that are being taken in this domain. In this regard, it is important to point out that contacts between, on the one hand, the Language Policy Division of the Council of Europe (in Strasbourg, France) and the European Center for Modern Languages (in Graz, Austria) and, on the other, ACALAN and other African language centers is bound to play a significant role in realizing the objectives of the latter and the African network of language professionals and language activists. At a global level, this 'alliance' may well help to counter some of the disabling effects of the global hegemony of English.

This sanguine statement should not, however, be misunderstood as some naïve belief that metropolitan countries and many of the donor groups that support these developments are purely altruistic in their support. Clayton's study of the evolution of Cambodian language policies (2000) shows very clearly that what he labels 'linguistic pragmatism', as opposed to 'linguistic imperialism', is becoming the preferred policy stance in these circles. There is, thus, a coincidence of interest that is developing in the 'North' and the 'South' and this is not problematic as long as it does not translate into exclusive benefits for the elite.

It is clear that the secular tendency will be for the establishment of an unstable diglossia in most countries and regions, one that involves one or more local languages in combination with an international language. At present, there is no doubt that in most cases, the preferred international language is English for all the reasons that are now almost taken for granted across the globe. In this connection, I believe that it is important to distinguish between the dominance and the hegemony of English. While the former is the result of 'force and money' (Wright 2004), the latter is inscribed in discourse. The former will change depending on the change in the balance of political forces in the world (Hobsbawm 2000:47–48). The latter is much more subject to the intervention of agents mobilized and organized in order to counter the negative impact of the discursive grids that come with the dominance of a particular language as the expression of the power of all or some of those who speak it.

Our experience in South Africa has led us to promote the notion of 'functional multilingualism', but not in the sense of a stable diglossic situation where the local languages are always used only in the primary, less powerful, spheres of the family, places of worship or the primary school, while the language of wider communication is used for government, big business, tertiary education and other high-status functions. It must be understood that as and when the users of the local language want it to be used in these 'controlling domains of language', there should be a principled commitment on the part of a democratic government that the relevant languages be so used. Of course, this is more easily said than done and it does not make it possible for us to avoid all the difficult decisions about questions such as prioritizing certain interventions rather than others, harmonizing varieties, negotiating agreements among language communities in the same polity and phasing in policy adaptations and all the other implications of democratic language planning. Above all, it must be understood that such a development takes time and that the initial investment in establishing the necessary infrastructure and trained language professionals cannot be avoided.

This is the message that must be transmitted to the political leadership. ACALAN itself is not mandated to do so, even though it can and should advise governments at their request. It is the civil society that will have to take the initiative in this regard. And, since it is now very obvious that the radical democratization of African societies is the only guarantee for a more equitable and just social order, the salience of the language issue and of appropriate language policies will become ever more evident.

In a nutshell, we are proposing a comprehensive, large-scale, long-term and systematic intervention on the part of NGOs, CBOs, language profession-als' associations (especially in the domain of education) with government support at the national, sub-regional and continental levels to create the condi-tions and the capacity that will enable the realization of the common goal of using as many African languages as possible in all the controlling domains (e.g., government administration, lawmaking, big business, education, etc.) within the next two–three generations. ACALAN itself is in the process of collating all the relevant data and the many different proposals and outlines of plans that are being proposed or executed by individual and clusters of projects. The official status accorded it by the Khartoum Summit of the Heads of State and of Government at the end of January 2006 means that it has the necessary authority and, possibly, the leverage to accelerate the tempo of change in this fundamental area.

Notes

[1] In recent history, only the strategic 'nationalities' program that was conceptual-ized and carried out with very contradictory results in the former USSR between 1920 and 1950, give or take a few years, is comparable to what the ACALAN lead-ership explicitly and implicitly wants to undertake. Postcolonial language planning on the Indian subcontinent is another source of insights and caveats.

[2] The application of world systems theory to the linguistic domain has been criticised for the tendency to underplay the relevance of 'agency' as opposed to 'structure' in human affairs and, therefore, to project a linear, one-way, quasi-deterministic causal effect from the 'core' to the 'periphery', from the dominant to the subaltern. See, for example, recent studies by Clayton (2000) and Sonntag (2003).

[3] Even though the paradigm within which NEPAD as an economic package has been conceptualized and is being executed is extremely controversial and problematic, I shall not discuss it any further here. Suffice it to say that as an attempt, at that level, to promote pan-African unity and economic development in its most conventional meaning, it necessarily opens up the political and cultural space within which dif-ferent contending ideas of what it means to be 'African' – with all its implications, including language policy – will be fought out (see Ngugi wa Thiongo 2003). In this connection, it is important to consider the similar, and related, developments in the European Union. De Swaan (2001) is very useful for such a comparison.

[4] The ACALAN core project of pan-African masters and doctoral degrees in Applied Linguistics and African Languages is intended to address this issue on a continen-tal scale.

[5] In an address to the International Federation of Translators, held in Finland in August 2005, I explored an important vein of this complex terrain, namely, that of re-establishing the continuity between tradition and modernity by means of such translation. This is an area of research and philosophical reflection that, in my view, needs to be mined much more consciously and systematically, especially by African scholars. (Alexander 2005a:12–19).

⁶ The progress of machine-assisted translation and of translation software packages is making this approach eminently feasible.

⁷ Professor Kwesi Prah, renowned for his promotion of and work on the standardization and harmonization of the languages of the continent, prefers to use the term 'core languages' (personal communication).

References

Alexander, Neville. 2004. New meanings of Panafricanism in the era of globalisation. *PeaceAfrika* 8(2).17–26.

—2005a. The potential role of translation as social practice for the intellectualisation of African languages. In *Proceedings of the XVII World Congress International Federation of Translators,* ed. by L. Salmi and K. Koskinen, 12–19. Tampere, Finland, 4–7 August 2005. Paris: FIT.

Alexander, Neville (ed.). 2005b. *The Intellectualisation of African Languages: The African Academy of Languages and the Implementation of the Language Plan of Action for Africa.* Cape Town: PRAESA.

Bamgbose, Ayo. 2002. Mission and vision of the African Academy of Languages. In ACALAN, *Special Bulletin,* 24–27 January 2002. Bamako: ACALAN.

—2003. Language and the African Renaissance: Lessons from the South African Experience. In *Tied Tongues: The African Renaissance as a Challenge for Language Planning,* ed. by H. Wolff, 39–60. Muenster: LIT Verlag.

Clayton, Thomas. 2000. *Education and the Politics of Language: Hegemony and Pragmatism in Cambodia, 1979–1989.* Hong Kong: Comparative Education Research Centre, The University of Hong Kong.

De Swaan, Abram. 2001. *Words of the World: The Global Language System.* Cambridge: Polity Press.

Eco, Umberto. 2003. *Mouse or Rat? Translation as Negotiation.* London: Weidenfeld and Nicolson.

Hobsbawm, Eric. 2000. *The New Century.* London: Abacus.

Makgoba, Malegapuru William (ed.). 1999. *African Renaissance. The New Struggle.* Cape Town: Mafube Publishing and Tafelberg.

Mazrui, Ali and Mazrui, Alamin. 1998. *The Power of Babel. Language and Governance in the African Experience.* Oxford: James Currey.

Newald, Richard. 1960. *Die deutsche Literatur vom Späthumanismus zur Empfindsamkeit 1570–1750.* München: C.H. Beck'sche Verlagsbuchhandlung.

Ngugi wa Thiongo. 2003. Consciousness and African Renaissance: South Africa in the Black Imagination. The Fourth Steve Biko Memorial Lecture, University of Cape Town, 12 September.

Sibayan, Bonifacio. 1999. *The Intellectualization of Filipino.* Manila: The Linguistic Society of the Philippines.

Sonntag, Selma K. 2003. *The Local Politics of Global English: Case Studies in Linguistic Globalization.* Lanham: Lexington Books.

Spolsky, Bernard. 2006. Language policy failures. In *Along the Routes to Power: Explorations of Empowerment through Language,* ed. by Martin. Puetz, Joshua A. Fishman and JoAnne Neff-van Aertselaer, 87–99. Mouton de Gruyter: Berlin and New York.

Tadadjeu, Maurice and Diakité, Salam. 2005. Understanding the language plan of action for Africa within the language policy of the African Union. In Alexander (ed.), 41–50.

Wright, Sue. 2004. *Language Policy and Language Planning: From Nationalism to Globalisation*. London: Palgrave Macmillan.

Author Index

Subject Index